INTERNATIONAL ACCOUNTING AND ECONOMIC DEVELOPMENT

INTERNATIONAL ACCOUNTING AND ECONOMIC DEVELOPMENT

The Interaction of Accounting, Economic, and Social Indicators

Ahmed Riahi-Belkaoui

QUORUM BOOKS
Westport, Connecticut • London

657
R48i

Library of Congress Cataloging-in-Publication Data

Riahi-Belkaoui, Ahmed, 1943–
   International accounting and economic development : the interaction of accounting, economic, and social indicators / Ahmed Riahi-Belkaoui.
      p.   cm.
   Includes bibliographical references and index.
   ISBN 1–56720–504–6 (alk. paper)
   1. Comparative accounting.   2. International economic relations.   3. Economic development.   I. Title.
   HF5625.R48   2002
   657—dc21   2001048116

British Library Cataloguing in Publication Data is available.

Library of Congress Catalog Card Number: 2001048116
ISBN: 1–56720–504–6

First published in 2002

Quorum Books, 88 Post Road West, Westport, CT 06881
An imprint of Greenwood Publishing Group, Inc.
www.quorumbooks.com

Printed in the United States of America

The paper used in this book complies with the Permanent Paper Standard issued by the National Information Standards Organization (Z39.48–1984).

10 9 8 7 6 5 4 3 2 1

Contents

Exhibits

Preface

International accounting development is essential to the creation of an accounting order that serves as a basis and a guarantee for a proper conduct of business activities and growth. Economic development is also essential to the creation of an economic order that serves as a basis and a guarantee for providing resources and economic and business opportunities to a country's citizens. A generally accepted thesis is that both accounting order and economic order work in tandem and rely on each other for equilibrium and stability. Accordingly, the basic objective of this book is to establish the relationship between accounting and economic development and the determinants of accounting development before presenting empirical evidence on:

- The determinants and implications of economic development
- The role and the determinants of disclosure adequacy that include: (1) economic freedom and human development; (2) political, financial, and economic risks; (3) human development and economic development; (4) managerial, academic, and professional influences; (5) welfare of the common man; (6) economic, political, and civil indicators; and (7) the determinants of prediction performance of earnings forecasts
- The role of country return and risk in: (1) disclosure adequacy; (2) prediction performance of earnings forecasts; and (3) levels of financial disclosure by European firms
- The role and impact of cultural determinism for: (1) systematic risk of global stock exchanges; (2) compensation practices; (3) professional self-regulation in accounting; and (4) the perception of accounting concepts

The book should be of interest to those interested in the relationship of accounting and economic development and the interactions of accounting, economic, and social indicators, including practicing accountants, business executives, accounting teachers and researchers, and students.

Many people have helped in the development of this book. I received considerable assistance from the University of Illinois at Chicago research assistants, especially Ewa Tomaszewska, Shahrzad Ghatan, and Vivian Au. I also thank Eric Valentine, R. A. Homiski, and the entire production team at Quorum Books for their continuous and intelligent support.

1
Accounting and Economic Development

Economic development requires in large part a well-established and monitored planning process. The planning process relies on the provision of relevant macro- and microinformation for a better deliberation of the activities required and the necessary standards of performance. Accounting appears to serve an important role in the provision of this information, resulting in a crucial role in the promotion of economic development. Accordingly, this chapter elaborates on the role of accounting in economic development. First the role of the planning process in economic development is presented, followed by a description of the role of social indicators and accounting.

DEVELOPMENT PLANNING

The Developing Economies

The developing economies form a third element in a world power structure dominated by the technologically more advanced nations of the Atlantic bloc and the former European Communist bloc. This third element has been seen for a long time as the "commonwealth of poverty," in spite of its niche and complex cultures, its immense human resources, and its possession of much of the world's metallic minerals, water power, oil and coal, timber, and potential cropland. This Third World is also seen as "a universe of radical scarcity." "Defining and determining every dimension of men's relationships to each other . . . the inadequacy of the means of livelihood is the first and distinguishing truth of this area" ("Editorial," 1963, p. 4).

In effect, for much of the Third World real GNP per capita is under $200, the daily intake of calories is under 2,200, and the daily intake of animal protein is under 15 grams. Added to this poverty is a legacy of warped economics facing continuous environmental difficulties—poor soils, erratic climates, floods and droughts, and diseases. This is particularly serious given that the economies of the Third World are plagued by two distortions: a grossly inflated agricultural sector and an overexpanding tertiary sector. In general, these countries are characterized by low per capita real income, limited stock of capital goods, dominance of subsistence agriculture, and relatively low levels of education and wealth. The rate of economic growth in these economies appears to be dependent on the rate of capital formation, the incremental capital output ratio, technological change, the growth of the labor force, and a favorable social and political environment.

To escape from this vicious cycle of underdevelopment, the Third World countries have begun searching for a new economic and social identity. In fact, since acquiring their independence, most developing economies have begun major efforts to improve their economic situations. Economic development is now the primary goal in the developing economies. It is understood to include both economic growth and social and institutional changes. The strategies adopted to spur economic development in the developing economies have been either of the kind putting a primacy on economic growth or of the kind emphasizing socioeconomic development.

Barriers and Impediments to Economic Development

There seems to be a consensus on the factors contributing to the economic problems of the developing countries, which include rapid population growth, resource limitations, and inefficiency in resource use.

Rapid population growth is an important concern for the developing countries. It has been further stimulated by improvements in health care and the eradication of major epidemic diseases. This improvement in health care has averted the doom predictions, known as the iron law of population growth, as envisioned by Malthus. Population growth remains serious, however, leading economists to talk about the "critical minimum effort" needed to increase capital quickly enough so that the increase in output exceeds the increase in population.

With respect to resource limitations, economic development must rest on an adequate presence of financial and physical capital, social-overhead capital, and human capital. Physical capital in terms of natural resources endowment is important for economic development, but its presence has never been an absolute precondition for economic growth. It needs to be complemented with an adequate supply of financial, social-overhead, and human capital.

Financial capital plays a vital role in economic development by spurring investment. It may be generated internally through the savings of households and firms if a healthy banking climate is maintained in the country. In most cases, the developing countries have to rely on external funding of their major projects.

The social-overhead capital of a country is also known as the infrastructure of the economy. It is composed of the system of supporting services, such as transportation and communications, necessary to an efficient conduct of the economy. Consequently, a dependable social-overhead capital is vital to the economic development of the developing countries.

Human capital, in the form of a well-developed, healthy, educated, and efficient workforce, is often missing in the developing countries. A precondition to economic development is a high-quality system of education, training, and health.

The developing countries are also plagued by an inefficient use of resources, in terms of both allocative efficiency and X-efficiency. Allocative efficiency results from the use of a nation's resources to make the wrong products. X-efficiency, to use a term introduced by Professor Harvey Liebenstein (1996, pp. 352–415), arises wherever resources are used poorly even in making the right products. The source of X-efficiency may be inadequate education, poor health, traditions, institutions, habitual ways of producing, custom, or cultural attitudes. The presence of X-efficiency in the developing countries is evident in the enormous differences in productivity from country to country, in particular in industries using the same technology.

It is generally believed that entrepreneurship is a vital ingredient for economic development. The lack of entrepreneurship in most developing countries is generally seen as one of the major ingredients for a maintained economic growth. Entrepreneurship is "a combination of the following attributes: imagination, daring, willingness to take risks, a sense of timing, and an ability to recognize profitable opportunities, all driven by a love of money, power, or some other such goal, which together combine to make up the quality of business leadership" (Baumol and Binder, 1982, p. 760). Moreover, the lack of entrepreneurship, political stability, and political freedom and civil liberties may act as a major barrier to economic growth. Instability may discourage local and foreign direct investment because of the constant fear of nationalization, harassment, and a poor business climate.

Approaches to Development

Two major approaches have been applied to development in the developing countries (Islam and Henault, 1979, pp. 253–267). The first strategy aimed at a high push to be achieved by a high rate of growth and industrialization, leading to a high rate of growth in per capita income. This view was reinforced by the works of S. Harrod and A. Domar, which transformed development into a process of growth resting on a few quantifiable variables (Islam and Henault, 1979, pp. 253–267), and by W. W. Rostow's theory of stages of economic growth and the idea of a takeoff (Rostow, 1959). The process of economic development consisted of transforming the underdeveloped societies from an ascriptive, particularistic, and functionally diffuse pattern to a pattern characterized by achievement, universalism, and functional specificity (Parsons, 1951). As stated by Nasir Islam and Georges Henault, an "underdeveloped society thus suffers from a lack of social and geographic mobility, a lack of division of labour, emphasizes status rather than achievement, and consequently leads to low productivity" (Islam and Henault, 1979, p. 254). This first strategy called for a direct involvement of the government in achieving industrialization and urbanization and in maintaining a high rate of sustained economic growth through the "planning" process.

Planning is seen as the essential ingredient of any development policy. At the microlevel, the "technology gap" was to be reduced by a transfer of relevant techniques and procedures taken from Western countries. All projects were to be conducted systematically using "development administration" as a way of designing, implementing, and evaluating policies and programs leading to socioeconomic changes. It relied on what is known in UN technical assistance circles as MMT (modern management technology), which refers to techniques such as linear programming, CPM, PERT, queuing theory, long-range planning and forecasting network analysis, modeling, and cost-benefit analysis. The total impact of this first strategy is far from perfect. For example, Islam and Henault state:

In our opinion, the net overall result of this gigantic effort of international and foreign-aid giving agencies in the area of administrative development was over-bureaucratization, excessive controls and regulation of the economy, proliferation of bureaucratic structure increase in the size of bureaucracies, and excessive concentration of power in the hands of the administrative elites. The impact of these factors on development at best remains questionable. In fact, the balance may tip toward the negative rather than the positive side. (Islam and Henault, 1979, p. 25)

The second strategy is usually traced back to the institutional school of C. E. Ayres, Thorstein Veblen, and Gunnar Myrdal, with their emphasis on the social and institutional preconditions for progress. Here the growth models of the first strategy were replaced by a new ideology of development. The main elements of this new ideology are supposed to include need orientation; endogenous, self-reliant, ecologically sound motives; and be based on agricultural transformation (Nefron, 1977, p. 10). The approach moves from a largely economic perspective to a wider, all encompassing, socioeconomic one aimed at the fulfillment of all basic needs: adequate nutrition, health, clean water, and shelter. The advocates of this second strategy are generally influenced by the center-periphery thesis in dependence theory, which holds that underdevelopment is a function of one society's dependence on another. This explains their constant demands for a new international economic order based on both a global redistribution of economic surpluses and major changes in the productive relations within the periphery sector (Cohen, 1973). In fact, a major cause of discontent in the center-periphery thesis (also known as the North-South controversy) is the price of commodities, which the periphery countries consider to be unfairly low and unstable.

The second strategy views development in terms of the fulfillment of basic needs, which have been eloquently described as follows:

The concepts of basic needs bring to any development strategy a heightened concern with meeting the consumption needs of the whole population, particularly in the areas of education and health, but also in nutrition, housing, water supply, and sanitation. In formulating policies aimed at reducing poverty, a good deal of attention has generally been paid to restructuring the patterns of production and income so that they benefit the poor. But similar attention has not been devoted to their needs for public services. (Ul Haq, 1980, p. 32)

The concept of basic needs was justified by the failure of the three types of justification used for the emphasis on a country's economic growth as the principal performance indicator. First, income did not automatically trickle down to the poor; second, governments did not always take steps to reduce poverty; third, a period of inequality is not needed in the early stages of development. The concept of basic needs is also perceived as a positive concept and has a broad appeal, politically and intellectually.

The performance of developing countries in meeting basic needs varies from one country to another. Frances Stewart used life expectancy as the single most significant indicator of performance on basic needs. She compared achievement in life expectancy with what may have been predicted on the basis of a country's level of income per capita as a way of classifying countries' performance. Three types of economies turned out to be notably successful: the rapidly growing, market-oriented economies; the centrally planned economies; and the "misled" economies with welfare intervention. The less successful cases are evident in three categories of developing economies: the very poor economies, the economies with rapid growth but without substantial poverty reduction, and the economies with moderate growth and moderate poverty impact. It is accepted, however, that most developing countries have made some progress in meeting basic needs, such as education, basic health, nutrition, water and sanitation, and shelter.

But is it possible that policies aimed at providing the poor and neglected with basic goods and services are the cause for a sacrifice of productive investments and economic growth? Proponents of the basic-needs approach argue on the basis of theoretical and empirical evidence that providing for basic needs can improve growth performance. In short, investing in people may be a good way to both eliminate the worst aspects of poverty and increase the growth rate of output.

The Planning Process

Development planning involves a coordinated governmental intervention in the direction of the economy of a nation through the setting of national economic targets, and the implementation of these targets. It involves primarily setting an economic plan that specifies quantitative economic targets, but also monitoring economic activities toward reaching specified goals. The definition of economic planning is subject to different interpretations. For example, four types of planning are viewed in a 1951 UN publication as follows:

First, . . . it [planning] refers only to the making of public expenditures, extending over from one to say ten years. Second, it refers sometimes to the setting of production targets, whether for private or for public enterprises, in terms of the input of manpower, of capital, or of other scarce resources, or use in terms of output. Thirdly, the word may be used to describe a statement which sets targets for the economy as a whole, purporting to allocate all scarce resources among the various branches of the economy. And fourthly, the word is sometimes used to describe the means which the government uses to try to enforce upon private enterprise the targets which have been previously determined. (UN Department of Economic Affairs, 1951, p. 63)

The economic planning route chosen by most developing countries in the context of a mixed economy is motivated by several variables. The most important variable is related to the market-failure argument. The imperfection of structure and operations of markets in the developing countries, with the results of distorted prices and inequities, renders the market concept an inefficient tool for economic development in these countries. Here is a great argument for the explicit market-failure theme for planning in the developing countries:

Governments cannot, and should not, take a merely passive role in the process of industrial expansion. Planning has become an essential and integral part of industrial development programs, for market forces, by themselves, cannot overcome the deep-seated structural rigidities in the economies of developing countries. . . . Today the need for some degree of economic planning is universally recognized. It is, of course, an integral part of the economy of the Soviet Union and the other centrally planned countries. . . . In developing countries, planning is more feasible and more desirable than in developed market economies. The greater feasibility is a result of the smaller number of variables that must be taken into consideration, and the greater desirability stems from the fact that the automatic mechanisms for co-ordination of individual actions function less satisfactorily in developing than in developed economies. Planning in developing countries is made necessary by, inter alia, the inadequacies of the market as a mechanism to ensure that individual decisions will optimize economic performance in terms of society's preferences and economic goals. . . . The inadequacy of the market mechanism as a means of allocating resources for industrial development sometimes results from government policy itself or because the theoretical assumptions (particularly with respect to the mobility of the factors of production) do not apply to the actual economic situation. Even more importantly, the market mechanism cannot properly allow for the external effects of investment. (Helfgoth and Schiano-Campo, 1920, p. 11)

Besides the market-failure argument, other arguments used to justify economic planning in the developing countries include a resource mobilization and allocation argument that gives to economic planning a better role in the channeling of scarce resources to development; an attitudinal or psychological argument that gives to economic planning a better success in rallying people behind development; and a foreign-aid argument that makes economic planning a better base used by donor countries in granting financial and technical assistance (Todaro, 1985, pp. 466–468).

The planning process is characterized by some common elements that are apparent in all contexts and some specific elements that characterize specific country and contexts. Common elements are apparent in the following characteristics of the planning process:

1. Starting from the political views and goals of the government, planning attempts to define policy objectives, especially as they relate to the future development of the economy.
2. A development plan sets out a strategy by means of which it is intended to achieve these objectives, which are normally translated into specific targets.
3. The plan attempts to present a centrally coordinated, internally consistent set of principles and policies, chosen as the optimal means of implementing the strategy and achieving the targets and intended to be used as a framework to guide subsequent day-to-day decisions.
4. It comprehends the whole economy (hence it is "comprehensive," in contrast to "colonial" or "public sector" planning).
5. In order to secure optimality and consistency, the comprehensive plan employs a more-or-less formalized macroeconomic model (which, however, will often remain unpublished), and this is employed to project the intended future performance of the economy.
6. A development plan typically covers a period of, say, 5 years and finds physical expression as a medium-term plan document, which may, however, incorporate a longer-term perspective plan and be supplemented by annual plans. (Killick, 1976)

Economic planning seeks the achievement of full employment of resources and social economic progress through existing and new institutions. Its aims are economic growth and structural change through a conscious effort by a state and its people. Development planning has spread all over the world, acquiring even in the special states in developed countries the form of "industrial policy." In socialized countries it took the form of central planning, with the state controlling, through regulations and directives, the level of savings, the amount and composition of output and investment, and the structure of prices. In mixed economies it is distinguished by three approaches: a project-by-project approach focusing on selected public investment projects; integrated public investment planning, focusing on a well-prepared investment plan rather than the piecemeal basis of the project-by-project approach; and comprehensive planning, focusing on an overall planning of the economy of a nation, including both an integrated public investment plan and a plan for the private sector (Waterson, 1969, pp. 61–65).

The desirability of comprehensive planning is stated as follows: "In the long run, comprehensive planning based on growth models may give better results than partial planning. Comprehensive planning's view of an economy as a whole and its emphasis on internal consistency allow economic comparisons and judgments to be made which are not generally possible with partial planning" (Waterson, 1969, p. 98). Comprehensive planning or development planning relies on a development plan or public investment plan that has the force of law, at least in administrative units accountable to the central government. Development plans are short-term, medium-term, and long-term, linked by a degree of flexibility and continuity. A short-term plan can be renewed and "rolled" forward in time.

The plan includes the basic development objectives of a given country to be carried out through a variety of economic and social policies. The size of a plan is a fraction of a country's willingness to accept current sacrifices for future benefits. Three approaches may be used for the determination of the size of a plan: "One is to have the country's requirements determine it; another is to have the country's resources fix it; the third is to set it somewhere between the two points where the requirements and resource approaches would have left it" (Waterson, 1969, p. 156). The requirements approach is the most useful for a developing country.

Planning Model

Planning models are generally divided into two basic categories: aggregate growth models and multisector input-output models (Todaro, 1985, p. 468).

Aggregate Growth Models

These, generally based on the Harrod-Domar model, are to predict output and employment growth by examining relationships between important macroeconomic variables, such as savings, investment, capital stocks, exports, imports, foreign assistance, and so on. A generally used modified Harrod-Domar growth equation is as follows (Todaro, 1985, p. 470):

$$k(g + \delta) = (S_\pi - S_w)(\pi/Y) + S_w \tag{1.1}$$

where

k = the average (equal to marginal) capital-output ratio

g = targeted growth rate of output

δ = the fraction of the capital stock depreciated in each period

s = share of output Y that is saved

π = profit income

W = wage income

s = propensity to save out of profit income

S_w = propensity to save out of wage income

The formula can be used for the evaluation of the adequacy of current saving out of profit and wage income. Taylor gives the following example:

For example, if a 4 percent growth rate is desired, while the following parameters values hold: $\delta = 0.033$, $K = 3.0$ $(\pi/y) = 0.5$, then [the growth equation] reduces to $0.42 = S_\pi + S_w$. If the savings rate out of capital income is 30 percent, then labor income recipients must save at a 12 percent rate to maintain the postulated rate of growth. This would be considered a considerable saving rate for low-income people. (Taylor, 1975, p. 391)

Using the same example as Taylor, Todaro reaches the following conclusions: "If savings out of capital income amount to 25%, then wage earners must save at a 17% rate to achieve the targeted rate of growth. In the absence of such a savings rate out of labor income, the government could pursue a variety of policies to raise domestic saving and/or seek foreign assistance" (Todaro, 1985, p. 470).

The Two-Gap Model

Rather than the strict Harrod-Domar models, the two-gap model is needed in these cases where the lack of foreign exchange reserves acts as a constraint over growth. The two-gap model is generally formulated as follows:

$$I \leq F + sY \qquad (1.2)$$

A saving-constraint or gap. It states that the savings generated by capital inflows (i.e., the difference between imports and exports) and the savings generated domestically for the national output are less than or equal to the investment needed. In other words:

F = difference between imports and exports

Y = national output

s = share of output Y that is always saved

A foreign exchange constraint or gap. It is stated as follows:

$$m_1 I + m_2 I - E \leq F \qquad (1.3)$$

m_1 = marginal import share from the investment
m_2 = marginal propensity to import out of a unit of GNP
E = exogenous level of exports

The term F enters both of the inequality constraints of the two-gap model and is critical in the analysis. If in addition to F, both output and exports are assigned an exogenous current value, then only one of the two inequalities will be binding—that is, investment (and, therefore, the output growth rate) will be restricted to a lower level by one of the inequalities. This dichotomy creates a classification of countries in the sense that countries can be classified according to whether the savings or foreign exchange constraint is binding. It also provides a crude means for the assignment of foreign aid since the impact of increased capital inflow on investment is greater when the trade on the foreign exchange gap rather than the savings gap is binding. Todaro suggests accordingly that "two gap models simply provide a crude methodology for determining the relative need and ability of different LDCs to use foreign aid effectively" (Todaro, 1985, p. 449).

Taylor gives a more positive assessment:

As with other models of the Harrod-Domar type, note the mechanistic nature of the forecasts. Imports are strictly linked with output and investment levels, as are savings, while exports and net capital inflows are exogenous. Trying to alter many of these "fixed" parameters is at the heart of planning in a developing economy experiencing structural change. However, for forecasting, this is a less serious objection, and the two-gap specification is widely used. Although extremely simple, two-gap models generalize Harrod-Domar in a relevant way and are consistent with the categories in which national accounts are usually arranged. (Taylor, 1975, p. 41)

Input-Output Models

These present the interrelations between the major sectors of the industrial economy by means of a set of simultaneous algebraic equations expressing the production processes of each industry. Each industry is viewed as a producer of output and a user of input. Two basic sets of equations characterize the mathematical input-output model.

The first set of equations states for each sector that the entire product produced is consumed either by other industries or by final demanders as follows: where

X_i = annual rate of total output of industry i
X_{ij} = amount of the product of industry i consumed annually by industry j as an intermediate product
Y_i = amount of product i consumed by a final demand

The second set of equations derives the technical coefficients of production a_{ij} for each industry as follows:

$$X_{ij} = A_{ij}X_j \qquad (1.4)$$

Therefore, the symbolic representation of the input-output model of the economy may be as follows:

$$a_{ij}X_j - X_i = Y_i \qquad (1.5)$$

or

$$
\begin{aligned}
X_i - A_{11}X_1 - A_{12}X_2 - A_{13}X_3 &= Y_1 \\
X_i - A_{11}X_1 - A_{12}X_2 - A_{13}X_3 &= Y_1 \\
X_i - A_{11}X_1 - A_{12}X_2 - A_{13}X_3 &= Y_1
\end{aligned}
\qquad (1.6)
$$

or

$$\overline{X} - \{A\} . \overline{X} = \overline{Y}$$

where X represents a *column vector* of total outputs consisting of n elements [in the above example $n = 3$], each of which numerically represents the total output of one of n industries; $[A]$ is a $n \times n$ square matrix of technical coefficients and Y is a column vector of total final demands.

Equation (1.7) can be solved to yield the following expression:

$$X = [I - A]^{-1}Y \qquad (1.7)$$

where

$$
\begin{aligned}
I &= \text{identity matrix} \\
[I - A]^{-1} &= \text{inverted Leontief matrix generally designed} \\
&\quad \text{by the block letter } R
\end{aligned}
$$

or

$$\overline{X} = \overline{RY} \qquad (1.8)$$

Equation (1.8) can be used to derive the level of output of $Xi_i = 1,2, \ldots n$ of commodity i for a planned final demand $Yj_{j=1,\ldots n}$

Obviously, the reliability of the matrix of technical coefficients is vital to the use of the input-output model in development planning. The reliability is hampered by critical assumption of the model (Todaro, 1985, p. 473). Linear or nonlinear programming or activity analysis models could be used to alleviate the above problem. However, they are considered not very feasible in most developing countries because of the lack of adequate information (Todaro, 1985, p. 480).

SOCIAL INDICATORS OF DEVELOPMENT

Social Indicators

Effective data and information are needed for the formulation, implementation, and monitoring of a development plan. Data are needed about natural and human resources. An integrated system of national accounts is a priority in development planning. Planning with inadequate data is a recipe for disaster. There is even the question of whether any planning should start before the creation of databases. Witness the following comment:

A county which seeks to improve its statistics for planning must set priorities. It must decide, for example, whether to build up its basic data first or whether it is more desirable to prepare aggregative national accounts estimates, even though the data on which they are based are inadequate. Some experts advocate the first course; others the second. There is also the question whether the available data, although inadequate, should be used to start planning immediately or whether planning should be postponed until improved information is obtained. Some planners prefer to postpone planning for a year or two until they accumulate more reliable information. But this causes great delays in meeting a country's problems through planning and most planners feel that it is preferable to start planning as soon as possible even if there is need to use statistics that are second-best. (Waterson, 1969, p. 199)

What is needed for effective development planning is the creation of development planning. Social indicators constitute one of the routes chosen in macrosocial accounting toward the evaluation, measurement, and disclosure of national social performance. The approach consists of focusing on a number of social issues to which "measures" are assigned to depict the extent of improvement in these issues. The approach has generated a rich literature on an international scale aimed at producing, testing, and refining an array of "social indicators" on all possible issues of interest to a particular society, nation, or government.

Social indicators have been described as mere statistics that reflect the human condition and that may be helpful to plan for social change. They go beyond economic indicators with their greater orientation toward the needs and goals within the full range of human social activities and a greater emphasis on all the social concerns, processes, and systems deemed essential for an adequate living standard and quality of life. They are essential to an assessment of the state and changing conditions of society, a discovery of the potential and actual social problems, and an evaluation of the effects of social policies and programs.

As such, they are a basic component of a macrosocial accounting aimed at measurement, evaluation, and monitoring of social performance of macroeconomic units, from cities to entire governments. In what follows, the origins of the social indicator movement, the nature of social indicators, the construction of social indicators, the actors involved in the production of social indicators, the research approaches and functions of social indicators, and examples of social indicators are examined.

Origins of the Social Indicator Movement

For good reason, the origins of the movement for the production and use of social indicators are generally traced back to biblical times. Concern with social justice and the application of new statistical techniques spurred the social indicators movement. The movement truly emerged, however, in 1966, when the National Aeronautics and Space Administration became concerned with the social effects of its space exploration program and R. A. Bauer and his colleagues examined the need to anticipate the consequences of rapid technological change through a comprehensive system of what they called social indicators (Bauer, 1966). This was followed by the publication of *Toward a Social Report* and Senator Walter Mondale's Full Opportunity and Social Accounting Act of 1967 (U.S. Department of Health, Education and Welfare, 1965). From there the social indicator movement found followers in many nations and international organizations and established itself as a legitimate research field of relative independence in the social sciences. This effort is evident in the surge of assessments and bibliographical publications (Wilcox et al., 1972; Land and Spilerman, 1975), a special newsletter (*Social Indicators Newsletter*), and a specialized journal (*Social Indicators Research*).

The Nature of Social Indicators

There is no agreed definition of social indicators. Various definitions are provided in the literature. Social indicators are:

Quantitative data that serve as indices to socially important conditions of society. (Bauer, 1966, p. 69)

Statistics, statistical services, and all other forms of evidence that enable us to assess where we stand and are going with respect to our values and goals, and to evaluate specific programs and determine their impact. (Bauer, 1966, p. 1)

Statistics which measure social conditions and changes there-in over time for various segments of the population. By social conditions, we mean both the external (social and physical) and the internal (subjective and perceptional) context of human existence in a given society. (Land, 1975b, p. 58)

Social indicators and social statistics are facts about society in a quantitative form. But social indicators involve not only quantitative measurement of an aspect of the social but also its interpretation in relation to some norm against which statistic represents advance or retrogression. (Hauser, 1975, p. 13)

The first common characteristic of these definitions is their reference to the functions of the social indicators, which are essentially to measure social changes and conditions. The second common characteristic of these definitions is their reference to the nature of the social indicator as a kind of statistic. From these two characteristics we may summarize the nature of social indicators as generally quantitative constructs designed to monitor, measure, and/or report social conditions and changes.

Following a social indicator model introduced and elaborated by Kenneth Land, these constructs may be categorized in one of several types of social indicators (Land, 1971, pp. 322–325):

1. Policy instruments descriptive indicators: These are exogenous descriptive variables that are manipulable by social policy. By exogenous it is meant that they are outside the social system model, a system of relationships connecting all variables and containing analytical indicators.

2. Nonmanipulable descriptive indicators: These are exogenous descriptive variables that are not manipulable by social policy.

3. Output or end-product descriptive indicators: These are endogenous descriptive variables that define the social conditions being measured and are the consequences of the social processes embodied within the model.

4. Side-effect descriptive indicators: These are endogenous descriptive variables that influence or are influenced by, but do not define, the social conditions and social processes under consideration.

Land emphasizes also that relationship between these indicators is more of an ideal rather than an actual description of the state of social indicators research (Land, 1975b, p. 35).

Social indicators as quantitative constructs generally meet some qualitative characteristics as well:

1. Social indicators are generally normative, in the sense that any move in a particular direction may be interpreted as either good or bad.

2. Social indicators generally relate to outputs rather than inputs of social programs.

3. Social indicators are generally comprehensive and aggregate measures.

4. Social indicators should be genuinely "indicative" of something in the sense that they should relate to economic theories and fit into models, whether explanatory or predictive (Moser, 1973, pp. 135–136).

5. Social indicators relate to subjects for which problems of measurement are not impossible to handle.

6. Social indicators should tap questions of importance to the general public and relate to shared goals. Good health, better education, lower crime rates, improved streets and lighting, and less traffic congestion are goals over which there would be reasonably limited disagreement, even though questions of relative priority inevitably persist (Clark, 1973, p. 6).

7. Social indicators are best showing the direct and indirect effects of alternative policies when they are integrated into a model. This last characteristic argues for analytical as opposed to descriptive indicators. This view is also supported as follows:

In summary development of a social indicator science requires that concentration be on explanatory not descriptive, models of social subsystems and attendant indicators. These models should leave operationalized concepts and causal relationships expressed in proportions which [are] tested to establish whether linkages exist between indicators and other unobservable variables. (Carley, 1979, p. 42)

The Construction of Social Indicators

The construction of social indicators ought to rely on a theoretical or formal approach to be able to provide power and precision in its measurement. This approach ought to be deductive, going from the abstract and general to the simple and particular. Such a model has been proposed by Michael Carley (1979, pp. 33–44) and includes the following steps:

development and statement of a theoretical proposition; formulation of an explicit causal model in words and/or some type of diagram, for example, a path diagram; operationalization, that is the statement in measurable terms of the postulated relationships between social indicators and empirically defined variables, for example equations; testing, and perhaps retesting, of the model. (Carley, 1979, p. 42)

This model allows, for one thing, for the continued development and improvement of social indicators and social theory. Each of the steps requires clear and rigorous thinking, including a precise statement of the theoretical proposition, a carefully defined causal model of the various social relationships underlying the concept being measured, a translation of the relationships into operational and empirically testable forms, and a continuous testing of the model. The "operationalization" step rests on making various computational or procedural choices as follows:

1. The construction and interpretation of social indicators generally follows accepted statistical standards.

2. The fact that most indicators may behave in linear or curvilinear forms does not preclude that some indicators may not always fit a well-behaved trend.

3. Ordinal measurement generally used for social indicators requires setting standards of adequacy and around that grade of inadequacy and abundance.

4. When percentage and index numbers are used to screen social indicators, the choice of the base period is important given the way it may affect the interpretation of the social indicators.

5. Indicators may be either open-ended in growth, such as population, or related to a maximum, such as mortality.

6. Indicators may be either "objective" indicators based on numerical counts of people, money, and things, or "subjective" indicators based on the appraisal of interviewed persons.

7. Indicators may be constructed for all types of goods: free goods, public goods, consumer goods, and/or capital goods.

8. The difficulties with finding indicator units and valuation of intangibles apply also to social indicators.

9. International comparison of indicators may be hampered by the calculation of purchasing power parities that may justify the use of nonmonetary indicators of production and consumption.

10. Social indicators are the result of aggregation of a mass of information into a single or several series.

11. Social indicators should be empirically correlated into the constituent variables of a social concern they are supposed to measure.

12. Social indicators may be based on a common scale, such as money, value, or people, or on different units.

13. Social indicators may be based on either implicit weighing through selection and scaling or explicit weighing. (Horn, 1980, pp. 440–441)

Actors in the Production of Social Indicators

Various actors are involved in the production of social indicators, including supranational and national agencies, scientific institutions, and individuals. Of the supranational agencies, the United Nations, the Organization for Economic Cooperation and Development, the European Community, and the Council for Mutual Economic Assistance are very much involved in the production of social indicators. For example, the UN interest started with attempts to define and measure standards and levels of living (United Nations, 1954, 1961), before moving to developing a socioeconomic system including a database and procedures for determining indicators, and finally extending the system into a system of demographic and social statistics (SDSS) (United Nations, 1976, 1973). The SDSS system used principles of economic bookkeeping to suppress the socioeconomic state of the population and its change over time as a set of demographic accounts in the form of an input-output matrix. The data pertain mainly to demographic structure, housing, public order, use of time, and social mobility. The most interesting development in the construction of social indicators is achieved by the OECD.

National agencies in various countries are continuously developing national compendia of social indicators and social reports.

Similarly, various scientific institutions and individual researchers are involved in social indicator research. In Sweden, two theoretical approaches have been used, one characterized by a conception of welfare based on command over resources (Johansson, 1973, 1976), and one based on a consideration of needs (Allardt and Uusitalo, 1972). This is translated on a practical level in welfare or level-of-living surveys in Sweden (Johansson, 1973), as well as in England (Roos, 1978), Norway (Ringen, 1973), Austria, and West Germany.

Research Approaches and Functions of Indicators

The term "social indicator" is not associated with a single specific research proposal. The number of approaches for systems of social indicators is on the rise. Most of them attempt to operationalize and measure the components of a multidimensional conception of welfare. Examples include the development of a net national welfare index by the Economic Council of Japan, which measures the annual value of the total economic production available for final consumption (Economic Council of Japan, 1973), the development of a level-of-living index, or index of measurable welfare, in natural units of goods and services by Jan Drewnovsky (1970), the development of a social indicators battery by J. Q. Wilson for the purpose of ascertaining differences in the quality of life in the United States (Wilson, 1969), the attempt by Nestor E. Terleckyj to calculate the improvements in the quality of life with thirty-one selected programs in relation to twenty-one national goals and relying on a large-scale input-output matrix (Terleckyj, 1978), the development at the United Nations of a system of social and demographic statistics to encourage the national statistical bodies to systematize their entire social statistics in the direction of an integrated system of "stocks" and "flows" (United Nations, 1973), and the development by Erik Allardt of a welfare model of national development based on the theories of social systems, social structure, and needs (Allardt, 1973a, pp. 63–74). These are only examples and are far from exhaustive of all the approaches to social indicator research. It is generally accepted to classify this research into three distinct approaches: those concerned with measuring the quality of life and welfare; those concerned with monitoring social change and socioeconomic development; and those concerned with forecasting social events and evaluation research (Glatzer, 1981, p. 224).

In fact, these three areas follow the main aspects of social reporting—namely, welfare measurement, observation of a social change, prognosis of a social change without intervention, social policy planning to steer society in desired direction, and monitoring of planning performance (Zapf, 1976, p. 432). R. V. Horn used this sequence to specify the most exhaustive list of the different functions of social indicators as follow (Horn, 1980, p. 432):

SOCIAL PROCESS	FUNCTIONS OF SOCIAL INDICATORS
Assessment of welfare elements	Cognition
Observation of welfare trends	Analysis
Clarification of societal interaction	Conceptualization
Prognosis of trend without intervention	Projections
Formulation of social policy alternatives, including priority-rating and trade-offs	Operationalization, direction
	Classification and targeting
Social policy decision	Monitoring
Audit of planning progress	Retrospective analysis
Review of plan performance	

Each of these functions constitutes a legitimate avenue in social indicator research.

Examples of Social Indicators of Development

The OECD list of social indicators was intended to measure and report changes in the relative importance of the social demands, aspirations, and problems that are, or could become in the decade ahead, major concerns of the socioeconomic planning process. They are to be viewed as an initial framework subject to any improvements to be brought by member countries. Seven major criteria were used in the final section of social indicators. The social indicators should:

a. be output-oriented or designed to describe a final outcome, leaving to other statistics the quantification of inputs, through puts or intermediate outputs;

b. be relevant to policy—i.e., descriptive of prevailing social conditions which are potentially amenable to improvement through collective actions or public policy;

c. be applicable over a long period of time in a substantial number of member countries. Actual values of the indicators may of course differ widely over time and access the whole OECD area;

d. apply to conditions of individual well-being, excluding a number of "indivisible public goods," however desirable these are as an aspect;

e. be independent of particular institutional arrangement, so as to be reasonably comparable between countries and over time;

f. form part of a comprehensive grid portraying all areas of social concerns;

g. correspond closely to the social concern which they relate, yet be more than a narrow description of social phenomena;

h. form an integrated framework of definitions, specifications, statistical guidelines, and disaggregation which should be compatible with other important sets of social and demographic statistics. (OECD, 1982, p. 10)

Based on these criteria a tentative list of eight social concerns and thirty-three indicators was developed. The indicators present systematically selected statistical measures of individual well-being that can be influenced by social policies and community actions (OECD, 1982, p. 12). To give meaningful basic information on the level of individual well-being, some disaggregations are presented as suggestions. The purposes of disaggregation relate to normative considerations, explanatory requirements, and program monitoring and evaluation (OECD, 1976, pp. 31–33). Examples of standard disaggregations include age, sex, household type, socioeconomic status, community size, ethnic group, citizenship, region, branch of economic activity, occupation, type of activity, working hours, level of education, tenure status, and/or age of dwelling.

In the developing countries, indicators represent some aspect of development, such as industrialization, equity, health, education, and so on, and play a crucial role in development policy. Examples of indicators, from the study of the contents and measurement of development carried by the UN Research Institute for Social Development (UNRISD), include the following:

1. Expectation of life at birth

2. Percent population in localities of 20,000 and over

3. Consumption of animal protein, per capita, per day

4. Combined primary and secondary enrolment

5. Vocational enrolment ratio

6. Average number of persons per room

7. Newspaper circulation per 1,000 population

8. Percent economically active population in electricity, gas, water, etc.

9. Agricultural production per male agricultural worker

10. Percent adult male labour in agriculture

11. Electricity consumption, kWh per capita

12. Steel consumption, kg. per capita

13. Energy consumption, kg. of coal equivalent per capita

14. Percent G.D.P. derived from manufacturing

15. Foreign trade per capita, in 1960 U.S. dollars

16. Percent salaried and wage earners to total economically active population (United Nations Research Institute for Social Development, 1970, p. 63)

Another study, by Adelman and Morris, suggests the following social indicators of development:

1. Size of the traditional agricultural sector

2. Extent of dualism

3. Extent of urbanization

 4. Character of basic social organization

 5. Importance of the indigenous middle class

 6. Extent of social mobility

 7. Extent of literacy

 8. Extent of mass communication

 9. Degree of cultural and ethnic homogeneity

10. Degree of social tension

11. Crude fertility rate

12. Degree of modernization of outlook

13. Degree of national integration and sense of national unity

14. Extent of centralization of political power

15. Strength of democratic institutions

16. Degree of freedom of political opposition and press

17. Degree of competitiveness of political parties

18. Predominant basis of the political party system

19. Strength of the labour movement

20. Political strength of the traditional elite

21. Political strength of the military

22. Degree of administrative efficiency

23. Extent of leadership commitment to economic development

24. Extent of political stability

25. Per capita G.N.P. in 1961

26. Rate of growth of real per capita G.N.P.: 1950/51–1963/64

27. Abundance of natural resources

28. Gross investment rate

29. Level of modernization of industry

30. Change in degree of industrialization since 1950

31. Character of agricultural organization

32. Level of modernization of techniques in agriculture

33. Degree of improvement in agricultural productivity since 1950

34. Level of adequacy of physical overhead capital

35. Degree of improvement in physical overhead capital since 1950

36. Level of effectiveness of the tax system

37. Degree of improvement in the tax system since 1950

38. Level of effectiveness of financial institutions

39. Degree of improvement in human resources

40. Structure of foreign trade (Adelman and Morris, 1967, pp. 16–17)

National Income Accounting

National income accounting constitutes the second route chosen in macroso-cial accounting toward the evaluation, measurement, and disclosure of national performance. The first approach taken in national income accounting was to rely on a system; the second approach aims at providing better measures of social well-being.

National income accounting is the set of rules and techniques for measuring the total flow of output (parts and services) produced and the total flow of input (factors of production) used by the economy.

1. The government outputs are valued at the cost of the input needed to produce them.
2. Inventories are treated as if they were "purchased" by the firms producing them.
3. A firm's output is defined to be its value added; that is to say, the value of output minus the value of the inputs it purchased from other firms.
4. Finally, current market prices are used in measuring the value of the economic output.

Conventionally Measured GNP

As stated earlier, the value of the output of the economy can be measured either as the sum of the values of the final products or as the sum of the payment to the various factors of production. In either case the value of the output of the national economy is best exemplified and known as the GNP of the nation. As conventionally known, the GNP is the sum of the values of all final goods and services produced in a specific period of time (usually a year) and valued at current market prices.

Two ways have been devised for the measurement of the GNP. The first method measured the GNP as the sum of all final goods and services:

$$GNP = C + I + G + EX - IM \tag{1.9}$$

where

C = sales of goods and services to consumers
I = gross sales of products to business for final use as producers' (capital) goods, including inventory changes
G = sales of goods and services to government
EX = exports
IM = imports

Exhibit 1.1 shows the GNP as the sum of final demands. The second method measures the GNP as the sum of all factor payments—in other words, as the sum of all the incomes in the economy:

Exhibit 1.1
GNP in 1981 as the Sum of Final Demands (billions of dollars)

Item	Amount
Personal consumption expenditures	1,858.1
Gross private domestic investment	450.6
Government purchases of goods and services	589.6
Net exports	23.8
Exports 366.7	
Imports 342.9	
GNP	2,922.1

$$GNP = W + R + I + P + T + X + D \tag{1.10}$$

where

W = wages
R = rental income of persons
I = net interest paid to households
P = profits
T = indirect business taxes
X = business transfer payments
D = depreciation or capital consumption

Exhibit 1.2 shows the GNP as the sum of incomes. Through some recombinations, some other useful macroeconomic measurements may be derived as follows:

Net National Product	= GNP − Depreciation
National Income	= $W + R + I + P$
Personal Income	= National Income − (Corporate Profit Taxes + Retained Earnings + Payroll Taxes) + Transfer Payments
Disposable Personal Income	= Personal Income − Personal Taxes

Both methods of measurement constitute the parts of a dualistic system to measure the output of a nation. Both, however, suffer from some limitations as follows. First, the GNP includes only market activity and does not include non-market activities such as work done by housewives and do-it-yourself-ers. It may be inapplicable to some of the Third World countries, where most activities are not conducted in organized markets. Second, the GNP does not include illegal activities; even though some of those activities produce goods and services, few are sold on the market, generating factor incomes. In addition, the GNP does not include factors affecting human welfare. For example, leisure is not included, although it is important for well-being. In brief, GNP is not a measure of well-being. Third, the GNP includes good as well as bad activities.

Exhibit 1.2
GNP in 1981 as the Sum of Incomes (billions of dollars)

Item	Amount
Compensation of employees (wages)	1,771.7
Net interest	215.0
Rental income	33.6
Profit	323.4
Corporate profits 189.0	
Proprietors' income 134.4	
National income	2,343.7
Indirect business taxes and miscellaneous items	257.0
Net national product	2,600.0
Depreciation	321.5
GNP	2,922.2

For example, the outlays necessary to correct the effect of a disaster may cause the GNP to rise. Finally, most of the undesirable effects of economic activities are not deducted from the GNP to give a better measure of net increase in economic welfare.

Toward a Better Measure of GNP

As stated earlier, the GNP is a measure of the nation's annual production of goods and services. It fails, however, to measure social well-being adequately. Accordingly, various attempts have been made to modify conventionally measured GNP to obtain a better measure of social well-being. First, W. Nordhaus and J. Tobin developed a measure of economic welfare as a result of a management of items in the national accounts and addition of items not covered in the GNP computations: household work, leisure, and the services consumers derive from the durable goods such as autos, boats, and appliances (Nordhaus and Tobin, 1967, pp. 16–17). A correction is also made for the "disamenities of urbanization," which include "litter, congestion, noise, insecurity, large buildings, and advertisements offensive to taste."

Second, as stated earlier in the social indicators section, the Economic Council of Japan has developed a net national welfare (NNW) measure to account for the impact on the environment (Economic Council of Japan, 1974). As in Nordhaus and Tobin, the NNW is a rearrangement of national accounts items, added to imputations for the services of government capital, consumer durables, leisure, and other nonmarket activities, and corrected for "urbanization" and "environmental maintenance costs"—that is, the costs of operating and maintaining pollution control equipment plus the annualized capital costs of purchasing it.

Other attempts were made to provide a framework of modifying the traditional account structure in order to measure the environmental changes. First, M. Olson suggested that the GNP be reduced by an amount equal to the social damage from pollution (Olson, 1977). Second, O. Herfindahl and A. Kneese suggested that a surrogate for the social damage from pollution is the pollution control expenditures and as such they should be deducted to reduce the GNP (Herfindahl and Kneese, 1973). Third, A. Marin also concluded that if we want national income to conform more closely to theoretical concepts of welfare indexes, then we need to include a proxy for the environmental services that would not be completely free goods if it were possible to overcome their inherent nonmarketability (Herfindahl and Kneese, 1973). The least unsatisfactory proxy considered for Mann would be spending on environmental protection. H. M. Peskin, building on an earlier work (Peskin and Peskin, 1978; Peskin 1976), suggested a procedure for the conventional income and product accounts so that they can capture features of the environment that are at present ignored (Peskin, 1981). It is based on a framework that views the environment as a separate sector subject to both "environmental services" and "environmental damages." As a result, two entries are required to account for these services and damages in a national accounting structure:

One will describe the productive services the environment provides to business and other consumers of environmental services. This will be entered on the lefthand side of the business accounts and the consolidated national account, along with the other productive inputs. A second entry will describe any loss of environmental services or damage to consumers resulting from the use of the environment by business and other sectors. Since this damage can be viewed as a "bad" produced by the business (as opposed to a "good"), it will be entered negatively on the righthand side of the business accounts and the consolidated national account, along with the other components output. Since in general, these two entries will not be equal, a balancing entry will be required if accounting balance is to be maintained. (Peskin, 1981)

Peskin has shown that the modified GNP can be defined alternatively as conventional GNP less images, conventional GNP plus environmental services, and conventional GNP plus net environmental benefits. Efforts to design and implement this modified accounting framework are underway (Peskin, 1981, p. 84). Finally, the per person gross domestic product (GDP) is only an economic measure that does not make any adjustments for quality-of-life considerations. To compensate for this limitation, the United Nations produces a Human Development Index that combines gross domestic products with other indicators of well-being. This index may be adjusted for life expectancy and literacy; for life expectancy, literacy, and income distribution; and for life expectancy, literacy, and sexual equality. Reliance on either measures of per person GDP or Human Development Index can provide different rankings of countries about their living standards. The developed countries can be used as a good example. The 1990 statistics for the ten best countries in the world are shown in Exhibit 1.3. There are surprising results. Although the United States is number 1 in terms of per

Exhibit 1.3
The Ten Best Countries in the World: It Depends on the Little Adjustments

	Per Person GDP in 1990, Using Purchasing Power Parity Exchange Rate	Per Person GNP in 1990, Using Market Exchange Rate	1990 U.N. Human Development Index Adjusted for Life Expectancy and Literacy	1990 U.N. Human Development Index Adjusted for Life Expectancy and Income Distribution	1990 U.N. Human Development Index Adjusted for Life Expectancy and Sexual Equality
United States	$21,449 (1)	21,790 (7)	0.976 (7)	0.994 (9)	0.809 (10)
Switzerland	20,997 (2)	32,680 (1)	0.981 (5)	0.961 (4)	—
Luxembourg	19,340 (3)	—	—	—	—
Canada	19,120 (4)	20,470 (8)	0.983 (2)	0.948 (7)	0.813 (9)
Germany	18,291 (5)	22,320 (5)	0.971 (10)	—	—
Japan	17,634 (6)	25,430 (3)	0.993 (1)	0.990 (1)	—
France	17,431 (7)	19,490 (10)	—	—	0.849 (4)
Sweden	16,867 (8)	23,660 (4)	0.982 (4)	0.963 (3)	0.886 (2)
Denmark	16,765 (9)	—	—	—	0.878 (3)
Finland	16,453 (10)	26,040 (2)	—	0.941 (10)	0.902 (1)
Norway	—	32,120 (5)	0.978 (6)	0.965 (5)	0.845 (5)
United Arab Emirates	—	19,860 (9)	—	—	—
Iceland	—	—	0.983 (3)	—	—
Netherlands	—	—	0.976 (8)	0.972 (2)	—
Australia	—	—	0.973 (9)	—	0.843 (6)
Belgium	—	—	—	0.951 (6)	—
Britain	—	—	—	0.948 (8)	—
Austria	—	—	—	—	0.832 (7)
Czechoslovakia	—	—	—	—	0.830 (8)

person GDP in 1990 using purchasing power parity exchange rates, it is number 7 using market exchange rates. With the 1990 UN Human Development Index adjusted for life expectancy and literacy, Japan comes first although its per capita income is less than two-thirds that of the United States. This is because Japanese citizens tend to live three years longer. The ranking of the United States using the 1990 UN Human Development Index adjusted for life expectancy, literacy, and income distribution sinks to the ninth level given the disparities in income distribution. Finally, the 1990 Human Development Index adjusted for life expectancy, literacy, and sexual equality shows Finland in first position and the United States in tenth position, owing to the high disparities existing between men and women in the United States. Czechoslovakia ranks higher than the United States in this dimension.

Other Possible Improvements in National Income Accounting

More and more economists are arguing that the government should keep its books like a business. As a first step the government should adopt a complete balance sheet and income statement that would separate its long-term investment in physical assets from its operating expenses, adjust its assets and debts for inflation, and clarify the way it records nontax revenues and outlays. In addition, the government should add a capital account to the government budget that would separate long-term investments from operating squares.

The complete balance sheet would require a detailed inventory of the nation's land and mineral holdings as well as a list of the condition and expected life span of its buildings and a complete record of its finances and investments. These assets and liabilities should be adjusted for inflation to reflect the real net worth of the nation.

ACCOUNTING DEVELOPMENT AND ECONOMIC DEVELOPMENT

Role of Capital Markets

Capital is a scarce but essential commodity for the economic development of developing countries. Capital formation, in the form of domestic capital formation, direct foreign investment, and/or foreign aid, is needed for increasing gross national products to the levels set by the development plans. In fact, a high rate of capital accumulation is one of the most important goals in economic planning. Institutional arrangements for channeling savings and foreign investments to economic development are, as a result, another important goal of economic planning. These institutional arrangements include commercial and savings banks; investment banks and development financial institutions; insurance, social security, and pension schemes; and securities markets (Enthoven, 1973, p. 196). Their principal operational functions are as follows.

(a) mobilizing and canalization of savings; (b) granting liquidity; (c) functioning as middlemen in buying and selling of securities, of between interested parties; (d) risk diversification for savers by means of loans and investment in various fields; (e) underwriting of securities; (f) apposing of financial and economic data for investment purposes; (g) supplying various types of auxiliary services to firms and individuals. (Enthoven, 1973)

In addition to these financial intermediaries, the growth of a capital market in the developing countries is crucial to the task of spurring capital formation. The growth of a capital market allows for the formation of some of the capital needed to sustain local and foreign firms and encourage investment. An efficient capital market, if at all possible, allows risk sharing and risk reduction, and provides through security prices aggregate information about investment opportunity. Unfortunately the capital markets in developing countries are best characterized by thinness and poor management. The following consequences emerge:

1. The individual investor is reduced to financing his or her project out of proper savings and to acting as the manager of the project.
2. The individual investor may shun risky investments and investments with long-term payoff as a result of hampering the risk-sharing fund of a financial market (Lee, 1987, p. 77).
3. There is a lack of communication between the management and the shareholders leading the potential investor to be unsure of the price to pay and of the quality of the security (Lee, 1987, p. 82).

4. The security's price is decomposed into fundamental value and "noise." In the inefficient and thin capital markets of the developing countries, the lack of knowledge about the fundamental value of the security reduces the determination of the security price to "noise." Investing in the capital market now has the equivalence of playing the lottery.

What is evident is that the functioning of capital markets, resource allocation, and the existence of a capital market are not enough if there is no confidence in corporate operation and the working of the capital market. Accounting plays an important role in creating the level of confidence needed for the success of a capital market in a developing country. A sound accounting system that focuses on the reliability and accuracy of the financial statements of corporations creates the right climate of confidence conducive to the functioning of capital markets, resource allocation, and economic growth. Quereshi draws attention to the relationship between financial accounting, capital formation, and economic development as follows:

The choice is also based on the idea that financial reporting, capital markets, and capital formation interrelate. Capital formation, a strategic factor in economic development, is closely dependent upon financial mechanisms and institutions. Studies by such eminent monetarists as Kuznets, Goldsmith, and McKinnon provide a convincing evidence on the parallel between the development of capital markets and economic growth. The development and proper functioning of capital markets in turn is intimately related to the availability of financial information which is provided by the accounting fraction of financial reporting. (Quereshi, 1975, p. 71)

The developed countries rely on conventional accounting information for resource allocation decisions. A certain level of market efficiency renders conventional accounting satisfactory in these countries. The developing countries do not have the required market efficiency and other supplementary systems to compensate for the deficiencies of the conventional accounting information system. Some of the reasons follow:

First, typically, developing countries have economic policies that accompany various forms of government control, which tends to distort the market's ability to make optional resource allocations in the economy. Second, separate information and economic data gathering systems normally do not exist, and even if they do, because of the short history of industrial development, systems are in the fledgling stage and their capacity is invariably limited. Third, apart from the information paucity problem, the flow of information and economic data that exist in the society is generally inhibited owing either to explicit government control or bureaucratic inefficiency. Fourth, the pace of industrial change imposed by internal and external factors is so rapid that the society's fragile information systems are incapable of adjusting themselves organically in the short run. Fifth, and most importantly, the accounting standards and practice in most developing countries are either so archaic or loose in application that information generated from such systems is unreliable or limited at best. All these factors of developing countries collectively add up to the condition in which resource allocation for economic development is likely to be distorted, and thus the problem of an information gap between accounting and the planner's needs is serious. (Yu and Lee, 1988)

Basically capital formation, as well as the efficiency of capital markets, depends on information production and disclosure. Gordian Ndubizu explains the relationships among financial information disclosure, capital market efficiency, and economic growth as follows:

a. Accounting information disclosure minimizes the capital market uncertainty. This is accomplished through the disclosure of the value and risk of each asset traded on the capital market.
b. The reduced capital market uncertainty encourages more investors to buy and sell securities in the capital market. It has been documented that higher capital market uncertainty induces security buyers to underprice high-quality security. Consequently the seller of such security will withdraw from the market, which reduces the size of the market.
c. The capital market size affects both the market information processing (denoted c) and risk sharing (denoted d). Other things being equal, the larger the capital market, the more efficient is the information processing. The capital market information processing generates the security prices. The security prices affect the ability of the capital market to efficiently allocate scarce resources (denoted e).
d. The larger the market portfolio, the smaller the market risk per asset is and the easier it is for investors to hold/purchase an efficient portfolio of securities. The optimal risk sharing leads to an efficient allocation of savings (denoted f).
e. The capital market helps in the development of savings which effect economic growth through investment. The capital market transfers the accumulated savings to the most efficient investment opportunity. This function of the capital market stimulates economic growth. (Ndubizu, 1992, p. 153)

The accounting infrastructure appears as the cause of capital market thinness. A well-developed accounting infrastructure improves the communication of information to users and allows security holders to better assess the fundamental value of securities and to monitor management effectively. As stated by C.W.J. Lee,

good communication makes it possible for the investment of better quality to command a higher price and hence will induce management to seek financing in an organized capital market. When the monitoring cost and signalling cost are zero, information would flow freely among the capital market participants. Consequently, when the accounting infrastructure is well developed, all investment projects would be financed in a centralized and well-organized capital market. (Lee, 1987, p. 82)

Role of Accounting Infrastructure

The accounting environment of developing countries differs depending on the characteristics used to depict it. The accounting environment of developing countries has been referred to as either the accounting establishment or the accounting infrastructure. H. P. Holzer and J. S. Chandler defined the accounting establishment as consisting of four components: "the accounting function in indigenous enterprises, the local accounting profession, the accounting function of governmental agencies, and the teaching of accountancy in educational institutions" (Holzer and Chandler, 1981, pp. 23–32).

As suggested by Lee, the accounting infrastructure is comprised of four elements: (1) the facilities of information production in the nature of the information producer and final user; (2) the framework of information diffusion in the nature of the information intermediaries; (3) the foundation of information monitoring in the nature of the laws and regulations that govern the production, transmission, and usage of information; and (4) the foundation of contract enforcement in the nature of the legal entity that monitors and implements the laws and regulations (Lee, 1987, p. 79). The thinness of the capital market in developing countries as well as the failure of security prices to reflect much of the underlying fundamental information can be attributed to deficiencies in the accounting infrastructure. The crucial role of the accounting infrastructure for capital market efficiency is argued as follows:

The cost of fundamental information depends on the development of the accounting infrastructure. The more advanced the infrastructure, the lower will be the cost of information. In a developing economy where the accounting infrastructure is not well developed, the cost of fundamental information would be high and the percentage of informed investors in the market would be low. As a result, the price of a security can deviate widely from its fundamental value. With a high volume of noise in security price, the uniformed investors cannot confidently use the security price as a reliable guide to investment decision. Hence, the intertemporal misallocation of resources is a serious issue in developing economies. The development of advanced accounting infrastructure can reduce the information cost and increase the information content of security prices. Because the market price can aggregate relevant fundamental information in the economy, the decision makers can use the market price to enhance their information set and reduce the possible decision bias caused by the bounded rationality. When the capital market is semi-strongly or strongly efficient, then the market price would reflect useful fundamental information and would provide useful guidance to the investment decision. (Lee, 1987, p. 83)

Another excellent description of accounting infrastructure in the developing countries is provided by R.S.O. Wallace and R. J. Briston (Wallace and Briston, 1992, pp. 201–224). The basic elements that make up this information infrastructure include:

(1) the supply function—the training and education of accountants and auditors (i.e., the information producers) and availability of institutions and equipment in sufficient number and quality to assist the information producer, (2) the demand function—the information user, including information intermediaries, information screening mechanisms such as inter-firm comparison, and stock exchanges and banks; and (3) quality control systems— the laws and regulations that govern the production, transmission and usage of information, the legal entities that monitor and implement the laws and regulations and the personnel that validate the information produced. These basic elements seem to influence, and are influenced by, the types of accounting which exist in a country. (Wallace and Briston, 1992, p. 202)

The complexity of this infrastructure points to the problems by developing countries in upgrading their accounting environments. Accounting academics have made various suggestions on how best to improve this accounting infrastructure; Wallace and Briston correctly argue, however, that the national accounting infrastructure development (NAID) program suitable for a country depends on the particular circumstances of a given country (Wallace and Briston, 1992, p. 206). They identified three approaches for developing accounting infrastructure: a dependency approach, a self-reliance (without foreign assistance) approach, and a self-reliance (with foreign assistance) approach (Wallace and Briston, 1992, pp. 206–210). The dependency approach exists generally between a developed country and a developing country that was a colony of the developed country. Basically money, personnel, technology, and administration and accounting systems are transferred from the developed to the developing country to stimulate development. The self-reliance (without foreign assistance) approach exists when the developing country has the appropriate knowledge, skills, and attitude to dictate the evolution of its accounting capability. The self-reliance (with foreign assistance) approach exists when the developing country relies on both its own abilities and external assistance to bring about improvements and upgradings in its accounting infrastructure.

Micro- Versus Macroaccounting

Information needs in the developing countries relate to the conduct of both business and government units and of the nation. Micro- and macroaccounting systems, whether or not integrated, are needed. The macro- or national accounting system serves to determine the structure, conduct, and performance of the nation's affairs and implement economic policies. Macroaccounting includes national income accounts, input and output accounts, flow of funds accounts, balance of payments, and national balance sheet. The microaccounting system serves to determine conduct and performance of private and public balance of payments, and national balance sheet. The microaccounting system serves to determine the structure, conduct, and performance of private and public enterprises. Microaccounting includes both enterprise and governmental accounting.

In the context of an integrated national accounting system, microaccounting is used to serve macroaccounting (Wallace, 1990, p. 20). In fact, in countries that rely on national economic planning, the two systems are more integrated than in countries relying on market forces. Various authors in international accounting argued for the superiority of an integrated macro-based accounting and advised its adoption by developing countries (Needles, 1976, pp. 45–62). Recommendations were also made for its adoption in Kuwait (Shuaib, 1980, pp. 143–58) and Syria (Abdeen, 1980, pp. 129–141). The suggestion for linkages between micro- and macroaccounting is made for the sake of success of development planning (Mirghani, 1982, pp. 57–68). The unavailability of reliable information and the unreliability of available information can have adverse effects upon exerted development efforts (Mirghani, 1982).

The linkage between micro- and macroaccounting allows for the determination of the type of information outputs for the microaccounting system that is intended to become the information inputs of the macroaccounting system, creating in the process an information feedback loop. The advantages of such a feedback loop are presumed as follows:

1. The preparers of the macroaccounting information would be able to keep track of the changing information needs of the development planning process.

2. The development planners would be able to indicate to the preparers of the macroaccounting information, through negative or positive feedback information, the effectiveness of the information provided in aiding the development planning process. This should, in turn, enable the macroaccounting system to adjust its operations in order to serve the development planning process better.

3. The macroaccounting system would be able to provide negative or positive feedback information to the development planners regarding the progress being made in achieving the objectives of the development plan. This would in turn enable the development planners to revise the development plan, on a timely basis, whenever it is necessary.

4. The developing country would have development planning and macroaccounting systems that are complementary to each other rather than having each system operating in a vacuum. This would save the particular developing country the cost of implementing and later scrubbing development strategies or policies that were ultimately found to have been formulated on the basis of unreliable information. (Mirghani, 1982, p. 63)

Mirghani also offers a structure of the macroeconomic system comprised of its method of classification, processing methodologies, and database. The classification system is threefold: the microunits comprising the economy divided into major economic sectors, the macroaccounting system grouped into accounts or subsystems intended to produce specific information output, and the economic transactions of each economic sector worked into the input data for each subsystem of the macroaccounting system. This integration of macroaccounting and microaccounting is prevalent in general in countries expressing some forms of indicative planning and in particular in most francophone countries where the French system of uniform accounting for the purpose of assisting national or macroaccounting is adopted. The merge of two systems, while desirable, is not required for an effective macroaccounting system.

Enterprise Accounting

Enterprise accounting, or private-enterprise accounting, contributes to the measurement of the efficiency of the allocation and use of economic resources. It plays a vital role in running firms in developed countries. The low level of enterprise accounting expertise in developing countries and the consequent low reliability of the information provided has the following consequences:

National investors are understandably disinclined to provide the capital necessary to expanding economies, and private-sector capital markets of adequate size fail to materialize. Management reporting is also usually of two calibers and often is almost nonexistent. In developing nations internal reporting may offer management little more than verification of past transactions and management may not realize the potential of accounting as a managerial tool. (Scott, 1986, p. 52)

This is an unfortunate situation given the importance of enterprise accounting for the integrity and development of capital markets and for economic development in general. Some of the merits of enterprise accounting follow:

1. The skills and techniques that make up enterprise accounting are essential to the development of commerce, industry, and public administration.
2. Economic development rests on successful industrialization and the efficient mobilization of capital. Accounting can help in evaluating the success of both endeavors, as stated by Seidler: "Enterprise accounting is a supplier of information, a device for increasing the efficiency of resource allocations, and a mechanism for controlling productive operations. It seems logical that these skills, normally considered to be tools of private enterprise management, should be equally useful to the management of the development process" (Seidler, 1967b, p. 7).
3. Through the production of reliable and timely information, enterprise accounting is essential to the efficient functioning of a capital market necessary to channel funds for development and investment, in the collection of taxes, and in the efficient allocation of scarce resources.
4. Enterprise accounting information is needed by government, capital markets, and business firms in developing nations. First, government needs such information for implementing public policy, controlling and regulating private enterprise, controlling economic cycles, analyzing expenditures for social overhead, measuring national income, constructing input-output and flow of funds systems, disseminating information, and, finally, collecting income taxes.
5. Enterprise accounting information is seen as vital to the emergence of a domestic private capital market, a domestic public capital market, an external private capital

market, an external public source of capital, and a capital market consisting of funds from international agencies.

6. Enterprise accounting information is necessary to assist management in its custodial functions, operating decisions, control of subsidiaries and branches, personnel control, real income measurement, budgeting and forecasting, and special management problems.

7. Finally, economic development depends on an efficient use of a country's economic resources. It rests on development planning to guide the efficient use of these resources. To be successful, development planning should be supported by an adequate supply of information, which is one of the prerogatives of accounting.

This last point is eloquently addressed by M. A. Mirghani:

Since development planning represents a system of decision making under conditions of great uncertainty, it should be supported by an information system capable of generating the types of information necessary for reducing the amount of uncertainty surrounding the economic choices that must be made. The development planning process can be likened to the resource allocation process in a micro-organization. The management of any organization would attempt to select the package of alternative uses that would yield maximum benefits in view of the constraints operating in that organization's specific environment. Such an exercise would not be fruitful without an information system that would enable management to make rational choices among alternative uses. (Mirghani, 1982, p. 593)

Enterprise accounting in the developing countries needs, however, to adapt to the specific problems faced by these countries and produce the appropriate report for an understanding of these problems. For example, J. M. Samuels suggested a list of the major problems of developing countries and the types of accounting statements for an understanding of these problems (Samuels, 1990, p. 80).

Specific economic data and information are required for economic planning. Some of this information includes competitive advantage, effective interest rates, value added, productivity employment, market structure, export and import dependence, local contents, effective tariff rates, shadow price, linkage relations, input-output ratios, investment coefficients, effect of price-level change, energy requirements, water requirements, environmental pollution, technology and skill level, and R&D capability (Yu and Lee, 1988, p. 472). Most of these data and information are not provided by the conventional accounting system of either developed or developing countries. The scope of accounting information obviously needs to be expanded to include the production and reporting of these important indicators of development planning. Enthoven advocated that critical information for economic planning—such as value added, profitability, capital coefficient, price level change, human resources, and productivity—should be included in the accounting scope in a manner that integrates enterprise, government, and macroaccounting in the whole process of economic analysis, policy, and planning (Enthoven, 1985).

Developing countries rely to a large extent on economic development planning to achieve a certain measure of growth. To avoid misallocation of resources in the planning process, reliable economic data and information are needed and are generally presumed to be provided by the accounting and information system. This is generally not the case. As stated by S. Yu and J. Lee, economic data and information required for industrial development planning by developing countries are much more diverse and intense than traditional accounting's income-based, one-dimensional approach. Development planning typically requires, apart from profitability at the microlevel and fiscal and monetary policy at the macrolevel, such information as value added, productivity, export dependence, local contents, linkage relations, investment coefficients, energy requirement, technology level, and capability. Most of this information is required not only at the project level, but also at the industry and national levels. Currently, it is obtained not through routine accounting information systems, but through ad hoc efforts or separate information and data-gathering systems established purposefully or developed indigenously within the economy (Yu and Lee, 1988, p. 472).

Accounting for Inflation

The differences between price change models rest in the differences in their implicit or explicit specification of a valuation model or a measured attribute for assets and liabilities, and a capital maintenance concept. Various studies provided a taxonomy of price change models based on a useful algebraic approach (Chambers, 1978, pp. 124–144; Barton, 1975; Chasteen, 1984, pp. 515–523). Lenny Chasteen's approach will be used here to illustrate the different price change models (Chasteen, 1984). He based his analysis on the assumptions and price change data in twelve price change models, based on an attribute measured/capital maintenance concept:

1. Historical cost/nominal dollars (HC/N$) model
2. Historical cost/constant dollars (HC/C$) model
3. Historical cost/constant dollars model a la Ijiri
4. Historical cost/constant dollars model using the one-line adjustment
5. Current cost/nominal dollars (CC/N$) model
6. Current cost/constant dollars (CC/C$) model
7. Current cost/physical capital (CC/PC) model
8. Current cost/physical capital model that incorporates purchasing power gains and losses on monetary items based on specific price changes

9. Current cost/physical capital model that incorporates both a specific price change adjustment as in the previous model and a "gearing" adjustment
10. Current exit value/nominal dollars (EV/N$)
11. Current exit value/constant dollars (EV/C$) a la Sterling
12. Current exit value/constant dollars a la Chambers

The algebraic formulations of each model follow.

1. The historical cost/nominal dollars model:

$$M + N = L + \underset{\top}{R} \tag{1.11}$$

$$(t = 1 \text{ capital})$$

Both inventory and equity security may be reported at $N(1 + s_1)$ or $N(1 + s_2)$ if s_1 and s_2 were negative.

2. The historical cost/constant dollars model:

$$M + N(1 + p) = L + R(1 + p) = L + \underset{\top}{R(1 + p)} \quad \underset{\top}{-p\,(M - L)} \tag{1.12}$$

$$(t{=}1 \text{ capital}) \text{ (income [loss])}$$

3. The historical cost/constant dollars model based on Ijiri's interpretation (Ijiri, 1976, pp. 227–243):

$$M + N(1 + p) = L + \underset{\top}{R(1 + p)} = \underset{\top}{Np - RP} \tag{1.13}$$

$$(t = 1 \text{ capital}) \quad \text{(income [loss])}$$

where Np is price level holding gain and Rp a price level capital change.

4. The historical cost/constant dollars model based on the one-line adjustment (Chambers, 1978; Grady, 1975, pp. 3–5; Agrawal and Roseinzweig, 1982, p. 29):

$$M + N = L + \underset{\top}{R(1 + p)} - \underset{\top}{Rp} \tag{1.14}$$

$$(t{=}1 \text{ capital}) \quad \text{(loss)}$$

5. The current cost/nominal dollars model (Edwards and Bell, 1961; Samuelson, 1980, pp. 254–268):

$$M + N(1 + s_1) = L + \underset{\mid}{R} + Ns_1 \tag{1.15}$$

$$(t = 1 \text{ capital})$$

allowing the disaggregation of the firm's replacement or current cost income into two elements: (1) the current operating profit (revenues less the current costs of earning the revenues) and (2) holding gains (Ns_1).

6. The current cost/constant dollars model:

$$M + N(1 + s_1) = \underset{\mid}{L + R(1 + p)}$$
$$(t = 1 \text{ capital}) \tag{1.16}$$
$$+ \frac{N(s_1 - p) - p(M - L)}{\mid}$$
$$(\text{income [loss]})$$

where $N(s_1 - p)$ is the holding gain or loss resulting from the specific price level changes, and $p(M - L)$ is the purchasing power gain or loss resulting from the general price level changes.

7. The current cost/physical capital model:

$$M + N(1 + s_1) = L + \underset{\mid}{R + Ns_1} \tag{1.17}$$
$$(t = 1 \text{ capital})$$

where, unlike the current cost/nominal dollars model, the holding gains are considered a capital maintenance adjustment rather than an element of income.

8. The current cost/physical capital model that incorporates purchasing power gains and losses on monetary items based on specific price changes (Gynther, 1966):

$$M + N(1 + s_1) = L + \underset{\mid}{R + Rs_1} - \underset{\mid}{s_1(M - L)} \tag{1.18}$$
$$(t = 1 \text{ capital}) (\text{income [loss]})$$

9. The current cost/physical capital model that incorporates losses, a specific price change adjustment, and a "gearing" adjustment:

$$M + N(1 + s_1) =$$
$$L + \underline{R + Ns_1[R/(L+R)]+Ms_1[R/(L+R)]}$$

$(t = 1 \text{ capital})$ (1.19)

$$+ \underline{Ns_1[R/(L+R)]-Ms_1[R/(L+R)]}$$

(income)

where the gearing adjustment is calculated by allocating the holding gain (specific price increase) on nonmonetary assets between income and capital as follows: income portion $= [L/(L + R)] Ns_1$; capital maintenance portion $= [R/(L + R)] Ns_1$.

10. The current exit value/nominal dollars model:

$$M + N(1 + s_2) = L + \underline{R} \qquad\qquad + \underline{Ns_2}$$
$$(t = 1 \text{ capital}) \text{ (income)}$$
(1.20)

11. The current exit value/constant dollars (EV/C\$) a la Sterling 1970; 1975, pp. 42–51):

$$M + N(1 + s_2) = L + \underline{R(1 + p)} \qquad + \underline{N(s_2 - p) - p(M-L)} \qquad (1.21)$$
$$(t = 1 \text{ capital}) \qquad\qquad (\text{income})$$

where the monetary assets are valued at exit prices instead of replacement costs.

12. The current exit value/constant dollars a la Chambers (1975, pp. 56–62):

$$M + N(1 + S_2) = L + \underline{R(1 + p)} + \quad \underline{Ns_2 - Rp}$$
$$(t = 1 \text{ capital}) \text{ (income)}$$
(1.22)

The twelve models described in this section represent some of the models that can be used or adapted by any country to deal with inflation. The easiest and most practical models that could be adopted by developing countries include the historical cost/constant dollars model (no. 1), the current cost/nominal dollars model (no. 5), and the current cost/constant dollars model (no. 6). They can provide relevant information about the impact of price changes on the financial structure, performance, and conduct of firms in the developing countries.

CONCLUSIONS

Macro- and microaccounting information is needed by governments, capital markets, and business firms to ensure a proper conduct of the planning process, generally required for the economic development of the developing countries. This chapter shows the importance of this role of accounting in both the planning process and economic development.

REFERENCES

Abdeen, A. 1980. "The Role of Accounting in Project Evaluation and Control: The Syrian Experience." *International Journal of Accounting Education and Research* 15: 143–158.

Abdelsalam, M. 1990. "The Use of Corporate Financial Reports by Investors in Saudi Arabia." In K. S. Most (ed.), *Advances in International Accounting* 3, pp. 25–39. Greenwich, Conn.: JAI Press.

Abdelsalam, M. and D. Satin. 1988. "The Impact of Published Annual Financial Reports on Share Prices in Saudi Arabia." *International Journal of Accounting Education and Research* 23: 113–124.

Adelman, I. and C. T. Morris. 1967. *Society, Politics and Economic Development.* Baltimore: Johns Hopkins University Press.

Agami, A. M. and Y. A. Alkafaji. 1987. "Accounting Education in Selected Middle Eastern Countries." *International Journal of Accounting Education and Research* 23: 145–168.

Agrawal, S. and K. Roseinzweig. 1982. "One-Line Adjustment Methods of Accounting for the Effects of Inflation." *Collected Abstracts of the AAA Annual Meeting* (AAA).

Aitken, M. J. and M. A. Islam. 1984. "Dispelling Arguments against International Accounting Standards." *International Journal of Accounting Education and Research* 19: 35–46.

Alhashim, D. D. 1977. "Social Accounting in Egypt." *International Journal of Accounting Education and Research* 12: 127–142.

Allardt, E. 1973a. "A Welfare Model for Selecting Indicators of National Development." *Policy Sciences* 4: 63–74.

———. 1973b. "Individual Needs, Social Structures and Indicators of National Development." In S. N. Eisenstadt and S. Rokkan (eds.), *Building States and Nations*, vol. 1. Beverly Hills, Calif.: Sage.

Allardt, E. and H. Uusitalo. 1972. "Dimensions of Welfare in a Comparative Study of the Scandinavian Societies." *Scandinavian Political Studies* 2: 15–24.

Amer, M. B. 1969. "Impact of Public Ownership on the U.A.R. Accounting Profession." *International Journal of Accounting Education and Research* 4: 49–62.

American Accounting Association. 1977. "Report of the 1975–76 Committee on International Accounting Operations and Education." *The Accounting Review* 52(Supplement): 65–132.

———. 1980. *Accounting Education and the Third World.* Sarasota, Fla.: AAA Report of the Committee on International Accounting Operations and Education 1976–1978.

American Institute of Certified Public Accountants (AICPA). 1964. *Professional Accounting in 25 Countries*. New York: AICPA.

———. 1975. *Professional Accounting in 30 Countries*. New York: AICPA.

Ariyo, A. 1988. "Economic Considerations in the Choice of Depreciation Methods: Some Additional Evidence from Nigeria." In K. S. Most (ed.), *Advances in International Accounting* 2, pp. 89–97. Greenwich, Conn.: JAI Press.

Ba-Eissa, M. O. 1984. *The Professionalisation of Accounting: A Study of the Development of Accounting Profession with Special Reference to Great Britain, the United States and Saudi Arabia*. Doctoral thesis, University of Kent at Canterbury.

Bai, Z. L. 1988. "Accounting in the People's Republic of China—Contemporary Situations and Issues." In V. K. Zimmerman (ed.), *Recent Accounting and Economic Developments in the Far East*. Center for International Education and Research in Accounting, University of Illinois at Urbana–Champaign, pp. 27–50.

Bait-et Mal, M. M., C. H. Smith, and M. E. Taylor. 1973. "The Development of Accounting in Libya." *International Journal of Accounting Education and Research* 8: 83–102.

Barton, A. 1975. *An Analysis of Business Income Concepts*, ICRA Occasional Paper No. 7, International Center for Research in Accounting (University of Lancaster).

Bauer, R. A. 1966. "Detection and Anticipation of Impact: The Nature of the Task." In *Social Indicators*. Cambridge, Mass.: MIT Press.

Baumol, W. J. and A. S. Binder. 1982. *Economics: Principles and Policy*, 2nd ed. New York: Harcourt Brace Jovanovich.

Benjamin, B. Y. Tei et al. 1990. "Non-compliance with Disclosure Requirements in Financial Statements; the Case of Hong Kong Companies." *International Journal of Accounting Education and Research* 25(2): 99–112.

Bernstein, M. H. 1955. *Regulating Business by Independent Commission*. Princeton, N.J.: Princeton University Press.

Berry, M. 1988. The Cultural Development of Accounting in the People's Republic of China." In V. K. Zimmerman (ed.), *Recent Accounting and Economic Developments in the Far East*. Center for International Education and Research in Accounting, University of Illinois at Urbana–Champaign, pp. 1–25.

Bond, R. R. 1970. "Emerging Nations and Emerging Institutions." *International Journal of Accounting Education and Research* 6: 83–90.

Bose, A. 1988. "The Indian Accounting Profession: Its Origins and Current Status." In V. K. Zimmerman (ed.), *Recent Accounting and Economic Developments in the Far East*. Center for International Education and Research in Accounting, University of Illinois at Urbana–Champaign, pp. 149–162.

———. 1977. "The Growth of Accountancy in India." *Accountancy* 88: 36–38.

Briston, R. J. 1974. "The Accountancy Profession in a Developing Country: An Indonesia Case Study." *The Accountant's Magazine* August: 314–315.

———. 1978. "The Evolution of Accounting in Developing Countries." *International Journal of Accounting Education and Research* 14: 105–120.

———. 1979. "The Changing Role of Government Audits in Developing Countries: Its Implications for UK Accounting Firms." *The Accountant's Magazine* August: 25–27.

———. 1984. "Accounting Standards and Host Country Control of Multinationals." *British Accounting Review* 16: 12–26.

Briston, R. J. and A. A. El-Ashker 1984. "The Egyptian Accounting System: A Case

Study in Western Influence." *International Journal of Accounting Education and Research* 19: 129–155.

Briston, R. J. and E. S. Liang. 1990. "The Evolution of Corporate Reporting in Singapore." In R.S.O. Wallace, J. M. Samuels, and R. J. Briston (eds.), *Research in Third World Accounting* 1, pp. 281–299. London: JAI Press.

Briston, R. J. and R.S.O. Wallace. 1990. "Accounting Education and Corporate Financial Reporting in Tanzania." In R.S.O. Wallace, J. M. Samuels, and R. J. Briston (eds.), *Research in Third World Accounting* 1, pp. 281–301. London: JAI Press.

Briston, R. J., F. S. Liang, and H. Yunus. 1990. "Accounting Education and Work Force Requirements in Indonesia." In B. E. Needles, Jr. and V. K. Zimmerman (eds.), *Comparative International Accounting Education Standards*. Center for International Education and Research in Accounting, University of Illinois at Urbana–Champaign, pp. 147–173.

Brookner, L. and E. Heilman. 1960. "Technical Assistance in Accounting in Turkey." *The Accounting Review* 25: 33–36.

Campbell, L. 1985. "Financial Reporting in Japan." In C. W. Nobes and R. H. Parker (eds.), *Comparative International Accounting*, 2nd ed. Deddington, U.K.: Philip Ailan.

Carley, M. J. 1979. "Social Theory and Models in Social Indicator Research." *International Journal of Social Economics* 6, 1.

Cassell, M. E. 1979. "Economic Development Accountancy." *Management Accounting* (UK) May: 23–24.

Chaderton, R. 1990. "The Education of Professional Accountants in the Barbados." In B. E. Needles and V. K. Zimmerman (eds.), *Comparative International Accounting Education Standards*. Center for International Education and Research in Accounting, University of Illinois at Urbana–Champaign, pp. 273–243.

Chambers, R. J. 1975. "NOD, COG and PuPu: See How Inflation Teases," *Journal of Accountancy* September: 56–62.

———. 1978. "The Use and Misuse of a Notation: The History of an Idea." *Abacus* December: 122–144.

Chan, A. M. 1988. "The Speculative Accounting System in Hong Kong; Understanding Hong Kong's Accounting Reality." In V. K. Zimmerman (ed.), *Recent Accounting and Economic Developments in the Far East*. Center for International Education and Research in Accounting, University of Illinois at Urbana–Champaign, pp. 197–218.

Chandler, J. S. and H. P. Holter. 1985. "Preconditions for the Introduction of Computer-Aided Accounting Systems in Less Developed Countries." *Management International Review* 25: 53–66.

Chasteen, L. 1984. "A Taxonomy of Price Change Models," *The Accounting Review* July: 515–523.

Cheng, C. 1980. "Political Accounting in China: What the West Should Know." *Journal of Accountancy* January: 76–82, 85.

Cheng, P. C. and T. N. Jain. 1973. "Economic Perspective and Accounting Practices in South Korea." *International Journal of Accounting Education and Research* 8: 123–142.

Chiu, J. S. and D. L. Chang. 1979. "Management Accounting in Taiwan." *Management Accounting* (U.S.) 60: 50–55.

Choi, F.D.S. 1979. "ASEAN Federation of Accountants: A New International Accounting Force." *International Journal of Accounting Education and Research* 15: 53–75.

Choi, F.D.S. and G. L. Mueller. 1984. *International Accounting*. Engelwood Cliffs, N.J.: Prentice-Hall.

Chow, C. W. and A. Wong-Boren. 1986. "Audit Firm Size and Audit Quality: Some Evidence from Mexico." *International Journal of Accounting Education and Research* 21: 1–25.

———. 1987. "Voluntary Financial Disclosure by Mexican Corporations." *The Accounting Review* 62:533–541.

Chu, J. M. 1973. "Accounting Principles and Practices in Panama." *International Journal of Accounting Education and Research* 9: 43–52.

Clapp, C. L. 1967. "National Variation in Accounting Principles and Practices." *International Journal of Accounting Education and Research* 3: 29–42.

Clark, T. N. 1973. "Community Social Indicators: From Analytical Models to Policy Applications." *Urban Affairs Quarterly* September: 15–37.

Cohen, B. J. 1973. *The Question of Imperialism: The Political Economy of Dominance and Dependence*. New York: Basic Books.

Cooke, T. E. and R.S.O. Wallace. 1990. "Financial Disclosure Regulation and its Environment: A Review and Further Analysis." *Journal of Accounting and Public Policy* 9: 79–110.

Costouros, G. J. 1975. "Accounting Education and Practices in Greece." *International Journal of Accounting Education and Research* 11:95–106.

da Costa, R. C., J. C. Bourgeois, and W. M. Lawson. 1978. "A Classification of International Financial Accounting Practices." *International Journal of Accounting Education and Research* 13: 73–85.

Dahmash, N. H. 1982. "Public Auditing Developments in the Arab States: A Comparative Study." *International Journal of Accounting Education and Research* 18:89–114.

Dev, S. and E. L. Inanga. 1979. "Educating Accountants in Nigeria." *Accountancy* 90: 127–129.

Drewnovsky, J. 1970. *Studies in the Measurement of Levels of Living and Welfare*. UNRISD Report no. 703. Geneva: United Nations.

Economic Council of Japan. 1973. *Measuring Net National Welfare of Japan*. Tokyo: Economic Research Institute.

———. 1974. NNW Measurement Committee. *"Measuring National Welfare of Japan."* (Report prepared for the Japanese Ministry of Finance. Tokyo). April 30.

"Editorial." 1963. *New Left Review*: 4.

Edwards, E. and P. Bell. 1961. *The Theory and Measurement of Business Income*. Berkeley: University of California Press.

Elliot, E. L. 1968. *The Nature and Stages of Accounting Development in Latin America*. Center for International Education and Research in Accounting, University of Illinois at Urbana-Champaign.

———. 1972. "Accounting and Economic Development in Latin America." *International Journal of Accounting Education and Research* 8: 89–98.

Elliot, E. L., J. Larrea, and J. M. Rivera. 1968. "Accounting Aid to Developing Countries: Some Additional Considerations." *The Accounting Review* 43: 763–768.

Engleman, K. 1962. "Accountancy Problems in Developing Countries." *Journal of Accountancy* January: 53–56.

Enthoven, A. H. 1985. *Mega Accountancy Trends: Extended Accountancy Dimensions in*

Challenging Social Patterns. Richardson, Tex.: Center for International Accounting Development, University of Texas at Dallas.

―――. 1973. *Accountancy and Economic Development Policy*. Amsterdam: North-Holland.

Enthoven, A.J.H. 1965. "Economic Development and Accountancy." *Journal of Accountancy* August: 29–35.

―――. 1967. "Accounting and Development Programming." *International Journal of Accounting Education and Research* 3: 107–120.

―――. 1969. "Accountancy for Economic Development." *Finance and Development* September: 24–29.

―――. 1973. *Accounting and Economic Development Policy*. Amsterdam: North-Holland.

―――. 1976. "Scope of Accountancy Planning in Developing Countries." *Accounting and Business Research*, No. 22: 135–139.

―――. 1979. *Accountancy Systems in Third World Economies*. Amsterdam: North-Holland.

―――. 1981a. "Accounting in Developing Countries." In C. W. Nobes and R. H. Parker (eds.), *Comparative International Accounting*, 1st ed., pp. 217–237. Deddington, U.K.: Philip Allan.

―――. 1981b. *Accounting Education in Economic Development Management*. Amsterdam: North-Holland.

―――. 1983. "Price-Level Accounting in a Developing Economy (the Case of Zaire)." *The Government Accountants Journal* Summer: 33–40.

Falk, H. S. Frumer and J. A. Heintz. 1974. "Accounting for Stock Reacquisitions: Israel and the United States Compared." *The International Journal of Accounting Education and Research* 9: 118–124.

Fantl, I. 1971. "The Case against International Uniformity." *Management Accounting* (UK) May: 13–25.

Fleming, R. 1979. "New Concepts in Brazilian Accounting for Inflation." *The Accountant's Magazine* April: 162–165.

Foroughi, T. K. 1981. "Accounting in Developing Countries before and after Social Crises: The Case of Iran." *Journal of International Accounting Education and Research* 17: 181–223.

Forrester, D. 1983. "Comment va-t-il in Africa?: A Study of the Influence of French Accounting." *AUTA Review* 15: 230–240.

Frank, W. G. 1979. "An Empirical Analysis of International Accounting Principles." *Journal of Accounting Research* 17: 593–605.

Frankel, H. S. 1949. "Psychic and Accounting Concepts of Income and Welfare." *Econometrica* 17 (Supplement) July.

Fu, P. Y. 1968. *A Study of Governmental Accounting in China: With Special Reference to the Sung Dynasty (960–1279)*. Doctoral dissertation, University of Illinois at Urbana-Champaign.

Gbenedio, P. O. 1977. *The Challenge to the Accounting Profession in a Developing Country: The Nigerian Case*. Doctoral dissertation, University of Cincinnati.

Ghandhi, N. W. 1976. "The Emergence of the Post Industrial Society and the Future of the Accounting Function." *International Journal of Accounting Education and Research* 11: 33–50.

Ghartey, A. 1978. "A New Perspective for Accounting Education in Ghana." *International Journal of Accounting Education and Research* 14: 121–132.

Ghartey, J. B. 1985. "Accountability, the Threshold of Political Instability, Underdevelopment and Misery: The Case of Africa." *International Journal of Accounting Education and Research* 21: 143–158.

Ghosh, S. N. 1990. "A Comparative International Study of the Education of Professional Accountants: A Case Study of Bangladesh." In B. E. Needles, Jr. and V. K. Zimmerman (eds.), *Comparative International Accounting Education Standards.* Center for International Accounting Education, University of Illinois at Urbana-Champaign, pp. 97–1080.

Glatzer, W. 1981. "An Overview of the International Development in Macro Social Indicators." *Accounting, Organizations and Society* 6 (3): 15–32.

Goodrich, P. S. 1980. "Grouping National Accounting Policies: A Q-Factor Analysis." School of Economic Studies, University of Leeds, Discussion Paper No. 96.

————. 1982. "Accounting and Political Systems." School of Economic Studies, University of Leeds, Discussion Paper No. 109.

Grady, P. 1975. "Purchasing Power Accounting." *Price Waterhouse Review.*

Graves, O. F. and M. Eery. 1989. "Accounting's Role in Successful Economic Development: Some Normative Evidence from the German Democratic Republic." *International Journal of Accounting* 24: 189–220.

Gul, F. A. and T. H. Yap. 1984. "The Effect of Combined Audit and Management Services on Public Perception of Auditor Independence in Developing Countries: The Malaysian Case." *Journal of International Accounting Education and Research* 20: 95–107.

Gynther, R. 1966. *Accounting for Price Level Changes.* New York: Pergamon Press.

Hardman, D. J. 1984. "Accounting Development in the Solomon Islands." *International Journal of Accounting Education and Research* 20: 141–152.

Hauser, P. M. 1975. *Social Statistics in Use.* New York: Russell Sage.

Heintz, J. A. and J. Han. 1985. "A Study of Audit Judgement of Korean CPAs." *The International Journal of Accounting Education and Research* 21: 21–38.

Helfgoth, R. and S. Schiano-Campo. 1920. "An Introduction to Development Planning." *United Nations Industrial Development Organization (UNIDO), Industrialization and Productivity Bulletin* 16: 15–35.

Hem, R. V. 1980. "Social Indicators: Meaning, Method and Applications." *International Journal of Social Economics* 7(8): 22–33.

Herfindahl, O. and A. Kneese. 1973. "Measuring Social and Economic Change: Benefits and Costs of Environmental Pollution." In M. Moss (ed.), *Measurement of Economic and Social Performance.* New York. Columbia University Press.

Hicks, N. L. 1980. "Is There a Tradeoff between Growth and Basic Needs?" In *World Bank, Poverty and Basic Needs* September: 16–22.

Holzer, H. P. and J. S. Chandler. 1981. "A Systems Approach to Accounting in Developing Countries." *Management International Review* Fall: 23–32.

Holzer, H. P. and D. Tremblay. 1973. "Accounting and Economic Development: The Cases of Thailand and Tunisia." *The International Journal of Accounting Education and Research* 9:67–80.

Horn, R. V. 1980. "Social Indicators: Meaning, Method and Applications." *International Journal of Social Economics* 7(8): 113–125.

Hove, M. R. 1986. "Accounting Practices in Developing Countries: Colonialism's Legacy of Inappropriate Technologies." *International Journal of Accounting Education and Research* 22: 81–100.

———. 1989. "The Inappropriate Uses of International Accounting Standards in Less Developed Countries: The Case of International Accounting Standard Number 24–Related Party Disclosures–Concerning Transfer Prices." *International Journal of Accounting* 24: 165–179.

IASC. 1988. *Survey of the Use and Application of International Accounting Standards.* London: IASC.

Iino, T. and R. Inouye. 1984. "Financial Accounting and Reporting in Japan." In H. Peter Holzer et al. (eds.), *International Accounting.* New York: Harper & Row.

Ijiri, Y. 1976. "The Price-Level Restatement and Its Dual Interpretation." *The Accounting Review* April: 15–25.

Inanga, E. L. 1976. "The Information Content of Published Accounts of Nigerian Public Limited Companies." *Nigerian Journal of Economic and Social Studies* 18: 237–259.

Islam, N. and G. M. Henault. 1979. "From GNP to Basic Needs: A Critical Review of Development and Development Administration." *International Review of Administrative Sciences* 2: 22–30.

Jagetia, L. C. and E. C. Nwadik. 1983. "Accounting Systems in Developing Nations: The Nigerian Experience." *International Journal of Accounting Education Research* 18: 69–81.

Jaggi, B. L. 1970. "A Review of the Accounting Profession in India." *International Journal of Accounting Education and Research* 6: 35–51.

———. 1973. "Accounting Systems in Developing Countries: An Assessment." *International Journal of Accounting Education and Research* 9: 159–170.

———. 1975. "The Impact of the Cultural Environment of Financial Disclosures." *International Journal of Accounting Education and Research* 10: 75–84.

Jaruga, A. A. 1980. "The Accounting Profession in a Centrally Planned Economy: The Polish Case." *Calcutta Management Association Newsletter* May. (Reprinted in *Accountants' Digest* September 1980, pp. 20–23.)

Johansson, S. 1973. "The Level of Living Survey: A Presentation." *Acta Sociologica* 10: 16–33.

———. 1976. *Toward a Theory of Social Reporting.* Stockholm: Swedish Institute for Social Research.

Johnson, T. L. and M. Caygill. 1971. "The Development of Accounting Links in the Commonwealth." *Accounting and Business Research* Spring: 155–173.

Jones, G. M. and J. Kinfu. 1971. "The Birth of an Accounting Profession: The Ethiopian Experience." *International Journal of Accounting Education and Research* 7: 89–98.

Juchau, R. H. 1978. "Accounting Practice Problems in Papua New Guinea and Fiji." *The Australian Accountant* March: 110–113.

Juchau, R. H., M. White, and R. Hopkins. 1986. "Tertiary Education Strategies for Accounting in Developing Societies—The South West Pacific as a Case Study." *International Journal of Accounting Education and Research* 21: 145–160.

Kapadia, G. P. 1973. *History of the Accounting Profession in India.* New Delhi: Institute of Chartered Accountants of India.

Killick, T. 1976. "The Possibilities of Development Planning." *Oxford Economic Papers* July: 17–21.

Kohlmeies, L. M. 1969. *The Regulators*. New York: Harper & Row.

Kraayenhof, J. 1963. "International Challenges in Accounting." *Journal of Accountancy* January: 36.

Kwang, C. 1966. "The Economic Accounting System of State Enterprises in Mainland China." *International Journal of Accounting Education and Research* 1: 61–99.

Land, K. C. 1975a. "Social Indicator Models: An Overview." In Kenneth C. Land and Seymor Spilerman (eds.), *Social Indicator Models*. New York: Russell Sage Foundation.

———. 1975b. "Theories, Models and Indicators of Social Change." *International Social Science Journal* No. 1: 31–73.

———. 1971. "On the Definition of Social Indicators." *American Sociologist* November: 13–40.

Land, K. C., and S. Spilerman (eds.). 1975. *Social Indicator Models*. New York: Russell Sage Foundation.

Lee, C.W.J. 1987. "Accounting Infrastructure and Economic Development." *Journal of Accounting and Public Policy* Summer: 13–21.

Lee, S.A.A. 1965. "Korean Accounting Revaluation Laws." *The Accounting Review* 40: 622–625.

Lev, B. 1976. "The Formulation of Accounting Standards and Rules: A Comparison of Efforts in Israel and the United States." *International Journal of Accounting Education and Research* ii: 121–132.

Lev, B. and B. Yahalomi. 1972. "The Effect of Corporate Financial Statements on the Israeli Stock Exchange." *Management International Review* 12: 145–150.

Liebenstein, H. 1966. "Allocative Efficiency v. X-Efficiency." *American Economic Review* June: 21–32.

Lowe, H. D. 1967. "Accounting Aid for Developing Countries." *The Accounting Review* 42: 356–360.

Mahon, J. J. 1965. "Some Observations on World Accounting." *Journal of Accountancy* January: 15–23.

Markell, W. 1968. "Accounting Education—Its Importance in Developing Countries: Israel—A Case Study." *International Journal of Accounting Education and Research* 3: 125–133.

Marston, C. 1986. *Financial Reporting in India*. London: Groom Helm.

Mason, A. K. 1978. "The Development of International Financial Reporting Standards." ICRA Occasional Paper No. 17, International Center for Research in Accounting, University of Lancaster.

Mensah, Y. W. 1979. *A Database Approach to the Design of Macro-Oriented Enterprise Accounting Systems in Developing Countries*. University of Illinois at Urbana-Champaign.

———. 1981. "Financial Reporting Model for Dependent Market Economies." *Abacus* 17: 161–173.

Mepham, M. J. 1977. "The Accountancy Profession in Jamaica." *The Accountant's Magazine* November: 468–470.

Mirghani, M. A. 1979. *The Role of Accounting in the Economic Development of Developing Countries: The Case of the Sudan*. Graduate School of Business, Indiana University.

———. 1982. "A Framework for a Linkage between Microaccounting and Macroaccounting for Purposes of Developing Planning in Developing Countries." *International Journal of Accounting Education and Research* 18: 57–68.

Mora, R. E. 1972. "The Accounting Profession in Mexico and Why." *International Journal of Accounting Education and Research* 8: 17–24.

Moser, Clause (Sir). 1973. "Social Indicators: Systems, Methods and Problems." *Review of Income and Wealth* June: 13–21.

Nair, R. D. and W. G. Frank. 1980. "The Impact of Disclosure and Measurement Practices on International Accounting Classifications." *The Accounting Review* 55: 426–450.

Ndubizu, G. A. 1984. "Accounting Standards and Economic Development: The Third World in Perspective." *Journal of International Accounting Education and Research* 19: 181–196.

———. 1992. "Accounting Disclosure Methods and Economic Development: A Criterion for Globalizing Capital Markets." *International Journal of Accounting Education and Research* 27 (2): 151–163.

Needles, B. E. 1976. "Implementing a Framework for the International Transfer of Accounting Technology." *International Journal of Accounting Education and Research* 12: 45–62.

———. 1988. "Auditing Standards in the Far East: An Overview." In V. K. Zimmerman (ed.), *Recent Accounting and Economic Developments in the Far East.* Center for International Education and Research in Accounting, University of Illinois at Urbana–Champaign, pp 65–95.

Nefron, M. 1977. "Introduction." In Marc Nefron (ed.), *Another Development: Approaches and Strategies.* Uppsala: Dag Hammarskjold Foundation.

Niarchos, N. and M. Georgkopulus. 1986. "The Effect of Annual Corporate Profit Reports on the Athens Stock Exchange: An Empirical Investigation." *Management International Review* 26(1): 64–72.

Ninsuvannakul, P. 1966. "Education for Accountancy in Thailand." *International Journal of Accounting Education and Research* 2: 77–114.

———. 1988. "The Development of the Accounting Profession of the ASEAN Countries: Past, Present, and Future." In V. K. Zimmerman (ed.), *Recent Accounting and Economic Developments in the Far East.* Center for International Education and Research in Accounting, University of Illinois at Urbana–Champaign, pp. 115–148.

Nobes, C. W. 1981. "An Empirical Analysis of International Accounting Principles: A Comment." *Journal of Accounting Research* 19: 268–270.

———. 1983. "A Judgemental International Classification of Financial Reporting Practices." *Journal of Business Finance and Accounting* 10: 1–19.

Nobes, C. W. and J. Matatko. 1980. "Classification of National Systems of Financial Accounting." *AUTA Review* 12: 57–78.

Nobes, C. W. and R. H. Parker. 1985. *Comparative International Accounting*, 2nd ed., pp. 174–184. Deddington, U.K.: Philip Allan.

Nordhaus, W. and J. Tobin. 1967. "Is Growth Obsolete?" In F. Thomas Juster (ed.), *Economic Growth.* Ann Arbor: University of Michigan, Institute of Social Research.

Ogundele, B. 1969. "The Accounting Profession in Nigeria: An International Perspective." *International Journal of Accounting Education and Research* 5 (10): 1–19.

————. 1970. *Accounting and Economic Development: The Case of Nigeria.* Doctoral dissertation, University of Illinois at Urbana–Champaign.

Olson, M. 1977. "The Treatment of Externalities in National Income Statistics." In L. Wings and A. Evans (eds.), *Public Economics and the Quality of Life.* Baltimore: Johns Hopkins University Press.

Organization for Economic Cooperation and Development. 1976. *Measuring Social Well-Being: A Progress Report on the Development of Social Indicators.* Paris: OECD.

————. 1982. *The OECD List of Social Indicators.* Paris: OECD.

Park, S. and I. S. Cho. 1988. "The Korean CPA Profession: Its Role in the Economic Development of Korea." In V. K. Zimmerman (ed.), *Recent Accounting and Economic Developments in the Far East.* Center for International Education and Research in Accounting, University of Illinois at Urbana–Champaign, pp. 97–113.

Parker, R. H. 1987. "Importing and Exporting Accounting: The British Experience." In *International Pressures for Accounting Change.* Englewood Cliffs, N.J.: Prentice-Hall/ICAEW.

Parsons, T. 1951. *The Social System.* Glencoe, Ill.: Free Press.

Pena, P. A. 1976. "Special Report: A Comparison of the Accounting Professions of Colombia and the United States." *International Journal of Accounting Education and Research* 11: 143–177.

Perera, M.H.B. 1975. "Accounting and Its Environment in Sri Lanka." *Abacus* 11: 85–96.

————. 1989. "Accounting in Developing Countries: A Case for Localized Uniformity." *British Accounting Review* 21: 141–157.

Peskin, H. M. 1976. "A National Accounting Framework for Environmental Assets." *Environmental Economics and Management* 15: 2–55.

————. 1981. "National Income Accounts and the Environment." In H. M. Peskin, P. R. Portney, and A. V. Kneese (eds.), *Environmental Regulation and the U.S. Economy.* Baltimore: Johns Hopkins University Press.

Peskin, H. M. and J. Peskin. 1978. "The Valuation of Nonmarket Activities in Income Accounting." *Review of Income and Wealth* 71 March: 115–132.

Price Waterhouse International. 1973. *Accounting Principles and Reporting Practices: A Survey in 38 Countries.* London: ICAEW.

————. 1975. *Accounting Principles and Reporting Practices: A Survey of 46 Countries.* London: ICAEW.

————. 1979. *International Survey of Accounting Principles and Reporting Practices in 64 Countries,* R. D. Fitzgerald, A. D. Stickler, and T. R. Watts (eds.). Scarborough, Ont.: Butterworths.

Quereshi, M. 1974. "Private Enterprise Accounting and Economic Development in Pakistan." *International Journal of Accounting Education and Research* 9: 125–142.

————. 1975. "Economic Development, Social Justice and Financial Reporting: Pakistan's Experience with Private Enterprise." *Management International Review* 2: 52–75.

Radebaugh, L. H. 1975. "Environmental Factors Influencing the Development of Accounting Objectives, Standards and Practices in Peru." *International Journal of Accounting Education and Research* 11: 39–56.

Rahman, M. Z. 1987. "Accounting Reports and Performance Measurement of Multinational Enterprises in Less Developed Countries." *Management International Review* 27, (2): 35–46.

Ringen, S. 1973. *An Introduction to the Level of Living Study*. Memorandum no. 23. Bergen, Norway.

Rivera, J. M. 1990. "The Accounting Profession and Accounting Education in Panama: A Survey." In B. E. Needles, Jr. and V. K. Zimmerman (eds.), *Comparative International Accounting Educational Standards*. Center for International Education and Research in Accounting, University of Illinois at Urbana–Champaign, pp. 175–192.

Rogness, E. C. 1977. "For Export: Accounting Expertise." *Management Accounting* (U.S.) 58: 19–20.

Roos, J. P. 1978. "The Way of Life in Social Change: A Comparative Study." *Acta Sociologica* 18: 15–32.

Rostow, W. W. 1956. "The Take-off into Self Sustainable Growth." *Economic Journal* 66: 25–48.

———. 1959. "The Stages of Economic Growth." *Economic History Review*. August: 23–44.

———. 1960. *The Stages of Economic Growth, a Non-Communist Manifesto*. London: Cambridge University Press.

Rydell, F. 1963. "The Accounting Profession in Pakistan, India, Burma and Thailand: A Comparative Study." Institute of Business Administration, University of Karachi, pp. 155–176.

Salas, C. A. 1976. "Accounting Education and Practice in Spanish Latin America." *International Journal of Accounting Education and Research* 3: 67–86.

Samuels, J. M. 1990. "Accounting for Development: An Alternative Approach." In R.S.O. Wallace, J. M. Samuels, and R. J. Briston (eds.), *Research in Third World Accounting* 1, pp. 67–86. London: JAI Press.

Samuels, J. M. and J. C. Oliga. 1982. "Accounting Standards in Developing Countries." *International Journal of Accounting Education and Research* 18: 69–88.

Samuels, J. M. and A. G. Piper. 1985. *International Accounting: A Survey*. London: Groom Helm.

Samuelson, R. A. 1980. "Should Replacement-Cost Changes Be Included in Income?" *The Accounting Review*. April: 254–268.

Scott, G. M. 1970. *Accounting and Developing Nations*. Seattle: University of Washington Graduate School of Business Administration.

———. 1986. "Private Sector Enterprise Accounting in Developing Nations." *International Journal of Accounting Education and Research* 14: 51–66.

Seidler, L. J. 1967a. "International Accounting—The Ultimate Theory Course." *The Accounting Review* 4: 775–781.

———. 1967b. *The Function of Accounting in Economic Development: Turkey as a Case Study*. New York: Praeger.

———. 1968. "Teaching Business Administration Overseas: The Case of the Ugly American." *International Journal of Accounting Education and Research* 4: 145–153.

———. 1969. "Nationalism and the International Transfer of Accounting Skills." *International Journal of Accounting Education and Research* Fall: 35–46.

Seidler, R. E. 1966. "Accounting Information Systems and Underdeveloped Countries." *The Accounting Review* 25: 652–656.

Shinawi, A.A.K. and W. F. Crum. 1971. "The Emergence of Professional Accounting in Saudi Arabia." *International Journal of Accounting Education and Research* 6: 103–110.

Shuaib, S. A. 1980. "Accounting Information and the Development Planning Process in Kuwait." *International Journal of Accounting Education and Research* 15: 129–141.

Singh, D. R. and B. N. Gupta. 1977. "Corporate Financial Disclosure in Indian Companies." *Indian Journal of Accounting* June and December: 21–37.

Singhvi, S. S. 1967. *Corporate Disclosure through Annual Reports in the USA and India.* Doctoral dissertation, Graduate School of Business, Columbia University.

———. 1968. "Characteristics and Implications of Inadequate Disclosure: A Case Study of India." *International Journal of Accounting Education and Research* 3: 29–44.

Sishtla, V. S. 1990. "Economic Change under Five-Year Plans and Accounting Education in India." In B. E. Needles, Jr. and V. K. Zimmerman (eds.), *Comparative International Accounting Education Standards.* Center for International Education and Research in Accounting, University of Illinois at Urbana-Champaign, pp. 213–236.

Solomons, D. 1980. "Foreword to AAA Report." In *Accounting Education and the Third World.* Sarasota, Fla.: AAA.

Sombart, W. 1902. *Der moderne Kapitalismus,* 6th ed. Munich and Leipzig: N.p.

"Statement of Standard Accounting Practice No. 16: Current Cost Accounting." 1980. *Accountancy* April: 13–55.

Sterling, R. R. 1970. *Theory of the Measurement of Enterprise Income.* Lawrence, Kans.: University of Kansas.

———. 1975. "Relevant Financial Reporting in an Age of Price Changes." *Journal of Accountancy* February: 15–35.

Stewart, F. 1980. "Country Experience in Providing Basic Needs." In World Bank, *Poverty and Basic Needs,* September.

SyCip, W. 1967. "Professional Practice in Developing Economies." *Journal of Accountancy* January: 41–45.

———. 1981. "Establishing and Applying Standards in Diverse Economic and Social Environments." In J. C. Burton (ed.), *The International World of Accounting Challenges and Opportunities* (1980 Proceedings of the Arthur Young Professors Roundtable), pp. 85–96. Reston, Va.: The Council of Arthur Young Professors' Roundtable.

Tai, B. Y. 1988. "The Accounting Profession in Hong Kong: Problems and Challenges." In V. K. Zimmerman (ed.), *Recent Accounting and Economic Developments in the Far East.* Center for International Education and Research in Accounting, University of Illinois at Urbana-Champaign, pp. 219–228.

Talaga, J. A. and B. Ndubizu. 1986. "Accounting and Economics Development: Relationships among the Paradigms." *International Journal of Accounting Education and Research* 21: 55–68.

Taylor, L. 1975. "Theoretical Foundations and Technical Implications." In C. R. Blitzer, P. B. Clark, and L. Taylor (eds.), *Economy-wide Models and Development Planning.* London: Oxford University Press.

Terleckyj, N. 1978. *Elements of Possibilities for Improvements in the Quality of Life in the USA 1971–1981.* Washington, D.C.: National Planning Association.

Tipgos, M. A. 1987. "A Comprehensive Model for Improving Accounting Education in Developing Countries." In K. Most (ed.), *Advances in International Accounting* 1, 383–404. Greenwich, Conn.: JAI Press.

Todaro, M. P. 1985. *Economic Development in the Third World.* New York: Longman.

Ul Haq, Mahbub. 1980. "An International Perspective on Basic Needs." In World Bank, *Poverty and Basic Needs*, September.

United Nations. 1954. *Report on International Definition and Measurement of Standards and Levels of Living*. New York: United Nations.

———. 1961. *International Definition and Measurement of Levels of Living, an Interim Guide*. New York: United Nations.

———. 1973. *Toward a System of Social and Demographic Statistics*. Prepared by Richard Stone. ST/STAT. 68. New York: United Nations.

———. 1976. *Social and Demographic Statistics: Draft Guidelines on Social Indicators*. New York: United Nations.

United Nations Department of Economic Affairs. 1951. *Measures of Economic Development of Underdeveloped Countries*. New York: UNDEA.

United Nations Centre on Transnational Corporations. 1985a. *International Accounting and Reporting Issues: 1984 Review*. New York: United Nations.

———. 1985b. *International Accounting and Reporting Issues: 1985 Review*. New York: United Nations.

United Nations Research Institute for Social Development. 1970. *Contents and Measurement of Socio-economic Development*. Geneva: UNRISD.

United States Department of Health, Education and Welfare. 1965. *Toward a Social Report*. Washington, D.C.: USDHEW.

Vanderdries, R. 1970. "Social Accounting and Its Applications in Peru." *International Journal of Accounting Education and Research* 6: 91–100.

Wallace, R. S. O. and R. J. Briston. 1987. *Disclosure of Accounting Information in Developing Countries: A Case Study of Nigeria*. Doctoral thesis, University of Exeter.

———. 1988a. "Corporate Financial Reporting in Nigeria." *Accounting and Business Research* 18: 352–362.

———. 1988b. "Intranational and International Consensus on the Importance of Disclosure Items in Financial Reports: A Nigerian Case Study." *British Accounting Review* 20, 223–265.

———. 1990. "Accounting in the Developing Countries: A Review of the Literature." *Research in Third World Accounting*: 16–34.

———. 1992. "Improving the Accounting Infrastructure in Developing Country." *Research in Third World Accounting* 2: 15–32.

Walton, P. 1986. "The Export of British Accounting Legislation to Commonwealth Countries." *Accounting and Business Research* 16: 353–357.

Waterson, A. 1969. *Development Planning: Lessons of Experience*. Baltimore: Johns Hopkins University Press.

Whiteley, J. 1976. "Third World Aid: How and Why Are We Going Wrong?" *Accountancy* 87: 42–44.

Whittle, J. D. 1980. "The Accountancy Profession in Thailand." *Accountant's Magazine* March: 112–113.

Wilcox, L. D. et al. 1972. *Social Indicators and Social Monitoring: An Annotated Bibliography*. Amsterdam: Elsevier Scientific.

Wilkinson, T. L. 1965. "United States Accounting as Viewed by Accountants of Other Countries." *International Journal of Accounting Education and Research* 1: 3–14.

Wilson, J. Q. 1969. *Quality of Life in the United States*. Kansas City, Mo.: Mid-West Research Institute.

Winjum, J. O. 1971. "Accounting and the Rise of Capitalism: An Accountant's View." *Journal of Accounting Research* 9: 333–350.

———. 1972. *The Role of Accounting in the Economic Development of England 1500–1750*. Center for International Education and Research in Accounting, University of Illinois at Urbana-Champaign.

World Bank. 1985. *World Development Report 1985*. New York: Oxford University Press.

Wu, F. H. and D. W. Hackett. 1977. "The Internationalization of US Public Accounting Firms: An Empirical Study." *International Journal of Accounting Education and Research* 12: 81–92.

Xu-Ying, Y. 1988. "The General Character of Chinese and U.S. Management Accounting and Analysis of the New Chinese Management Accounting Style." In V. K. Zimmerman (ed.), *Recent Accounting and Economic Developments in the Far East*. Center for International Education and Research in Accounting, University of Illinois at Urbana-Champaign, pp. 51–64.

Yamey, B. S. 1964. "Accounting and the Rise of Capitalism: Further Notes on a Theme by Sombart." *Journal of Accounting Research* 2: 117–136.

Yu, S., and Jungho Lee. 1988. "Functions of Accounting in Developing Countries for Economic Planning." In Kyqllro Someya (ed.), *Accounting Education and Research to Promote International Understanding*. Westport, Conn.: Greenwood Press.

Zapf, W. 1976. "Soziale Indikatoren fine Zwischenbilanz." *Allgerneines Statistisches Archiv* 1: 16–33.

Zeff, S. A. 1972. *Forging Accounting Principles in Five Countries*. Champaign, Ill.: Stripes Publishing.

Zhou, Z. H. 1988. "Chinese Accounting Systems and Practices." *Accounting, Organizations and Society* 13: 207–224.

Zimmerman, K. (ed.). *Comparative International Accounting Education Standards*. Center for International Education and Research in Accounting, University of Illinois at Urbana-Champaign, pp. 97–108.

2
Diversity in International Accounting

INTRODUCTION

There is diversity in the international accounting discipline and profession. This diversity is not necessarily a minus, as it forced those concerned with attempts at explaining the diversity and/or correcting the diversity to allow for a smooth conduct of accounting internationally. The diversity in international accounting comes at three levels:

Accounting diversity, which translates into diversity in the accounting practices and principles used in the various countries of the world.

Accounting judgment diversity, which translates into variations in the judgments made by accountants and managers from different parts of the world when faced with the preparation and/or use of accounting data.

Standard setting diversity, which translates into different approaches used by different international institutions for the setting of accounting standards.

Each of these forms of diversity is explained in this chapter for a better understanding of the international accounting mystique, arena, and folklores.

ACCOUNTING DIVERSITY

Nature of Accounting Diversity

Financial reporting and disclosure practices vary from country to country. The differences include presentation differences, differences in the degree of flexibility in the accounting practices, and differences in the accounting practices themselves.

The presentation differences vary between the U.S. case, when the balance sheet items are listed in decreasing order of relative liquidity, with shareholders' equity shown on the bottom right, and the U.K. case, where assets are shown in reverse order of liquidity with shareholders' equity (reserves) as the first line item on the credit side.

The degree of flexibility in the accounting practices adopted varies, with international reporting entities having greater flexibility in their choice of accounting practices than their U.S. counterparts.

The differences in accounting practices cover most of the financial accounting areas, especially the areas of consolidation, basis of presentation, business combination, valuation of fixed assets, accounting for goodwill, inventory costing, contingency reserve policy, income tax allocation, pension accounting, research and development, foreign currency translation, accounting for long-term leases and long-term contracts, to name only a few.

Proposed Classification Systems

Various researchers have attempted to provide some classification schemes that could explain some of the observed accounting diversity in the world.

Mueller identified four elements of differentiation:

State of economic development: National economies vary in terms of their extent of development and in terms of nature, from the developed to the developing countries.

State of business complexity: National economies vary in terms of their technological and industrial know-how, creating differences in their business needs as well as their business output.

Shade of political persuasion: National economies vary in terms of their political systems, from the centrally controlled economy to the market-oriented economy.

Reliance on some particular system of law: National economies vary in terms of their supporting legal system. They may rely on either a common-law or code-law system; they may use protective legislation and unfair trade and antitrust laws, for example. (Mueller, 1968, pp. 92–93).

These differences in the business environment cause differences in multinational accounting practices and a clustering of financial accounting principles. Mueller, for example, employs the four elements of differentiation to identify ten distinct sets of business environments:

United States/Canada/the Netherlands: There is minimum of commercial or company legislation in the environment. Industry is highly developed; currencies are relatively stable. A strong orientation to business innovation exists. Many companies with widespread international business interests are headquartered in these countries.

British Commonwealth (excluding Canada): Comparable company legislation exists in all Commonwealth countries, and administration procedures and social order reflect strong ties to the mother country. There exists an intertwining of currencies through the so-called "sterling bloc" arrangement. Business is highly developed but often quite traditional.

Germany/Japan: Rapid economic growth has occurred since World War II. Influences stemming from various U.S. military and administrative operations have caused considerable imitation of many facets of the U.S. practices, often by grafting U.S. procedures to various local traditions. The appearance of the new class of professional business managers is observable. Relative political, social, and currency stability exists.

Continental Europe (excluding Germany, the Netherlands, and Scandinavia): Private business lacks significant governmental support. Private property and the profit motive are not necessarily in the center of economic and business orientation. Some national economic planning exists. Political swings from far right to far left, and vice versa, have a long history in this environment. Limited reservoirs of economic resources are available.

Scandinavia: Here we have developed economies but characteristically slow rates of economic and business growth. Governments tend toward social legislation. Company acts regulate business. Relative stability of population numbers is the rule. Currencies are quite stable. Several business innovations (especially in consumer goods) originated in Scandinavia. Personal characteristics and outlooks are quite similar in all five Scandinavian countries.

Israel/Mexico: These are the only two countries with substantial success in fairly rapid economic development. Trends of a shift to move reliance on private enterprise are beginning to appear; however, there is still a significant governmental presence in business. Political and monetary stability seem to be increasing. Some specialization in business and the professions is taking place. The general population apparently has a strong desire for higher standards of living.

South America: Many instances are present of significant economic underdevelopment along with social and educational underdevelopment. The business base is narrow. Agricultural and military interests are strong and often dominate governments. There is considerable reliance on export/import trade. Currencies are generally soft. Populations are increasing heavily.

The developing nations of the Near and Far East*: Modern concepts and ethics of business have predominantly Western origins. These concepts and ethics often clash with the basic oriental cultures. Business in the developing nations of the Orient largely means trade only. There is severe underdevelopment on most measures, coupled with vast population numbers. Political scenes and currencies are shaky. Major economic advances are probably impossible without substantial assistance from the industrialized countries. OPEC member countries have developed more rapidly since 1973.

Africa (excluding South Africa)*: Most of the African continent is still in early stages of independent civilization, and thus little native business environment presently exists. There are significant natural and human resources. Business is likely to assume a major role and responsibility in the development of African nations.

*These areas are obviously treated very generally; exceptions exists for a few given countries.

Communist nations: The complete control by central government places these countries in a grouping all their own (Mueller, 1968, pp. 93–95).

These groupings are assumed to affect the development of accounting and the formulation of accounting principles and to explain the diversity of practices used from one country to another.

A more elaborate classification scheme was provided by the American Accounting Association's 1975–76 Committee on International Accounting Operations and Education (American Accounting Association, 1977, pp. 65–101). Its proposed morphology for the classification of accounting systems rests on the eight parameters of (1) *political system*, (2) *economic system*, (3) *stages of economic development*, (4) *objectives of financial reporting*, (5) *source of, or authority for, standards*, (6) *education, training, and licensing*, (7) *enforcement of ethics and standards*, and (8) *clients*.

More elaborate conceptual models were proposed by Mueller (1967) and Nobes (1984).

Mueller classified accounting systems among Western nations with market-oriented economic systems into four patterns of accounting development. These are:

1. *Accounting within a macroeconomic framework.* In this case accounting is developed to facilitate the implementation of national economic policies. Sweden is generally used as a good example of a country where accounting is set to serve the national economic policies.

2. *The macroeconomic approach.* In this case accounting is developed to serve the needs of business and business enterprises. The influence translates in the focus on reflecting economic reality in measurement and valuation and in choosing a current valuation method for asset valuation. The Netherlands is generally used as an example of a country where microeconomics plays an important role in the development of accounting.

3. *Accounting as an independent discipline.* In this case, accounting is developed as a service function in business by adopting solutions that worked in particular problems, relying on considerations of pragmatism and usefulness. The United States and United Kingdom are generally used as examples of countries where accounting has developed as an independent discipline, leading to the formulation of "generally accepted accounting principles."

4. *Uniform accounting.* In this case accounting is developed as part of the administrative control of business, designed to monitor business through rigid systems of definitions, measurements, and presentations. France is generally used as an example of a country that relies on uniform accounting in the form of an accounting plan. In fact, the *plan comptable general* was produced in 1947, revised in 1957 and (as partial implementation of the Fourth Directive) in 1982. The *plan* comprises a chart of accounts, definitions of terms, model financial statements, and rules for measurement and valuation. The first two digits (out of a total of five digits) of the present French chart are shown in Exhibit 2.1.

Nobes' classification is based on the general differentiation of micro-based versus macro-uniform as a class, and the importance of the influence of law or economics as a subclass.

A more recent classification by Mueller et al. (1994, pp. 8–13) reduced the accounting groups to:

A.) A *British American* model (a sometimes *Anglo-Saxon* model), where the accounting approach is the one found predominately in the United States, United Kingdom and the Netherlands, with an orientation towards the needs of investors and creditors. Countries included in this group are:

Australia	India	Papua New Guinea
Bahamas	Indonesia	Philippines
Barbados	Ireland	Puerto Rico
Benin	Israel	Singapore
Bermuda	Jamaica	South Africa
Botswana	Kenya	Tanzania
Canada	Liberia	Trinidad & Tobago
Cayman Islands	Malawi	Uganda
Central America	Malaysia	United Kingdom
Colombia	Mexico	United States
Cyprus	Netherlands	Venezuela
Dominican Republic	New Zealand	Zambia
Fiji	Nigeria	Zimbabwe
Ghana	Pakistan	
Hong Kong	Panama	

B.) A *Continental* model, where the accounting approach used is the one found in Continental Europe, Japan, and French-speaking countries, with an orientation towards meeting government-imposed economic, tax or legal restrictions. Countries included in this group are:

Algeria	Germany	Portugal
Angola	Greece	Senegal
Austria	Guinea	Sierra Leone
Belgium	Italy	Spain
Burkina	Ivory Coast	Sweden
Cameroon	Japan	Switzerland
Denmark	Luxembourg	Togo
Egypt	Mali	Zaire
Finland	Morocco	
France	Norway	

C.) A *South American* model, where the accounting approach used parallels those in South America, with a focus on accounting for inflation, taxation and compliance with the national government's macroeconomic plan. Countries included in this group are:

Exhibit 2.1
The First Two Digits of the French Chart of Accounts

Class 1: Capital accounts (capital, loans, and similar creditors)	Class 2: Fixed asset accounts	Class 3: Stock and work-in-progress accounts	Class 4: Personal accounts	Class 5: Financial accounts	Class 6: Expense accounts	Class 7: Income accounts	Class 8: Special accounts	Class 9: Cost accounts
10 Capital and reserves	20 Intangible assets	30	40 Suppliers and related accounts	50 Trade investments	60 Purchases and stock movements (supplies and goods for resale)	70 Sales of goods	80 Contingent and asset and liabilities	90 Reciprocal accounts
11 Profit or loss brought forward	21 Tangible assets	31 Raw materials	41 Trade debtors and related accounts	51 Trade investments	61 Purchases from subcontractors and external charges (related to investment)	71 Movements in finished goods during the accounting period	81	91 Cost reclassifications
12 Profits or loss for the financial year	22 Fixed assets under concession	32 Other consumables	42 Employees and related accounts	52	62 Other external charges (related to operations)	72 Work performed by the undertaking for its own purposes and capitalized	82	92 Cost analysis centres
13 Investment grants	23 Fixed assets in course of construction	33 Work in progress (goods)	43 Social Security and other public agencies	53 Cash in hand	63 Taxes, direct and indirect	73 Net income recognized on long-term contracts	83	93 Manufacturing costs
14 Provisions created for tax purposes	24	34 Works in progress (services)	44 The government and other public bodies	54 Interest accounts and credits	64 Staff costs	74 Operating subsidies	84	94 Stocks

15 Provisions for liabilities and charges	25	35 Finished goods	45 Accounts current—group companies and proprietors	55	65 Other operating charges	75 Other operating income	85	95 Costs of goods sold
16 Loans and similar creditors	26 Participating interests and debts relating thereto	36	46 Sundry debtors and creditors	56	66 Financial income	76 Financial income	86 Intra-company exchanges of goods and services (charges)	96 Standard cost variances
17 Debts related to participal interests	27 Other financial assets	37 Goods for resale	47 Suspense accounts	57 Internal transfers	67 Extra-ordinary	77 Extra-ordinary	87 Intra-company exchanges of goods and services (income)	97 Differences in accounting treatments
18 Branch and inter-company accounts	28 Provisions for depreciation of fixed assets	38	48 Prepayments and accruals	58	68 Depreciation amortization, transfers to	78 Depreciation and provisions written back provisions	88	98 Manufacturing profit and loss account
19	29 Provisions for loss in value of fixed assets	39 Provisions for loss in value of stocks and work in progress	49 Provisions for loss in value on personal accounts	59 Provisions for loss in value on financial accounts	69 Profit sharing by employees, taxes on profits and similar items	79 Charges transferred	89	99 Internal transfers

Argentina	El Salvador	Nicaragua
Bolivia	Guatemala	Paraguay
Brazil	Guyana	Peru
Chile	Honduras	Uruguay
Ecuador		

D.) A *Mixed-Economy* model, where accounting meets the needs of both central economic planning and market-oriented enterprise activities. Countries using this dual approach include:

Albania	Georgia	Russia
Armenia	Hungary	Serbia
Azerbaijan	Kazakhstan	Slovak Republic
Belorussia	Kirgizia	Slovenia
Bosnia-Herzegovina	Latvia	Tadzhikstan
Bulgaria	Lithuania	Turkmenistan
Croatia	Moldavia	Ukraine
Czech Republic	Poland	Uzbekistan
Estonia	Romania	Vietnam

E.) Various *Emerging* models, including an Islamic model focusing on theological compliance and an international standards model focusing on compliance with accepted international financial accounting standards.

A classification system purposed by Nobes is also shown in Exhibit 2.2. Two "classes" (micro-based and macro-uniform) correspond to a certain extent to two types of legal systems (common and code law, respectively). The first variable differentiating accounting development is therefore the legal system, with accounting in common law countries labeled *nonlegalistic* or *Anglo-Saxon*, and

Exhibit 2.2
Nobes' Classification of Accounting Systems: A Hypothetical Classification of Financial Reporting Measurement Practices in Developed Western Countries in 1980

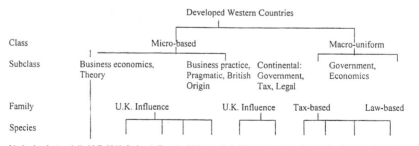

Source: C. W. Nobes, "A Judgmental International Classification of Financial Reporting Practices," *Journal of Business Finance and Accounting* (Spring 1983): 7. Reproduced by permission.

accounting in code law countries labeled *legalistic*. The subclasses in Nobes' model correspond to Mueller's four comparative development patterns: "business economics, theory" is the microeconomic pattern; "business practices, pragmatic" is the independent discipline approach; "government, tax, legal" is the uniform approach; and "government, economies" is the macroeconomic pattern.

Toward a Contingency Framework for International Accounting

Empirical attempts were first made to classify nations by deriving "clusters" of existing accounting practices through factor analysis exercises. These studies attempted to classify the accounting patterns in the world of accounting into different historical "zones of accounting influence." The proposed classification systems and the attempts at identifying zones of accounting influence were helpful in guiding the early international accounting research toward identifying the important conceptual determinants of accounting development internationally. To date, the search has identified new research avenues that may give a better explanation of accounting diversity. These avenues include: (1) the impact of culture, (2) impact of political systems, (3) the impact of economic systems, and (4) the unit act of legal and tax systems. When combined these avenues present a contingency framework for international accounting.

The Impact of Culture

A good definition of culture follows:

Culture consists of patterns, explicit and implicit, of and for behavior acquired and transmitted by symbols, constituting the distinctive achievements of human groups, including their embodiments in artifacts; the essential core of culture consists of traditional (i.e. historically derived and selected) ideas and especially their attached values; cultural systems may on the one hand be considered as products of action, on the other as conditioning elements of further action. (Kroeber and Kluckhorn, 1952, p. 181)

The cultural relativism hypothesis attempts to link cultural values to accounting development. Jaggi was the first to introduce two hypotheses on the issue of the impact of cultural environment and individual value orientations on financial disclosures (Jaggi, 1975, pp. 75–84).

Hypothesis 1: The reliability of disclosures in financial statements is likely to differ with differences in the value orientations of managers from different countries. Accounting principles and procedures will vary to respond to the needs of individual countries and to ensure reliability in a given set of cultural environments.
Hypothesis 2: As a result of the prevailing cultural environment in the developing countries, the reliability of financial disclosure is not accepted to be high unless legal disclosure standards are set. (Jaggi, 1975, p. 83)

Other attempts at linking culture and accounting development relied on Hofstede's four cultural values: power distance, individualism, masculinity, and uncertainty avoidance (Hofstede, 1980). They may be defined as follows:

Individualism versus collectivism is a dimension that represents the degree of integration a society maintains among its members. While individualists are expected to take
care of themselves and their immediate families only, collectivists are expected to remain
emotionally linked in cohesive groups that protect them in exchange for unquestioning
loyalty.
Large versus small power distance is a dimension that represents the extent to which
members of a society accept the fact that power in institutions and organizations is
distributed unequally. In large power distance societies, there is a tendency for people
to accept a hierarchical order in which everybody has a place that needs no justification,
whereas in small power distance, there is a tendency for people to ask for equality and
demand justification for any existing power inequalities.
Strong versus weak uncertainty avoidance is a dimension that represents the degree to
which the members of a society feel uncomfortable with uncertain and ambiguous situations. In strong uncertainty avoidance societies, people are intolerant of ambiguity and
try to control it at all cost, whereas in weak uncertainty avoidance, people are more
tolerant of ambiguity and accept living with it.
Masculinity versus femininity is a dimension that represents the nature of social divisions of sex roles. Masculine roles imply a preference for achievement, assertiveness,
making money, sympathy for the strong, etc. Feminine roles imply a preference for warm
relationships, modesty, care for the weak, preservation of the environment, equality of
life, etc. (Hofstede, 1980)

Gray hypothesized that "accounting values" are derived from their respective
societal cultural values, as defined by Hofstede. The model is shown in Exhibit
2.3. His four accounting values are as follows:

Professionalism versus statutory control—a preference for the exercise of individual
professional judgement and the maintenance of professional self-regulation as opposed
to compliance with prescriptive legal requirements and statutory control.
Uniformity versus flexibility—a preference for the enforcement of uniform accounting
practices between companies and for the consistent use of such practices over time as
opposed to flexibility in accordance with the perceived circumstances of individual companies.
Conservatism versus optimism—a preference for a cautious approach to measurement so
as to cope with the uncertainty of future events as opposed to a more optimistic, laissez-
faire, risk-taking approach.
Secrecy versus transparency—a preference for confidentiality and the restriction of disclosure of information about the business only to those who are closely involved with
its management and financing as opposed to a more transparent open and publicly accountable approach. (Gray, 1988, pp. 1–15)

Exhibit 2.4 summarizes proposed relationships between Gray's "accounting values" and Hofstede's four cultural dimensions. Empirical results are, however,
mixed.

Exhibit 2.3
Theory of Cultural Influence

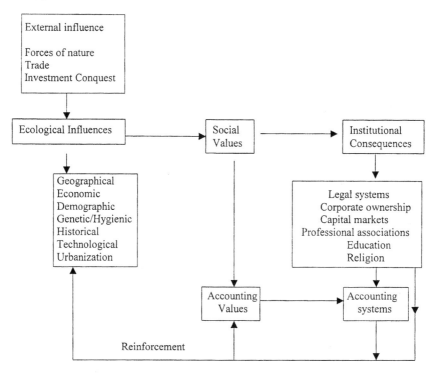

Source: S. J. Gray, "Towards a Theory of Cultural Influence on the Development of Accounting Systems Internationally," *ABACUS* (March 1988): 7. © Accounts Foundation at the University of Sydney. Reproduced by permission.

Finally, the present author attempted to determine the association between a professional self-regulation score and the cultural dimensions of power distance, uncertainty avoidance, individualism, and masculinity (Riahi-Belkaoui, 1989, pp. 93–101). His results suggest that the degree of professional self-regulation in accounting internationally is influenced negatively by the uncertainty avoidance and individualism dimensions and positively by the masculinity dimension. In other words, societies where people are essentially tolerant of ambiguity, are collectivist in their relations with others, and show a preference for competitiveness, achievement motivation, assertiveness, and the enjoyment of material success have strong conditions for professional self-regulation.

The Impact of Political Systems and Civil Liberties

Countries can be ranked in terms of the degree of political rights and civil liberties they offer. Dr. Raymond Gastil, director of Freedom House, has constructed and provided since 1973 indexes of political rights and civil liberties

Exhibit 2.4
Relations between Gray's Accounting Values and Hofstede's Cultural Dimensions

Cultural Dimensions (Hofstede)	Accounting Values (Gray)			
	Professionalism	Uniformity	Conservatism	Secrecy
Individualism	+	-	-	-
Power Distance	-	+	?	+
Uncertainty Avoidance	-	+	+	+
Masculinity	?	?	-	-

Note: "+" indicates a direct relationship between the variables; "−" indicates an inverse relation-
    ship. Question marks indicate that the nature of the relationship is indeterminate. Gray hy-
    pothesizes that individualism and uncertainty avoidance will influence accounting the most,
    followed by power distance, then masculinity.
Source: N. Baydoun and R. Willett, "Cultural Relevance of Western Accounting Systems to De-
    veloping Countries," *ABACUS* 31 (March 1995): 71. © Accounts Foundation at the University
    of Sydney. Reproduced by permission.

(Gastil, 1978). He defines civil liberties as the rights of the individual against
the state and the rights to freedom of expression and a fair trial. He then develops
a civil liberties index composed of seven levels:

- Level 1 for states where the rule of the law is not mistaken and which include various
  news media and possible and evident freedom of expression.

- Level 2 for states where civil liberties are less effective than in states ranked (1) because
  of violence and ignorance or lack of sufficient or free media of expression, created
  either by special laws that restrain rights or authoritarian civil tradition or by the influence of religion.

- Level 3 for states where civil liberties exist but are hampered by serious imperfections
  such as repeated reliance on martial law, jailing for sedition, or suppression of
  publications.

- Level 4 for states where there are broad areas of freedom and free publication along
  with broad areas of repression.

- Level 5 for states where civil liberties are often denied and complaints of violation are
  ignored because of weak government-controlled or frequently censored media.

- Level 6 for states where the rights of the State and the government are given legal
  priority over the rights of groups and individuals, although a few individuals are allowed considerable freedom.

- Level 7 for states where citizens have no rights *vis-à-vis* the State and where internal
  criticism is only known to the outside world because of the government's condemnation
  of it. (Gastil, 1978)

Gastil defines political rights as the right to play a part in determining the
laws and the government of the community. He then develops a political rights
index composed of seven levels:

- Level 1 for states where almost everybody has both rights and opportunities to partic-ipate in the political process, to compete for political office, and to join freely formed political parties.
- Level 2 for states where the effectiveness of the open electoral processes is reduced by factors such as extreme poverty, a feudal social structure, violence or agreements to limit opposition.
- Level 3 for states where the effectiveness of the open electoral process is reduced by nondemocratic procedures such as coups.
- Level 4 for states where there is either a constitutional block to the full democratic significance of elections or the power distribution is not affected by the elections.
- Level 5 for states where either elections are closely controlled or limited or the results have very little significance.
- Level 6 for states where either there is no operational electoral system or opposition candidates are not allowed to compete.
- Level 7 for states which may be characterized as tyrannies with little legitimacy either in a national tradition or a modern ideology. (Gastil, 1978)

An emerging political and civil relativism in accounting rests on the funda-mental assumption that accounting concepts in any given country rest on the political and civil context of that country.

The political freedom of a country is important to the development of ac-counting in general and reporting and disclosure in particular. When people cannot choose the members of a government or influence government policies, they are less likely to be able to create an accounting profession based on the principle of full and fair disclosure. Political repression involves a general loss of freedom, which may hinder to some extent the development of such a pro-fession of accounting. There is likely to be a negative relationship between accounting freedom to report or to disclose and political freedom. The degree of political freedom in a given country is generally assumed to depend on the degree of political rights, the civil liberties, and the type of political system. Violations of political rights and civil liberties associated with various forms of political structure restrict political freedom in general and may act as a hindrance to the tradition of full and fair disclosure. While these propositions may be viewed as intuitive and hardly self-evident, one of the objectives of international accounting research would be to empirically test their validity.

The Impact of Economic Systems

Countries differ in their choices of economic systems. Gastil makes a useful distinction among the following from economic systems: capitalist, capitalist-statist, capitalist-socialist, and socialist. Capitalist states are those states that "rely on the operation of the market and on private provision for individual welfare" (Gastil, 1978, p. 46). Capitalist-statist states are those states that have "very large government productive enterprises, either because of an elitist development philosophy or a major dependence on a key resource as oil" (Gastil, 1978). Capitalist-socialist states are those states that "provide social services on a large scale through governmental or other nonprofit institutions, with the result that private control over property is sacrificed to egalitarian purposes" (Gastil, 1978, p. 47). Finally, socialist states are those states that "strive programmatically to place an entire national economy under direct or indirect control" (Gastil, 1978).

The economic environment is important to the development of accounting in general and reporting and disclosure in particular. Economic development constitutes economic growth and various structural and social changes. One such change is the need for financial and reporting devices to measure the performance of each sector of the economy in terms of efficiency and productivity. Lowe notes that, from a historical point of view, "accounting development is an evolutionary process dependent upon and interwoven with economic development" (Lowe, 1967, p. 360). Similarly, Elliot et al. state that the "social function of accounting, to measure and communicate economic data, cannot be considered simply as the effect of economic development, but should be considered a valuable tool for promoting the development process" (Elliot, Larrea and Rivera, 1968, p. 764). However, economic development may be achieved by various forms of economic policies depending on the type of economic system chosen, the level and growth rate of income, the extent of government intervention and expenditures, and the level of exports. Each of these factors may imply a specific impact on accounting development that needs to be investigated.

The Impact of Law and Tax Systems

Legal and tax relativism in accounting rests on the fundamental assumption that accounting concepts in any given country rest on the legal and tax content of that country.

First, countries have different national legal systems. The national law of each country defines most directly and most frequently the conduct of business and hence the practice of accounting. Given that there are differences in the national legal systems of different countries, there is by definition an implication that there will be differences in their accounting systems. The differences in national legal systems include, for example, the difference between the Roman, or "civil," law and the common law. While civil law is a *legislative* system, common law is basically nonlegislative. Other general differences include the size and sophistication of government and proliferation of regulatory agencies and commissions. In the United States, examples of regulatory agencies include the Food and Drug Administration, the Federal Trade Commission, and the U.S. Tariff Commission; British examples include the Board of Trade. Other differences are in the nature of legal entities, welfare policy, property-ownership restrictions, monopoly policy, and applicability of national laws.

All these legal differences imply different accounting practices internationally, since accounting may be used to implement some of these laws. In fact, the

Exhibit 2.5
A Hierarchical Classification of Legal Systems

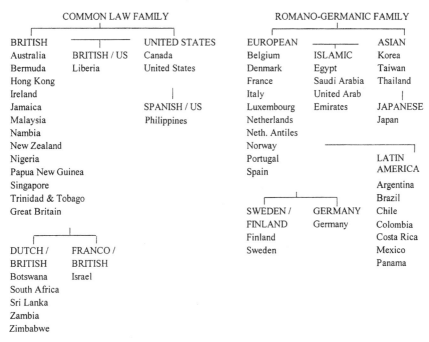

COMMON LAW FAMILY   ROMANO-GERMANIC FAMILY

BRITISH		UNITED STATES	EUROPEAN		ASIAN
Australia	BRITISH / US	Canada	Belgium	ISLAMIC	Korea
Bermuda	Liberia	United States	Denmark	Egypt	Taiwan
Hong Kong			France	Saudi Arabia	Thailand
Ireland			Italy	United Arab	
Jamaica		SPANISH / US	Luxembourg	Emirates	JAPANESE
Malaysia		Philippines	Netherlands		Japan
Nambia			Neth. Antilles		
New Zealand			Norway		
Nigeria			Portugal		LATIN
Papua New Guinea			Spain		AMERICA
Singapore					Argentina
Trinidad & Tobago					Brazil
Great Britain			SWEDEN /	GERMANY	Chile
			FINLAND	Germany	Colombia
			Finland		Costa Rica
DUTCH /	FRANCO /		Sweden		Mexico
BRITISH	BRITISH				Panama
Botswana	Israel				
South Africa					
Sri Lanka					
Zambia					
Zimbabwe					

Source: Reprinted from S. B. Salter and T. S. Doupnik, "The Relationship between Legal Systems and Accounting Practices: A Classification Exercise," *Advances in International Accounting* 5, copyright 1992, pp. 3–22, with permission from Elsevier Science.

legalistic approach to accounting is predominant in most countries, with some countries completely relying on it and others permitting other approaches. In the countries relying completely on the legalistic approach, accounting becomes effectively a process of compliance with the laws of the country. Similarly, official audits are performed by statutory auditors to certify that financial statements have been prepared in accordance with the law. A thirteen-category hierarchical classification system for the world's legal systems shown in Exhibit 2.5 can be very helpful in identifying clusters of countries employing similar accounting practices.

Second, countries have different national tax systems. The tax system of each country defines most directly and most frequently the conduct of business and hence the practice of accounting. Seidler makes this point:

Worldwide tax collections constitute the greatest source of demand of accounting services. The tax on income, both on the individual and business enterprises level, is the largest source of revenue for governments of countries with literate populations. Clearly, the collection on tax revenues, the life-blood of government, outweighs the niceties of accounting theory. Income tax evasion in frequently grounded in distortions of records or in absence of records. Therefore, tax collecting governments initially become involved in the bookkeeping and accounting procedures followed by individuals and companies, to provide some assurance of collecting taxes. (Seidler, 1981, p. 41)

International Accounting Research

The contingency framework presented in this chapter with its implications for the role of culture, political systems and civil liberties, economic systems, legal and tax systems on accounting development internationally calls for theoretical and empirical international accounting research (IAR) on the framework. To make the connection between accounting and practices in different countries and their environment, IAR needs to rely on different theories and different methodologies (Gernon and Wallace, 1995, pp. 54–106). For example Exhibit 2.6 shows the different frameworks that can be used for the study of the accounting profession while Exhibit 2.7 shows the differences between three approaches to cross-national accounting research. The different frameworks that can be used for the study of the accounting profession include (a) Weberian: market control theories, (b) Marxist: production-based theories, and (c) Dunkheim: social conflict theories (Gernon and Wallace, 1995, p. 70). Similarly, three approaches that can be used for cross-national research include (a) the global approach, (b) the contextual approach, and (c) the synthetic approach (Gernon and Wallace, 1995, p. 81). They offer different configurations for the study of international accounting.

JUDGMENT DIVERSITY

The diversity of judgment in an international accounting context may be examined by reference to (1) cognitive relativism, (2) cultural relativism, (3) linguistic relativism, (4) organizational culture relativism, and (5) contractual relativism. Each of these relativisms is examined next.

Cognitive Relativism in Accounting

The essence of cognitive relativism in accounting is the presence of a cognitive process that is assumed to guide the judgment/decision process. The model presented by the present author on cognitive relativism presents the judgment and decision made about an accounting and/or auditing phenomenon as the product of a set of social cognitive operations that includes the observation of information of the phenomenon and the formation of a schema to represent the phenomenon that is stored in memory and later retrieved to allow the formation of a judgment and decision when needed. Therefore, an understanding of the knowledge structures or schemata used by individuals facing an accounting or

Exhibit 2.6
Differences between Three Approaches to Cross-National Accounting Research

Area of Difference	Global Approach	Contextual Approach	Synthetic Approach
Primary Research	What are the similarities and differences among national accounting systems?	What are the effects of contextual features like culture on accounting practices?	What accounts for national variations in accounting practices?
Orientation	Descriptive and diagnostic analysis of past events, some ex post facto hypotheses testing	Predictive theory building and analytical	Explanation of differences and similarities Embedding on contextual with empirical analysis
Research Focus	National accounting practices and profiles	Contextual features such as culture, industrialization, economic development, legal and political systems as explanatory variables	Accounting numbers and practices as global phenomena
Research Design	Begins with the selection of the countries to compare based on either method of agreement or indirect method of difference Dependent variables (accounting practices) are then selected based on the researcher's interest Independent variables are usually not explicitly stated prior to cross-national comparisons	Begins with the selection of independent variables (contextual factors) often in conjunction with the comparison countries Dependent variables (accounting practices) are selected next based on the researcher's interests (if descriptive) or postulated effects of the independent variables (if predictive theories are being built)	Begins with the selection of dependent variables (accounting practices) of interest Independent variables (societal or cultural factors) are selected next based on their theoretical relevance to the independent variable(s) Comparison countries are selected last based on their relative standing on the independent variable(s)
Data Analysis	Comparisons of within-country relationships or country mean scores on dependent variables	Comparison of within-country relationships or country mean scores on the dependent variable(s)	Assessment of statistical and contextual relationships between societal-level and accounting variables

Source: Helen Gernon and R. S. Olusegun Wallace, "International Accounting Research: A Review of Its Ecology, Contending Theories and Methodologies," *Journal of Accounting Literature* 14 (1995): 81. Reproduced by permission.

Exhibit 2.7
Theoretical Framework for the Study of the Accounting Profession

Frameworks	Theoretical Thrusts
Weberian: Market Control Theories	In addition to categorizing accounting professionals on the basis of trait and functionalist characteristics, this framework is concerned with how accountants seek and attain competitive advantage within a relatively free market; that is, structured by the state but dominated by the private sector. This may be achieved through the control of the market for accounting and auditing services by such strategies as social closure (i.e., excluding others from the market through professional associations, recruitment policies, training, and legal control); defining what the market needs and the ways such needs can be met; setting high professional kill level and ethical code of professional conduct.
Marxist: Production-Based Theories	Marxist-inspired theories emphasize the supply side, the means of production. They are also concerned with the role of the accounting profession within—the ongoing class struggle between capital and labor—whether they align themselves with capital or labor or constitute an independent class. This set of theories is also concerned with questions relating to the increasing role of accountants as employers in the private sector and as employees in both the private and public sectors. The theories also dwell on and describe the contracts between accounting professionals and society as well as the rewards that ensue from such contracts. Underlying these theories is the assumption that accounting professionals use their skills and status in society's best interests.
Durkheim: Social Conflict Theories	This set of theories is best described as structural functionalism and is concerned with the delicate balance pursued by the accounting professions as they seek to render service to society in an altruistic manner while pursuing their self-interest and self-regulating their services and conduct in the market. The theories also seek to explain or predict different roles of the major players or those affected by the contract.

Source: Helen Gernon and R. S. Olusegun Wallace, "International Accounting Research: A Review of Its Ecology, Contending Theories and Methodologies," *Journal of Accounting Literature* 14 (1995): 70. Reproduced by permission.

auditing phenomenon is important to an understanding of the judgment/decision process in accounting. A similar assessment is made about auditing:

The role of schemata is particularly relevant in auditing, because the schemata developed by auditors through experience and prior knowledge of client situations may affect the manner in which the auditor perceives the evaluation of assertions and the need to accumulate and interpret evidence about these assertions. Thus, understanding the nature of audit expertise may depend on understanding schematic structures, including the differences in complexity of knowledge structures, recall ability, and speed of access among auditors with varying levels of experience. In addition, understanding knowledge structures through descriptive research is essential to the development and valuation of expert systems in auditing. (Ashton, 1988, pp. 108–109)

In fact, all accounting and auditing phenomena involve the cognitive use of a knowledge structure or schema, developed by individuals through experience, learning, and prior knowledge. For example, Frederick characterized a schematic representation of internal control evaluation with respect to transaction cycles (Frederick, 1986). Each transaction cycle (e.g., purchasing and disbursements) was decomposed into a series of functions (e.g., receiving), which were decomposed into a set of specific control procedures (e.g., physical verification of goods received). Each of these knowledge structures and schemata shapes the manner in which an accounting phenomenon is approached, and guides the judgment/decision process in accounting. A schema-driven information search or strategy where the decision maker relies on an experience-based mental model is assumed to occur when an individual faces an accounting and/or auditing phenomenon.

Cultural Relativism in Accounting

The essence of cultural relativism in accounting is the presence of a cultural process that is assumed to guide the judgment/decision process. The model as presented by the present author on cultural relativism postulates that culture through its components, elements, and dimensions dictates the organizational structures adopted, microorganizational behavior, the accounting environment, and the cognitive functioning of individuals faced with an accounting and/or auditing phenomenon. Basically each culture is distinguished from others by thoroughgoing, seemingly fundamental themes. Each culture creates taken-for-granted models of the world that are widely shared by members of the society and are crucial in their understanding of that world and their behavior in it. Such models are used to perform a variety of different cognitive tasks:

Sometimes, these cultural models serve to set goals for action, sometimes to plan the attainment of said goals, sometimes to direct the actualization of these goals, sometimes to make sense of the actions and fathom the goals of others, and sometimes to produce verbalization that may play various parts in all these projects as well as in the subsequent interpretations of what has happened. (Quinn and Holland, 1987, pp. 3–40)

What may result is that people will comply with certain social behavior because it directly satisfies some culturally defined need—what Spiro called "intrinsic cultural motivation" (Spiro, 1961, pp. 93–177). Basically, "through the process of socialization individuals come to find achieving culturally prescribed goals and following cultural directives to be motivationally satisfying, and to find not achieving culturally prescribed goals and not following cultural directives to be anxiety producing" (Spiro, 1961).

These cultural models represent the schemata that individuals invoke for the performance of such naturally occurring cognitive tasks as categorizing, reasoning, remembering, problem solving, and decision making. In the context of the cognitive relativism model in accounting introduced earlier, individuals from different cultures may invoke different knowledge structures or schemata when faced with an accounting or auditing phenomenon. Culture plays a central role in the organization of everyday understanding in accounting and auditing and the retrieval of that information for a judgment/decision process. It implies that accounting and auditing knowledge is organized in a culturally standardized and hence familiar event sequence that tells the individual how to react to a particular accounting and/or auditing phenomenon. This point is also acknowledged in cognitive science as "well-developed belief systems about the world" (D'Andrade, 1984, pp. 88–115).

Linguistic Relativism in Accounting

The essence of linguistic relativism in accounting is the presence of a linguistic process that is assumed to guide the judgment/decision process. The model presented by the present author on linguistic relativism postulates that accounting as a language affects the judgment/decision process in accounting as a result of the theory and the findings underlying the Sapir-Whorf hypothesis of a linguistic relativity, the sociolinguistic thesis, and the bilingualism or diglossia hypothesis (Schank and Abelson, 1977, p. 132).

The basis of the linguistic relativity hypothesis in accounting is that the characteristics of the accounting language, lexical or grammatical characteristics, have a marked influence on the cognitive processes preceding the judgment/decision process in accounting (Riahi-Belkaoui, 1990a, p. 22). Basically, the cognitive organization underlying the development, storage, and retrieval of schemes about accounting or auditing phenomena is constrained by the linguistic structure. The degree of fluency and mastery of the accounting language acts as a major determinant in the organization of everyday understanding of accounting and auditing and the retrieval of that information for a judgment/decision process. It implies that accounting and auditing knowledge is organized in linguistically standardized and hence familiar event sequences that tell the individual how to react to a particular accounting and auditing phenomenon.

The basis of the sociolinguistic thesis in accounting is that different linguistic repertoires exist in accounting as a result of the different social role relations espoused by individuals facing the accounting and/or auditing phenomena (Belkaoui, 1978, pp. 97–129). These different role relationships result from membership in different professional associations, differences in educational levels, expertise, and fluency in accounting, and differences in economic social positions. These role relationships result in the use of either an elaborated accounting communication code if the role system is open or a restricted accounting communication code if the role system is closed. Basically, the nature of the social role held by an individual acts as a major determinant in the organization of everyday understanding in accounting and/or auditing and the retrieval of that information for the judgment/decision process. It implies that accounting and auditing knowledge is organized as an elaborated or restricted communication code, depending on the nature of the social role, that tells the individual how to react to and interpret an accounting and/or auditing phenomenon.

Speakers of different languages or dialects experience different worldviews in their use of accounting languages than unilinguals (Belkaoui, 1980, pp. 362–374). The capacity to converse in more than one communication code provides these individuals with different levels of creativity, cognitive feasibility, concept formation, verbal intelligence, and psycholinguistic abilities when faced with an accounting/auditing phenomenon. Basically, the mastery of more than one language or more than one dialect acts as a major determinant in the organization of everyday understanding in accounting and/or auditing and the retrieval of that information for a judgment/decision process. It implies that accounting and auditing knowledge is organized in multilinguistically standardized and hence familiar event sequences that tell an individual how to react to a particular accounting and/or auditing phenomenon in each language.

Organizational Culture Relativism in Accounting

Organizational cultural efficiency requires the sharing of frameworks, language, and referents that shape the schemata individuals use when faced with an accounting and/or auditing phenomenon. The model presented by the present author on organizational culture argues in favor of such relativism whereby the organizational culture to which an individual belongs ultimately determines the judgment/decision process in accounting, by providing him/her with schemata of good and bad solutions that will increase the ability to determine how to operate in the organizational culture or clan (Monti-Belkaoui and Belkaoui, 1983, pp. 111–127). Therefore, membership in an organizational culture acts as a major determinant in the organization of everyday understanding of accounting and/or auditing phenomena and the retrieval of that information for a judgment/ decision process. It implies that the organizational culture gives the individual faced with an accounting and/or auditing phenomenon categories, processing routines, and schemata that help solve the problems in the best interests of the culture.

Contractual Relativism in Accounting

The essence of the model on contractual relativism presented by the present author is that contracts define permissible behavior and actions that ultimately determine the judgment/decision process in accounting (Belkaoui, 1980, p. 123). The importance of these contracts results from the assumptions and implications inherent in the four models of agency theory—namely, the stewardship/account-ability model, the transaction-cost economics model, the principal-agent model, and the positivist agency model. Basically, the cognitive organization underlying the development, storage, and retrieval of schemata about accounting and/or auditing phenomena are constrained by the covenants of the contracts entered between individuals and the firm. These covenants act as a major determinant in the organization of everyday understanding of accounting and auditing and the retrieval of that information in the judgment/decision process.

Judgment in International Accounting

The judgment/decision process in accounting and auditing is determined by a cognitive process that is itself altered and uniquely shaped by the particular national culture of the individual faced by the accounting and/or accounting phenomenon (cultural relativism), the particular linguistic repertoire used by the individual (linguistic relativism), the organizational culture of the entity of which the individual considers himself/herself a dedicated and loyal member (organizational culture relativism), and the covenants and requirements of the contracts binding the individual to a set of norms and allegiances to the firm (contractual relativism).

While the cognitive process is viewed as essential in explaining the judgment/decision process in accounting, the impact of culture, language, organizational culture, and contracts is assumed to be present in some cases and absent in others. When all the factors are present, the theory postulates that the order of importance of these factors is as follows: cognition, culture, language, organizational culture, and contracts (see Exhibit 2.8).

STANDARD-SETTING DIVERSITY

In addition to practice diversity, there is also a standard-setting diversity created by the existence of diverse standard-setting bodies from each country and region of the world using different standard-setting procedures. The problems created are imposing great pressure for more uniformity in the accounting and auditing system and frequent call for accounting harmonization. At the same

Exhibit 2.8
An International Accounting Theory

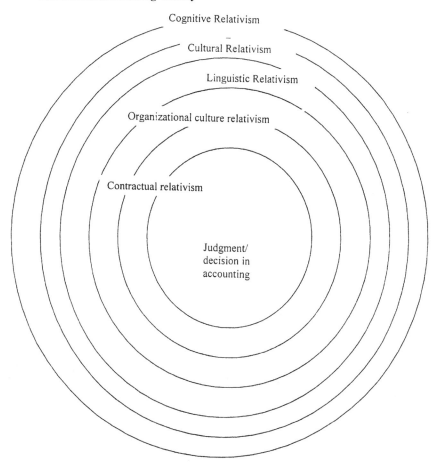

Cognitive Relativism

Cultural Relativism

Linguistic Relativism

Organizational culture relativism

Contractual relativism

Judgment/
decision in
accounting

time the standard-setting bodies of various countries have started to develop conceptual frameworks as a guide to developing accounting techniques.

Harmonization of Accounting

Harmonization is not to be confused with standardization. Wilson presents a useful distinction:

The term harmonization as opposed to standardization implies a reconciliation of different points of view. This is a more practical and conciliatory approach than standardization, particularly when standardization means that the procedures of one country should be adopted by all others. Harmonization becomes a matter of better communication of information in a form that can be interpreted and understood internationally. (Wilson, 1969, p. 40)

Harmonization consists of recognizing the international differences and attempting to reconcile them with other countries' objectives as a first step. The second step is to correct or eliminate some of these barriers in order to achieve an acceptable degree of harmonization.

There are various advantages to harmonization. The most often cited favorable arguments include the following. First, for many countries, there are still no adequate codified standards of accounting and auditing. Internationally accepted standards not only would eliminate the setup costs for those countries but would allow them to immediately be part of the mainstream of accepted international accounting standards.

Second, the growing internationalization of the world's economies and the increasing interdependence of nations in terms of international trade and investment flows act a major argument for some form of internationally accepted standards of accounting and auditing. Such internationalization would also facilitate international transactions, pricing, and resource allocation decisions and might render the international financial markets more efficient.

Third, the need for companies to raise outside capital, given the insufficiency of retained earnings to finance projects and the availability of foreign loans, has increased the need for accounting harmonization. In effect, supplies of capital, here and abroad, tend to rely on financial reports to make the best investment and loan decisions and tend to show a preference for comparable reporting.

Fourth, comparability of financial statements will be enhanced through harmonization, making them easier to understand and use between countries. The end result may be comparable and credible data for use across borders.

Current trends, however, seem to indicate that there is little chance of ever achieving international harmonization. The following arguments are usually advanced to justify this pessimistic expectation. First, tax collections in all countries are one of the greatest sources of demand for accounting services. Because tax-collection systems vary internationally, it can also be expected that there will be a corresponding diversity in the accounting principles and systems used internationally.

Second, accounting policies are known to be fashioned sometimes to achieve either political or economic goals compatible with the economic or political system espoused by a given country. Since there is little hope of having a single political or economic system internationally, it can be expected that the differences in political and economic systems will continue to act as a barrier to international accounting harmonization.

Third, some of the obstacles to international harmonization are created by accountants themselves, through national strict licensing requirements. An extreme example occurred in 1976, when the French accountancy profession required foreign accountants practicing in France to sit for an oral examination.

As a result of the French experience, the European Community (EC) became involved with the qualification of auditors. The first published version of the draft Eighth Directive created several restraints on the ability of foreign accountants to practice in the EC member countries. Consider the following paragraphs from the version of the draft Eighth Directive:

The partners, members, persons responsible for management, administration direction or supervision of such professional companies or associations who do not personally fulfill the Directive [i.e., non-EC-qualified accountants] shall exercise no influence over the statutory audits carried out under the auspices of such approved professional companies or associations. The law shall in particular, ensure:

- that the above mentioned persons may not participate in the appointment or removal of auditors and that they may not issue to the latter any instructions regarding the carrying out of audits; . . .
- that the confidentiality of audit reports produced by the auditors and all documents relating thereto are protected and that these are withheld from the knowledge of the above-mentioned persons.

Fourth, opponents of harmonization fear that the accounting systems of the developed Western countries will end up dominating the global harmonization attempts. Naturalism is a powerful obstacle to harmonization as well as the absence of strong professional bodies in a number of countries.

It is fair to notice that there is ample evidence of a harmonization drive. The European Union, through the enforcement of its directors, seems to be achieving a higher level of harmonization among the member countries. This regional harmonization approach should be tried in other parts of the world. The emergence of the International Accounting Standards Committee (IASC) and the adoption of its standards by countries may result finally in a global harmonization. The research on harmonization needs reliable measures of harmonization. Tay and Parker (1990, pp. 71–88) and Van der Tas (1988, pp. 157–169) made a distinction between material (de facto) and formal (de jure) harmonization. Material (de facto) harmonization refers to the harmony of actual accounting practices while formal (de jure) harmonization refers to the harmony of financial accounting regulations. Van der Tas (1988) also makes a useful distinction between disclosure harmonization, which is the harmonization of the extent of information disclosure, and measurement harmonization, which is the harmonization of the nature of information disclosed. He derived material measurement harmonization as follows: "Material measurement harmonization means that more companies in the same circumstances apply the same accounting method to an event or give additional information in such a way that the financial reports of more companies can be made comparable" (Van der Tas, 1988). Based on this definition, Van der Tas offered a statistical concentration index, the "I" index to measure international comparability from the point of view of an international standard setter. The general formula of the I index is as follows:

$$I^x = \left(\sum_{i=1}^{n} (f_i^1 \times f_i^2 xL \; L \; f_i^m x) \right)^{1/(m-1)} \tag{2.1}$$

where

L_1 = relative frequency of method i in country m

M = number of countries

N = number of alternative methods (Van der Tas, 1988, p. 167)

Tay and Parker make the following useful distinctions (Van der Tas, 1988, p. 168):

1. between harmonization as a movement from total diversity and standardization, a movement toward uniformity,
2. between regulation, a de jure state and process, and practice, a de facto state and process,
3. between strict regulation, a law that applies to all companies, and less strict regulation, a standard that applies to more companies, and
4. between harmony and uniformity as states and harmonization and standardization as processes.

These distinctions are illustrated in Exhibit 2.9. In addition, Tay and Parker offer an alternative approach to harmonization measurement based on the following four specific recommendations:

First if harmonization activities are the result of concern about the comparability of accounts produced by companies from different countries, then a measurement study should focus on actual reporting practices rather than regulations, that is, on *de facto* rather than *de jure* harmonization.

Second, actual reporting practices may be assessed most accurately from annual accounts, or detailed surveys of such accounts. Thus the appropriate data sources would be published accounts, or national surveys based on samples of company accounts (if the companies in the sample are appropriate to the research objective), rather than surveys of legal and professional accounting regulation.

Third, given the sources suggested, data on proportions of companies using different accounting methods can be obtained. An operational definition of harmony could then take the form of comparing the observed distribution or some expected distribution. A suitable proxy for the former could be a uniform/equal/rectangular distribution, that is, a distribution in which equal numbers of companies would be expected to use each of the available alternatives. (This would represent no preference for, or bias towards, any one available method.) Evidence of harmony would then be the existence of a significant difference between the observed and expected distributions, as measured by some appropriate significance test, for example, chi-square.

Finally, the level of harmony could be quantified by using a concentration index, preferably one describing the entire distribution, rather than just a portion of it. Com-

Exhibit 2.9

Terminology of Harmonization and Standardization Accounting Methods

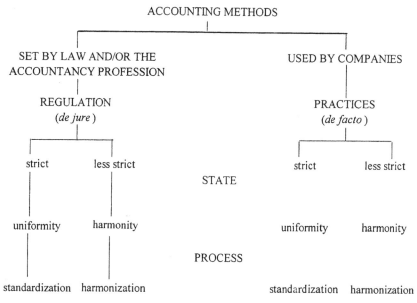

Source: J.S.W. Tay and R. H. Parker, "Measuring International Harmonization and Standardization," *ABACUS* (March 1990): p. 74. © Accounts Foundation at the University of Sydney. Reproduced by permission.

parison of levels of harmony over different periods would yield evidence of harmonization or disharmonization. (Tay and Parker, 1990, pp. 71–88)

Actors Involved in the Harmonization Drive

International Accounting Standards Committee (IASC)

The IASC was founded in 1973 with the following objectives contained in its constitution:

1. to formulate and publish in the public interest accounting standards to be observed in the presentation of financial statements and to promote their worldwide acceptance and observance;
2. to work generally for the improvement and harmonization of regulations, accounting standards and procedures relating to the presentation of financial statements. (Tay and Parker, 1990, pp. 84–85)

This translates into a goal of developing a common international approach to standards setting in accounting aimed at a worldwide harmonization and improvement of accounting principles used in the preparation of financial statements for the benefit of the public.

The IASC has an operating structure composed of the IASC Board, the consultative group, and various steering committees. Its procedure of exposure and comment is as follows:

1. After discussion, the IASC Board selects a topic that is felt to need an International Accounting Standard, and assigns it to a steering committee. All IASC member bodies are invited to submit material for consideration.
2. The steering committee, assisted by the IASC secretariat, considers the issues involved and presents a point outline on the subject to the Board.
3. The steering committee receives the comments of the Board and prepares a preliminary draft on the proposed standard.
4. Following review by the Board, the draft is circulated to all member bodies for their comments.
5. The steering committee prepares a revised draft, which, after approval by at least two-thirds of the Board, is published as an Exposure Draft. Comments are invited from all interested parties.
6. At each stage in the consideration of drafts, member bodies refer for guidance to the appropriate accounting research committees in their own organizations.
7. At the end of an exposure period (usually six months) comments are submitted to the IASC and are considered by the steering committee responsible for the project.
8. The steering committee then submits a revised draft to the Board for approval as an International Accounting Standard.
9. The issue of a Standard requires approval by at least three-quarters of the Board, after which the approved text of the Standard is sent to all member bodies for translation and publication.

As of 1999 the following standards had been produced:

IAS 1   Presentation of Financial Statements
IAS 2   Inventories
IAS 3   No longer effective. Replaced by IAS 27 and IAS 28
IAS 4   Withdrawn. Replaced by IAS 16, IAS 22, and IAS 28
IAS 5   No longer effective. Replaced by IAS 1
IAS 6   No longer effective. Replaced by IAS 15
IAS 7   Cash Flows Statement
IAS 8   Profit or Loss for the Period, Fundamental Errors and Changes in Accounting Policies
IAS 9   Research and Development Cost (to be superseded by IAS 38 effective 1/7/99)
IAS 10 Events after the Balance Sheet Date
IAS 11 Construction Contracts

IAS 12 Income Taxes

IAS 13 No longer effective. Replaced by IAS 1

IAS 14 Segment Reporting

IAS 15 Information Reflecting the Effects of Changing Prices

IAS 16 Property, Plant, and Equipment

IAS 17 Leases

IAS 18 Revenue

IAS 19 Employee Benefits

IAS 20 Accounting for Government Grants and Disclosure of Government Assistance

IAS 21 The Effects of Changes in Foreign Exchange Rates

IAS 22 Business Combinations

IAS 23 Borrowing Costs

IAS 24 Related-Party Disclosures

IAS 25 Accounting for Investments

IAS 26 Accounting and Reporting by Retirement Benefit Plans

IAS 27 Consolidated Financial Statements and Accounting for Investments in Subsidiaries

IAS 28 Accounting for Investments in Associates

IAS 29 Financial Reporting in Hyperinflationary Economies

IAS 30 Disclosures in the Financial Statements of Banks and Similar Financial Institutions

IAS 31 Financial Reporting of Interests In Joint Ventures

IAS 32 Financial Instruments: Disclosures and Presentation

IAS 33 Earnings Per Share

IAS 34 Interim Financial Reporting

IAS 35 Discontinuing Operations (1/1/99)

IAS 36 Impairment of Assets (1/7/99)

IAS 37 Provisions, Contingent Liabilities and Contingent Assets

IAS 38 Intangible Assets

IAS 39 Financial Instruments: Recognition and Measurement

IAS 40 Investment Property

The success of the IASC's efforts naturally rests on acceptance of the standards by member countries and recognition and support internationally. Noncompliance with international standards has been attributed to the following factors by Sir Henry Benson, the founder of IASC:

Some countries take the view that they cannot require compliance locally until they are satisfied that the Standards are internationally acceptable. Some see local legislations as an obstacle to the introduction of international standards. Some accounting bodies do not have the power to discipline their members, all cannot therefore impose compliance with either national or international standards. Some countries have not yet overcome stubborn local resistance from the business community. (Benson, 1976, p. 34)

Besides these obstacles there is definite evidence that effort toward harmonization is not equally shared by all members of IASC. Douglas summarized that situation as follows:

Some accountancy bodies have declared to their members that international accounting standards are to be accorded the same status as domestic accounting standards. Each IAS is accompanied by an explanation of the relationship between the international standard and any domestic standard dealing with the same subject.

Other accountancy bodies have issued statements declaring support for the concept of international standards and strongly encouraging their members to accept them. Some of these bodies indicate the extent to which an international standard differs from the related domestic standard. They often offer to review, or encourage the relevant body to review, the basis of the domestic standard, with the objective of eliminating any differences.

There are some member countries, however, that have not yet presented any format statement of the status of IASs to the members of the accountancy profession. (Douglas, 1977, pp. 49–50)

There is good evidence, however, of increasing compliance and national support of IASC pronouncements (Group of Experts on International Standards of Accounting and Reporting, 1977, p. 17).

Wallace argues that an enlarged perspective on contingency theory with the inclusion of contextual, environmental, and sociocultural variables can provide a comprehensive understanding of the determinants of the organizational patterns and effectiveness of the IASC (Wallace, 1990, p. 3).

The integrative model shown in Exhibit 2.10 provides a means of conceptualizing the variables by offering three successive environments: (A) the IASC's internal environment (the core); (B) its tasks and constituencies (the inner boundary); and (C) the varying international environment (the outer boundary). The survival of the IASC depends on the efficient management of (a) the technical core resources, (b) the procedural process, and (c) the external environment. Exhibit 2.11 summarizes IASC's survival strategies.

One survival strategy used by IASC is to coordinate its activities with the standard-setting bodies of the United Kingdom, Australia, Canada, and the United States, uniting in a group referred to as the G4+1. It meets four times a year to discuss key financial reporting issues with the objective of ensuring that future accounting standards are harmonized among the members.

The United Nations (UN)

The United Nations became interested in accounting and the need for improved corporate reporting when the Group of Eminent Persons appointed to

Exhibit 2.10
Environmental Factors Influencing IASC's Patterns and Survival

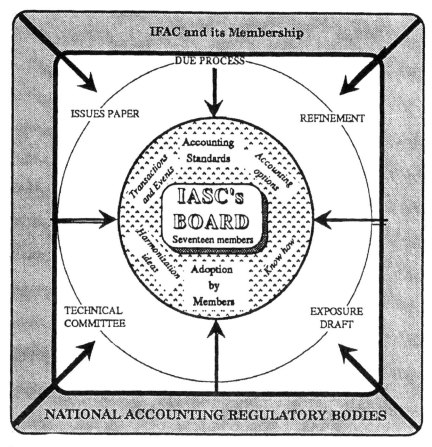

Source: R.S.O. Wallace, "Survival Strategies of a Global Organization: The Case of the International Accounting Standards Committee," *Accounting Horizons* (June 1990): 3. Reproduced by permission of the American Accounting Association and R. S. Olusegun Wallace.

study the impact of multinational corporations advocated the formulation of an international, comparable system of standardized accounting and reporting. It also recommended the creation of a Group of Experts on International Standards of Accounting and Reporting. The group was created in 1976 with the following objectives:

1. To review the existing practice of reporting by transnational corporations and reporting requirements in different countries.
2. To identify gaps in information in existing corporate reporting and to examine the feasibility of various proposals for improved reporting.

Exhibit 2.11
IASC's Survival Strategies

	Managing Technical Core Resources	Managing Procedural Process	
Technological Demands and Managerial Policies	1. Institutional Competence: a) Expertise/ Professionalism b) Independence 2. Research capability 3. Size of staff and budget 4. Mission and Goals	1. Substantive Authority a) Adequate justification for the exercise of authority b) Adequate rationale for rule promulgation 2. Procedural Due Process a) Members' opportunities to be heard b) Members' opportunities to Influence action	Market Demands and Emerging Issues
	Managing External Environment		
Political and Legal Factors	1. Seeking clear mandate 2. Satisfying diverse constituencies 3. Links with other organizations 4. Diluting the concentration of accountants on IASC's Board		Economic Factors

Sociological Factors

Source: R.S.O. Wallace, "Survival Strategies of a Global Organization: The Case of the International Accounting Standards Committee," *Accounting Horizons* (June 1990): 5. Reproduced by permission of the American Accounting Association and R. S. Olusegun Wallace.

3. To recommend a list of minimum items, together with their definitions, that should be included in reports by transnational corporations and their affiliates, taking into account the recommendations of various groups concerned with the subject matter.

As a result the group issued a report that included a thirty-four-page list of recommended items to be disclosed (1) by the "enterprise as a whole," that is, consolidated data, and (2) by individual member companies, including the parent company. Following publication of the report, an Intergovernmental Working Group of Experts on International Standards of Accounting and Reporting was formed with the objective of contributing to the harmonization of accounting standards. It does not function as a standards-setting body; its mandate is to review and discuss accounting and reporting standards. The various UN efforts to regulate transnational corporations (TNCos) are illustrated in Exhibit 2.12. Needless to say, this effort by the UN has had a mixed international reaction. Most of the concerned institutions have expressed the feeling that accountancy standards at the domestic or the international level are best set in the private sector. These same institutions are united in their support for the work of the

Exhibit 2.12
The ECOSOC and Relevant UN Bodies Involved in the Regulation of Accounting and Reporting by International Corporations

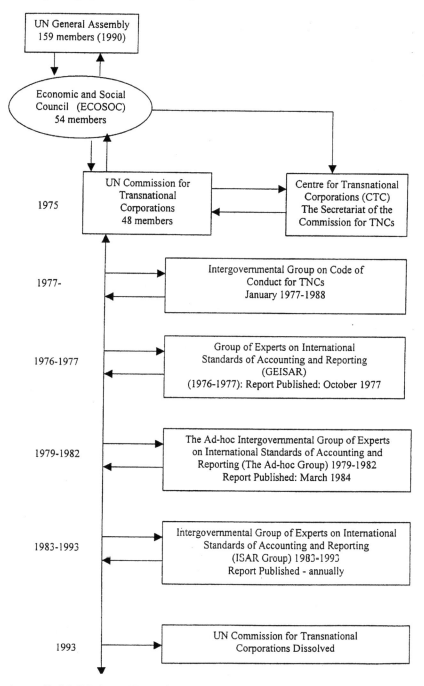

Exhibit 2.13
OECD Member Countries and Their Dates of Joining

Austria (1961)	Australia (1971)	Belgium (1961)
Canada (1961)	Czech Republic (1995)	Denmark (1961)
Finland (1969)	France (1961)	Germany (1961)
Greece (1961)	Hungary (1996)	Iceland (1961)
Ireland (1961)	Italy (1961)	Japan (1964)
Korea (1996)	Luxembourg (1961)	Mexico (1994)
The Netherlands (1961)	New Zealand (1973)	Norway (1961)
Poland (1996)	Portugal (1961)	Spain (1961)
Sweden (1961)	Switzerland (1961)	Turkey (1961)
United Kingdom (1961)	United States (1961)	

IASC and national accountancy groups. Member countries and their dates of joining are shown in Exhibit 2.13.

The Organization for Economic Cooperation and Development (OECD)

The OECD is an organization whose members include twenty-four relatively industrialized noncommunist countries in Europe, Asia, North America, and Australia. A Declaration on International Investment and Multinational Enterprises was issued in 1976, including an annex entitled "Guidelines for Multinational Enterprises," a section of which is subtitled "Disclosure of Information." The major elements suggested to be disclosed are listed below.

Enterprises should publish within reasonable time limits, on a regular basis, but at least annually, financial statements and other pertinent information relating to the enterprise as a whole comprising in particular:

- the structure of the enterprise, showing the name and location of the parent company, its main affiliates, its percentages, direct and indirect, in these affiliates, including shareholdings between them;
- the geographical areas . . . where operations are carried out and the principal activities carried on therein by the parent company and the main affiliates;
- the operating results and sales by geographical areas and, as far as practicable, by major lines of business for the enterprise as a whole;
- significant new capital investment by geographical area and, as far as practicable, by major lines of business for the enterprise as a whole;
- a statement of the sources and uses of funds by the enterprise as a whole;
- the average number of employees in each geographical area;
- research and development expenditures for the enterprise as a whole;

- the policies followed in respect of intra-group pricing;
- the accounting policies, including those on consolidation, observed in compiling the published information. (OECD, 1976, p. 14).

The European Community (EC)

The EC has also been active in achieving regional harmonization of accounting principles through a series of Directives, which, within the Treaty of Rome, are not as binding as regulations. Directives anticipate given results, but the mode and means of implementation are left to the member countries. The EC is in fact the first supranational body to have an important authority in the area of financial reporting and disclosure. Its influence is so pervasive that its directives are perceived to have important effects on non-EC-based multinationals operating in the Community. Particularly relevant to international accounting are the Fourth, Fifth, and Seventh Directives.

The Fourth Directive: The Fourth Directive, formally adopted in 1978, deals with the annual financial statements of public and private companies, other than banks and insurance companies (Commission of the European Communities, 1974). Its purposes have been summarized as follows:

a. Coordinating national laws for the protection of members and third parties relating to the publication, presentation, and content of annual accounts and reports of limited liability companies, and the accounting principles used in their preparation.

b. Establishing in the EC minimum equivalent legal requirements for disclosure of financial information to the public by companies which are in competition with one another.

c. Establishing the principle that annual accounts should give a true and fair view of a company's assets and liabilities, and of its financial position and profit and loss.

d. Providing the fullest possible information about limited companies to shareholders and third parties (with some relief to smaller companies). (The Fourth Directive, 1978)

The major aspects relevant to international accounting were articles 1 and 2 on types of companies covered by the Directive and the general reporting requirements, articles 3–27 on the format of annual reports, articles 28–39 on the valuation rules, articles 44–50 on publication requirements, and articles 51–52 on the procedural, statutory changes in national laws required for compliance.

The Fifth Directive: The proposed Fifth Directive, revised in 1984, deals with the structure, management, and external audits of limited liability corporations. The Directive proposed to require a company that employs more than 1,000 workers in the EC (or is part of a group of companies that employs more than 1,000 workers in the EC) to allow the employees to participate in the company's decision-making structure. In addition, it specifies certain rules concerning annual meetings of shareholders, the adoption of the company's annual financial statements, and the appointment, compensation, and duties of the company's auditors.

The Seventh Directive: Issued in June 1983, the Seventh Directive addresses the issue of consolidated financial statements and offers more guidelines for more standardization of accounting reporting. Companies in EC member countries and non-EC corporations with subsidiaries in a member country are required to file consolidated financial statements in that country.

The Eighth Directive: The Eighth Directive, issued on April 10, 1984, presents the minimum qualifications of auditors, to include educational and professional training of at least university-entrance-level qualifications. Both theoretical and practical training are required before the individual is required to pass a professional examination.

Other Actors

The preceding sections have identified the most important actors involved in the harmonization drive. Various other national, regional, and international groups are emerging as active in the same drive. They include basically the following:

ASEAN Federation of Accountants (AFA)

African Accounting Council (AAC)

Union Européenne des Experts Comptables Économiques et Financiers (UEC)

Association Interamericana de Contabilidad (AIC)

Confederation of Asian and Pacific Accountants (CAPA)

Nordic Federation of Accountants (NFA)

Association of Accountancy Bodies in West Africa (ABWA)

American Accounting Association (AAA)

Canadian Association of Academic Accountants (CAAA)

European Accounting Association (EPA)

Japan Accounting Association (JAA)

Association of University Instructors in Accounting (AUIA)

Financial Analysts Federations (FAF)

Financial Executives Institute (FEI)

Arab Society of Certified Accountants (ASCA)

Given the proliferation of actors involved or willing to be involved in the harmonization drive, one would expect some interrelationships among these bodies and cross-presentation in an attempt to exercise some influence in the international accounting arena.

Toward an International Conceptual Framework

Nature of an International Conceptual Framework

The credibility of international financial reporting has eroded and is subject to various criticisms. To correct the situation and provide a more rigorous way of setting standards and increasing financial statement users' understanding and confidence in financial reporting, an international conceptual framework may be needed. A good definition suitable to the international conceptual framework follows:

A conceptual framework is a *constitution*, a coherent system of interrelated objectives and fundamentals that can lead to consistent standards and that prescribes the nature, function, and limits of financial accounting and financial statements. The objectives identify the goals and the purposes of accounting. The fundamentals are the underlying concepts of accounting, concepts that guide the selection of events to be accounted for, the measurement of those events, and the means of summarizing and communicating them to interested parties. Concepts of that type are fundamental in the sense that other concepts flow from them and repeated reference to them will be necessary in establishing, interpreting, and applying accounting and reporting standards. (FASB, 1976, p. 2)

A conceptual framework, therefore, is intended to act as a constitution for the international standards-setting process. It would guide in resolving disputes in the standards-setting process by narrowing the question to whether specific standards conform to the conceptual framework. In fact, four specific benefits that would result from any conceptual framework have been identified. A conceptual framework, when completed, will (1) guide the standards-setting body in establishing accounting standards, (2) provide a frame of reference for resolving accounting questions in the absence of specific promulgated standards, (3) determine the bounds for judgments in preparing financial statements, and (4) enhance comparability by decreasing the number of alternative accounting methods.

At this time there is no international conceptual framework project. Instead, we are witnessing separate national efforts at creating a national conceptual framework in countries like the United States, Canada, Great Britain, and Australia. Whether these separate efforts will lead ultimately to a final harmonization in the form of an international conceptual framework is either a long-term goal or merely wishful thinking, depending on one's perceptions of the likelihood of an international consensus on such theoretical projects as an international conceptual framework for accounting. The separate efforts are examined as a first step in an international conceptual framework.

U.S. Efforts

U.S. efforts to formulate a conceptual framework started first with the publication by the AICPA of APB Statement No. 4, *Basic Concepts and Accounting Principles Underlying Financial Statements of Business Enterprises*. Although it was basically descriptive, which diminished its chances of providing the first accounting conceptual framework, the Statement did influence most subsequent attempts to formulate the objectives of financial statements and to develop a basic conceptual framework for the field of accounting. In response to the criticisms of corporate financial reporting and the realization that a conceptual framework for accounting is needed, in April 1971 the board of directors of the AICPA announced the formation of two study groups. The study group on the establishment of accounting principles, known as the "Wheat Committee," was charged with the task of improving the standards-setting process. Its report resulted in the formation of the Financial Accounting Standards Board (FASB). A second study group, known as the "Trueblood Committee," was charged with the development of the objectives of financial statements. It published the *Report of the Study Group on the Objective of Financial Statements*, which presented twelve objectives of accounting. Following the publication of this report the FASB began its work on the conceptual framework. It first identified nine important issues:

- *Issue 1*: Which view of earnings should be adopted?
- *Issue 2 through 7*: What are the definitions of assets, liabilities, earnings, revenues, expenses, and gains and losses?
- *Issue 8*: Which capital maintenance or cost recovery concepts should be adopted for a conceptual framework for financial accounting and reporting?
- *Issue 9*: Which measurement method should be adopted?

The overall scope of the conceptual framework is as follows:

1. At the first level the *objectives* identify the goals and purposes of accounting. Statement of Financial Accounting Concept No. 1, *Objectives of Financial Reporting by Business Enterprises*, presents the goals and purposes of accounting for business enterprises. Statement of Financial Accounting Concepts No. 4, *Objectives of Financial Reporting by Nonbusiness Organizations*, presents the goals and purposes of accounting for nonbusiness organizations.
2. At the second level the *fundamentals* identify and define the *qualitative characteristics* of accounting information (Statement of Financial Accounting Concepts No. 4) and the *elements* of financial statements (Statement of Financial Accounting Concepts No. 3, *Elements of Financial Statements of Business Enterprises*).
3. At the third level the *operational guidelines* that the accountant uses in establishing and applying accounting standards include the recognition criteria, financial statements versus financial reporting, and measurement (Statement of Financial Accounting Standards No. 33, *Financial Reporting and Changing Prices*).
4. At the fourth level the *display* mechanisms that accounting uses to convey accounting information include reporting earnings, reporting funds flow and liquidity, and reporting financial position.

Canadian Efforts

The Canadian Institute of Chartered Accountants (CICA) published a research study in June 1980, *Corporate Reporting: Its Future Evolution*, written by Edward Stamp and hereafter referred to as the Stamp Report (Stamp, 1980). The main motivations behind this effort are, first, the FASB conceptual framework is not suitable for Canada, given the environmental, historical, political, and legal differences between the United States and Canada and, second, it will provide a Canadian solution to the problem of improving the quality of corporate financial accounting standards.

The approach advocated in the Stamp Report is an evolutionary one. It identifies problems and conceptual issues and provides solutions in terms of identification of the objectives of corporate financial reporting, the users of corporate reports, the nature of the users' needs, and the criteria for assessment of the quality of standards and of corporate accountability as the possible components of a Canadian conceptual framework. Unlike the FASB's conceptual framework, which is deemed too normative (if not axiomatic) and too narrow in its scope (its primary concern is with investors), the Canadian conceptual framework would be based on an evolutionary (rather than revolutionary) approach and would be less narrow in its scope (its primary concern is with the reasonable needs of the legitimate users of published financial reports). Furthermore, a public justification and explanation of the standards is suggested to win general acceptance of the framework.

It is now up to the CICA to evaluate the recommendations of the Stamp Report and develop a truly Canadian conceptual framework. The report is successful in listing major conceptual problems in developing any framework.

Reactions to the report have been mixed. It has been perceived as an opinion document: "In the final analysis, *Corporate Reporting* is an opinion document. It is not, nor do I believe it attempts to be, a classic inquiry type research study. Rather, it is based on the informed opinion of a group of experienced and capable accountants" (Archibald, 1988, p. 229).

It has also been characterized as confusing before finally opting for a socio-economic political worldview.

We might conclude that the Stamp Report, though arriving at many blind alleys, going through several iterations, and making several detours, does arrive at a position on a world view that might prove to be very fruitful in the development of public accounting theory and standards—the socioeconomic-political world view. (Dewhurst, 1982, p. 253)

British Efforts

In July 1975, the Accounting Standards Steering Committee of the Institute of Chartered Accountants in England and Wales published its *Corporate Report* as a discussion paper intended as a first step toward a major review of users, purposes, and methods of modern financial reporting in the United Kingdom (Accounting Standards Steering Committee, 1975, p. 50).

The paper's basic philosophy and starting point is that financial statements should be appropriate to their expected use by the potential users. In other words, they should attempt to satisfy the informational need of users. The report assigns responsibility for reporting to the "economic entity" having an impact on society through its activities. Economic entities are itemized as limited companies, listed and unlisted, pension schemes, charitable and other trusts, not-for-profit organizations, noncommerically oriented central government departments and agencies, partnerships and other forms of unincorporated business enterprises, trade unions and trade and professional associations, local authorities, and national industries, and other commercially oriented public-sector bodies (Accounting Standards Steering Committee, 1975, p. 16).

The report defines users as those having a reasonable right to information and whose information needs should be recognized by corporate reports. The users are identified as the equity investor group, the loan creditor group, the employer group, the analyst-advisor group, the business contact group, the government, and the public. To satisfy the fundamental objectives of annual reports set by the basic philosophy, seven desirable characteristics are cited—namely, that the corporate report be relevant, understandable, reliable, complete, objective, timely, and comparable.

After documenting the limitations of current reporting practices, the report suggests the need for the following additional statements:

1. A *statement of value added*, showing how the benefits of the efforts of an enterprise are shared among employees, providers of capital, the state, and reinvestment.

2. An *employment report*, showing the size and composition of the workforce relying on the enterprise for its livelihood, the work contribution of employees, and the benefits earned.

3. A *statement of money exchange with government*, showing the financial relationship between the enterprise and the state.

4. A *statement of transactions in foreign currency*, showing the direct case dealings between the United Kingdom and other countries.

5. A *statement of future prospects*, showing likely future profit, employment, and investment levels.

6. A *statement of corporate objectives*, showing management policy and medium-term strategic targets.

Finally, after assessing six measurement bases (historical cost, purchasing power, replacement cost, net realizable value, value to the firm, and net present value) against three criteria (theoretical acceptability, utility, and practicality), the report rejected the use of historical cost in favor of current values accompanied by the use of general index adjustment.

STANDARD SETTING IN THE DEVELOPING COUNTRIES

After World War II, many developing countries gained their independence and started developing their societies and economics. Their political independence rested on developing their own national economics.

To escape from the vicious cycle of underdevelopment, the developing countries began searching for a new social and economic identity. Economic development became the primary goal in the developing economies. Various strategies were used to spur economic growth. In spite of these efforts, most of these countries are still confronted with difficult economic and social problems. Some of these problems include unbalanced development, backward agriculture and food shortage, deteriorating trade conditions, heavy foreign borrowing, and a widening gap between the rich and the poor and between the towns and the countryside, aggravated by high unemployment.

Faced with this bleak situation, the developing countries began asking for a new international economic order. Of the many aspects of a new international economic order, the demands of the developing countries are:

- To raise the prices of raw materials and primary goods.
- To reform industrial and trade structure.
- That developed countries should increase their foreign debt.
- To reform the present international financial system, enabling it to provide capital for the developing countries.
- To reform the international economic structure and its decision making structure. (San, 1982, p. 26)

The implementation of this new economic order requires the development of adequate and reliable accounting systems in the developing countries that are capable of providing the necessary information for firms operating in these nations to function efficiently and be part of the global network of manufacturing and service firms.

The developing countries are characterized, however, by relatively inadequate and unreliable accounting systems and generally new and untested standard-setting institutions. Theory development and academic and professional accounting research add to the economic, social, political and institutional problems that may be acting as deterrents to effective standard setting. In spite of these limitations, however, the development of basic accounting systems and procedures and the process of standard setting has accelerated, as evidenced by the increasing number of professional organizations, standard-setting books, and academic accounting associations, as well as by the increasing membership of these groups in international standard-setting bodies.

The standard-setting process in the developing countries has not followed a unique strategy proper to these countries and their context. In fact, four strategies may be identified (Amenkhienan, 1986, pp. 22–26): (1) the evolutionary approach, (2) the development through transfer of accounting technology, (3) the adoption of international accounting standards, and (4) the development of accounting standards based on analysis of accounting principles and practices in the advanced nations against the backdrop of their underlying investment. These strategies are reviewed below.

The Evolutionary Approach

The evolutionary approach consists of an isolationist approach to standard setting whereby the developing country develops its own standard without any outside interferences or influences. The particular developing country defines its own specific accounting objectives and needs and proceeds to meet them by developing its own techniques, concepts, institutions, profession, and education in isolation. The particular country may feel its context to be unique enough to justify this drastic approach of standard setting. The learning process in this approach has to come from the local experiences, rather than the international experiences. It assumes the foreign partners will adapt to its own idiosyncratic rules and may have to if they want to continue to trade with the country and/ or maintain operations. Naturally, it may create an additional cost to the foreign partners, who may feel the conditions onerous enough to justify complete co-operation. In addition, the absence of an adequate local accounting technology may hamper not only the local firms but also the foreign firms operating in the country.

The Transfer-of-Technology Approach

The development through transfer of accounting technology may result from either the operations and activities of international accounting firms, multinationals, and academicians practicing in the developing countries, or the various international treaties and cooperative arrangements calling for exchanges of information and technology. Adolf Enthoven, for example, described the benefits of U.S. accounting assistance to the developing world as follows:

US accounting and accountants have already had a positive effect on accounting systems, procedures and training in many developing countries. For example, the affiliates of US MNEs have developed sound financial management systems. Other US companies have entered into joint ventures with foreign companies or have set up their own organizations in these countries for the production and sale of goods and services. Good financial and managerial accounting methods have accompanied these investments. Many US CPA firms have either established corresponding relationships with foreign firms or set up branch offices aboard. Although much of value has been accomplished by US accountants in CPA firms and in industry developing economies, such activities have generally been directed toward certain companies or to serve CPA firm clients. More might be done; however, I recognize that this task isn't the first priority of accountants in public practice and industry. (Enthoven, 1983, p. 112)

Because most developing countries may not have given formal attention to the formation and implementation of a strategy that facilitates the transfer of accounting technology, or the development of an indigenous accounting profession, Belverd Needles, Jr., proposed a conceptual framework by which a country might formulate a strategy for the international transfer of accounting technology as part of its overall economic plan (Needles, 1976, p. 59). Basically, national goals combine with the social, political, and economic environment and general resources and constraints to influence the overall economic plan. The economic plan itself contains as a subplan a strategy for the transfer of accounting technology, composed of (1) objectives for the accounting technology transfer, (2) strategy, (3) channels of transfer, and (4) levels of accounting technology. The three types of technology, individual, organizational, and independent professional, are defined as follows:

T1—level of technical accounting knowledge possessed by individuals;

T2—level of sophistication of accounting techniques used by government and business organizations;

T3—level of advancement of an independent accounting profession. (Needles, 1976, p. 59)

While the mere transfer of accounting technology may appear to be a direct benefit to the developing countries, there is the cost associated with (1) the transfer of the wrong or inapplicable technology, (2) the lack of appropriate infrastructure for the correct application of the technology, (3) the increased dependence on outside experts, (4) the lack of incentives for developing local standards, and (5) the horrible loss of pride by some culture groups. These costs ought to be compared with the benefits of technology transfer by each of the developing countries. It is a strategic decision that is an integral part of the overall economic plan as suggested earlier. The whole process of development ought to include not only economic growth strategies but accounting growth strategies, and therein lies the question of the desirability of accounting technology transfer by the developing countries.

The Adoption of International Accounting Standards

The strategy available to the developing countries consists of joining the International Accounting Standards Committee (IASC) or some other international standards bodies identified earlier and adopting wholesale their pronouncements. The rationale behind such strategy may be to (1) reduce the setup and production costs of accounting standards, (2) join the international harmonization drive, (3) facilitate the growth of foreign investment that may be needed, (4) enable its profession to emulate well-established professional standards of behavior and conduct, and (5) legitimize its status as a full-fledged member of the international community. In fact, some of the developing countries give more credence to the IASC and other standards than do some of the developed countries that have a dominant influence in the preparation of such standards.

The question is whether the benefits described as accruing to the developing countries from the mere adoption of the international accounting standards may be outweighed by the misspecifying of costs. Indeed, the international standards for accounting for various transactions occurring in the advanced countries may be totally irrelevant to some of the developing countries, as these transactions have little chance of occurring or may be occurring in a fashion more specific to the context of the developing countries. The particular situations occurring in the developing countries call for specific and local standard setting. In addition, the institutional and market factors of these countries are different enough in some contexts to justify a more "situationist" approach to standards setting.

This situationist strategy has also been labeled as the "zero-based option," or what George Scott refers to as "fresh start" because it uses established international standards as a basis toward a better fitting with the particular economic development context of the developing country. Scott elaborates as follows: "The major alternative is to effect a relatively clean break with accounting tradition in developing nations and to attempt to develop accounting with a 'fresh start' on the basis of the standards of accounting education, practices and professionalism that are embodied in economic evaluation accounting" (Scott, 1970, p. 12).

The Situationist Approach

The situationist strategy was also labeled as the "development of accounting standards based on an analysis of accounting principles and practices in the advanced nations against the backdrop of their underlying environments" (Scott, 1970, p. 25). Basically, it calls for a consideration of the diagnostic factors that determine the development of accounting in the developing countries. A standard meeting the constraints imposed by these factors can be deemed relevant and useful to the developing countries. The total of these standards constitutes the system of reporting and disclosure of the developing country. The factors influencing it may be represented as being influenced by the cultural linguistics, political and civil rights, economic and demographic characteristics, and legal and tax environment of the country in question. In other words, based on cultural relativism, linguistic relativism, political and civil relativism, economic and demographic relativism, and legal and tax relativism, the accounting concepts and the reporting and disclosure systems in any given country rest on the varying aspects of that country.

CONCLUSIONS

The harmonization of accounting systems is taking place. It will, however, take a long time before a complete harmony takes place in the accounting world

internationally. Differences abound and demand careful consideration and interpretation.

APPENDIX 2.A: IASC Constitution

Name and Objectives

1. The name of the organization shall be the International Accounting Standards Committee
    (IASC).

2. The objectives of the IASC are:

    a. To formulate and publish in the public interest accounting standards to be observed in the
       presentation of financial statements and to promote their worldwide acceptance and obser-
       vance.

    b. To work generally for the improvement and harmonization of regulations, accounting stan-
       dards and procedures relating to the presentation of financial statements.

Membership

3. As from 1 January 1984 membership of the International Accounting Standards Committee
    shall consist of all professional accountancy bodies that are members of the International
    Federation of Accountants (IFAC). Until 1 January 1984 membership shall be as laid down
    in the previous Constitution.

The Board

4. The business of the Committee shall be conducted by a Board of up to seventeen members
    consisting of:

    a. up to thirteen countries as nominated and appointed by the Council of IFAC that shall be
       represented by representatives from the professional accountancy bodies that are members
       of IFAC in these countries (in this Constitution the term "country" shall include two or
       more countries that may be nominated to accept jointly a single seat on the Board), and
    b. up to four organizations co-opted under clause 12(a).

5a. The term of appointment of the Board Member selected under clause 4(a) shall be no more
    than five years. A retiring Board Member shall be eligible for reappointment. The first ap-
    pointments under clause 4(a) shall be as of 1 January 1983.

5b. The term of appointment to the Board of a Member selected under clause 4(b) shall be de-
    termined by the Board at the time of appointment.

6. The professional accountancy bodies referred to in clause 4(a) and the organizations co-opted
    under clause 12(a) may nominate not more than two representatives from their Board Member
    country or their organization to serve on the Board. The nominated representatives from each
    country or organization may be accompanied at meetings of the Board by a staff observer.

7. The representatives on the Board and the persons nominated to carry out particular assignments
    or to join steering committees/working parties/groups shall not regard themselves as repre-
    senting sectional interests but shall be guided by the need to act in the public interest.

8. The President of IFAC, or his designate, accompanied by not more than one technical adviser,
    shall be entitled to attend meetings on the Board of IASC, be entitled to the privilege of the
    floor, but shall not be entitled to vote.

9. A report on its work shall be prepared by the Board each year and sent to the professional
    accountancy bodies and organizations which are represented on the Board and to the Council
    of IFAC for dissemination to the member bodies.

Chairman

10. The Board shall be presided over by a Chairman elected for a term of two-and-a-half years by the Members of the Board from among their number. The Chairman shall not be eligible for re-election. The member country providing the Chairman shall be entitled to a further representative.

Voting

11. Each country represented on the Board and each organization co-opted under clause 12(a) shall have one vote which may be taken by a show of hands or by written ballot. Except where otherwise provided either in this Constitution or in the Operating Procedures, decisions shall be taken on a simple majority of the Board.

Responsibilities and Powers

12. The Board shall have the power to:

   a. invite up to four organizations having an interest in financial reporting to be represented on the Board;

   b. remove from membership of the Board any country or organization co-opted under clause 12(a) whose contribution is more than one year in arrears or which fails to be represented at two successive Board meetings;

   c. publish documents relating to international accounting issues for discussion and comment provided a majority of the Board votes in favour of publication;

   d. issue documents in the form of exposure drafts for comment (including amendments to existing Standards) in the name of the International Accounting Standards Committee provided at least two-thirds of the Board votes in favor of publication;

   e. issue International Accounting Standards provided that at least three-quarters of the Board votes in favor of the publication;

   f. establish operating procedures so long as they are not inconsistent with the provisions of the Constitution;

   g. enter into discussions, negotiations or associations with outside bodies and generally promote the worldwide improvement and harmonization of accounting standards.

Issue of Discussion Documents, Exposure Drafts and Standards

13a. Discussion documents and exposure drafts shall be distributed by the Board to all Member Bodies. A suitable period shall be allowed for respondents to submit comments.

   b. Dissentient opinions will not be included in any exposure drafts or standards promulgated by the Board.

   c. Exposure drafts and standards may be distributed to such governments, standard setting bodies, stock exchanges, regulatory and other agencies and individuals as the Board may determine.

   d. The approved text of any exposure draft or standard shall be that published by IASC in the English language. The Board shall give authority to the individual participating bodies to prepare translations of the approved text of exposure drafts and standards. These translations should indicate the name of the accountancy body that prepared the translation and that it is a translation of the approved text. The responsibility for and cost of translating, publishing, and distributing copies in any country shall be borne by the professional body(ies) of the country concerned.

Financial Arrangements

14a. An annual budget for the ensuing calendar year shall be prepared by the Board each year and sent to the accountancy bodies and organizations which are represented on the Board, and to the Council of IFAC.

b. IFAC shall contribute 5% of the budget of IASC in January and 5% in July of each year to defray the costs of participation in Steering Committee by member bodies not represented on the Board of IASC. The remainder of the budget of IASC shall be borne by the members of the Board, except that the Council of IFAC may decide to reimburse wholly or in part the share of the budget charged to one or more Board members.

c. The countries or organizations represented on the Board shall contribute on 1st January and 1st July each year a sum in such proportions as shall be decided by three-quarters vote on the Board. Unless otherwise agreed, members of the Board shall contribute equally to the annual budget. Members who are represented on the Board for part only of a calendar year shall contribute a pro rata proportion calculated by reference to the period of their representation on the Board in that year. All Board member contributions shall be billed and collected by IASC.

d. The Board shall determine in its operating procedures what other expenses shall be a charge against the revenues of the Committee.

e. The Board shall annually prepare financial statements and submit them for audit and send copies thereof to the professional accountancy bodies and organizations which are represented on the Board and to the Council of IFAC for dissemination to the member bodies.

Meetings

15. Meetings of the Board shall be held at such times and in such places as the members on the Board may mutually agree.

16. In conjunction with the General Assembly of IFAC a meeting of the members of IASC shall be held during or immediately prior to each International Congress of Accountants at the location chosen for the congress.

Administrative Office

17. The location of the administrative office of the International Accounting Standards Committee shall be London, England.

Amendments to Constitution

18. Amendments to this Constitution shall be discussed with the Council of IFAC and shall require a three-quarters majority of the Board and approval by the membership as expressed by a simple majority of those voting.

APPENDIX 2.B: Members of IASC

Australia	Belgium	Colombia
Austria	Bolivia	Croatia
Bahamas	Botswana	Cyprus
Bahrain	Brazil	Czech Republic
Bangladesh	Canada	Denmark
Barbados	Chile	Dominican Republic

Ecuador	Kuwait	Singapore
Egypt	Lebanon	South Africa
Fiji	Lesotho	Spain
Finland	Liberia	Sri Lanka
France	Libya	Sudan
Germany	Luxembourg	Swaziland
Ghana	Malawi	Sweden
Greece	Malaysia	Switzerland
Hong Kong	Malta	Syria
Hungary	Mexico	Taiwan
Iceland	Netherlands	Tanzania
India	New Zealand	Thailand
Indonesia	Nigeria	Trinidad and Tobago
Iraq	Norway	Tunisia
Ireland	Pakistan	Turkey
Israel	Panama	United Kingdom
Italy	Paraguay	United States of America
Jamaica	Peru	Uruguay
Japan	Philippines	Zambia
Jordan	Poland	Zimbabwe
Kenya	Portugal	
Korea	Saudi Arabia	

REFERENCES

Accounting Standards Steering Committee. 1975. *The Corporate Report.* London: The Institute of Chartered Accountants in England and Wales.

Al-Hashim, Ahia. 1980. "Regulation of Financial Accounting: An International Perspective." *International Journal of Accounting* Fall: 47–68.

Amenkhienan, F. E. 1986. *Accounting in the Developing Countries: A Framework for Standard Setting.* Ann Arbor, Mich.: UMI Research Press.

American Accounting Association. 1977. "Report of the American Accounting Association Committee on International Accounting Operation and Education 1975–1976." *The Accounting Review* 4 (Supplement): 67–119.

Archibald, T. R. 1988. "A Research Perspective on Corporate Reporting: Its Future Evolution." In S. Basu and J. Alex Milburn (eds.), *Research to Support Standard Setting in Financial Accounting: A Canadian Perspective.* Toronto: The Clarkson Gordon Foundation.

Ashton, R. H. et al. 1988. "Audit Decision Making." In *Research Opportunities: The Second Decade.* Sarasota, Fla.: American Accounting Association.

Bailey, Derek T. (ed.). 1988. *Accounting in Socialist Countries.* London: Croom Helm/ Routledge.

Basu, A. K. 1988. *International Accounting Harmonization.* Calcutta, India: DSA in Commerce.

Baydoun, N. and R. Willett. 1955. "Cultural Relevance of Western Accounting Systems to Developing Countries." *ABACUS* 31(1): 67–92.

Belkaoui, Ahmed. 1978. "Linguistic Relativity in Accounting." *Accounting Organizations and Society* October: 97–129.

———. 1980. "The Interprofessional Linguistic Communication of Accounting Concepts: An Experiment in Sociolinguistics." *Journal of Accounting Research* Fall: 362–374.

Benson, Sir Henry. 1976. "The Story of International Accounting Standards." *Accountancy* July: 1–12.

Briston, R. J. 1978. "The Evolution of Accounting in Developing Countries." *International Journal of Accounting* 13(1): 105–120.

Commission of the European Communities. 1974. *Amended Proposal for a Fourth Council Directive for Co-ordination of National Legislation regarding the Annual Accounts of Limited Liability Companies.* Brussels: 1 CEC.

D'Andrade, R. 1984. "Cultural Meaning Systems." In R. Shuseder and R. Levine, (eds.), *Cultural Theory: Essays on Mind, Self, and Emotion.* Cambridge: Cambridge University Press.

Dewhurst, J. F. 1982. "An Evaluation of Corporate Reporting: Its Future Evolution Based on Different World Views." In A. K. Basu and J. S. Milburn (eds.), *Research to Support Standard Setting.* Toronto: The Clarkson Gordon Foundation.

Douglas, T. R. 1977. "International Accounting Standards." *CA Magazine* October: 15–19.

Elliot, Edward L., Jose Larrea, and Juan M. Rivera. 1968. "Accounting Aid to Developing Countries: Some Additional Considerations." *The Accounting Review* October: 763–768.

Enthoven, Adolf J. H. 1983. "US Accounting and the Third World." *Journal of Accountancy* June: 110–118.

FASB. 1976. *Conceptual Framework for Financial Accounting and Reporting: Elements of Financial Statements and Their Measurement.* Stamford, Conn.: FASB.

The Fourth Directive. 1978. London: Deloitte, Haskins & Sells.

Frederick, D. 1986. "Auditor's Representations and Retrieval of Knowledge in Internal Control Evaluation." Unpublished doctoral dissertation, University of Michigan.

Gastil, R. D. 1978. *Freedom in the World—Political Rights and Civil Liberties 1978.* New York: Freedom House.

Gernon, Helen and R. S. Olusegun Wallace. 1995. "International Accounting Research: A Review of Its Ecology, Contending Theories and Methodologies." *Journal of Accounting Literature* 14: 54–106.

Ghartey, James B. 1987. *Crisis Accountability and Development in the Third World.* Aldershot: Avebury (Grower Publishing).

Gray, S. J. 1988. "Towards a Theory of Cultural Influence on the Development of Accounting Systems Internationally." *ABACUS* May: 1–15.

Group of Experts on International Standards of Accounting and Reporting. 1977. *International Standards of Accounting and Reporting for Transnational Corporations.* New York: United Nations.

Hoarau, C. 1995. "International Accounting Harmonization: American Hegemony or Mutual Recognition with Benchmarks?" *European Accounting Review* 4(2): 217–234.

Hofstede, Geert. 1980. *Culture's Consequences: International Differences in Work-Related Values.* Beverly Hills, Calif.: Sage Publications.

Hove, M. R. 1986. "Accounting Practices in Developing Countries: Colonialism's Legacy of Inappropriate Technologies." *International Journal of Accounting* 21(1): 81–100.

Jaggi, B. 1975. "The Impact of the Cultural Environment on Financial Disclosure." *International Journal of Accounting Education and Research* January: 75–84.

Kroeber, A. L. and Kluckhorn, C. 1952. *Culture: A Critical Review of Concepts and Definitions.* Cambridge, Mass.: Peabody Museum.

Lowe, Howard D. 1967. "Accounting Aid for Developing Countries." *The Accounting Review* April: 356–360.

Monti-Belkaoui, Janice and Ahmed Belkaoui. 1983. "Bilingualism and the Perception of Professional Concepts." *Journal of Psycholinguistic Research* 12: 111–27.

Mueller, Gerhard G. 1967. *International Accounting.* New York: Macmillan.

———. 1968. "Accounting Principles Generally Accepted in the United States versus Those Generally Accepted Elsewhere." *International Journal of Accounting* Spring: 91–103.

Mueller, Gerhard G., Helen Gernon, and Gary Meek. 1994. *Accounting: An International Perspective.* Homewood, Ill.: Irwin.

Needles, B. E., Jr. 1976. "Implementing a Framework for the International Transfer of Accounting Technology." *International Journal of Accounting Education and Research* Fall: 45–62.

Nobes, Christopher. 1984. *International Classification of Financial Reporting.* London: Croom Helm.

OECD. 1976. "Declaration on International Investment and Multinational Enterprise." *The OECD Observer* July/August: 13–18.

Perera, M.H.B. 1989. "Accounting in the Developing Countries: A Case for Localized Uniformity." *The British Accounting Review* July: 141–57.

Perera, M.H.B. and M. R. Mathews. 1990. "The Cultural Relativity of Accounting and International Patterns of Social Accounting." *Advances in International Accounting* 2: 205–214.

Quinn, N. and D. Holland. 1987. "Culture and Cognition." In D. Holland and N. Quinn (eds.), *Cultural Models in Language and Thought.* Cambridge: Cambridge University Press.

Rahman, Sheikh F. 1998. "International Accounting Regulation by the United Nations: A Power Perspective." *Accounting, Auditing, & Accountability Journal* 11(5): 593–623.

Riahi-Belkaoui, Ahmed. 1989. "Cultural Determinism and Professional Self-Regulation in Accounting." *Research in Accounting Regulation* 3: 93–101.

———. 1990a. "Managerial, Academic and Professional Influences and Disclosure Adequacy: An Empirical Investigation." *Advances in International Accounting* Summer: 13–22.

———. 1990b. *Judgement in International Accounting.* Westport, Conn.: Greenwood Publishing.

———. 1993. *The Cultural Shaping of Accounting.* Westport, Conn.: Greenwood Publishing.

————. 1994. "Levels of Financial Disclosure by European Firms and Relation to Country Return and Risk." *Advances in International Accounting* 7: 171–181.

————. 1995a. "Accounting Information Adequacy and Macroeconomic Determinants of Economic Growth: Cross-Country Evidence." *Advances in International Accounting* 8: 87–98.

————. 1995b. *The Linguistic Shaping of Accounting.* Westport, Conn.: Greenwood Publishing.

————. 1996. "Political, Financial and Economic Risks and Accounting Disclosure Requirements of Global Stock Exchanges." *Research in Accounting Regulation* 10: 179–191.

————. 1997. *Disclosure Adequacy: Nature and Determinants.* Westport, Conn.: Greenwood Publishing.

————. 1998. "Human Development, Economic Development and Accounting Disclosure Requirements of Global Stock Exchanges: An Empirical Investigation." *Journal of Global Business* Spring: 49–56.

Riahi-Belkaoui, Ahmed, Claude Perochon, M. A. Mathews, Bruno Bernardi, and Youssef A. El-Adly. 1991. "Report on the Cultural Studies and Accounting Section of the American Accounting Association, 1988–89." *Advances in International Accounting* 4: 175–98.

San, Fu Zhao. 1982. "The Winding Road to Growth with Social Justice." *South* December: 15.

Schank, R. and R. Abelson. 1977. *Scripts, Plans, Goals and Understanding: An Inquiry into Human Knowledge Structure.* Hillsdale, NJ: Erlbaum.

Scott, G. M. 1970. *Accounting and the Developing Nations.* Seattle: University of Washington, Graduate School of Business Administration.

Seidler, Lee J. 1981. "Technical Issues in International Accounting." In F.D.S. Choi (ed.), *Multinational Accounting: A Research Framework for the Eighties.* Ann Arbor, Mich.: UMI Research Press.

Spiro, M. 1961. "Social Systems, Personality, and Functional Analysis." In B. Kaplan (ed.), *Studying Personality Cross-Culturally.* New York: Harper & Row.

Stamp, E. 1980. *Corporate Reporting: Its Future Evolution.* Toronto: CICA.

Tay, J. S. and R. H. Parker. 1990. "Measuring International Harmonization and Standardization." *ABACUS* 26(1): 71–88.

Van der Tas, L. G. 1988. "Measuring Harmonization of Financial Reporting Practice." *Accounting and Business Research* 19(2): 157–169.

Violet, William J. 1983. "The Development of International Accounting Standards: An Anthropological Perspective." *International Journal of Accounting Education and Research* Spring: 1–13.

Wallace, R.S.O. 1990. "Survival Strategies of a Global Organization: The Case of the International Standards Committee." *Accounting Horizons* June: 1–22.

————. 1993. "Development of Accounting Standards for Developing and Newly-Industrialized Countries." *Research in Third World Accounting* 1: 121–165.

Wallace, R.S.O. and H. Gernon. 1991. "Frameworks for International Comparative Financial Accounting." *Journal of Accounting Literature* 10: 209–264.

Wilson, John A. 1969. "The Need for Standardization of International Accounting." *Touche Ross Tempo* Winter: 16–31.

3
Accounting Information Adequacy and Macroeconomic Determinants of Economic Growth: Cross-Country Evidence

INTRODUCTION

The question "What determines the rate of economic growth?" has been and is still a subject of research interest (Lucas, 1988; Romer, 1986, 1990a; Stern, 1991; Barro, 1990). The search is for empirical linkages between long-run average growth rates and fiscal, trade, and monetary indicators as suggested by theory (Levine and Renelt, 1992). The research to date has not considered the potential impact of accounting information adequacy on economic growth.

Economic research assumes either that accounting is given or that the impact of accounting is inconsequential, or both (Talaga and Ndubizu, 1986). As accounting is assumed to establish the links of firms to the economy (Prakash and Rappaport, 1975; Riahi-Belkaoui, 1992) and perform a critical function in any economy (Scott, 1968; Ghartey, 1987; Enthoven, 1973; Larson, 1992; Riahi-Belkaoui, 1994), its inclusion in macroeconomic models of growth is warranted. Accordingly, based on a set of hypotheses, this chapter examines the cross-sectional relationship between economic growth on one hand and macroeconomic and accounting information adequacy variables on the other hand. Specifically, the chapter relies on 1980–1988 data from thirty-one countries to construct a pooled cross-sectional data set and examines the association of five variables with economic growth. These variables are: (1) gross domestic investment as a percentage of GDP, (2) annual rate of inflation, (3) terms of trade,

Adapted from Ahmed Riahi-Belkaoui, "Accounting Information Adequacy and Macroeconomic Determinants of Economic Growth: Cross-Country Evidence," *Advances in International Accounting* Vol. 8, copyright 1995, pp. 87–98, with permission from Elsevier Science.

(4) total expenditures on health and education as percentage of GDP, and (5) accounting information adequacy. The results support the significant impact of accounting information adequacy, in addition to the other four macroeconomic variables, on economic growth.

HYPOTHESES AND EMPIRICAL DESIGN

General Growth Model

The empirical growth literature has relied on the following cross-sectional specification:

$$Y = B_i I + B_i M + B_i Z + u \tag{3.1}$$

where Y is the per capita growth in GNP, I is a set of variables always included in the regression, M is a variable of interest, and Z is a subset of variables generally believed to be important explanatory variables of growth (Levine and Renelt, 1992). The I variables are inspired by new growth models that rely on constant returns to reproducible inputs or endogenous technological change (e.g., Barro, 1990; Romer, 1990b). Gross domestic investment as a percentage of GDP is used as the I variable in this study. M, the variable of interest, is accounting information adequacy. Finally, the Z variables represent fiscal, trade, and monetary indicators as suggested by theory and earlier research. This study uses annual rate of inflation, terms of trade, and total expenditures on health and education as a percentage of GDP as Z variables included in the model. The next section considers a set of hypotheses that support the variables included in the model.

HYPOTHESES AND VARIABLES

The hypotheses are drawn on the basis of the following characteristics: (1) they include the impact of accounting information adequacy, (2) they rely on macroeconomic rationales, (3) they yield testable implications for economic growth, and (4) they can be supported by available data.

Gross Domestic Investment as a Percentage of GDP

Out of forty-one growth studies, thirty-three included gross domestic investment as a percentage of GDP as an I variable. In addition, economic theory holds that higher rates of saving and investment are essential to the long-run rate of growth of a nation (Plossner, 1992). The intuition behind Solow's (1956) framework is that higher investment or savings rates lead to more accumulated capital per worker, resulting in an increase in the per capita output of the economy, but at a decreasing rate. In endogenous growth models with an emphasis on broader concepts of capital, such as Rebelo (1991) and Barro (1990), per capita growth and the investment ratio tend to move together. Delong and Summers (1992), looking at a cross-section of countries in the postwar period, find a positive association between investment in machinery and equipment and faster rates of growth. Based on the above empirical and theoretical evidence, this study relies on gross domestic investment as a percentage of GDP as a potential positive determinant of economic growth.

Annual Rate of Inflation

The Tobin-Mundell hypotheses imply that anticipated inflation causes more rapid shifts from real money balances toward real capital, raising investment and economic growth. Conversely, Stockman (1981) implied that, in economies with "cash-in-advance" constraints, anticipated inflation reduces economic activity and economic growth. Based on the above theoretical rationales, this study relies on the annual rate of inflation as a potential determinant of economic growth. A positive relationship will support the Tobin-Mundell hypotheses, while a negative relationship will support Stockman's hypothesis.

Terms of Trade

Export promotion policies have a beneficial impact on economic growth (Feder, 1982). Similarly, trade restrictions are expected to have an adverse effect on the efficiency of the economy by causing the failure to exploit comparative advantage and the reduction of aggregate output (Kormendi and Meguire, 1985). One factor associated with higher exports and lower trade restrictions is the commodity or net barter terms of trade. Terms of trade is a ratio of two indices: (1) the average price of a country's exports, which are approximated by dividing an index of export volume into an index of export revenue, and (2) the average price of its imports determined by the same method. Terms of trade is used as a determinant of economic growth. Thus, countries in which terms of trade are greater may be expected to experience greater economic growth.

Total Expenditures on Health and Education as a Percentage of GDP

The impact of government expenditures on economic growth has led to a policy debate among developmental economists. Supply-side theorists argue that the taxes required for financing government expenditures distort incentives and reduce efficient resource allocation and the level of output (Grier and Tullock, 1989; Kormendi and Meguire, 1985; Denison, 1985). Basically, countries with greater mean growth in governmental expenditures experience lower economic growth. The empirical growth literature uses (1) measures of overall size of the government in the economy, (2) disaggregated measures of government expenditures, and (3) measures of the growth rates of government expenditures. Dis-aggregated measures of government expenditures have been adopted in this study because of data availability. Thus, countries with greater total expenditures on health and education as a percentage of GDP should experience lower economic growth in the short run. Accounting information adequacy is assumed to be an important positive determinant of economic growth. This hypothesis is based on the following arguments:

1. Information produced by the accounting system serves the economy by allowing for increases in the efficiency of resource allocation among competing interests (Talaga and Ndubizu, 1986; Larson, 1992).

2. An important element of the efficient capital market is the existence of a sophisticated accounting infrastructure comprised of the facilities of information production, the framework of information monitoring, and contract enforcement (Lee, 1987).

3. Accounting information disclosure stimulates economic growth through its beneficial effect on the market capital accumulation (Ndubizu, 1992).

4. Accounting information is vital to the planning, decision-making, performance evaluation, and data-structuring processes of various economic institutions vital to economic growth (Prakash and Rappaport, 1975).

5. Three alternative perspectives on accounting method choice—the opportunistic behavior, efficient contracting, and information perspectives—may be relevant to the accounting information adequacy thesis (Holthausen, 1990; Healey, 1985). The efficient contracting hypothesis implies that accounting methods are chosen in order to minimize agency costs among the various parties to the firm, hence resulting in maximizing the value of the firm (Watts, 1977). According to the opportunistic behavior perspective, the same choice allows managers to behave opportunistically to transfer wealth (Watts and Zimmerman, 1978). Finally, the information perspective implies that the accounting methods are selected to provide information about the future cash flows of the firm but do not affect them directly (Holthausen and Leftwich, 1983). The opportunistic behavior and efficient contracting hypotheses link accounting to cash flows and wealth transfer implying that accounting ultimately affects economic growth. Thus, countries with higher accounting information adequacy may be expected to experience greater economic growth.

To measure accounting information adequacy, research examining the relationship between accounting and its environment has generally relied on disclosure indices based on the disclosure practices of large corporations in developed and developing countries (Wallace and Gernon, 1991; Meek and Saudaragaran, 1990). One exception is a recent study by Adhikari and Tondkar (1992) that relied on an alternative proxy, the operationalization of listing and filing requirements of stock exchanges in different countries, for measuring the general level of accounting disclosures in different countries. The level of stock exchange disclosure requirements as obtained from Adhikari and Tondkar (1992) was used in this study as the measure of accounting information adequacy and is hypothesized as a positive determinant of economic growth. Thus,

Exhibit 3.1
List of Countries

1. Australia	12. India	23. South Africa
2. Austria	13. Italy	24. Spain
3. Brazil	14. Japan	25. Sweden
4. Canada	15. Korea	26. Switzerland
5. Colombia	16. Malaysia	27. Thailand
6. Denmark	17. Mexico	28. Turkey
7. Egypt	18. Netherlands	29. United Kingdom
8. Finland	19. New Zealand	30. United States
9. France	20. Norway	31. Venezuela
10. Germany	21. Pakistan	
11. Greece	22. Singapore	

countries in which the general level of disclosure required by stock exchanges is greater may be expected to experience greater economic growth.

Empirical Design

The hypotheses were tested using a two-stage regression specified as follows:

$$GNPG_j = a_0 + a_1 GDIG_j + a_2 AIA_j + a_3 ARI_j \qquad (3.2)$$
$$+ a_4 TOT_j + a_5 TEHEG_j + u'_j$$

where

$GNPG$ = GNP per capita annual growth

$GDIG$ = gross domestic investment as a percentage of gross domestic product (GDP)

AIA = accounting information adequacy

ARI = the annual rate of inflation

TOT = term of trade

$TEHEG$ = total expenditures on health and education as a percentage of GDP

j = country j

A two stage regression was used because of the possibility that economic growth also causes accounting information adequacy. All the variables are measured for the 1980–1988 period. The data for this study come from the *Human Development Report* of the United Nations (1990) and the *International Financial Statistics* of the International Monetary Fund. Accounting information adequacy is measured by the level of accounting disclosure required by stock exchanges (Adhikari and Tondkar, 1992). The thirty-one countries were chosen because they had available data for all the variables used in this study. The list of countries is shown in Exhibit 3.1.

THE EMPIRICAL RESULTS

The correlation coefficients are reported in Exhibit 3.2. There is no evidence of serious multicollinearity among all the independent variables. The RESET (regression specification error test), as suggested by Ramsey (1969) and Thursby (1981, 1985), and the Hausman test (1978), as suggested by Wu (1973) and Hausman (1978), were used as specification tests. The results of the RESET test, used to check omitted variables, incorrect functional form, and noninde-pendence of regressors, show that the model used in this study is not misspe-cified (see diagnostic check statistics in Exhibit 3.3).

Exhibit 3.3 provides the results of estimating Equation (3.2) for the sample of thirty-one countries using the two-stage regression. The model explains about 57 percent of the variation in measured economic growth. The residuals appear normally distributed and include no clear outliers (the standard deviation of residuals based on N-K degrees of freedom is s.d. $2 = 0.086$). The F-statistic for the regression, $F = 6.42$, rejects the null hypothesis of no explanatory power for the regression as a whole at better than the 1 percent level.

The individual coefficients on the macroeconomic variables were all signifi-cant with the expected sign: (1) positive for gross domestic investment as a percentage of GDP as expected from the new growth models, (2) positive for the term of trade as expected by the export promotion policy implications, (3) negative for inflation as advocated by Stockman's (1981) hypothesis, and (4) negative for total expenditures on health and education as a percentage of GDP, as expected from the "supply-side" hypothesis. Of more relevance to this study is the significant and positive influence of accounting information adequacy as measured by the general level accounting disclosure required by stock ex-changes. A stepwise regression identified the relative importance of each of the independent variables in explaining economic growth in the following order: (1) gross domestic investment as percentage of GDP, (2) terms of trade, (3) annual rate of inflation, (4) total expenditures on health and education as percentage of GDP, and (5) accounting information adequacy.

In addition, the results of the Hausman *F-test* show that the hypothesis of the econometric exogenity of accounting information disclosure adequacy cannot be rejected at the 0.01 level, indicating that no simultaneous equation bias was observed. More specifically, based on previous empirical studies (Belkaoui, 1983; Belkaoui and Maksy, 1985; Cook and Wallace, 1990; Adhikari and Tond-kar, 1992), the instrumental variables used in the equation specifying accounting adequacy included economic growth and the UN Human Development Index (United Nations, 1990). This index is considered a more realistic measure of human development than mere GNP per head. It is included in this equation in order to relate disclosure adequacy to both economic and human development. The equation in the second stage of the two-stage regression was as follows:

$$AIA_j = b_0 + b_1 GNPG_j + HDI_j + u''_j \qquad (3.3)$$

Exhibit 3.2
Summary Statistics and Correlation Coefficients of Independent Variables

Variables	Mean	Standard Deviation	Median	AIA	ARI	TOT	TEHEG
GDIC	23.7	4.8	23.0	.1188 (.474)	-.1201 (.5123)	.0567 (.7577)	-.1619 (.3758)
AIA	68.8	9.6	70.6	1.000 (.555)	-.1064 (.3750)	.1595 (.0331)	.3718
ARI	16.2	33.8	7.1		1.000	.0394 (.8277)	-.3142 (.0798)
TOT	96.9	22.3	103.0			1.000	.2598 (.1509)
TEHEG	9.9	4.5	10.5				1.000
GNPG	3.0	1.6	2.7				

Note: GDIC = gross domestic investment as a percentage of GDP; *AIA* = accounting information adequacy; *ARI* = annual rate of inflation; *TOT* = terms of trade; *TEHEG* = total expenditures on health and education as a percentage of GDP; *GNPG* = per capita annual growth in GNP.

Exhibit 3.3
Results of the Regression Model

Variables	Intercept	GDIG	AIA	ARI	TOT	TEHEG	R^2	RESET F-value	Hausman F-value
B-value	-4.878	0.112*	0.058	-0.015	0.028	-0.141			
t-ratio	-1.814**	2.641*	2.652*	-2.59*	3.065*	-2.56*	.57	0.005	6.42*

Note: *Significant at alpha = 0.01; **significant at alpha = 0.10.

Exhibit 3.4
Results of the Second Regression

Variables	Intercept	GNPG	HDI	R^2	F
B value	46.090	0.821	23.530	0.81	3.727**
t-ratio	5.345*	0.622	2.655*		

Note: *Significant at alpha = 0.01; **significant at alpha = 0.05.

where *HDI;* = human development index for country *j*.

The results, as shown in Exhibit 3.4, indicate that economic growth is not a significant explanator of accounting adequacy. *HDI*, however, is found to be a significant explanator of accounting adequacy. Both results add more strength to the main result of this study that accounting adequacy causes economic growth.

CONCLUSION

This study presents the results of an exploratory empirical study on the impact of macroeconomic factors and accounting disclosure adequacy on economic growth.

There are two major empirical results in this chapter. First, in accordance with macroeconomic hypotheses, economic growth was found to be positively related to gross domestic investment as a percentage of GDP and terms of trade, and negatively related to inflation rate and total expenditure on health and education as a percentage of GDP. Second, accounting disclosure adequacy, as measured by the accounting disclosure requirements of the stock exchanges of the countries included in the sample, was found to be positively related to economic growth. Accounting appears as a major associate of economic growth as it provides the information links needed for the efficient functioning of the investment, trade, fiscal, and monetary forces in the economy. More work needs to be done with alternative measures for all the independent variables used in this study as well as different periods of analysis.

REFERENCES

Adhikari, A. and R. H. Tondkar. 1992. "Environmental Factors Influencing Accounting Disclosure Requirements of Global Stock Exchanges." *Journal of International Financial Management and Accounting* 4: 75–105.

Barro, R. J. 1990. "Economic Growth in a Cross Section of Countries." *Quarterly Journal of Economics* May: 407–444.

Belkaoui, A. 1983. "Economic, Political and Civil Indicators and Reporting and Disclosure Adequacy: Empirical Investigation." *Journal of Accounting and Public Policy* Fall: 207–221.

Belkaoui, A. 1989. "Language and Accounting." *Journal of Accounting Literature* 8: 16–32.

Belkaoui, A. and M. Maksy. 1985. "Welfare of the Common Man and Accounting Disclosure Adequacy: An Empirical Investigation." *International Journal of Accounting* Spring: 81–94.

Blitzen, C. R. et al. 1975. *Economy-wide Models and Development Planning*. London: Oxford University Press.

Bornschier, V., C. Chase-Dunn, and R. Rubinstein. 1978. "Cross-National Evidence of the Effects of Foreign Investment and Aid on Economic Growth and Inequality: A Survey of Findings and Reanalysis." *American Journal of Sociology* 84: 651–683.

Chenery, H. B., S. Robinson, and M. Syrguin. 1986. *Industrialization and Growth: A Comparative Study*. London: Oxford University Press.

Chenery, H. B. and T. N. Srivivasan (eds.). 1985. *Handbook of Development Economics*, Vol. 2. Amsterdam: North-Holland.

Chenery, H. B. and L. J. Taylor. 1968. "Development Patterns: Among Countries and Over Time." *Review of Economics and Statistics* November: 391–416.

Cook, T. E. and R.S.O. Wallace. 1990. "Financial Disclosure Refulation and Its Environment: A Review and Further Analysis." *Journal of Accounting and Public Policy* 9: 79–110.

De Gregorio, J. 1992. "The Effects of Inflation on Economic Growth." *European Economic Review* 36: 417–425.

Delong, J. B. and L. H. Summers. 1992. "Macroeconomic Policy and Long-Run Growth." In *Policies for Long-Run Economic Growth*, pp. 93–128. Kansas City: Federal Reserve Bank of Kansas.

Denison, E. F. 1985. *Trends in American Economic Growth: 1929–82*. Washington, D.C.: The Brookings Institution.

Enthoven, A.J.H. 1973. *Accountancy and Economic Development Policy*. Amsterdam: North-Holland.

Feder, G. 1982. "On Exports and Economic Growth." *Journal of Development Economics* 12: 59–73.

Ghartey, J. B. 1987. *Crisis Accountability and Development in the Third World*. Aldershot, UK: Avebury.

Grier, K. B. and G. Tullock. 1989. "An Empirical Analysis of Cross-National Economic Growth, 1951–80." *Journal of Monetary Economics* 29: 259–276.

Hausman, J. A. 1978. "Specification Tests in Econometrics." *Econometrics* 4: 1251–1270.

Healey, P. 1985. "The Effects of Bonus Schemes on Accounting Decisions." *Journal of Accounting and Economics* 7: 85–107.

Holthausen, R. 1990. "Accounting Method Choice, Opportunistic Behavior, Efficient Contracting, and Information Perspectives." *Journal of Accounting and Economics* 12: 207–218.

Holthausen, R. and R. Leftwich. 1983. "The Economic Consequences of Accounting Choice: Implications of Costly Contracting and Monitoring." *Journal of Accounting and Economics* 5: 77–117.

Kohn, M. L. (ed.). 1989. *Cross National Research in Sociology*. Newbury Park, Calif.: Sage.

Kormendi, R. C. and P. G. Meguire. 1985. "Macroeconomic Determinants of Growth: Cross-country Evidence." *Journal of Monetary Economics* 16: 141–163.

Larson, R. K. 1992. "International Accounting Standards and Economic Growth: An Empirical Investigation of Their Relationship in Africa." *Research in Third World Accounting* 2: 27–43.

Lee, C. J. 1987. "Accounting Infrastructure and Economic Development." *Journal of Accounting and Public Policy* 6: 75–85.

Levine, R. and D. Renelt. 1992. "A Sensitivity Analysis of Cross-Country Growth Regressions." *American Economic Review* September: 942–963.

Lucas, R. 1988. "On the Mechanics of Economic Development." *Journal of Monetary Economics* July: 3–42.

Maddison, A. 1987. "Growth and Slowdown in Advanced Capitalist Economies: Techniques of Quantitative Assessment." *Journal of Economic Literature* June.

Mankiw, N. G., D. Romer, and D. N. Wed. 1992. "A Contribution to the Empirics of Economic Growth." *Quarterly Journal of Economics* 107: 407–437.

Meek, G. K. and S. M. Saudaragaran. 1990. "A Survey of Research on Financial Reporting in a Transnational Context." *Journal of Accounting Literature* 9: 296–314.

Ndubizu, G. A. 1992. "Accounting Disclosure Methods and Economic Development: Criteria for Globalizing Capital Markets." *International Journal of Accounting* 27: 151–163.

Plossner, C. I. 1992. "The Search for Growth." In *Policies for Long-Run Economic Growth*, pp. 57–86. Kansas City: Federal Reserve Bank of Kansas.

Prakash, P. and A. Rappaport. 1975. "Informational Interdependencies." *The Accounting Review* October: 723–734.

Ramsey, F. I. 1969. "Test for Specification Errors in Classical Linear Least Squares Regression Analysis." *Journal of the Royal Statistical Society* 31 (Series B): 31.

Rebelo, S. 1991. "Long-Run Policy Analysis and Long-Run Growth." *Journal of Political Economy* 99: 500–521.

Riahi-Belkaoui, A. 1989. "Cultural Determinism and Professional Self-Regulation of Accounting Concepts." *Research in Accounting Regulation* 3: 93–101.

———. 1992. *Accounting Theory*, 3rd ed. London: Academic Press.

———. 1994. *International and Multinational Accounting*. Fort Worth, Tex.: Dryden Press.

Romer, P. M. 1986. "Increasing Returns and Long-Run Growth." *Journal of Political Economy* October: 1002–1037.

———. 1990a. "Capital, Labor, and Productivity." *Brooking Papers on Economic Activity* 10: 337–420.

———. 1990b. "Endogenous Technological Change." *Journal of Political Economy* October: 71–102.

Scott, G. M. 1968. "Private Enterprise Accounting in Developing Nations." *International Journal of Accounting* 4: 51–65.

Solow, R. 1956. "A Contribution to the Theory of Economic Growth." *Quarterly Journal of Economics* 70: 65–94.

Stern, N. 1991. "The Determinants of Growth." *The Economic Journal* January: 122–123.

Stockman, A. 1981. "Anticipated Inflation and the Capital Stock in a Cash-in-Advance Economy." *Journal of Monetary Economics* 8: 387–393.

Talaga, J. A. and G. Ndubizu. 1986. "Accounting and Economic Development: Relationships among Paradigms." *International Journal of Accounting Education and Research* 21 (2): 55–68.

Thursby, F. I. 1981. "A Test for Strategy for Discriminating between Auto-correlation and Misspecification in Regression Analysis." *Review of Economics and Statistics* 63: 117–123.

———. 1985. "The Relationship among the Specification Test of Hausman, Ramsey and Chow." *Journal of the American Statistical Association* 80: 926–928.

United Nations. 1990. *Human Development Report*. New York: United Nations.

Wallace, R.S.O., and H. Gernon. 1991. "Frameworks for International Comparative Financial Reporting." *Journal of Accounting Literature* 19: 209–264.

Watts, R. 1977. "Corporate Financial Statements, a Product of the Market and Political Processes." *Australian Journal of Management* 2: 53–78.

Watts, R. and J. Zimmerman. 1978. "Towards a Positive Theory of the Determination of Accounting Standards." *The Accounting Review* 53: 112–134.

Wu, P. 1973. "Alternative Tests of Independence between Stochastic Regressors and Disturbances." *Econometrics* 15: 733–750.

4
Basic Needs and Economic Systems: A Sensitivity Analysis

INTRODUCTION

An important empirical question addressed in the field of social economics is one of allocation. Given a certain level of income, does one system of social organization systematically devote more of its resources to basic needs than another? Or, stated differently, does the welfare of man differ from one economic system to another, and is it better in one system than in others? The question was empirically examined by Horvat (1974), who found that the countries he labeled "etatist" achieved "unambiguously higher basic welfare than other countries" (p. 32). He also found that the countries with a long welfare or social tradition fared better than did capitalist countries where such a tradition was less popular. Horvat, however, acknowledges that the welfare ranking of the high-income countries is biased downward while that of the poor countries may be biased upward, which may explain his results. To correct for this bias and determine whether it influenced Horvat's conclusion, Mandle (1980) replicated the study and eliminated both the richest and poorest countries. He failed, however, to reject Horvat's findings. Hella (1983) examined some questions about data, methodology, and interpretation in both papers but failed to reject their conclusions.

As we see it, there are two problems with these studies. First, they are all based on Horvat's data, which cover the period 1970–1976. A replication with more recent data is justified because following the turbulent sixties and during the seventies, the so-called capitalist countries moved aggressively to provide various forms of social welfare ("safety nets") to individuals. Second, these studies rely on one combination of three measures of basic needs (life expectancy, education, and health services) used by Horvat to define the welfare of the common man. This combination may be biased toward certain countries and does not reflect all possible dimensions of life expectancy, education, and health. Therefore, a replication using various combinations of measures of life expectancy, education, and health is necessary before making any statement about the impact of different economic systems on the welfare of man.

Given these two issues, this study proposes to use recent data and various combinations of measures of life expectancy, education, and health to examine the following hypothesis:

H_0: There is no difference in the levels of welfare of the common man between countries adopting different economic systems.

METHODOLOGY

Welfare of the Common Man

Following earlier studies, which we are replicating here using more recent data, the welfare of the common man is operationally computed as the difference between the ranking of basic welfare and the ranking of economic welfare. If the difference in ranking is positive, the common man is not being treated as well as elsewhere. If it is negative, the country is assumed to be efficiently employing its resources to satisfy the welfare needs of its population.

To determine their economic ranking, countries were ordered on the basis of their per capita GNP for 1979. To determine the basic welfare ranking, Hella's methodology is used; namely, we calculate a standardized value for each measure of need (health, life expectancy, and education), add the standardized value, and rank the countries on the basis of the new variables. To choose the measures of need, we used the World Bank's values for life expectancy (three), for health (three), and for education (four), which were available for most of the countries in the survey, to create thirty-six welfare measures for each country. These measures will serve as the database for an analysis of variance testing of the hypothesis (World Bank, 1981).

Types of Economic Systems and the Sample

The groupings used by the World Bank were used to differentiate between economic systems. These were (a) low-income countries (36 countries), (b) middle-income countries (60 countries), (c) industrial market economies (18 countries), (d) capital surplus oil exporters (4 countries), and (e) nonmarket industrial economies (6 countries). The complete list of the countries in each of the categories of the World Bank report was used in the study. Note that this classification is not only similar in most respects to the Horvat/Mandle classification, it is exhaustive in that it includes all the countries of the world.

EMPIRICAL RESULTS

The hypothesis is operationally intended to investigate the relationships between the thirty-six measures of the welfare of the common man and the type of economic system adopted by the countries in our sample. First, one-way ANOVA with F distribution was used. However, because of the possibility of a nonnormal distribution of welfare values and inequality of variances, a nonparametric test, the Kruskal-Wallis one-way ANOVA, is also used. The H-statistic is computed as follows:

$$H = \frac{12}{N(N + 1)} \sum_{j=1}^{k} \frac{Rj}{nj} - 3(N + 1) \tag{4.1}$$

where

k = number of categories for each independent variable

Nj = number of countries in the j category

N = number of countries in the total sample

Rj = sum of the ranks in the j category.

The values of the H-statistic were compared with the chi-square critical values to test the hypothesis. The results of the F- and x^2-statistics are shown in Exhibit 4.1.

As Exhibit 4.1 shows, the results for the types of economic system were significant. Basically, as noted in other studies, the welfare of the common man is dependent mainly on the type of economic system adopted by the given country.

An examination of the mean welfare-of-man scores for each of the thirty-six cases considered in this study showed the following for the five types of economic systems:

a. For low-income countries, the 36 means were positive.

b. For middle-income countries, 29 out of the 36 means were positive.

c. For industrial market economies, the 36 means were negative.

d. For capital surplus oil exporters, the 36 means were negative.

e. For the nonmarket industrial economies, 21 out of the 36 means were positive.

It appears that the welfare of man fares better in the industrial market economies and capital surplus oil exporters than in nonmarket industrial economies and low- and middle-income countries. The results are contrary to the other em-

Exhibit 4.1
Parametric and Nonparametric Results

Welfare of Man	F^*	x^{2*}	Welfare of Man	F	x^{2*}
W_1	12.43	33.65	W_{20}	26.60	42.51
W_2	14.57	31.35	W_{21}	8.48	51.33
W_3	10.87	35.27	W_{22}	7.73	20.17
W_4	23.63	48.45	W_{23}	13.45	19.29
W_5	17.58	38.32	W_{24}	24.43	26.59
W_6	29.43	32.70	W_{25}	13.87	45.26
W_7	25.49	39.33	W_{26}	15.39	37.40
W_8	13.35	53.86	W_{27}	26.77	32.62
W_9	11.87	18.89	W_{28}	29.80	38.43
W_{10}	21.07	18.50	W_{29}	15.47	45.97
W_{11}	11.64	27.98	W_{30}	12.44	43.04
W_{12}	18.08	45.08	W_{31}	20.30	32.74
W_{13}	28.11	49.54	W_{32}	29.33	41.69
W_{14}	9.18	28.18	W_{33}	10.06	52.47
W_{15}	9.00	37.73	W_{34}	9.64	21.78
W_{16}	15.90	48.50	W_{35}	16.69	21.61
W_{18}	26.51	49.95	W_{36}	25.97	29.57
W_{19}	16.13	34.36			

Note: *Significant at 0.0001.

pirical studies investigating the differences in the welfare of man among the various economic systems. The results of this study show that the countries labeled as industrial market economies and capital surplus oil exporters achieved unambiguously higher basic welfare than other countries.

CONCLUSIONS

Using recent data and different combinations of the welfare-of-man measure, this study found that the level of the welfare of man is markedly correlated with the socioeconomic systems in the following order: industrial market economies and capital surplus oil exporters (highest welfare), nonmarket industrial economies, and low- and middle-income countries (lowest welfare). Unlike the Horvat, Hella, and Mandle studies, we find that, relative to their income levels, the basic needs performance of the industrial market economies and capital surplus countries is superior to that of other countries.

REFERENCES

Hella, Karl N. 1983. "Basic Needs and Economic Systems: Notes on Data, Methodology and Interpretation." *Review of Social Economy* October: 172–177.

Horvat, Branko. 1974. "Welfare of the Common Man in Various Countries." *World Development* 2: 29–39.

Mandle, Jay R. 1980. "Basic Needs and Economic Systems." *Review of Social Economy* October: 179–189.

World Bank. 1981. *World Development Report, 1981*. Washington, D.C.: World Bank.

5

Lending to Developing Countries and the "Welfare of Man": An Empirical Investigation

INTRODUCTION

Concerns over foreign debt and the potential of default risk continue to preoccupy economists, financial institutions, and world political leaders. In particular, the ability of official and private creditors to correctly price their loans to the developing countries and the extent to which certain key factors are taken into account have been questioned in various empirical studies. Sand and Mascarenhas (1989) provide a summary of these studies as well as the actors found significant in explaining Eurocredit spread. These factors generally fall into four classes: (i) objective economic indicators of country risk; (ii) subjective bankers' country risk-taking (ICCR); (iii) intercountry systemic factors; and (iv) loan characteristics. The study by Sand and Mascarenhas provides a finer treatment of the problem by first developing and employing a more accurate measure of the return variable including both spread and front fees, instead of spread alone, and second examining the four classes of variables in addition to regional patterns of the loan characteristics of maturity, grace period, and size. What is, however, missing is the determinants of the "welfare of the common man," as it is termed in the social economic literature, and how these determinants affect the pricing of loans to developing countries. The term "welfare of the common man" is defined as the extent to which economic welfare is translated into achievement in social welfare or "basic welfare" (to use the language of social

Exhibit 5.1
Lending Model

```
Health
Index
                    Ranking of
Education            Basic Welfare
Index                Index
                                        Credit Pricing
                                        in Lending to
Life                                    Developing
Index                                   Countries by:


                    minus


                    Ranking of
                    Economic            a: Official Creditors
                    Welfare Index       b. private Creditors


                    equals


                    "Welfare of
                    Man"
```

economics literature) (see, e.g., Horvat, 1976; Mandle, 1980; Hella, 1983). Our review of the literature suggests that one important question is in need of investigation: to what extent are components of the welfare of man, economic and basic welfare, taken into account in the pricing of loans to developing countries by both official and private creditors? The objective of our study is the investigation of this question.

ELEMENTS INFLUENCING LENDING

The model to be investigated in this study postulates that credit pricing to developing countries is related to the components of the welfare of man: economic welfare and basic welfare. The model is described in Exhibit 5.1. The dependent variable is credit pricing in lending to developing countries by both official and private creditors. Official creditors include international organizations like the World Bank, regional development banks, and other multilateral and intergovernmental agencies, as well as governments and their agencies (including central banks) and official export credit agencies (World Bank, 1988). Private creditors include the bond markets, commercial banks, manufacturers, exporters and other suppliers of goods.

The welfare of man is the difference between the rankings of the economic welfare index and the basic welfare index. The basic welfare index itself is a composite of three indices: a health index, an education index, and a life index.

The Welfare of the Common Man

The concept of the welfare of the common man originated when development economists turned their attention from economic growth per se to the issue of the "basic needs" of the population (Ul Haq, 1980; Morawetz, 1977). The development approach moved from a largely economic perspective to a wide, all-encompassing socioeconomic one aimed at the fulfillment of all basic needs: adequate nutrition, health, clean water, and shelter. Where the basic welfare ranking is lower than the economic welfare ranking, the "common man" is considered to be worse off than in other countries. Where, however, the basic welfare ranking is higher than the economic welfare ranking, the country is assumed to be using its resources efficiently to better the welfare needs of its population (Morawetz, 1977). The "welfare of man" is operationally defined as the difference between the ranking of economic welfare (as measured by GNP) and the ranking of basic welfare (a composite ranking of three indices on health, life, and education). Horvat's study, in 1974, found the countries of the socialist bloc, labeled "etatist," to have achieved higher basic welfare rankings than other countries. In addition, countries with a long welfare or social tradition had a better performance on these rankings than capitalist countries where such a tradition was weak or missing. The results may be explained, however, by the fact that the welfare ranking of high-income countries was biased downward while that of poor countries may have been biased upward, a fact acknowledged by Horvat. A replication of the study by Mandle (1980), after elimination of the richest and poorest countries, supported Horvat's findings. Another replication was undertaken by Belkaoui and Maksy (1986) using data covering the more recent period from 1960 to 1976. Their rationale was that during the seventies and following the turbulent decade of the sixties, the so-called "capitalist" countries made much progress in introducing and/or expanding social welfare to their citizens. Their results supported the thesis that the welfare of the common man has drastically improved in the industrial market economies compared to the years reported in Horvat's study.

Welfare of the Common Man and Lending to Developing Countries

Earlier studies in the determinants of credit pricing in sovereign lending investigated the significance of objective economic indicators of country risk, subjective bankers' risk rating, intercountry systemic factors, and loan characteristics. These factors were deemed useful by banks when attempting to detect in advance which countries are likely to experience repayment problems and when these difficulties may arise. While we agree that these factors may indicate whether a loan and interest will likely be fully paid, the existence of a default risk in a given country is much more linked to the relative success it achieved in satisfying basic needs compared to other countries. Where the basic welfare ranking is lower than the economic welfare ranking, the common man in that country is considered worse off than elsewhere and the probability of default is perceived to be high. Where the basic welfare ranking is higher than the economic welfare ranking, the country is assumed to be employing its resources efficiently to satisfy the welfare need of its population, thereby creating a better atmosphere of international lending and reducing the probability of a high default rate. In other words, creditors may perceive countries with high economic and basic welfare rankings to be less risky than those with lower rankings. We predict that this thesis will apply more to official than to private creditors. Private creditors may be more interested in other financial considerations that have an impact on the probability of default than the welfare-of-man criterion.

PROCEDURES

Methodology and Sample

As presented in Exhibit 5.1, this study investigates the relationship between credit pricing in lending to developing countries and the components of the welfare of man: the basic welfare index ranking and the economic welfare index ranking. First, each of these variables is explained and measured. Then, a multiple regression analysis is used to test the model.

All the countries listed in the World Bank's *World Development Report 1988* and *World Debt Tables 1989–90* and for which there are available data on the variables included in the model were included in the study. These amounted to sixty-seven countries (see Exhibit 5.2).

Credit Pricing in Lending to Developing Countries

Credit pricing in lending to developing countries is operationalized by the grant element of a loan, a measure of the overall cost of borrowing (World Bank, 1989b). The grant element of a loan is the grant equivalent expressed as a percentage of the amount committed, where the grant equivalent of a loan is its commitment (present value), less the discounted present value of its contractual debt service. For each country and each year, the average grant element, as weighted by the amounts of the loans, is used (World Bank, 1989b). The average

Exhibit 5.2
List of Countries

1. Ethiopia	35. Ivory Coast
2. Bhutan	36. Egypt
3. Burkina Faso	37. Nicaragua
4. Nepal	38. Thailand
5. Bangladesh	39. El Salvador
6. Malawi	40. Botswana
7. Zaire	41. Jamaica
8. Mali	42. Cameroon
9. Mozambique	43. Paraguay
10. Madagascar	44. Peru
11. Uganda	45. Turkey
12. Togo	46. Tunisia
13. Benin	47. Mauritius
14. Central African Republic	48. Chile
15. Rwanda	49. Costa Rica
16. China	50. Jordan
17. Kenya	51. Syria
18. Zambia	52. Brazil
19. Sierra Leone	53. Malaysia
20. Sudan	54. Mexico
21. Haiti	55. Uruguay
22. Pakistan	56. Hungary
23. Lesotho	57. Poland
24. Ghana	58. Portugal
25. Sri Lanka	59. Yugoslavia
26. Senegal	60. Panama
27. Indonesia	61. South Korea
28. Philippines	62. Algeria
29. Morocco	63. Venezuela
30. Bolivia	64. Gabon
31. Zimbabwe	65. Greece
32. Nigeria	66. Oman
33. Papua New Guinea	67. Trinidad and Tobago
34. Honduras	

grant element for each year used related to official creditors and private creditors for both 1986 and 1987.

The Welfare of the Common Man

The detailed procedures for the computation of the components of the welfare of man follow:

Exhibit 5.3
Summary Statistics

Variable	Standard Mean	Deviation	Minimum	Maximum
Grant Element				
Official Creditors, 1986	37.518	24.233	-0.90	93.90
Grant Element				
Private Creditors, 1986	8.304	7.902	-18.30	35.00
Grant Element				
Official Creditors, 1986	41.470	23.969	7.30	88.80
Grant Element				
Private Creditors, 1986	8.831	7.200	-10.80	28.10

First, countries were ranked on the basis of their per capita GNP for 1985 to determine their economic ranking.

Second, three social indicators of health, life, and education were aggregated into a single one to represent a country's basic welfare.

Because there is no objective way of weighing the component indicators, Horvat (1976) and Mandle (1980) assigned equal weight to the three indicators and computed the aggregate indicator for basic welfare as the average of the three component ranks of life, education, and health. There really is no mathematical basis for creating an average rank in this manner. Hella (1983) and Belkaoui and Maksy (1986) approached this serious difficulty in Horvat's methodology by calculating a standardized value for each of the three measures of need, adding the standardized values together and ranking the countries on the basis of this new variable. This methodology was adopted in this study for the computation of the ranking of basic welfare. In order to select the three measures of need (health, life, and education), the authors examined the World Bank's *World Development Report 1988*, which yielded the following measures available for all countries in this study:

X_1 = population per physician, 1981, as a measure of health.

X_2 = percentage of age group enrolled in tertiary education, 1985, as a measure of education

X_3 = life expectancy at birth, 1986, as a measure of life

EMPIRICAL RESULTS

Summary statistics for the dependent and independent variables are shown in Exhibit 5.3. The means of the grant element of the official creditors exceeded

Exhibit 5.4
Regression Results: Official Creditors

Variable	1986	1987
Intercept	-2.386	1.7892
	(-0.647)	(0.490)
Basic Welfare	0.1543	0.1776
	(1.659)***	(1.887)***
Economic Welfare	0.9780	0.9986
	(9.411)*	(9.512)*
R^2 adjusted	67.47%	68.57%
F	66.337*	70.826*

Note: t statistics are in parentheses; *significant at 0.01; ***significant at 0.10.

25 percent. Loans with an original element of 25 percent or more are defined by the World Bank as *concessional*. Eighteen out of sixty-seven countries had concessional loans from official creditors in 1986 and 1987. Only five of the sixty-seven countries had concessional loans from private creditors in 1986 and 1987. This is an additional piece of information on the seriousness of the foreign debt crisis, particularly for official creditors.

The results of the regression results for 1986 and 1987 relating the grant elements of official creditors and private creditors to basic and economic welfare are shown in Exhibits 5.4 and 5.5. The results show that the grant elements of official creditors are significantly related to the components of the welfare of man as hypothesized. The relationship was not significant for private creditors.

CONCLUSION

The ability of creditors to distinguish between "good" and "bad" risks in lending to developing countries has up to now focused on financial, economic, and perception indicators as well as loan characteristics. No distinction was made between official and private creditors and no consideration was given to the welfare of man as an important consideration in lending to developing countries. This study examined the relationships between the overall cost of borrowing by developing countries, as measured by the average grant element of loans in 1986 and 1987, and the components of the welfare of man, as measured by the ranking of basic welfare and economic welfare. As expected, the average grant element of official creditors was found to be related to the basic and economic welfare for sixty-seven developing countries. The relationship was insignificant for private creditors as these creditors are focusing on other indicators of the probability of default in international borrowing. The focus by official creditors on the components of the welfare of man shows a concern for those institutions with the general well-being of the citizens of developing coun-

Exhibit 5.5
Regression Results: Private Creditors

Variable	1986	1987
Intercept	8.884	9.641
	(3.354)*	(4.110)*
Basic Welfare	0.0016	0.0073
	(-0.024)	(0.121)
Economic Welfare	0.0006	0.0327
	(0.008)	(0.0727)
R^2 adjusted	0.0417	-0.0397
F	0.997	0.9021

Note: t statistics are in parentheses; *significant at 0.01.

tries and the extent to which economic welfare in those nations has translated into achievement in social welfare. This finding is very much compatible with the emphasis in economic development literature on the primacy of the achievement of basic needs as an essential impetus to effective takeoff and/or continuous development.

In fact, the results may also be interpreted in support of the following scenario: when governments of developed nations lend money to less developed countries (LDCs), the developed countries' governments tend to control how the LDC governments will use the loans. In general, the LDC governments are encouraged to spend on social welfare, which in some cases may explain the results of the positive relationship between governmental loans and the condition of social welfare.

This study focused on the relationship between the overall cost of borrowing and the components of a social indicator known as the welfare of man. Future research in this area needs to examine the same relationships with other known social indicators. One indicator that merits further research is the human development index introduced by the United Nations in its 1992 *Human Development Report*. One question of particular interest is how the analyses based on the Human Development Index will affect the pricing loans to developing countries by both official and private creditors.

REFERENCES

Belkaoui, A. and Maksy, M. 1986. "Basic Needs and Economic Systems: A Security Analysis." *Review of Social Economy* October: 178–182.

Hella, K. 1983. "Basic Needs and Economic Systems: Notes on Data, Methodology and Interpretation." *Review of Social Economy* October: 16–22.

Horvat, B. 1974. "Welfare of the Common Man in Various Countries." *World Development* July: 29–30.

Mandle, J. 1980. "Basic Needs and Economic Systems." *Review of Social Economy* October: 15–30.

Morawetz, D. 1977. *Twenty-Five Years of Economic Development, 1950 to 1975*. Washington, D.C.: World Bank.

Sand, O. C. and Mascarenhas, B. 1989. "Eurocredit Pricing in Sovereign Lending." *Journal of International Financial Management and Accounting* Autumn: 244–258.

Ul Haq, M. 1980. "An International Perspective on Basic Needs, in World Bank," *Poverty and Basic Needs* September: 32.

World Bank. 1989a. *World Development Report 1988*. Oxford: Oxford University Press.

————. 1989b. *World Debt Tables, 1989–90*, Vol. 2. Washington, D.C.: World Bank.

6

Economic Freedom, Human Development, and Accounting Disclosure Requirements of Global Stock Exchanges: An Empirical Investigation

INTRODUCTION

The present study is an attempt to quantify relationships between economic freedom, human development, and accounting disclosure requirements of global stock exchanges. The two main objectives of the chapter are (1) to verify that the accepted thesis in nonnative international accounting research that economic freedom and human development increase and promote disclosure in general and the mandatory requirements of global stock exchanges in particular has empirical foundations, and (2) to indicate desirable directions for further research and policy implications. The attempt is now made possible owing to data on human development provided by the United Nations (1991), ahd the meticulous work of the Fraser Institute on economic freedom (Gwartney et al., 1996). Both books provide detailed measures on human development and economic freedom internationally.

There is now ample anecdotal and empirical evidence that suggests that countries that have allowed a lower role of governments in economic activities and greater promotion of human development show rising rates of economic growth (United Nations, 1991; Barro, 1996; Ayal and Karras, 1998). There is also ample evidence connecting the disclosure level in general and the mandatory requirements of global stock exchanges in particular to the level and changes in rates of economic growth (Wallace and Gernon, 1991; Adhikari and Tondkar, 1992; Cooke and Wallace, 1990; Riahi-Belkaoui, 1995, 1996, 1998, 1999). The two results imply a potential link between the disclosure level, in general, and the mandatory requirements of global stock exchanges, in particular, and economic freedom and human development. In this study, we propose to test whether economic freedom and human development have contributed to the level of mandatory information requirements of global stock exchanges.

GENERAL DISCLOSURE MODEL

Let's consider a simple international disclosure model. Suppose that Y = Af (HDI) is a measure of the level of disclosure, A is an efficiency factor, HDI is a human development index, and f is a disclosure function. The function hypothesizes that the level of disclosure is a function of human development (Belkaoui and Maksy, 1986). Basically, just as economic growth is necessary for accounting development, human development is critical to accounting development. Human development is hampered by conditions of poverty, malnutrition, ill health, inadequate education, and gender disparities (United Nations, 1991). When people face low human development conditions, they are less likely to be able to devote the resources and the energy to create an adequate accounting system. Obstacles to human development are also obstacles to accounting development.

Let's now hypothesize that the reason the disclosure level is promoted by economic freedom, EF, is that the efficiency factor is an increasing function: $A = A(EF)$, with $A > 0$. This amounts to hypothesizing that economic freedom enhances the efficiency by which human development increases the level of disclosure. Substituting the efficiency factor function in the level of disclosure function, we obtain:

$$Y = q(HDI, EF) \tag{6.1}$$

This last equation implies that, under the hypothesis that the efficiency factor is enhanced by economic freedom, the latter must have significantly positive effects on the level of disclosure, in addition to the effect of human development.

METHODOLOGY

Sample

The level of disclosure requirements of a stock exchange is used to operationalize the dependent variable (Adhikari and Tondkar, 1992). Independent variables are the following: (1) human development and (2) economic freedom. To be included in our sample, a country must have available data to measure both the dependent and the independent variables. Thirty-three countries met this test. The countries are shown in Exhibit 6.1.

Adhikari and Tondkar's Disclosure Index

Adhikari and Tondkar's (1992) composite disclosure index, intended to measure the quantity and intensity of disclosure required as part of the listing and

Exhibit 6.1
Sample

Sydney (Australia)	Vienna (Austria)
Rio de Janeiro (Brazil)	Toronto (Canada)
Bogota (Colombia)	Copenhagen (Denmark)
Cairo (Egypt)	Helsinki (Finland)
Paris (France)	Frankfurt (Germany)
Athens(Greece)	Hong Kong (P.R.C)
Bombay (India)	Milan (Italy)
Tokyo (Japan)	Seoul (S. Korea)
Mexico (Mexico)	Kuala Lumpur (Malaysia)
Wellington (New Zealand)	Amsterdam (Netherlands)
Karachi (Pakistan)	Oslo (Norway)
Singapore (Singapore)	Lisbon (Portugal)
Madrid (Spain)	Stockholm (Sweden)
Zurich (Switzerland)	Bangkok (Thailand)
Istanbul (Turkey)	New York (United States)
Johannesburg (South Africa)	Caracas (Venezuela)
London (United Kingdom)	

filing requirements of stock exchanges, includes a list of forty-four items. An actual score for each stock exchange was obtained by summing all the scores received by the stock exchange for forty-four items that are required by the stock exchange as part of its listing and filing requirements. The disclosure score was obtained by dividing the actual score attained by a stock exchange by the maximum attainable score. To account for differences among different user groups, each disclosure score was weighted by its relevance to a list of experts from each of the countries examined. As a result, a weighted score was computed. The index is shown in Exhibit 6.2. The variables included in Adhikari and Tondkar's study (1992), including the disclosure index, were computed for the period 1986–1988.

Human Development

Human development is measured by the 1990 UN Development index (HDI) for the same period (United Nations, 1991). It is generally considered a more realistic measure of human development than mere GNP per head. The HDI is composed of three indicators: life expectancy, education, and income.

Economic Freedom

The economic freedom index is made possible by the meticulous work of the Eraser Institute, the results of which were published in *Economic Freedom of the World: 1975–1995* by James D. Gwartney, Robert Lawson, and Waiter

Exhibit 6.2
Adhikari and Tondkar's Disclosure Scoring Sheet

	Required
General Information	
Brief narrative history of the company	3.13
Statement of company objectives and mission	3.62
Description of major plants and properties, including location, function, and size	3.13
Description of major products, including an indication of those products that are new	3.58
Information relating to research and development activities including a narrative description of the progress with new product development and planned expenditures	3.66
Information on employees such as number, type, and description of employee benefits	2.73
Dependence on patents, licenses, contracts, where such factors are of fundamental importance to the company's business	4.00
Capital expenditures—narrative and quantitative data on expenditures in past year and planned expenditures	3.85
Information on corporate social responsibility such as expenditures on environment and community, etc.	2.75
Extent of dependence on major customers	3.68
Information on major industry trends and the relative position of the company in the industry	3.89
Information on the principal contents of each significant contract (not being a contract entered into in ordinary course of business)	3.28
Information on any recent or planned mergers or acquisitions	4.33
Information on management	
Information on company directors, such as their names, salaries, and major outside affiliations	3.17
Information on management, such as their names, salaries, and functional responsibilities	3.16
Information on significant transactions of directors, officers, and principal holders of securities	3.33
Information about the company's capital	
General information noncapitalization resignation of each class of stock, per value, authorized capital, issued, and outstanding stock	3.86
Summary statement of changes in share capital in past three years and any future planned change	3.72
Summary of rights, preferences, privileges, and priorities of different classes of stock	3.79

Exhibit 6.2 (continued)

Number and types of stockholders	3.00
Names and size of stock holdings of largest stockholders	3.59
Information on any options, warrants, conversion rights outstanding	3.83
Historical summary of price range and trading volume of ordinary (common) shares	3.19
Information on the loan, other borrowings, and indebtedness of the company and its subsidiaries	4.50

Financial Information

Historical summary of important operation and financial data	3.53
Audited financial statements (income statement and balance sheet)	4.56
Statement of sources and application of funds (statement of changes in financial positions or statements of cash flows)	4.03
Interim reports (quarterly or semiannual reports)	3.96
Information related to post–balance sheet events	4.13
Dividends records, including a statement of future dividends/dividends policies	3.97
Information about consolidated/unconsolidated subsidiaries, including consolidated statement	4.09
Information about investment in firms not qualifying as subsidiaries	3.44
Breakdown of earnings by major product lines, customer classes, and geographical locations	3.74
Breakdown of sales revenue by major product lines, customer classes, and geographical locations	3.63
Discussion of company's results for the past year	3.83
More detail or supplementary information in cases where financial statements do not "fairly" present or do not give a "true and fair view" of the company's financial position	4.33
Information on all pending and potential litigation that has had or may have a significant effect on the financial position	4.13
Pro forma or "giving effect" statements in classes where there has been or is contemplated any major financing, recapitalization, acquisition, or reorganization	4.25
Discussion of significant accounting policies	3.69

Recent developments and prospects

General information on the trend of the business since the end of the last financial year	4.22
Any significant information that may affect the market for a company's securities	4.30
Discussion of the major factors that will influence next year's results with special emphasis on the financial and trading prospects of the company	4.20
Profit forecast	4.33

Exhibit 6.3
Summary Statistics

Variables	Mean	Standard Deviation	Maximum	Medium	Minimum
WTD Score	68.768	9.638	90.75	70.68	48.02
HDI	0.657	0.185	0.993	0.952	0.308
Ie	6.317	1.396	9	6.45	2.8
Is 1	6.070	1.265	9.1	5.9	3.3
Is 2	6.638	1.684	9.1	6.9	2.4
AVG	6.341	1.423	9	6.55	2.8
GRADE	3.735	1.638	6	4	1

Note: WTD Score = weighted disclosure index; HDI = human development index; Ie = an equal impact index of economic freedom; Is1 = a survey of knowledgeable people-based index of economic freedom; Is2 = a survey of a large number of people-based index of economic freedom; AVG = an average of the above three indexes of economic freedom; GRADE = a letter grade index of economic freedom (A = 6; B = 5; C = 4; D = 3; E = 2; F = 1).

Block (1996). The index of economic freedom has seventeen components that are allocated to four major areas: (1) money and inflation, (2) government operations and regulations, (3) takings and discrimination taxation, and (4) international exchange. In aggregating these components of economic freedom into a summary index, various alternatives are used to attach different weights to the components. What results are five possible summary indices: (a) an equal impact index: Ie, (b) a survey of knowledgeable people based index: Is1, (c) a survey of a large number of people based index: Is2, (d) an average of the above three indices: AVG, and (e) a letter grade index: GRADE. Each of these five summary indices, Ie, Is1, Is2, AVG, and GRADE, will be used in this study to evaluate the impact of economic freedom (EE) on the level of disclosure of global stock exchanges.

Empirical Design

The two hypotheses were tested by the following regression:

$$WTDSCORE_j = a_0 + a_1 HDI_j + a_2 Ef_j + e' \qquad (6.2)$$

where

WTDSCORE = weighted disclosure index for country j

HDI   = human development index for country j

EF   = economic freedom index for country j, to be measured by Ie, Isl, Is2, AVG, and GRADE

Exhibit 6.4
Correlation Coefficients of Independent Variables (t-coefficients are in parentheses)

	HDI	Ie	Is 1	Is2	AVG	GRADE
HDI	1.000	0.558	0.484	0.639	0.5774	0.5935
		(0.0007)	(0.004)	(0.0001)	(0.0004)	(0.0003)
Ie		1.000	0.973	0.972	0.999	0.952
			(0.0001)	(0.0001)	(0.0001)	(0.0001)
Is 1			1.000	0.898	0.968	0.912
				(0.0001)	(0.0001)	(0.0001)
Is 2				1.000	0.954	0.948
					(0.0001)	(0.0001)
AVG					1.000	0.954
						(0.0001)
GRADE						1.000

Note: Variables are as defined in Exhibit 6.3.

RESULTS

The summary statistics and the correlation coefficients are shown in Exhibits 6.3 and 6.4, respectively. The RESET (regression specification error test) was used as specification tests. The results of the RESET test, used to check omitted variables, incorrect functional form, and nonindependence of repressors, show that the model used in this study is not misspecified.

Exhibit 6.5 provides the results of estimating Equation (5.1), using five different measures of economic freedom. The model explains 24.11 percent to 33.76 percent of the variation in the level of disclosure of global stock exchanges. The F statistic for the regression F, varying from 6.082 to 8.430, rejects the null hypothesis of no explanatory power for the regression as a whole at better than the 1 percent level.

The individual coefficients on the human development variable were all significant with the expected positive sign. Of more practical relevance to this study is the significant and positive influence of economic freedom as measured by each of the five measures on the level of disclosure global stock exchanges.

CONCLUSION

This study presents two empirical results on the impact of human development and economic freedom on the level of disclosure of global stock exchanges. Based on the data set from thirty-three countries, the results of the regression model show that when the accounting disclosure requirements of global stock exchanges and human development are higher, the demand for accounting disclosure by stock exchanges is higher. Economic freedom and human development create a good climate for the development of accounting. Harmonizing efforts may be more successful with countries with similar economic freedom

Exhibit 6.5
Results of the Regression Model (t-coefficients are in parentheses)

	Regression1	Regression2	Regression3	Regression4	Regression5
Intercept	40.082 (5.171)[*]	36.718 (4.629)[*]	43.765 (5.939)[*]	40.475 (5.291)[*]	48.020 (6.941)[*]
HDI	16.563 (1.7728)[**]	16.497 (1.861)	17.299 (1.834)[**]	16.036 (1.847)[**]	14.528 (1.888)[**]
Ie	2.302 (1.813)[**]				
Is 1		2.971 (2.300)[**]			
Is 2			1.539 (1.825)[**]		
AVG				2.302 (1.820)[**]	
GRADE					2.230 (2.027)
Adjusted R^2	27.60%	31.71%	24.11%	27.66%	33.76%
F	7.100	8.430[*]	6.082[*]	7.116[*]	7.644[*]

Note: Variables are as defined in Exhibit 6.3; *significant at a 0.01 level; **significant at a 0.05 level.

and human development profiles. In addition, cross-sectional investments should be considered not only on the level of disclosure in a given country but also in the economic freedom and human development contexts.

REFERENCES

Adhikari, Ajay and Rasoul H. Tondkar. 1992. "Environmental Factors Influencing Accounting Disclosure Requirements of Global Stock Exchanges." *Journal of International Financial Management and Accounting* 2: 75–105.

Ayal, E. B. and G. Karras. 1998. "Components of Economic Freedom and Growth: An Empirical Study." *Journal of Developing Areas* 32: 327–338.

Barro, R. 1996. "Democracy and Growth." *Journal of Economic Growth* 1: 1–27.

Belkaoui, A. and M. Maksy. 1986. "Welfare of the Common Man and Accounting Disclosure Adequacy: An Empirical Investigation." *International Journal of Accounting* 20 (Spring): 178–182.

Cooke, T. E. and R.S.O. Wallace. 1990. "Financial Disclosure Regulation and Its Environment: A Review and Further Analysis." *Journal of Accounting and Public Policy* 9: 79–110.

Gwartney, James, Robert Lawson, and Waiter Block. 1996. *Economic Freedom of the World: 1975–1995*. Vancouver, B.C.: Fraser Institute.

Hausman, J. A. 1978. "Specification Tests in Econometrics." *Econometrics* 13: 1251–1270.

Ramsey, P. 1969. "Test for Specification Errors in Classical Least Squares Regression Analysis." *Journal of the Royal Statistical Society* 31 (Series B): 31.

Riahi-Belkaoui, Ahmed. 1995. "Accounting Information Adequacy and Macroeconomic Determinants of Economic Growth: Cross-Country Evidence." *Advances in International Accounting* June: 87–98.

————. 1996. "Political, Financial and Economic Risks and Accounting and Disclosure Requirements of Global Stock Exchanges." *Research in Accounting Regulation* 10: 179–191.

————. 1998. "Human Development, Economic Development and Accounting Disclosure Requirements of Global Stock Exchanges." *Journal of Global Business* 9: 49–56.

————. 1999. "Disclosure Adequacy and Country Risk." *American Business Review* June: 1–4.

Thursby, T. 1981. "A Test for Strategy for Discriminating between Auto-correlation and Misspecification in Regression Analysis." *Review of Economics and Statistics* 63: 117–123.

————. 1985. "The Relationship among the Specification Tests of Hausman, Ramsey and Chow." *Journal of the American Statistical Association* 80: 926–928.

United Nations. 1991. *Human Development Report, 1991.* New York: United Nations.

Wallace, R.S.O. and H. Gernon. 1991. "Frameworks for International Comparative Financial Accounting." *Journal of Accounting Literature* 19: 209–264.

7

Political, Financial, and Economic Risks and Accounting Disclosure Requirements of Global Stock Exchanges

INTRODUCTION

As a direct result of the globalization of capital markets, firms are increasingly listing their shares on foreign stock exchanges. The exchange choice is shown to be influenced by the financial disclosure levels, lending credence to official concerns that stringent disclosure levels could reduce access to foreign capital and foreign investment opportunities (Saudagaran and Biddle, 1992; Biddle and Saudagaran, 1989). Competitive pressures may lead the stock exchanges to move in the long run to similar disclosure levels. There are, however, environmental factors that are causing the differences in disclosure levels and that need to be identified and considered in any harmonization strategy (Adhikari and Tondkar, 1992). An examination of the impact of economic and equity factors on the level of disclosure requirements of stock exchanges found only the size of the equity market to be a significant explanatory variable (Adhikari and Tondkar, 1992). The environmental determinism theory, which suggests a positive relationship between accounting and its total environment, calls for examination of the impact of the political, economic, and financial environment (Wallace and Gernon, 1991; Meek and Saudagaran, 1990; Cooke and Wallace, 1990). Accordingly, this study seeks to extend Adhikari and Tondkar's study by examining the relationship between political, financial, and economic risks on the one hand and levels of disclosure requirements of stock exchanges on the other

Adapted from Ahmed Riahi-Belkaoui, "Political, Financial and Economic Risks and Accounting Disclosure Requirements of Global Stock Exchanges," *Research in Accounting Regulation* Vol. 10, copyright 1996, pp. 179–191, with permission from Elsevier Science.

Exhibit 7.1
Model of Accounting Development

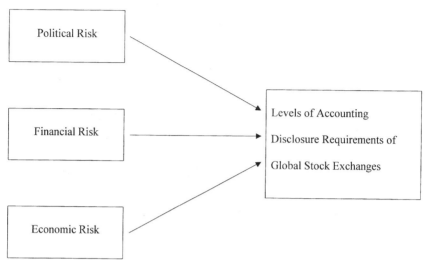

hand. The hypothesis of this chapter is that the differences in the levels of disclosure requirements of stock exchanges, observed by Adhikari and Tondkar (1992), are attributable to political, financial, and economic risks. Knowledge of these factors would be vital to formulate harmonization strategies and would allow users of cross-national accounting data to evaluate more properly accounting information and make rational economic decisions.

THEORETICAL JUSTIFICATION AND HYPOTHESIS

In attempting to identify the elements influencing the development of accounting, this study considers Adhikari and Tondkar's level of disclosure requirements of global stock exchanges as one representative of the state of accounting development in a given country. If we view this reporting and disclosure index as an expression of social behavior, then, based on a well-accepted thesis in sociology that social structure determines social behavior, we may hypothesize that the index is a direct product of its environment. This index, as shown in Exhibit 7.1, may be represented as being influenced by the political, financial, and economic risks in a given country. This is also in conformity with the environmental determinism theory, which suggests a positive relationship between accounting and its economic, financial, and political environment (Mueller, 1967, p. 2; Mueller, 1968; Seidler, 1967; Previts, 1975; Radebaugh, 1975; AAA, 1977, p. 100; AAA, 1980, pp. 13–18; Choi and Mueller, 1984; DaCosta et al., 1978; Frank, 1979; Nair and Frank, 1980; Belkaoui, 1983; Belkaoui and Maksy, 1986). The environment considered in this study is depicted by the economic, political, and financial risks. Market efficiency considerations compel stock exchanges to determine a level of financial disclosure that is compatible with these risks. Basically, global stock exchanges compete with each other for the type of securities listed and the terms and expected returns promised. There is uncertainty about the quality of the stock exchange and its securities, and there is a cost of being perceived as risky. As a result capital markets and stock exchanges have an incentive to provide information that enables them to attract quality stock and allows listed firms to raise capital on the best available terms. This is basically similar to Choi's (1973) "competitive disclosure hypothesis," in the sense that global stock exchanges need to be competitive by requiring adequate disclosure. In addition, international investors need the confidence and extra information available through a higher level of financial disclosure in the exchanges dominated by high political, economic, and financial risks. The higher these risks, the higher the demand for accounting disclosure by stock exchanges (Riahi-Belkaoui, 1994). The rationale for this thesis is presented next.

Political Risk

Political risk is defined as the "uncertainty stemming from unanticipated and unexpected acts of governments or other organizations which may cause loss to the business firm" (Greene, 1974, p. 21). It is manifested through a climate of uncertainty dominated by a probable loss to the business enterprise. It is most prevalent when Global Stock Exchanges suffer from the following risks: (1) discontinuities occur in the business environment, (2) they are difficult to anticipate, and (3) they result from political change (Robock and Simmonds, 1973, p. 356). In addition, politically risky countries are characterized by both government corruption and a divergence of economic expectations from reality (Janah, 1991, p. R4). A global stock exchange is compelled to take into account the political risk in the determination of the required level of disclosure, suggesting a higher level of disclosure requirements by stock exchanges in politically risky countries.

On the basis of this a priori analysis, the following hypothesis is proposed:

H_1: The higher the political risk in a given country, the higher the level of disclosure requirements of the stock exchange.

Financial Risk

Financial risk arises from varying exchange rates, divergent tax laws, and balance-of-payments problems (Kim and Kim, 1993, p. 5). It is manifest in higher likelihood of losses from exchange controls and loan defaults. One would expect that this climate of uncertainty would motivate a global stock exchange to require a higher level of accounting disclosure to provide potential data users with a full and fair disclosure of the situation. Accordingly, the following hypothesis is proposed:

H_2: The higher the financial risk in a given country, the higher the level of disclosure requirements of the stock exchange.

Economic Risk

Economic risk arises from instability in economic factors. It is manifest in higher inflation and debt-servicing costs (Janah, 1991). Various attempts have failed to find a relationship between the economic environment and differences in accounting reporting and disclosure adequacy (Belkaoui, 1983; Adhikari and Tondkar, 1992). These studies relied on per capita GNP as a measure of the degree of economic development. This study views economic risk as a better choice given that a given per capita GNP can be associated with either high or low economic risk. Accordingly, the following hypothesis is proposed:

H_3: The higher the economic risk in a given country, the higher the level of disclosure requirements of the stock exchange.

PROCEDURES

Methodology and Sample

The dependent variable in this study is Adhikari and Tondkar's level of disclosure requirements of a stock exchange. Independent variables are the following: (1) political risk, (2) financial risk, and (3) economic risk.

To be included in our sample, a country must have available data to measure both the dependent and independent variables. Thirty-four countries met this test. The data set used is shown in Exhibit 7.2. The independent variable scores are derived from Janah (1991) and the disclosure indices from Adhikari and Tondkar (1992).

Adhikari and Tondkar's Disclosure Index

Adhikari and Tondkar's composite disclosure index, intended to measure the quantity and intensity of disclosure required as part of the listing and filing requirements of stock exchanges, includes a list of forty-four items. An actual score for each stock exchange was obtained by Adhikari and Tondkar by summing all the scores received by the stock exchange for the forty-four information items that are required by the stock exchange as part of its listing and filing requirements. The disclosure score was obtained by dividing the actual score attained by a stock exchange by the maximum attainable score. To account for differences among different user groups, each disclosure score was weighted by its relevance to a list of experts from each of the countries examined. As a result, a weighted (WTDSCORE) and an unweighted (UNWTSCORE) score were computed. They are shown in Exhibit 7.3.

Political, Financial, and Economic Risks

This study relies on the risk-rating scores provided by International Country Risk Guide (ICRG) of International Business Communication Ltd. ICRG receives the most attention from foreign investors (Kim and Kim, 1993). ICRG provides a composite risk rating, as well as individual ratings for political, financial, and economic risk. The political component—which makes 50 percent of the composite score—includes factors such as government corruption and how economic expectations diverge from reality. The financial component includes such factors as the likelihood of losses from exchange controls and loan defaults. Finally, the economic component includes such factors as inflation and debt-service costs (Janah, 1991). The maximum, or least risky, score is 100 for the political category and 50 each for the financial and economic risk. For the composite score, 85–100 is considered very low risk; 70–84.5 low risk; 60–69.5 moderate risk; 50–59.5, moderately high risk; and 0–49.5 very high risk. The risk scores are shown in Exhibit 7.3.

RESULTS

The three hypotheses state that the higher the political financial and economic risks, the higher the level of disclosure requirements of stock exchanges. Because the ICRG scores used for the measurement of risks are the highest when these risk are low, *the signs of the relationships between the three risks and the dependent variables are expected to be negative.*

Exhibit 7.3. presents the results of the regression analysis. As the F-statistic indicates, the general regression was significant with the three risk variables explaining 38.47 percent of the weighted score or 37.39 percent of the unweighted score of the level of disclosure requirements of stock exchanges. The only significant variables were political risk and financial risk. Economic risk was not significant.

Political risk was significant in the exact direction to the stated Hypothesis H_0. In other words, the results show that the higher the political risk measure, the higher the level of disclosure requirements of stock exchanges. They indicate that in politically risky situations, cost and uncertainty are created in the minds of investors that need to be compensated by a higher level of disclosure. The situation that is characterized by high political risk appears to be judged by stock exchanges to be seriously threatening to international investors and warrants additional disclosure.

Financial risk also was significant, but in the opposite direction than stated in Hypothesis H_1. In other words, the higher the financial risk, the lower the

Exhibit 7.2
Data Used in This Study

Stock Exchange(Country)	Political Risk	Financial Risk	Economic Risk	Disclosure Scores Weighted	Disclosure Scores Unweighted
1. Zurich (Switzerland)	93.0	50.0	39.5	52.24	52.39
2. Luxembourg (Luxembourg)	93.0	49.0	36.0	66.62	66.64
3. Oslo (Norway)	87.0	47.0	42.0	60.63	60.59
4. Vienna (Austria)	88.0	47.0	39.5	54.17	53.52
5. Frankfurt (Germany)	83.0	50.0	38.5	67.20	66.86
6. Amsterdam (Netherlands)	85.0	46.0	40.5	73.19	72.84
7. Tokyo (Japan)	80.0	50.0	39.0	77.68	77.68
8. Singapore (Singapore)	79.0	48.0	39.5	80.89	80.32
9. New York (United States)	78.0	49.0	39.5	90.31	90.75
10. Toronto (Canada)	81.0	48.0	37.0	79.00	78.64
11. Copenhagen (Denmark)	86.0	41.0	37.0	67.20	66.86
12. Stockholm (Sweden)	81.0	47.0	35.0	60.54	60.05
13. Taipei (Taiwan)	71.0	49.0	43.0	72.19	71.70
14. London (United Kingdom)	76.0	50.0	36.0	86.21	86.21
15. Helsinki (Finland)	85.0	44.0	32.0	70.54	71.05
16. Paris (France)	79.0	46.0	34.5	76.20	76.16
17. Wellington (New Zealand)	78.0	46.0	35.0	67.13	65.19
18. Sydney (Australia)	76.0	45.0	37.0	74.60	74.64
19. Kuala Lumpur (Malaysia)	71.0	45.0	38.5	75.69	75.41
20. Milan (Italy)	72.0	47.0	25.0	68.46	68.39
21. Caracas (Venezuela)	75.0	40.0	36.0	73.67	73.32
22. Lisbon (Portugal)	69.0	42.0	38.5	65.68	65.50
23. Seoul (South Korea)	63.0	47.0	36.5	71.43	72.00
24. Madrid (Spain)	65.0	42.0	35.0	68.84	68.36

25. Mexico (Mexico)	71.0	41.0	28.5	70.55	70.68
26. Bangkok (Thailand)	57.0	42.0	37.0	74.75	75.41
27. Bogota (Colombia)	60.0	41.0	34.0	54.58	54.48
28. Hong Kong (Hong Kong)	58.0	42.0	35.0	77.04	75.77
29. Athens (Greece)	65.0	33.0	39.5	60.00	59.41
30. Rio de Janeiro (Brazil)	67.0	34.0	23.0	67.28	68.75
31. Cairo (Egypt)	54.0	30.0	29.0	49.02	48.02
32. Istanbul (Turkey)	52.0	19.0	27.5	50.68	50.68
33. Karachi (Pakistan)	34.0	22.0	32.0	55.71	55.82
34. Bombay (India)	34.0	25.0	27.0	58.23	58.84

Exhibit 7.3
Results of Cross-Sectional Regressions

Dependent Variables	Intercept	Independent Variables			R^2	F
		Political Risk	Financial Risk	Economic Risk		
1. WTDSCORE[1]	44.1616	-0.3150	1.1654	-0.0795	38.47%	6.253*
	(4.093)*	(-1.877)**	(3.642)*	(-0.215)		
2. UNWTSCORE[2]	45.3880	-0.3163	1.1743	-0.1259	37.39%	5.973
	(4.144)*	(-1.857)**	(3.615)*	(-0.335)		

Notes: [1]Weighted score; [2] unweighted score; *significant at $\alpha = 0.01$; **significant at $\alpha = 0.05$.

149

level of disclosure requirements of stock exchanges. This result might indicate that the financial risks, arising from varying exchange rates, divergent tax laws, and balance of payments problems, are best disclosed through macroeconomic data from market and governmental sources. The situation that is characterized by high financial risk is not deemed by stock exchanges to be detrimental to investors. In situations of high financial risks, disclosures other than accounting disclosures are deemed important.

Economic risk was not significant, a result consistent with previous studies (Belkaoui, 1983; Adhikari and Tondkar, 1992). One possible reason for the lack of significance of this relationship between economic factors and the level of disclosure requirement may be misspecification in the economic measure used. Economic development in general and economic risk in particular constitute a multidimensional phenomenon that can only be measured adequately by an index or composite of individual measures, or an economic growth factor. The suggested measures may be more indicative of the nature of the differences in the level of disclosure requirements by global stock exchanges.

SUMMARY AND CONCLUSIONS

This study examined international differences in the level of disclosure requirements of stock exchanges and related these differences to the political, financial, and economic risks of each country. The results indicate that the level of disclosure requirements of stock exchanges is positively influenced by political risk and negatively by financial risk. Influences in political and financial risks create different social environments for the demand of information by global stock exchanges. Politically risky countries require disclosure of more accounting information while financially risky countries require disclosure of other types of nonaccounting information, mainly macroeconomic indicators.

The results support the environmental determinism theory, in that the environmental factors of political and economic risks can contribute to explaining the differences in mandated disclosures by global stock exchanges. A first implication is that international investors need to judge the level of disclosure by the corresponding level of political and financial risks. A high or low level of disclosure does not necessarily connote a good or bad investment category but the responses of a global stock exchange to levels of political and financial risks. A second implication is that harmonization strategies may be more successful with countries having similar levels of political and financial risks, suggesting a risk-based cluster approach rather than a global approach to harmonization (Choi, 1981; Rivera, 1989).

Future research needs to examine the impact of more complex measures of economic risks on accounting development, the use of bigger samples to include emerging capital markets, the use of a longitudinal design where data are available, and the inclusion of other environmental variables, for a complete environmental determinism theory of international accounting.

NOTE

This thesis derives from the structuralist paradigm in sociology, which holds that structural determinants, that is, social facts, constitute the primary methodological foci for explanation of social behavior. One classical statement of this method can be found in Durkheim (1933, 1964), and more contemporary discussions can be found in Parsons (1971) and Ritzer (1975).

REFERENCES

Adhikari, A. and R. H. Tondkar. 1992. "Environmental Factors Influencing Accounting Disclosure Requirements of Global Stock Exchanges." *Journal of International Financial Management and Accounting* 4: 76–105.

American Accounting Association. 1977. "Report of the 1975–76 Committee on International Accounting Operations and Education." *The Accounting Review* 52: 65–132.

———. 1980. *Accounting Education in the Third World.* Report of the Committee on International Accounting Operations and Education 1976–78. Sarasota, Fla.: American Accounting Association.

Belkaoui, A. 1983. "Economic, Political and Civil Indicators and Reporting and Disclosure Adequacy: Empirical Investigation." *Journal of Accounting and Public Policy* Fall: 207–221.

Belkaoui, A. and M. Maksy. 1986. "Welfare of the Common Man and Accounting Disclosure Adequacy: An Empirical Investigation." *International Journal of Accounting Education and Research* 20: 178–182.

Biddle, G. C. and S. M. Saudagaran. 1989. "The Effects of Financial Disclosure Levels on Firms' Choices among Alternate Foreign Stock Exchanges." *Journal of International Financial Management Accounting* Spring: 55–87.

Choi, D.F.S. 1973. "Financial Disclosure and Entry to the European Capital Market." *Accounting and Business Research* Autumn: 282–292.

———. 1981. "A Cluster Approach to Accounting Harmonization." *Management Accounting* 63: 26–31.

Choi, D.F.S. and G. G. Mueller. 1984. *International Accounting.* Englewood Cliffs, N.J.: Prentice-Hall.

Cooke, T. E. and R.S.O. Wallace. 1990. "Financial Regulation and Its Environment: A Review and Further Analysis." *Journal of Accounting and Public Policy* Summer: 79–110.

DaCosta, R. C., J. C. Bourgeois, and W. M. Lawson. 1978. "A Classification of International Financial Accounting Practices." *International Journal of Accounting Education and Research* 2: 73–85.

Durkheim, E. 1933. *The Division of Labor in Society*, translated by G. Simpson. New York: Macmillan.

———. 1964. *The Rules of Sociological Method*, translated by S. S. Solovay and J. H. Mueller and edited by G.E.G. Catlin. New York: Free Press.

Frank, W. G. 1979. "An Empirical Analysis of International Accounting Principles." *Journal of Accounting Research* 2: 593–605.

Greene, F. 1974. "The Management of Political Risk." *Best's Review* July: 15.

Janah, M. 1991. "Rating Risk in the Hot Countries." *Wall Street Journal* September 20: R4.

Kim, S. H. and S. H. Kim. 1993. *Global Corporate Finance: Text and Cases*, 2nd ed. Miami, Fla.: Kolb Publishing.

Meek, G. K. and S. M. Saudagaran. 1990. "A Survey of Research on Financial Reporting in a Transnational Context." *Journal of Accounting Literature* 9: 145–182.

Mueller, G. G. 1967. *International Accounting*. New York: Macmillan.

———. 1968. "Accounting Principles Generally Accepted in the United States versus Those Generally Accepted Elsewhere." *International Journal of Accounting Education and Research* 3: 61–77.

Nair, R. D. and W. G. Frank. 1980. "The Impact of Disclosure and Measurement Practices on International Accounting Classifications." *International Journal of Accounting Education and Research* 1: 61–77.

Parsons, T. 1971. *The System of Modern Societies*. Englewood Cliffs, N.J.: Prentice-Hall.

Previts, G. J. 1975. "On the Subject of Methodology and Models for International Accounting." *International Journal of Accounting Education and Research* 2: 1–12.

Radebaugh, L. H. 1975. "Environmental Factors Influencing the Development of Accounting Objectives, Standards and Practices in Peru." *International Journal of Accounting Education and Research* 1: 39–56.

Riahi-Belkaoui, A. 1994. *International and Multinational Accounting*. London: Academic Press.

Ritzer, G. 1975. *Sociology: A Multiple Paradigm Science*. Boston: Allyn & Bacon.

Rivera, J. M. 1989. "The Internationalization of Accounting Standards: Past Problems and Current Prospects." *International Journal of Accounting* 24: 1–11.

Robock, S. H. and K. Simmonds. 1973. *International Business and Multinational Enterprises*. Homewood, Ill.: Richard D. Irwin.

Saudagaran, S. M. and G. C. Biddle. 1992. "Financial Disclosure Levels and Foreign Stock Exchange Listing Decisions." *Journal of International Financial Management Accounting* Summer. 10: 64–68.

Seidler, L. J. 1967. "International Accounting—The Ultimate Theory Course." *The Accounting Review* 4: 775–781.

Wallace, R.S.O. and H. Gernon. 1991. "Frameworks for International Comparative Financial Accounting." *Journal of Accounting Literature* 19: 209–264.

8

Human Development, Economic Development, and Accounting Disclosure Requirements of Global Stock Exchanges: An Empirical Investigation

INTRODUCTION

A fundamental research question in international accounting is to explain the diversity of accounting reporting and disclosure internationally. The diversity is best expressed by the different accounting and disclosure requirements of global stock exchanges. Factors that may explain the differences in accounting and disclosure requirements of global stock exchanges can be used by investors in the global economy to correct for differential information and by policymakers in identifying the areas for accounting harmonization. Both economic and non-economic factors may be used in the analysis. This chapter focuses mainly on the impact of human development and economic development as essential factors in understanding the diversity of accounting practice in general, and the mandatory requirements of global stock exchanges in particular.

STATEMENT OF PURPOSE

The purpose of this chapter is to investigate human development and economic development as potential determinants of the accounting disclosure requirements of global stock exchanges. The chapter uses data from thirty-four countries to construct a cross-sectional data set and examines the effects of the United Nations Human Development Index (HDI) as a measure of human de-

This chapter is adapted from "Human Development, Economic Development and Accounting Disclosure Requirements of Global Stock Exchanges" by Ahmed Riahi-Belkaoui. *Journal of Global Business* 9, no. 16 (1998): 49–56.

velopment and the percentage change in GNP as a measure of economic growth on the level of disclosure requirements of stock exchanges as measured by a disclosure index (Adhikari and Tondkar, 1992). The overall results obtained from the cross-sectional regression indicate that the level of disclosure requirements of stock exchanges is positively related to human development, as measured by the HDI and economic development, as measured by the percentage change in GNP.

REVIEW OF LITERATURE

The question of how to justify the variation among countries on accounting disclosure levels has been and is still a subject of research interest (Wallace and Gernon, 1991). There is a search for empirical linkages between measures of accounting disclosure levels and environmental factors. Knowledge and understanding of these factors is essential in formulating any strategy dealing with accounting diversity, helpful to users of cross-national accounting data in a proper evaluation of accounting information and making rational economic decisions (Adhikari and Tondkar, 1992). It is also essential to the success of accounting harmonization efforts (Meek and Saudagaran, 1990). These environmental factors include economic and noneconomic variables (Belkaoui, 1983; Belkaoui and Maksy, 1986; Cooke and Wallace, 1990; Adhikari and Tondkar, 1992). The research to date has not considered, however, the potential impact of human development on disclosure level. International accounting research takes human development as a given or assumes that the impact of human development is inconsequential, or both. As human development is assumed to trigger and/or facilitate the development of accounting (Ghartey, 1987), its inclusion in disclosure models as a noneconomic variable is justified. Accordingly, based on a set of hypotheses, this paper examines the cross-sectional relation between a measure of disclosure levels of stock exchanges and human and economic development.

GENERAL DISCLOSURE MODEL

The international accounting literature (Belkaoui, 1983) relied partly on the following cross-sectional specification:

$$Y = B_{ev}\text{EV} + B_{nev}\text{NEV} + U \qquad (8.1)$$

where Y is a measure of the level of disclosure, EV is a set of economic variables, and NEV is a set of noneconomic variables. Each of these variables is discussed.

1. The development variable has been measured in one of two ways. In examining the relationship between accounting and its environment, international accounting research relied generally on disclosure indices based on the disclo-

sure practices of large corporations in developed and developing countries (Wallace and Gernon, 1991; Meek and Saudagaran, 1990). One noticeable exception is a study by Adhikari and Tondkar (1992) that relied on an alternative proxy, the operationalization of listing and filing requirements of stock exchanges in different countries. This study relies on this new proxy as a measure of Y as it tends to be more representative of the general level of disclosure in a country than the disclosure practices of large corporations (Adhikari and Tondkar, 1992; Cooke and Wallace, 1990).

2. The economic variables were measured in a variety of ways in the main empirical studies (Belkaoui, 1983; Belkaoui and Maksy, 1986; Cooke and Wallace, 1990; Adhikari and Tondkar, 1992). The various measures used are shown in Exhibit 8.1. The results on these measures were either insignificant or mixed. The results may be insignificant if the explanatory variable is captured by other explanatory variables in the regression (i.e., these variables are multicollinear). For example, economic growth, as measured by the percentage change of GNP, has been found to be related to various fiscal, trade, and monetary indicators as suggested by theory (Levine and Renelt, 1992). To avoid this problem, this study limits the economic variable set to the economic growth variable.

3. The noneconomic variables were also measured in a variety of ways in the same empirical studies. The various measures are shown in Exhibit 8.1. They include political and demographic variables. The results on these variables were also either insignificant or mixed. To avoid the potential multicollinearity problem, as outlined earlier, this study limits the noneconomic variable set to the human development variable.

Two hypotheses that support the variables included in the model are discussed and developed.

IMPACT OF ECONOMIC GROWTH

Economic growth is important to the development of accounting in general and disclosure in particular. Lowe (1967) noted that, from a historical point of view, accounting adequacy is an evolutionary process dependent upon, and interwoven with, economic growth. Accounting is also considered vital to the planning, decision-making performance evaluation, and data-structuring processes of various economic institutions crucial to economic growth (Prakash and Rappaport, 1975). Economic growth requires various structural and social changes. One of these changes is the need for financial and reporting mechanisms for measurement of the performance of the economy in terms of efficiency and productivity. For example, an important element of the efficient capital market is the existence of a sophisticated accounting infrastructure comprised of the facilities of information production, the framework of information monitoring, and contract enforcement (Lee, 1987). Various authors (Talaga and Ndubizu, 1986; Larson, 1992) linked the efficiency of resource allocation among

Exhibit 8.1
Independent Variables Used in Previous Research Studies

Studies and Variables	Significance
Belkaoui (1983)	
Economic Variables	
Economic System	NS
Per Capita GNP	NS
Growth Rate of Income	NS
Government Expenditures Over GNP	S
Exports Over GNP	NS
Non-Economic Variables	
Population	NS
Political Right Index	NS
Civil Liberties Index	NS
Political System Index	NS
Belkaoui and Maksy (1985)	
Economic Variables	
Welfare of the Common Man	NS
Cooke and Wallace (1990)	
Economic Variables	
Per Capita GNP (as a single independent variable)	NS
Per Capita GNP (with other independent variables)	NS
Non-Economic Variables	
Environment Index	S
Density as the number of persons per accountant	NS
Adhikari and Tondkar (1992)	
Economic Variables	
Per Capita GNP	NS
Agricultural Sector Output	NS
Size of the Equity Market	S
Market Turnover	NS
Dispersion of Stock Ownership	NS

Note: NS = insignificant; S = significant.

competing interests to the information produced by the accounting system. Accordingly, the following proposition is suggested:

H₁: In countries with higher percentage changes in GNP, stock exchanges are likely to have more rigorous levels of disclosure requirements.

IMPACT OF HUMAN DEVELOPMENT

Just as economic growth is necessary for accounting development, human development is critical to accounting development. Human development is hampered by conditions of poverty, malnutrition, ill health, inadequate education, and gender disparities (United Nations, 1991).

When people face low human development conditions, they are less likely to be able to devote the resources and the energy to create an adequate accounting system. Obstacles to human development are also obstacles to accounting development (Ghartey, 1987). Accordingly, the following hypothesis is proposed:

H₂: In countries with high human development, stock exchanges are likely to have more rigorous levels of disclosure requirements.

METHODOLOGY

Sample

The level of disclosure requirements of a stock exchange is used to operationalize the dependent variable (Adhikari and Tondkar, 1992). Independent variables are the following: (1) economic growth and (2) human development.

To be included in our sample, a country must have available data to measure both the dependent and independent variables. Thirty-four countries met this test. The countries used are shown in Exhibit 8.2.

Adhikari and Tondkar's Disclosure Index

Adhikari and Tondkar's (1992) composite disclosure index, intended to measure the quantity and intensity of disclosure required as part of the listing and filing requirements of stock exchanges, includes a list of forty-four items. An actual score for each stock exchange was obtained by summing all the scores received by the stock exchange for forty-four items that are required by the stock exchange as part of its listing and filing requirements. This disclosure score was obtained by dividing the actual score attained by a stock exchange by the maximum attainable score. To account for differences among different user groups, each disclosure score was weighted by its relevance to a list of experts from each of the countries examined. As a result, both a weighted (WTDSCORE) and an unweighted (UNWTSCORE) were computed. The un-

Exhibit 8.2
Sample Countries

Sydney (Australia)	Vienna (Austria)
Rio de Janeiro (Brazil)	Toronto (Canada)
Bogota (Colombia)	Copenhagen (Denmark)
Cairo (Egypt)	Helsinki (Finland)
Paris (France)	Frankfurt (Germany)
Athens (Greece)	Hong Kong (Hong Kong)
Bombay (India)	Milan (Italy)
Tokyo (Japan)	Seoul (Korea)
Luxembourg (Luxembourg)	Kuala Lumpur (Malaysia)
Mexico (Mexico)	Amsterdam (Netherlands)
Wellington (New Zealand)	Oslo (Norway)
Karachi (Pakistan)	Lisbon (Portugal)
Singapore (Singapore)	Madrid (Spain)
Johannesburg (South Africa)	Stockholm (Sweden)
Zurich (Switzerland)	Bangkok (Thailand)
Istanbul (Turkey)	New York (United States)
London (United Kingdom)	Caracas (Venezuela)

weighted score is a measure of the level of disclosure while the weighted score is a measure of the relative importance of the disclosures to selected users. The index is shown in Chapter 6 (Exhibit 6.2). The variables included in Adhikari and Tondkar's study (1992), including the disclosure index, were computed for the period 1986–1988.

Economic Growth and Human Development

Economic growth (EG) is measured by the percentage change in GNP for the 1986–1988 period.

Human development is measured by the 1990 UN Human Development Index (HDI) for the same period (United Nations, 1991). It is generally considered a more realistic measure of human development than mere GNP per head. The HDI is composed of three indicators: life expectancy, education, and income.

Empirical Design

The hypotheses were tested by the following regressions:

$$\text{WTDSCORE}_j = a_0 + a_1\text{EG}_j + a_2\text{HDI}_j + e^1 \tag{8.2}$$

$$\text{UNWTDSCORE}_j = b_0 + b_1\text{EG}_j + b_2\text{HDI}_j + e^{11} \tag{8.3}$$

Exhibit 8.3
Regression Results

Dependent/Independent Variables	Intercept	Human Development	Economic Growth	F	R2
WTDSCORE (1)	43.094	24.046	1.5366	5.484*	0.2613
	(5.519)* (3)	(2.868)*	(1.329)		
UNWTDSCORE (2)	42.485	25.310	1.5227	6.617*	0.2992
	(5.755)*	(3.192)*	(1.603)**		

Note: ^{1}Weighted score; ^{2}unweighted score; T-statistics are in parentheses; *significant at a 0.01 level; **significant at a 0.10 level.

where $WTDSCORE_j$ is the weighted disclosure index for country j, $UNWTDSCORE_j$, is the unweighted disclosure index for country j, EG_j is the economic growth for country j, HDI_j is the human development index for country j. All the variables were measured for the 1986–1988 period and for each country. The data for this study come from *Human Development Report of the United Nations* and the *International Financial Statistics* of the International Monetary Fund.

RESULTS

The two hypotheses state that the higher the percentage change in GNP and human development, the more rigorous and higher will be the level of disclosure requirements of stock exchanges. Exhibit 8.3 presents the results of the regression models (2) and (3).[1] As the F-statistic indicates, the general regression is significant with the two independent variables explaining 26.13 percent of the weighted score or 29.92 percent of the unweighted score of the level of disclosure requirements of stock exchanges. The human development index was significant in the exact positive direction to stated hypotheses regardless whether the disclosure level of stock exchanges was measured by the weighted or unweighted scores. The economic growth, as measured by the percentage change in GNP, was significant only in the case where the disclosure level was measured by the unweighted score. Because the unweighted scores represent the exact level of disclosure, rather than the importance of the disclosure to a group of users, the results of this study show that the higher the economic growth, as measured by the percentage change in GNP, and human development, as measured by the UN Human Development Index, the higher the level of disclosure requirements of stock exchanges. It appears that the demand for accounting disclosures by stock exchanges, rather than the importance of such disclosure, is higher when both economic growth and human development are higher. The results of this study reiterate the importance of noneconomic variables in the explanation of accounting disclosure diversity internationally. The study adds to the literature that the importance of economic variables depends on whether the dependent variable is the level of disclosure or the importance of such disclosure. In this study, the level of disclosure rather than the importance of disclosure appears to be related to economic growth.

CONCLUSION

Previous empirical studies examining the determinants of the differences in accounting disclosure among countries considered a set of economic and noneconomic factors. The results were mixed because most of the independent variables may be measuring the same phenomenon resulting from potential multicollinearity and leading to insignificance. This study eliminated the problem by reducing the economic and noneconomic variables to two factors: economic growth and human development. Based on a data set from thirty-four countries, the results of a regression model show a positive relationship between the accounting disclosure requirements of global stock exchanges and economic and human development. Where economic growth and human development are higher, the demand for accounting disclosure by stock exchanges is higher. Economic growth and human development create a favorable climate for the development of accounting and also rely on the development of accounting. Harmonizing efforts may be more successful with countries with similar economic growth and human development profiles. In addition, cross-sectional investments should consider not only the level of disclosure in a given country, but also the economic growth and human development context.

NOTE

1. Similar results were reported by Riahi-Belkaoui (1997).

REFERENCES

Adhikari, Ajay and Rasoul H. Tondkar. 1992. "Environmental Factors Influencing Accounting Disclosure Requirements of Global Stock Exchanges." *Journal of International Financial Management and Accounting* 2: 75–105.

Belkaoui, A. 1983. "Economic, Political and Civil Indicators and Reporting and Disclosure Adequacy: Empirical Investigation." *Journal of Accounting and Public Policy* 3: 207–219.

Belkaoui, A. and M. Maksy. 1985. "Welfare of the Common Man and Accounting Disclosure Adequacy: An Empirical Investigation." *International Journal of Accounting* 3: 81–94.

Cooke, T. E. and R.S.O. Wallace. 1990. "Financial Disclosure Regulation and Its Environment: A Review and Further Analysis." *Journal of Accounting and Public Policy* 9: 79–110.

Ghartey, J. B. 1987. *Crisis Accountability and Development in the Third World.* Aldershot, U.K.: Avebury.

Larson, Robert K. 1992. "International Accounting Standards and Economic Growth: An Empirical Investigation of Their Relationship in Africa." *Research in Third World Accounting* 2: 27–42.

Lee, Chi-Wen Jevons. 1987. "Accounting Infrastructure and Economic Development." *Journal of Accounting and Public Policy* 6: 75–85.

Levine, Ross and David Renelt. 1992. "A Sensitivity Analysis of Cross-Country Growth Regressions." *American Economic Review* 3: 213–224.

Lowe, H. D. 1967. "Accounting Aid for Developing Countries." *The Accounting Review* 2: 356–360.

Meek, G. K. and S. M. Saudagaran. 1990. "A Survey of Research on Financial Reporting in a Transnational Contest." *Journal of Accounting Literature* 9: 145–182.

Prakash, Prem and Alfred Rappaport. 1975. "Informational Interdependencies." *The Accounting Review* 4: 723–734.

Riahi-Belkaoui, Ahmed. 1997. *The Nature and Determinants of Disclosure Adequacy,* Westport, Conn.: Greenwood Publishing.

Talaga, James A. and Gordian Ndubizu. 1986. "Accounting and Economic Development: Relationships among the Paradigms." *International Journal of Accounting* 2: 55–68.

United Nations. 1991. *Human Development Report 1991.* New York: United Nations.

Wallace, R.S.O. and H. Gernon. 1991. "Frameworks for International Comparative Financial Accounting." *Journal of Accounting Literature* 19: 209–264.

9

Managerial, Academic, and Professional Influences and Disclosure Adequacy: An Empirical Investigation

INTRODUCTION

Despite international efforts of harmonization, accounting objectives, standards, policies, and techniques continue to differ among countries. Various attempts have been made to identify the environmental conditions likely to affect the determination of accounting principles (Previts, 1975; Radebaugh, 1975; American Accounting Association, 1977; Da Costa et al., 1978; Frank, 1979; Nair and Frank, 1980; Belkaoui, 1983; Belkaoui and Maksy, 1986). However, these studies assumed that the economic, political, and social factors were the only factors that explain the differences in accounting principles and techniques between the various countries. The results were mixed. Also, an important factor that affects accounting development was not included in these studies, namely, the extent of managerial, academic, and professional influences on accounting development. Consequently, the objective of this study is to examine the international differences in disclosure adequacy and to relate these differences to the extent of managerial, academic, and professional influences on accounting development in each country.

DETERMINANTS OF THE DEVELOPMENT OF ACCOUNTING

To identify the determinants of the development of accounting, a disclosure index is used as one of the representatives of the state of accounting develop-

Adapted from Ahmed Riahi-Belkaoui, "Managerial, Academic and Professional Influences and Disclosure Adequacy: An Empirical Investigation" *Advances in International Accounting* Vol. 3, copyright 1990, pp. 205–214, with permission from Elsevier Science.

Exhibit 9.1
Model of Accounting Development

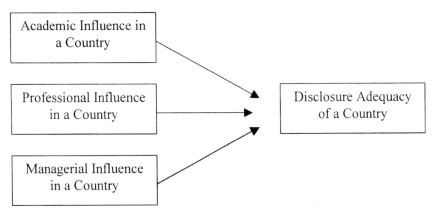

ment in a given country (Belkaoui, 1983; Belkaoui and Maksy, 1986). If this disclosure index is viewed as an expression of a social behavior, we may hypothesize that the index is a direct product of its environment based on a well-accepted thesis in sociology that social structure determines social behavior.[1] This index, as shown in Exhibit 9.1, may then be represented as being influenced by the extent of academic, professional, and managerial influences on accounting development.

Managerial Influence

The managerial class of a given country is of particular importance to the development of accounting in general and financial disclosure. When managers do not exert any influence on accounting development, they are less likely to be supportive of its standards of reporting and disclosure. An increase in their influence and their participation generates a willingness to abide by its rules and improve the disclosure adequacy of accounting reports. There is likely to be a positive relationship between disclosure adequacy and managerial influence because managers feel bound to abide by the disclosure rules they helped shape. While these propositions may be perceived as intuitive, the objective of this study is to empirically test their validity.

Academic Influence

The academic class of a given country is also important to the development of accounting in general and financial disclosure in particular. When academicians are not asked to participate in standard setting, there is less of a likelihood that important research findings will be incorporated in those standards; consequently, their usefulness and credibility may suffer. Academicians asked to participate and exert some influence lend more credibility to the disclosure standards, especially if the same standards have been subjected to intense research scrutiny. There is likely to be a positive relationship between disclosure adequacy and academic influence as academicians bring a "cultural" capital, crucial to the soundness of the standards (Peasnell and Williams, 1986).

Professional Influence

The professional accountant class of a given country is also important to the development of accounting in general and financial disclosure in particular. Not only its existence but its active participation in standard setting is crucial to the development and successful implementation of objectives of accounting (Buckley and Buckley, 1975; Carey, 1969). Without the participation and influence of this professional accountant class, accounting development may suffer as its technical and demanding requirements may be misunderstood, or misapplied by an "alienated" profession. Its participation and influence on accounting development, however, will generate a more solid commitment to its goals and a desire to improve its image. In such a case there is likely to be a positive relationship between disclosure adequacy and professional influence on accounting development. For the professional influence to be unconstrained the profession needs to be to a large extent self-regulated. On the basis of these a priori analyses, the following hypothesis is proposed.

H_0: The disclosure adequacy will differ with differences in the academic, professional, and managerial influences on accounting development.

PROCEDURES

Methodology and Sample

The dependent variable in this study is a disclosure adequacy index. Independent variables are: (1) the academic influence on accounting development, (2) the professional influence on accounting development, and (3) the managerial influence on accounting development. First, each of these variables is explained and measured. Second, a regression model is run to identify the significant determinants of the development of accounting internationally.

To be included in our sample a country must have available data to measure both the dependent and independent variables. Thirty countries met this test. They are shown in Exhibit 9.2.

Disclosure Adequacy Index

Most studies investigating the determinants of disclosure adequacy have relied on the database in the Price Waterhouse *International Survey of Accounting*

Exhibit 9.2
Countries Included in the Study

Argentina	Japan
Australia	Malaysia
Belgium	Mexico
Brazil	New Zealand
Channel Islands	Philippines
Chile	Portugal
Colombia	South Africa
Denmark	Spain
Finland	Switzerland
France	Thailand
Germany	United Kingdom
Hong Kong	United States
Indonesia	Uruguay
Ireland	Zambia
Italy	Zimbabwe

Principles and Reporting Practices (1979). The data relate to 1978. This study relied instead on a more recent database, which relates to 1982 and was produced by the University of Glasgow in collaboration with Deloitte Haskins and Sells International (Gray et al., 1984). Unlike Price Waterhouse's data, the Gray et al. data distinguish between measurement and disclosure. First, as this study is concerned with the *regulation* of disclosure adequacy only the disclosure items were considered in the measurement of the index. Second, unlike Belkaoui's (1983) study, which included all the propositions on a subject that refers to the same item, this study included the proposition yielding the highest score. These two transformations resulted in the reduction of the disclosure variables in the Gray et al. data to 107. Their database indicates for each of the 107 variables the extent of application in each country in terms of a fivefold classification: (1) required, (2) recommended, (3) permitted, (4) not applicable, and (5) non-permitted. In this study each of the five classifications are coded as:

Classification	Scale for the Extent of Application
1. Required	4
2. Recommended	3
3. Permitted	2
4. Not applicable	0
5. Nonpermitted	-1

The scale for the extent of application of each of the 107 variables constituted a separate observation for each of the thirty countries. The sum of these observations per country is used as the actual disclosure adequacy index.

A high score on the "actual disclosure adequacy index" indicates a willingness by the given country to adhere to and enforce 107 disclosure practices deemed necessary for enhancing the quality of accounting disclosure and encourage international harmonization (Gray et al., 1984). Where differences in disclosure practices exist, this either reflects the degree of professional, academic, and managerial influences on accounting development or indicates that a different measure of disclosure adequacy is considered appropriate. This study favors the former interpretation, which is (1) that the conformity with each of the 107 disclosure practices is a desired goal for each of the countries in the study, and (2) that the degree of conformity depends on the extent of academic, professional, and managerial influences on accounting development. That conformity is the desired goal is evident in the efforts of the various international standard-setting bodies. That the degree of conformity is a reflection of the extent of academic, professional, and managerial influences on accounting development is the subject of this study.

Academic, Professional, and Managerial Influences

The first chapter of Gray et al. (1984) included questions on influences on accounting development. Three of the questions and answers were used for the measurement of the extent of academic, professional, and managerial influences on accounting development.

A. The managerial influence was determined by the following question: "What is the attitude of business management to information disclosure and accounting standards?" The answer was determined in terms of a fivefold classification: (1) strongly against, (2) moderately against, (3) indifferent, (4) moderately support, and (5) strongly support. For the purposes of this study each of the several classifications is coded as follows:

Classification	Scale for the Extent of Application
1. Strongly against	-2
2. Moderately against	-1
3. Indifferent	0
4. Moderately support	1
5. Strongly support	2

B. The professional influence was determined by the following question: "To what extent can it be said that the government keeps its intervention to a minimum, relying instead on self-regulation within the financial country (based on

Exhibit 9.3
Regression Results

Independent	Intercept	Managerial Influence	Academic Influence	Professional Influence
Coefficients	2.272	0.1076	0.1553	0.1648
T- Statistic	14.18	2.15**	2.05**	2.63*
R^2	38.91			
F	5.52*			
N	30			

Note: *Significant at $\alpha = 0.01$; ** significant at $\alpha = 0.05$

professional standards, training, and a high standard of ethical behavior)?" The answer was threefold: (1) low professional self-regulation, (2) medium professional self-regulation, and (3) high professional self-regulation. For the purposes of this study each of the three classifications is coded as follows:

Classification	Scale for the Extent of Application
1. Low professional self-regulation	1
2. Medium professional self-regulation	2
3. High professional self-regulation	3

C. The academic influence was determined by the following question: "Does the academic side of the profession influence the setting of standards relating to external financial reporting?" The answer was either a yes or a no, coded respectively as 1 or 0.

RESULTS: DETERMINANTS OF FINANCIAL DISCLOSURE ADEQUACY

A multiple regression analysis was used to determine the association between the extent of academic, professional, and managerial influences on accounting development and the actual disclosure adequacy of each country in the sample. Exhibit 9.3 presents the results of the regression. The three independent variables of academic, professional, and managerial influences appear to be significant. They are positively related to actual disclosure adequacy. The overall regression was also significant (F significant at $a = 0.01$) and the three independent variables explain 38.9 percent of the variations in the dependent variable of actual disclosure adequacy: This indicates that while academic, professional, and managerial influences are important to the financial disclosure adequacy in a given country, other factors are also important and need to be included in the model.

Future research may inquire into the nature of the variables that need to be added to the model to increase its explanatory power. In any case, the results show the crucial role of academicians, managers, and professional accountants in promoting accounting development and improving financial disclosure adequacy in the process.

DISCUSSION

The significant findings that academic, professional, and managerial inputs into the financial reporting process determine the disclosure adequacy internationally have serious implications.

The first question that needs to be asked relates to whether disclosure is more or less adequate where the academics have inputs into the financial reporting process internationally. The answer rests on solving whether academicians are *ersatz* academics, as suggested by Watts and Zimmerman (1979), or scholar saints, as suggested by Peasnell and Williams (1986). Watts and Zimmerman make the assumption that individuals act to maximize their wealth and perquisites (including creative fulfillment, prestige, and leisure). Two conclusions are made: (1) sectional interest will "demand" accounting theories that will provide excuses for the policies they prefer and (2) incentives exist to ensure a "supply" of such theories. This close relationship to a policymaker, whether it is a standard-setting agency or another, makes the accounting academicians, like all other academicians, "bureaucratic" intellectuals who exercise advisory and technical functions within a bureaucracy as opposed to those intellectuals who elect to stay unattached to a bureaucracy. The bureaucratic intellectual is reduced to being an "ideologue" because he subordinates the search for a universally comprehensive understanding of social, cultural, and physical reality in favor of an immediately instrumental arbitration of competing policies or courses of action (Barrow, 1987, p. 423). Such a role is unfortunate if one subscribes to the prevailing assumption that a "particularization" of intellectual activity which links or constrains academic inquiry to specific social interests or needs leads to a fall from the "sacred" and a descent into the dishonorable realm of "ideology."

Peasnell and Williams (1986) disagree with this view of academicians and suggests that the academic reward system in the leading universities does not encourage the *ersatz* academics. One way of solving this problem is to determine the value systems of accounting academics internationally. A first attempt at studying the professional value systems of academic accountants found them not to be clearly defined, and personal and professional values not to be easily separated (Belkaoui and Chan, 1988).

The second question that needs to be asked relates to whether professional and managerial influences on accounting disclosure are inevitably restrictive. The professional influence may be restrictive as public accountants favor regulation that may benefit them in three ways: (1) barriers to entry, (2) increased demand for auditing services, and (3) reduction in negative externalities from free riders (Benston 1985, p. 53). The managerial influence is central to the determination of standards internationally. Moonitz (1974) supports this view: "Management is central to any discussion of financial reporting, whether at the statutory or regulatory level, or at the level of official pronouncements of accounting bodies" (p. 64). But that role is inevitably restrictive with the evidence of the beginnings of a positive theory of accounting that explores those factors influencing management's attitudes on accounting standards that are likely to affect corporate lobbying on accounting standards (Watts and Zimmerman, 1978). Managers' position is a function of the proposed standard's effect on the firm's value and on earnings used in compensation plans. "Ceteris paribus managers are more likely to oppose standards that restrict accounting procedures used in contracts (increasing agency costs) and reduce reported earnings than standards that do not restrict accounting procedures used in contracts and/or do not reduce reported earnings" (Watts and Zimmerman, 1986, p. 333). The evidence of the restrictive nature of managerial and professional influence is, for the time being, restricted to the U.S. context. Evidence in other national contexts is needed for a better evaluation of those influences on accounting disclosure adequacy internationally.

SUMMARY AND CONCLUSIONS

This chapter examined the international differences in financial disclosure adequacy and related these differences to the extent of academic, managerial, and professional influences on accounting development. The results indicate that the financial disclosure adequacy in terms of conformity to 107 disclosure practices is likely to differ with differences in the extent of academic, professional, and managerial influences on accounting development. The main conclusion to be derived from these results is that for a country to improve its financial disclosure adequacy the supportive role of its academicians, managers, and professional accountants is crucial. For the developing countries the results suggest a reinforcing of the institutions and enactment of laws to allow the academicians, managers, and professionals to have an active and constructive role in accounting development.

The implications of these findings are that these influences can be restrictive. Evidence is needed on (a) the professional value systems of accounting academicians internationally and (b) the lobbying behavior of managers and professionals internationally.

NOTE

1. This thesis results from the sociological paradigm of structural functionalism, which holds that structural determinants—social facts—constitute the primary methodological foci for explanation of social behavior.

REFERENCES

American Accounting Association. 1977. "Report of the 1975–76 Committee on International Accounting Operations and Education." *The Accounting Review* 11 (Supplement): 65–132.

Ashcroft, R. 1980. "Political Theory and the Problem of Ideology." *Journal of Politics* August: 687–705.

Barrow, C. W. 1987. "Intellectuals in Contemporary Social Theory: A Radical Critique." *Sociological Inquiry* 3: 15–22.

Belkaoui, A. 1983. "Economic, Political and Civil Indicators and Reporting and Disclosure Adequacy: Empirical Investigation." *Journal of Accounting and Public Policy* Fall: 207–221.

Belkaoui, A. and J. Chan. 1988. "Professional Value System of Academic Accountants." *Advances in Public Interest Accounting* Spring 1–28.

Belkaoui, A. and M. Maksy. 1986. "Welfare of the Common Man and Accounting Disclosure Adequacy: An Empirical Investigation." *International Journal of Accounting Education and Research* Spring: 81–94.

Benston, G. J. 1985. "The Market for Public Accounting Services: Demand, Supply and Regulation." *Journal of Accounting and Public Policy* Spring: 33–80.

Buckley, J. W. and M. H. Buckley. 1975. *The Accounting Profession.* New York: Melville.

Carey, J. L. 1969. *The Rise of the Accounting Profession*, Vols. 1 and 2. New York: AICPA.

DaCosta, R. C., J. C. Bourgeois, and W. M. Lawson. 1978. "A Classification of International Financial Accounting Practices." *International Journal of Accounting Education and Research* Spring: 73–85.

Durkheim, E. 1933. *The Division of Labor in Society*, translated by G. Simpson. New York: Macmillan.

———. 1964. *The Rules of Sociological Method*, translated by S. S. Solovay and J. H. Mueller, edited by G.E.G. Cathin. New York: Free Press.

Frank, W. G. 1979. "An Empirical Analysis of International Accounting Principles." *Journal of Accounting Research* Spring: 593–605.

Gray, S. J., L. G. Campbell, and J. C. Shaw (eds.) 1984. *International Financial Reporting: A Comparative International Survey of Accounting Requirements and Practices in 30 Countries.* New York: Macmillan.

Merton, R. K. 1968. *Social Theory and Social Structure.* New York: Free Press.

Moonitz, M. 1974. *Obtaining Agreements on Standards.* Studies in Accounting Research No. 8. New York: ARA.

Nair, R. D. and W. G. Frank. 1980. "The Impact of Disclosure and Measurement Practices on International Accounting Classification." *The Accounting Review* July: 426–450.

Nettle, J. P. 1969. "Power and the Intellectuals." In C. C. O'Brien and W. D. Vanech (eds.), *Power and Consciousness*, pp. 53–125. New York: New York University Press.

Parsons, T. 1971. *The System of Modern Societies.* Englewood Cliffs, N.J.: Prentice-Hall.

Peasnell, K. V. and D. J. Williams. 1986. "Ersatz Academics and Scholar Saints: The Supply of Financial Accounting Research." *ABACUS* September: 121–135.

Previts, G. J. 1975. "On the Subject of Methodology and Models for International Accountancy." *International Journal of Accounting Education and Research* Spring: 1–12.

Price Waterhouse International. 1979. *International Survey of Accounting Principles and Reporting Practices.* Scarborough, U.K.: Butterworths.

Radebaugh, L. H. 1975. "Environmental Factors Influencing the Development of Accounting Objectives, Standards and Practices in Peru." *International Journal of Accounting Education and Research* Fall: 39–56.

Ritzer, G. 1975. *Sociology: A Multiple Paradigm Science.* Boston: Allyn & Bacon.

Watts, R. L. and J. L. Zimmerman. 1978. "Towards a Positive Theory of the Determination of Accounting Standards." *The Accounting Review* January: 112–134.

———. 1979. "The Demand for and Supply of Accounting Theories: The Market for Excuses." *The Accounting Review* April: 273–305.

———. 1986. *Positive Accounting Theory.* Englewood Cliffs, N.J.: Prentice-Hall.

10

Welfare of the Common Man and Accounting Disclosure Adequacy: An Empirical Investigation

INTRODUCTION

Comparative accounting literature cites the possibility of classifying certain patterns in the world of accounting into different historical "zones of accounting influences" (Mueller, 1967; DaCosta, Bourgeois, Lawson, 1978, pp. 92–102). As a result, various attempts were made to identify the environmental variables likely to explain the grouping of countries in these zones of accounting influences. Most of the early attempts focused on cultural, social, and economic factors as possible explanatory variables of the differences in accounting principles and techniques among the various countries. The results were generally supportive of the hypothesis that the cultural and economic environment in a country influences its accounting principles and reporting practices (Frank, 1979, pp. 595–605; Nair and Frank, 1980, pp. 426–450). More recent studies have attempted to relate these differences to the economic and political environment of each country (Belkaoui, 1983, pp. 207–220; Goodrich, 1982). The results were far from conclusive.

Basically, the empirical literature on the determinants of differences in the reporting and disclosure adequacy among countries can be grouped into two types. The first type focuses on indices of economic and social welfare as possible explanatory variables, and the second focuses on political and civil welfare. What is missing in both types of studies is the welfare of the common man and

This chapter is adapted from "Welfare of the Common Man and Accounting Disclosure Adequacy: An Empirical Investigation" by Ahmed Belkaoui and Mostafa Maksy. *International Journal of Accounting* Vol. 20, No. 2 (1986): 178–182. Used by permission of CIERA.

how that welfare may affect the determination of accounting principles in a given country. The welfare of the common man, as introduced in the social economics literature, is defined as the extent to which economic welfare is translated into achievement in social welfare or "basic welfare" (to use the social economics terminology) (Horvat, 1974, pp. 29–39; Mandle, 1980, pp. 179–189; Hella, 1983, pp. 172–177). Two important questions are open to empirical examination in the comparative accounting literature. First, how do countries of different economic systems rate as to the welfare of the common man? Second, are the actual accounting reporting and disclosure adequacy of a given country related to the welfare of the common man? The objective of this study is to investigate these questions.

ELEMENTS INFLUENCING THE DEVELOPMENT OF ACCOUNTING

In most comparative empirical accounting research, the development of accounting is viewed in terms of the development of an adequate reporting and disclosure tradition. Therefore, in attempting to identify the elements influencing the development of accounting, this study considers a reporting and disclosure index as the representative of the state of accounting development in a given country (Mueller, 1977). If we view this reporting and disclosure index as an expression of social behavior, we may hypothesize that the index is a direct product of its environment, based on a well-accepted thesis in sociology that social structure determines social behavior (Durkheim, 1933, 1964; Parsons, 1971; Ritzer, 1975). Although this environment was defined as either the economic and social environment in some studies (Frank, 1979; Choi and Mueller, 1978; Seidler, 1967, pp. 775–781) or the political and civil environment in other studies (Belkaoui, 1984, 1985), this study views the environment as the welfare of the common man, a combination of economic and social environments.

Therefore, the index, as shown in Exhibit 10.1, may then be represented as being influenced by the welfare of the common man in a given country. The welfare of the common man is shown as the difference between the rankings of the economic welfare index and the basic welfare index. The basic welfare index itself is a composite of three indices: a health index, an education index, and a life index. Notice that the welfare of the common man is assumed to be moderated by the type of economic system adopted by the given country. All these variables and the hypothesized relationships will now be examined.

WELFARE OF THE COMMON MAN AND DETERMINANTS

The concept of the welfare of the common man originated when development economists turned their attention from economic growth per se to the issue of the "basic needs" of the population. Basically, the development approach moved from a largely economic perspective to a wider, all-encompassing socioeco-

Exhibit 10.1
Model of Accounting Development

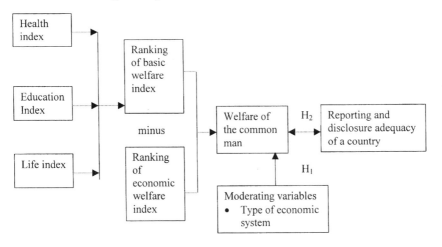

nomic one aimed at the fulfillment of all basic needs: adequate nutrition, health, clean water, and shelter (Belkaoui, 1984). This strategy views development in terms of the fulfillment of basic needs, which have been eloquently defined by Ul Haq as follows:

The concepts of basic needs bring to any development strategy a heightened concern with meeting the consumption needs of the whole population, particularly in the areas of education and health, but also in nutrition, housing, water supply, and sanitation. In formulating policies aimed at reducing poverty, a good deal of attention has generally been paid to restructuring the patterns of production and income so that they benefit the poor. But similar attention has not been devoted to their needs for public services. (Ul Haq, 1980, p. 32)

Morawetz identified sixteen indices of basic human needs, covering such essentials as three on nutrition, six on health, three on housing, and four on education. In doing so, he noted that "the ultimate goal is provision to the poor of the goods and services required to fulfill their basic needs: food, health care, shelter and the like" (Morawetz, 1977, p. 14). His attempt to relate these variables to economic development as measured by per capita output resulted in a statistically significant relationship for only five of the sixteen variables. He gloomily concluded that "GNP per capita and its growth rate do not seem to provide satisfactory proxies for fulfillment of basic needs and improvements in the same" (Morawetz, 1977, pp. 55–58). His efforts were continued by Horvat, who compared the per capita output ranking of sixty countries with a composite ranking of social indicators (Horvat, 1974). He was able to evaluate the relative success a country achieved in satisfying basic needs compared to other countries.

Where the basic welfare ranking is worse than the economic welfare ranking,

Horvat stated that the common man is not treated as well as elsewhere. Where, however, the basic welfare ranking is better than the economic welfare ranking, the country is assumed to be efficiently employing its resources to satisfy the welfare needs of its population (Horvat, 1974, p. 31). The welfare of the common man was operationally defined as the difference between the ranking of the economic welfare (measured by GNP) and the ranking of the basic welfare (a composite ranking of three indices on health, life, and education). Horvat found that the countries of the socialist bloc, the countries he labeled "etatist," achieved "unambiguously higher basic welfare than other countries" (Horvat, 1974, p. 32). He also found that the countries with a long welfare or social tradition fared better than capitalist countries, where such a tradition was less popular. Horvat, however, acknowledged that the welfare ranking of the high-income countries is biased downward and the welfare status of the poor countries may be biased upward, which may explain his results. To try to correct for this bias and to determine whether it influenced Horvat's conclusion, Mandle replicated the study and eliminated both the richest and the poorest countries. He failed, however, to reject Horvat's findings. His general and rather "political" conclusion stated: "It is thus that Marx may well turn out to be right. Capitalism does appear to be capable of generating long-term growth. What it may not be competent to achieve is development while alleviating the poverty of the bulk of the population. Furthermore, the evidence suggests that the institutional structure of the "etatist" countries is favorably organized to accomplish both" (Mandle, 1980, p. 189).

This debate will surely continue. In effect, Hella examined some questions concerning data, methodology, and interpretation in both Horvat's and Mandle's papers, but failed to reject their conclusions (Hella, 1983). One aspect of this study will be an attempt to replicate and verify Horvat's conclusion using more recent data. Horvat's data cover the period 1960–1976. The replication may be justified by the fact that during the seventies and following the turbulent sixties, the "so-called" capitalist countries have moved more aggressively to provide various forms of social welfare and "safety nets" to individuals. The first hypothesis to be tested is as follows:

H_1: There is no difference in the levels of the welfare of the common man between countries adopting different economic systems.

Basically, if the welfare of the common man is to be defined as the difference between the ranking of the economic welfare and the ranking of the basic welfare, we may easily assume that the type of economic system will have an impact on both the economic welfare and the social welfare and henceforth on the welfare of the common man.

WELFARE OF THE COMMON MAN AND REPORTING AND DISCLOSURE ADEQUACY

Earlier studies in the comparative accounting literature examining the determinants of reporting and disclosure adequacy found either little significance with various expressions of economic and social welfare and/or no significance with political welfare. The reason may be that the choice of determinants may have failed to include the combined effect of these determinants. As noted earlier, the combined effect of economic welfare and social or basic welfare is the concept of the welfare of man. The higher the welfare of man, the better the conditions for the creation of an accounting profession and tradition based on full and fair disclosure. Where the basic welfare ranking is worse than the economic welfare, the common man may not be treated as well as elsewhere, and the reporting and disclosure adequacy of a given nation will suffer equally. Where, however, the basic welfare ranking is better than the economic welfare ranking, the country may be assumed to be efficiently employing its physical and human resources to satisfy the welfare needs of its population, and the reporting and disclosure adequacy will be better than where the conditions are worse.

Therefore, the second hypothesis to be tested is as follows:

H_2: There is no difference between the reporting and disclosure adequacy of a country and the level of the welfare of man.

PROCEDURES

Methodology and Sample

As presented in Exhibit 10.1, the study investigates the relationships between two main variables: the welfare of the common man and an accounting reporting and disclosure adequacy index. The moderating variable is the type of economic system. First, each of these variables is explained and measured. Second, various correlation statistics are computed to test the two hypotheses.

All the countries listed in the World Bank's *World Development Report 1981*, which amounted to 124 countries, were included in this study. They are listed in Exhibit 10.2.

Reporting and Disclosure Adequacy Index

Adequacy refers to the coverage of events and transactions in the financial statements. A financial statement is considered adequate if all the relevant information has been reported and disclosed. The measurement of actual adequacy is then determined quantitatively as the extent of coverage of relevant infor-

Exhibit 10.2
List of Countries

Low-Income Countries

1. Kampuchea, Dem.	13. Burundi	25. Tanzania
2. Laos, PDR	14. Upper Volta	26. Zaire
3. Bhutan	15. India	27. Niger
4. Bangladesh	16. Malawi	28. Guinea
5. Chad	17. Rwanda	29. Central African Rep.
6. Ethiopia	18. Sri Lanka	30. Madagascar
7. Nepal	19. Benin	31. Uganda
8. Somalia	20. Mozambique	32. Mauritania
9. Mali	21. Sierra Leone	33. Lesotho
10. Burma	22. China	34. Togo
11. Afghanistan	23. Haiti	35. Indonesia
12. Viet Nam	24. Pakistan	36. Sudan

Middle-Income Countries

37. Kenya	57. Peru	77. Korea, Rep. of
38. Ghana	58. Morocco	78. Algeria
39. Yemen Arab Rep.	59. Mongolia	79. Mexico
40. Senegal	60. Albania	80. Chile
41. Angola	61. Dominican Rep.	81. South Africa
42. Zimbabwe	62. Colombia	82. Brazil
43. Egypt	63. Guatemala	83. Costa Rica
44. Yemen PDR	64. Syrian Arab Rep.	84. Rumania
45. Liberia	65. Ivory Coast	85. Uruguay
46. Zambia	66. Ecuador	86. Iran
47. Honduras	67. Paraguay	87. Portugal
48. Bolivia	68. Tunisia	88. Argentina
49. Cameroon	69. Korea, Dem. Rep.	89. Yugoslavia
50. Thailand	70. Jordan	90. Venezuela
51. Philippines	71. Lebanon	91. Trinidad and Tobago
52. Congo. People's Rep.	72. Jamaica	92. Hong Kong
53. Nicaragua	73. Turkey	93. Singapore
54. Papua New Guinea	74. Malaysia	94. Greece
55. El Salvador	75. Panama	95. Israel
56. Nigeria	76. Cuba	96. Spain

Exhibit 10.2 (continued)

Industrial Market Economies

97. Ireland	103. Japan	109. Norway
98. Italy	104. Australia	110. Belgium
99. New Zealand	105. Canada	111. Germany, Fed. Rep.
100. United Kingdom	106. France	112. Denmark
101. Finland	107. Netherlands	113. Sweden
102. Austria	108. United States	114. Switzerland

Capital-Surplus Oil Exporters

115. Iraq	117. Libya	118. Kuwait
116. Saudi Arabia		

Nonmarket Industrial Economies

119. Bulgaria	121. Hungary	123. Czechoslovakia
120. Poland	122. USSR	124. German Dem. Rep.

mation. The same approach is used here to compute an actual disclosure index for a country. The first requirement was to select a set of reporting and disclosure practices on which countries were likely to differ.

Price Waterhouse's *International Survey of Accounting Principles and Reporting Practices* provides such a database (Price Waterhouse International, 1979). It indicates for each of 267 accounting principles and practices the extent of application in each country in terms of a sevenfold classification: (1) required, (2) insisted upon, (3) predominant practice, (4) minority practice, (5) rarely or not found, (6) not accepted, or (7) not permitted. In this study, each of the seven classifications is coded as follows:

Classifications	Scale for the Extent of Application
1 = required	7
2 = insisted upon	6
3 = predominant practice	5
4 = minority practice	4
5 = rarely or not found	3
6 = not accepted	2
7 = not permitted	1

The scale for the extent of application of each of the 267 accounting principles and reporting practices constituted a separate observation for each of forty-eight countries surveyed by Price Waterhouse. The sum of these observations per country is used as the actual reporting and disclosure adequacy index.

Exhibit 10.3
Parametric and Nonparametric Results

Welfare of man	F^*	χ^{2*}	Welfare of man	F	χ^{2*}
W_1	12.43	33.65	W_{18}	26.51	49.95
W_2	14.57	31.35	W_{19}	16.13	34.36
W_3	10.87	35.27	W_{20}	26.60	42.51
W_4	23.63	48.45	W_{21}	8.48	51.33
W_5	17.58	38.32	W_{22}	7.73	20.17
W_6	29.43	32.70	W_{23}	13.45	19.29
W_7	25.49	39.33	W_{24}	24.43	26.59
W_8	13.35	53.86	W_{25}	13.87	45.26
W_9	11.87	18.89	W_{26}	15.39	37.40
W_{10}	21.07	18.50	W_{27}	26.77	32.62
W_{11}	11.64	27.98	W_{28}	29.80	38.43
W_{12}	18.08	45.08	W_{29}	15.47	45.97
W_{13}	28.11	49.54	W_{30}	12.44	43.04
W_{14}	9.18	28.18	W_{31}	20.30	32.74
W_{15}	9.00	37.73	W_{32}	29.33	41.69
W_{16}	15.90	48.50	W_{33}	10.60	52.47
			W_{34}	9.64	21.78
			W_{35}	16.69	21.61
			W_{36}	25.97	29.57

Note: *Significant at 0.0001.

A high score on the "actual reporting and disclosure adequacy index" suggests a willingness by a given country to adhere to and enforce 267 accounting principles and practices deemed necessary for enhancing the quality of accounting practice and helping to move toward a greater degree of harmonization (Price Waterhouse International, 1979, p. 3). That differences in accounting principles and financial reporting practices exist reflects the level of the welfare of the common man of separate nations and regions, or indicates that a different measure of reporting adequacy is considered appropriate. This study is based on the former interpretation, which is, first, that the conformity with each of the 267 practices and principles by the business community and accountancy profession is a desired goal of each of the countries in the study, and, second, that the degree of conformity depends on the welfare of the common man. That conformity is the desired goal is evident in efforts of various organizations, which include the United Nations Commission on Transnational Corporations, the Organization for Economic Cooperation and Development, the European Economic Community, and the International Accounting Standards Committee, aimed at a greater harmonization of international reporting. That the degree of conformity is a reflection of the welfare of the common man is the subject of this study.

Type of Economic Systems

The groupings used by the World Bank were used to differentiate among different economic systems. As shown in Exhibit 10.1, these were low-income countries (36 countries), middle-income countries (60 countries), industrial market economies (18 countries), capital surplus oil exporters (4 countries), and nonmarket industrial economies (6 countries).

Welfare of the Common Man

Following earlier studies that are replicated here using more recent data, the welfare of the common man is operationally computed as the difference between the ranking of basic welfare and the ranking of economic welfare (Horvat, 1974; Mandle, 1980; Hella, 1983). The main assumption in all these studies, including this one, is that if the social ranking is higher (better) than the economic ranking, it means that the given country has achieved higher relative basic welfare for its population than is generally the case in the sample of countries examined (Horvat, 1974, p. 31). The ranking of the economic welfare minus the ranking of each of the thirty-six different measures of basic welfare yielded thirty-six different measures of welfare of man for each of the countries.

EMPIRICAL RESULTS

Comparative Results on the Welfare of the Common Man: Hypothesis 1

The first hypothesis is intended to investigate the relationships between the welfare of the common man on one hand and the types of economic system adopted by the countries in our sample on the other hand. First, one-way ANOVA with F distribution was used for each of the independent variables, namely, type of economic system. Because of the possibilities of nonnormal distribution of welfare-of-man values and inequality of variances, a nonparametric test, the Kruskal-Wallis one-way ANOVA, is also used. The H-statistic is computed as follows:

$$H = \frac{12}{N(N + 1)} \sum_{j=1}^{k} \frac{R_j}{n_j} - 3 (N + 1)$$

where

k = number of categories for each independent variable
n_j = number of countries in the jth category
N = number of countries in the total sample
R_j = sum of the ranks in the jth category

The values of the H-statistic were compared with the chi-square critical values to test the hypothesis. The results of the F and χ_2 statistics are shown in Exhibit 10.3.

According to the information in Exhibit 10.3, the result for the impact of the type of economic system was significant. Basically, as noted in other related studies, the welfare of the common man is dependent mainly on the type of economic system adopted by the given country.

An examination of the mean welfare-of-man scores for each of the thirty-six combinations in this study showed the following results for the five types of economic systems:

1. For low-income countries, thirty-six of the thirty-six means were positive.
2. For middle-income countries, twenty-nine of the thirty-six means were positive.
3. For industrialized market economies, the thirty-six means were negative.
4. For capital surplus oil exporters, the thirty-six means were negative.
5. For the nonmarket industrial economies, the thirty-six means were positive.

From this examination of the mean scores of the welfare of man for the various combinations, the welfare of man appears to fare better in the industrial market economies and capital surplus oil exporters than in the nonmarket industrial economies and low- and middle-income countries. The results are contrary to other empirical studies investigating the differences in the welfare of man among the various economic systems. The results of this study indicate that the countries labeled as industrial economies and capital surplus oil exporters achieved unambiguously higher basic welfare than other countries.

Relationship Between Actual Reporting and Disclosure Adequacy and the Welfare of the Common Man

As discussed earlier, Hypothesis 2 attempted to test whether a relationship exists between accounting reporting and disclosure adequacy of a country and the level of the welfare of the common man. Because of the lack of accounting data in the Price Waterhouse survey for some countries in general and the nonmarket industrial economies in particular, we ranked only forty-eight countries from our sample with respect to reporting and disclosure adequacy in a descending order. The new sample is shown in Exhibit 10.4. The same ranking procedure was applied to each of the thirty-six measures of the welfare of man. We then correlated the ranking or reporting and disclosure adequacy of the thirty-six rankings of the welfare of the common man. Using the Spearman correlation coefficient, only one of the measures of the welfare of man was significant at $\chi = 0.09$ (Spearman correlation coefficient was equal to 0.2472). Therefore, with one minor exception, Hypothesis 2 cannot be accepted. The main finding is that, with the exception of a weak significant case, the reporting and disclosure adequacy in a given country is not significantly affected by the welfare of man in that country.

Exhibit 10.4
Countries for Which a Disclosure Adequacy Is Available

Argentina	Honduras	Pakistan
Australia	India	Panama
Austria	Ireland	Paraguay
Belgium	Italy	Peru
Bolivia	Jamaica	Philippines
Brazil	Japan	Portugal
Canada	Kenya	Singapore
Chile	Malawi	Spain
Costa Rica	Malaysia	Sweden
Dominican Republic	Morocco	Switzerland
Ecuador	Mexico	United Kingdom
El Salvador	Netherlands	United States
France	New Zealand	Uruguay
Germany	Nicaragua	Venezuela
Greece	Nigeria	Zaire
Guatemala	Norway	Zambia

SUMMARY AND CONCLUSIONS

This study attempted to investigate empirically whether the welfare of the common man has an impact on the development of accounting principles and practices. The welfare of the common man was defined as the difference between the ranking of economic welfare and the ranking of social welfare in a given country with respect to the countries included in the study sample. As a surrogate for economic welfare, we used per capita GNP. As a surrogate for social welfare, we used three indices: health, life, and education.

The development of accounting principles and practices is represented by a reporting and disclosure adequacy index composed of 267 accounting principles and practices and the extent of their application in 48 countries.

We first tested whether the welfare of the common man as defined is influenced or moderated by the type of economic system. We found that the economic system affects the welfare of the common man. We then tested the relationship between the welfare of the common man and the development of accounting principles and practices.

We found that no statistically significant relationship exists between the welfare of the common man and the development of accounting principles and practices.

Our second result is, however, subject to at least two limitations.

First, the reduction of our original sample from 124 to 48 countries and the elimination in the process of various interesting countries in general and the socialist countries in particular may have affected the nonsignificant results. This is basically due to the absence of accounting data for those countries.

Second, the choice of the disclosure adequacy index may be biased toward a concept of adequacy more appropriate to developed rather than developing countries. Other measures of adequacy may be more appropriate to developing countries and may need to be tailored to the specific information needs of business and government in each of those countries.

REFERENCES

American Accounting Association. 1977. "Report of the American Accounting Association Committee on International Accounting Operations and Education, 1975–1976." *The Accounting Review* 4 (Supplement): 67–119.

Belkaoui, A. 1983. "Economic, Political, and Civil Indicators and Reporting and Disclosure Adequacy: Empirical Investigation." *Journal of Accounting and Public Policy* Fall: 207–221.

———. 1984. *Socioeconomic Accounting*. Westport, CT: Greenwood Press.

———. 1985. *International Accounting*. Westport, CT: Greenwood Press.

Choi, F.D.S. and G. G. Mueller. 1978. *An Introduction to Multinational Accounting*. Englewood Cliffs, N.J.: Prentice-Hall.

DaCosta, R. C., J. C. Bourgeois, and W. M. Lawson. 1978. "A Classification of International Financial Accounting Practices." *International Journal of Accounting* Spring: 92–102.

Durkheim, E. 1933. *The Division of Labor in Society*. New York: Macmillan.

Frank, W. G. 1979. "An Empirical Analysis of International Accounting Principles." *Journal of Accounting Research* Autumn: 595–605.

Goodrich, P. S. 1982. "Accounting and Political System." *Discussion Paper No. 109*. School of Economic Studies, University of Leeds.

Hella, K. N. 1983. "Basic Needs and Economic Systems: Notes on Data, Methodology, and Interpretation." *Review of Social Economy* October: 172–177.

Horvat, B. 1974. "Welfare of the Common Man in Various Countries." *World Development* July: 29–39.

Mandle, J. R. 1980. "Basic Needs and Economic Systems." *Review of Social Economy* October: 179–189.

Morawetz, D. 1977. *Twenty-Five Years of Economic Development, 1950 to 1975*. Washington, D.C.: World Bank.

Mueller, G. G. 1967. *International Accounting*. New York: Macmillan.

———. 1968. "Accounting Principles Generally Accepted in the United States versus Those Generally Accepted Elsewhere." *International Journal of Accounting* Spring: 91–103.

———. 1977. "State of the Art of Academic Research in Multinational Accounting." *Canadian Chartered Accountant* February: 3–14.

Nair, R. D., and W. G. Frank. 1980. "The Impact of Disclosure and Measurement Practices on International Accounting Classifications." *The Accounting Review* July: 426–450.

———. 1981. "The Harmonization of International Accounting Standards." *International Journal of Accounting* Fall: 61–77.

Parsons, T. 1971. *The System of Modern Societies*. Englewood Cliffs, N.J.: Prentice Hall.

Price Waterhouse International. 1979. *International Survey of Accounting Principles and Reporting Practices*. Scarborough, U.K.: Butterworths.

Ritzer, G. 1975. *Sociology: A Multiple Paradigm Science*. Boston, Mass: Allyn and Bacon.

Seidler, L. J. 1967. "International Accounting—The Ultimate Theory Course." *The Accounting Review* October: 775–781.

Ul Haq, M. 1980. "An International Perspective on Basic Needs." In *World Bank Poverty and Basic Needs*. Washington, D.C.: World Bank.

11
Levels of Financial Disclosure by European Firms and Relation to Country Return and Risk

INTRODUCTION

This chapter reports on the level of financial disclosure of a set of European companies and tests the effects of country return and risk. The objective is to provide additional evidence on the factors behind voluntary financial disclosure. While most of the previous studies investigated either the impact of firm characteristics (Chow and Wong-Boren, 1987; Barrett, 1975, 1976) or the impact of political, economic, and social indicators (Belkaoui, 1983; Cooke and Wallace, 1990; Belkaoui and Maksy, 1986; Radebaugh, 1975), this study hypothesizes that firms' voluntary accounting and disclosure choices are aimed at controlling the conflicts created by favorable or unfavorable signals about the quality of investment in a given country. The signals considered are the country return and risk.

The chapter is organized as follows. The first section provides a rationale for the hypothesis. The next section describes the measurement procedures and sample selection. Results of cross-sectional regressions for 1987 and 1989 are then presented.

Adapted from Ahmed Riahi-Belkaoui, "Levels of Financial Disclosure by European Firms and Relation to Country Return and Risk" *Advances in International Accounting* Vol. 7, copyright 1994, pp. 171–181, with permission from Elsevier Science.

RATIONALE

Country's Quality of Investment

Research in international finance focused on the investigation of whether markets are segmented internationally or not (Stulz, 1981, 1984; Gultekin and Gultekin, 1983; Gultekin et al., 1989; Gultekin, 1983; Solnik, 1977). While the results are not conclusive, there is growing evidence of international equity integration, on the one hand, and of different average stock returns among countries, on the other hand. From the asset pricing theory perspective, and viewing countries as stock portfolios in a global market, the cross-sectional variations in expected returns should be explained by country risk exposures (Harvey, 1991). Country risk is defined as the conditional sensitivity (or covariance) of the country return to the world stock return. The reward per unit of risk is the world price of covariance risk. Harvey (1991) tested whether conditional versions of the Sharpe (1964) and Lintner (1965) asset pricing model are consistent with the behavior of returns in seventeen countries and provided evidence that countries' risk exposures help explain differences in performance. The quality of investment in a given country can then be characterized by a country return and risk exposure.

Levels of Financial Disclosures and Country Return and Risk

The quality of investment in a given country is signaled by the country return and risk exposure. International investors form an opinion of the investment climate through the information conveyed by both signals. The implication for firms in each country is to control the conflicts created by either favorable or unfavorable information about the general investment climate. The control is contingent on whether the information is conveyed by the return or the risk signals. More specifically, if a country return is high (low), firms in the particular country may adjust their levels of disclosure toward less (more) disclosure; in other words, there is a negative relationship between the level of disclosure of a firm and the country return. The action for less disclosure in the case of high return may be motivated by the cost associated with unnecessary disclosures. Similarly, if a country risk exposure is high (low), firms in the particular country may adjust their levels toward more (less) disclosure; in other words, there is a positive relationship between the level of disclosure and the country risk exposure. The following hypothesis is offered:

H_1: The level of disclosure by a firm in a given country is negatively related to the country return and positively related to the country risk exposure.

METHODS

Levels of Financial Disclosure

The following multiple-step procedure was used for determination of the level of financial disclosure:

1. A list of financial items that European firms may disclose was determined by referring to the pronouncements of European authorities, European accounting texts, and prior studies (Barrett, 1976, 1977; Choi, 1973: Firth, 1979; Cooke, 1989; Stanga, 1976; Peyrard, 1990; Most, 1964).
2. Following a procedure used by Van Offeren and Bavishi (1991), the financial items were grouped into 5 groups: (a) a general group including 12 items, (b) an income statement group including 3 items, (c) a funds cement group including 5 items, (d) a balance sheet group including 8 items, and (e) an accounting policies group including 31 items. The final instrument is shown in Exhibit 11.1.
3. The percentage of items disclosed for each group was determined for each firm resulting in an overall score for each group and each firm.
4. A total unweighted score for each firm was computed equal to the sum of the overall scores for each group. Unlike other studies, which used a weighted score (Chow and Wong-Boren, 1987; Buzby, 1975; Belkaoui and Kahl, 1978), this study relies on an unweighted score because the interest is with the level of disclosure rather than the importance of disclosure.

Measurement of Country Return

Country returns are drawn from Morgan Stanley Capital International (MSCI), and monthly data on the equity issues for twelve European countries from December 1969 to May 1989 are included in this study. These indices are composed of stocks that broadly represent stock composition in each of the countries. The country returns used are calculated in U.S. dollars in excess of the holding period return on the treasury bill that is closest to thirty days to maturity on the last trading day of the month. Holding-period returns are calculated in the same way as Fama (1984).

Measurement of the Country's World Risk Exposure

To measure the country world risk exposure, the model used by Harvey (1991, p. 116) is used. It gives estimates of a conditional CAPM with time-varying expected returns and a constant price of covariance risk. It is expressed as follows:

Exhibit 11.1
Levels of Disclosure

General
1. Brief narrative history of the firm.
2. Information on major industry trends.
3. Information on senior management.
4. Information related to research and development activities.
5. Information related to capital expenditures.
6. Information related to foreign sales.
7. Information related to foreign income.
8. Statement of company objectives.
9. Description of major products produced.
10. Share of market in major product areas.
11. Information related to geographic segmentation.
12. Information related to the number and nature of subsidiaries.

Income Statement
1. Cost of goods sold.
2. Breakdown of sales revenue by major product lines, customer classes and geographic location.
3. Breakdown of earnings by major product lines, customer classes and geographic location.

Balance Sheet
1. Allowance for doubtful debts.
2. Market value of inventory.
3. Fixed assets and receivables.
4. Liabilities and equities.
5. Total assets.
6. Fiscal year end date.
7. Retained earnings.
8. Non-equity reserves.

Funds Flow Statement
1. Disclosure of funds flow statement.
2. Total funds from operations.
3. Cash flow from investing activities.
4. Cash flow from financing activities.
5. Increase/ decrease in funds.

Accounting Policies
1. Statement of accounting principles used in the preparation of accounts.
2. Definition of Funds Statement.
3. Audit opinion.
4. Depreciation method.
5. Research and development costs.
6. Pension costs.
7. Extraordinary items.
8. Computation of earnings per share.
9. Valuation of marketable securities.
10. Inventory costing method.
11. Valuation of long term investment.
12. Acquisition method.
13. Accounting for goodwill.
14. Accounting for other intangibles.
15. Accounting for deferred taxes.
16. Foreign currency method.
17. Foreign currency translation gain/loss.
18. Discretionary reserves.
19. Contingent liabilities.
20. Minority interest effect reported.
21. Audit report date.
22. Historical summary of important operating and financial data.

Exhibit 11.1 (continued)

23. Summary of the age of debtors at the balance sheet date.
24. Treasury stock method reported.
25. Long term financial leases.
26. More than 50% long-term investment.
27. 20% long-term investment.
28. 21-50% long-term investment.
29. Current resale value of the firm's assets.
30. Information related to advertising and publicity.
31. Consolidation policies.

$$\eta = (u_m e_t) = \begin{bmatrix} (r_{mt} - Z_{t-1}\delta_m)^1 \\ r_t - \lambda(u_{mt}\eta_t) \end{bmatrix}$$

where

r = excess return on the world portfolio

δ_m = coefficients associated with the instrumental variables for estimating the conditional mean of world return

u_m = forecast error in the conditional mean of the world return

λ = world price of covariance risk

Three sets of instrumental variables Z are used in the estimation, a common instrument and two local instruments (Harvey, 1991). The common set of predetermined instrumental variables includes a constant, the excess return on the world index, a dummy variable for the month of January, the 1-month return for holding a 90-day U.S Treasury bill less the return on a 30-day bill, the yield on Moody's Baa rated bonds less the yield on Moody's Aaa rated bonds, and the dividend yield on the Standard and Poor's 500 stock index less the return on a 30-day bill. Local instrument one includes the common installment set augmented with the country-specific dividend yield. Local instrument two includes the country-specific dividend yield and the country-specific excess return in place of the world excess return (Harvey, 1991, p. 144).

Sample

European countries were selected on the basis of the available information on country return and risk exposure. The countries used and their returns and risk are shown in Exhibit 11.2.

European firms were selected on the basis of their importance and the availability of annual report information for both 1987 and 1989. The total number of firms used was 155. They include 54 banks and 101 nonfinancial firms.

Exhibit 11.2
Country Return and Risk

Country	Mean Country Return (1979-1989)	Risk
Austria	0.0554	-0.2664
Belgium	0.0867	9.7415
Denmark	0.0718	9.6631
France	0.0647	3.6508
Germany	0.0502	1.4478
Italy	0.0221	0.6391
Netherlands	0.0767	9.3435
Norway	0.0930	4.3466
Spain	0.0355	0.9848
Sweden	0.0938	8.3814
Switzerland	0.0462	3.6684
United Kingdom	0.0736	8.8903
World	0.0533	

Procedure

Cross-sectional regressions are run between the levels of disclosure of the European firms for 1987 and 1989 and the corresponding country return and risk. Membership in the European Community (EC) was introduced as an additional variable in the regression to control for potential additional disclosure requirements in the member countries and to investigate the potential increased disclosure requirements in the member countries between 1987 and 1989.
The final model is as follows:

$$LOD_t = a_{t0} + a_{t1}CRET_t + a_{t2}CRISK_t + a_{t3}Ec_t + a_{t4}LMS_t + t$$

where

LOD_t = level of financial disclosure

$CRET_t$ = country return

$CRISK_t$ = country risk

Ec_t = membership in the Common Market (membership coded 1; nonmembership coded 0)

LMS_t = law-mandated accounting systems as identified in Nobes' classification scheme (1989) (law-mandated accounting coded 1; non-law-mandated coded 0).

Exhibit 11.3
Multiple Regressions of Levels of Disclosure on Country Return and Risk ($LODt$ = $at0$ + $at1CRET$ + $at2CRISK$ + $at3ECt$ + $at4LMS$ + t)

Year	$at0$	$at1$	$at2$	$at3$	$at4$	F	R (%)
1st Part: All Firms (155 firms)							
1987	2.0966	(−1.894)	(0.067)	0.025	0.057	13.19	20.88
	(20.4)***	(−2.34)**	(5.10)***	(0.25)	(0.30)		
1989	1.202	−1.046	0.054	0.103	0.047	9.07	15.35
	(12.4)***	(−2.20)**	(4.36)***	(1.10)	(0.45)		
2nd Part: All Nonfinancial Firms (101 Firms)							
1987	2.1457	−3.482	0.080	0.104	0.038	20.94	39.12
	(20.9)	(−3.58)	(6.13)	(1.06)	(0.40)		
1989	2.2415	−0.974	0.0676	0.157	0.028	17.25	34.57
	(27.1)	(2.93	(6.39)	(1.99)	(0.45)		

Note: t-statistics are in parentheses.
Kolomogorov-Smirnov Z (sign) for the residuals.
***Significant at = 0.01; **significant at = 0.05.

The model controls for both membership in the common market and law-mandated accounting systems as identified in Nobes' classification scheme (1989). The regressions were run with banks included in the sample and with banks excluded to control for the potential additional reporting regulations.

RESULTS

Exhibit 11.3 reports the results of the multiple regressions of the levels of disclosure on country risk, return, and membership in the European Common Market. The results using either all the firms or limited to the nonfinancial firms are statistically significant and the Kolomogorov-Smirnov test indicates that neither set of residuals deviates significantly from normality. The independent variables of country return and risk have statistically significant coefficients. The positive signs of the country risk coefficient and the negative signs of the country return coefficient are consistent with less extensive voluntary disclosure by firms from countries with higher risk. The predicted effect of membership in the European Common Market was only supported for 1989 in the case of all the nonfinancial firms. The effect of law-mandated accounting systems was not significant in all cases.

The results also show that the models have a higher explanatory power when restricted to nonfinancial European firms. The specific regulatory requirements of each country imposed on banks may be a reason for the differential disclosure levels and impact of nonfinancial versus financial firms.

DISCUSSIONS

This study examined the relationship between the levels of disclosure of a selected set of European firms and the country return and risk. The results show that the levels of disclosure for 1987 and 1989 vary widely within the sample of 155 European-based firms and are related positively to the country world risk exposure and negatively to the country return. Basically, to control the signals conveyed by the country return and risk, European firms adjusted their disclosure level strategies. A low country return and a high country risk strategy dictated an expanded disclosure strategy, and vice versa. While international corporate disclosure has been shown to depend on internal and external environmental influences (Cooke and Wallace, 1990; Belkaoui, 1983) and capital market influences (Meek and Gray, 1989), this study extends the influence to country return and risk. A firm's intrinsic financial position can be healthy and yet the signals conveyed by country return and risk can affect the interests of potential local and foreign investors. Disclosure is one mechanism, shown in this study, that can be used to counteract the conflicting signals conveyed by the firm's return and risk on the one hand, and by the country's return and risk on the other.

Various factors limit the generalizability of these results. First, this study examined only disclosure items that can best be qualified as mandatory disclosures in the European context. A distinction between mandatory and voluntary disclosure and their respective potential association with country return and risk deserve careful examination.

Second, because most of these firms are multinationals with varying proportions of their assets and sales outside the countries in which they are registered, their disclosure levels may also be related to the country risk and return of other countries where they do most of their business. Future research should examine the plausibility of this scenario.

CONCLUSION

There is evidence that countries' risk exposures and returns help explain differences in market performance. It follows that the quality of investment in a given country can be characterized by a country return and risk exposure as determined by international CAPM. Firms in each country then need to control the conflicts created by either favorable or unfavorable information about the general investment climate, as conveyed by the country return and risk signals. A control mechanism used is the level of disclosure. If a country return is high (low), the levels of disclosure are adjusted toward less (more) disclosure to reduce the cost associated with unnecessary disclosures. If a country risk is high (low), the levels of disclosure are adjusted toward more (less) disclosure to reduce the unfavorable information about the general investment climate. In other words, increased firm disclosure improves the subjective probability distributions of a security's expected returns in the mind of an investor by reducing not only the uncertainty (risk) associated with that return stream but also the uncertainty (risk) associated with the country return stream.

REFERENCES

Barrett, M. E. 1975. "Annual Report Disclosure: Are American Reports Superior?" *Journal of International Business Studies* 6: 15–24.

———. 1976. "Financial Reporting Practices: Disclosure and Comprehensiveness in An International Setting." *Journal of Accounting Research* Spring: 10–26.

———. 1977. "The Extent of Disclosure in Annual Reports of Large Companies in Seven Countries." *International Journal of Accounting* Spring: 1–25.

Belkaoui, A. 1983. "Economic, Political and Civil Indicators and Reporting and Disclosure Adequacy: An Empirical Investigation." *Journal and Accounting and Public Policy* Fall: 207–221.

Belkaoui, A. and A. Kahl. 1978. *Corporate Financial Disclosure in Canada.* Research Monograph No. 1. Vancouver, Canada: Canadian Certified General Accountants Association.

Belkaoui, A. and M. Maksy. 1986. "Welfare of the Common Man and Accounting and Disclosure Adequacy: An Empirical Investigation." *International Journal of Accounting Education and Research* 20: 178–182.

Buzby, S. 1975. "Company Size, Listed versus Unlisted Stocks and the Extent of Financial Disclosure." *Journal of Accounting Research* Spring: 16–37.

Choi, F. 1973. "Financial Disclosure and Entry to the European Capital Market." *Journal of Accounting Research* Autumn: 159–175.

Chow, C. W. and A. Wong-Boren. 1987. "Voluntary Financial Disclosure by Mexican Corporations." *The Accounting Review* July: 533–541.

Cooke, T. E. 1989. "Voluntary Corporate Disclosure by Swedish Companies." *Journal of International Financial Management and Accounting* Summer: 171–195.

Cooke, T. E. and R. S. Olusegun Wallace. 1990. "Financial Disclosure Regulation and Its Environment: A Review and Further Analysis." *Journal of Accounting and Public Policy* 9: 79–110.

Fama, E. P. 1984. "The Information in the Term Structure." *Journal of Financial Economics* 13:509–529.

Firth, M. 1979. "The Impact of Size, Stock Market Listing, and Auditors on Voluntary Disclosure in Corporate Annual Reports." *Accounting and Business Research* Autumn: 273–280.

Gultekin, M. N. and N. B. Gultekin. 1983. "Stock Market Seasonality: International Evidence." *Journal of Financial Economics* 12. 469–481.

Gultekin, N. B. 1983. "Stock Market Returns and Inflation: Evidence from Other Countries." *Journal of Finance* 38: 49–65.

Gultekin, N. B., M. N. Gultekin, and A. Perrati. 1989. "Capital Controls and International Capital Market Segmentation: The Evidence from the Japanese and American Stock Markets." *Journal of Finance* 44: 849–869.

Harvey, R. C. 1991. "The World Price of Covariance Risk." *Journal of Finance* March: 111–158.

Lintner, J. 1965. "The Valuation of Risk Assets and the Selection of Risky Investments in Stock Portfolios and Capital Budgets." *Review of Economics and Statistics* February: 13–37

Meek, G. K. and S. J. Gray. 1989. "Globalization of Stock Markets and Foreign Listing Requirements: Voluntary Disclosures by Continental European Companies Listed on the London Stock Exchange." *Journal of International Business Studies* Summer: 315–336.

Most, K. S. 1964. "How Bad Are European Accounts?" *Accountancy* January: 15–32.

Nobes, C. 1989. *Interpreting European Financial Statements: Towards 1992.* London: Butterworths.

Peyrard, J. 1990. *Gestion Financiere avec Exercises.* Paris: Presses Universitaires de France.

Radebaugh, L. H. 1975. "Environmental Factors Influencing the Development of Accounting Objectives Standards and Practices in Peru." *International Journal of Accounting Education and Research* 11: 39–56.

Sharpe, W. F. 1964. "Capital Asset Prices: A Theory of Market Equilibrium under Conditions of Risk." *Journal of Finance* June: 425–442.

Solnik, B. 1977. "Testing International Asset Pricing: Some Pessimistic Views." *Journal of Finance* 32: 503–511.

Stanga, K. 1976. "Disclosure in Published Annual Reports." *Financial Management* Winter: 50–59.

Stulz, R. 1981. "A Model of International Asset Pricing." *Journal of Financial Economics* 9: 383–406.

Van Offeren, D. and V. B. Bavishi. 1991. "Financial Reporting Practices of Leading European Companies." Paper presented at the International Seminar in Accounting, University of Illinois at Champaign, March 22–29.

12

Determinants of Prediction Performance of Earnings Forecasts Internationally: The Effects of Disclosure, Economic Risk, and Alignment of Financial and Tax Accounting

INTRODUCTION

With the gradual growth and integration of global financial markets, financial analysts' accurate provisions of earnings forecasts, buy/sell recommendations, and other information to brokers, money managers, and institutional investors are acquiring international importance. Analysis and/or comparison of analysts' forecasts internationally shows marked differences in the prediction performance of earnings forecasts internationally (Mande, 1996; Capstaff et al., 1995; Arnold and Moizer, 1984; Rivera, 1991; Riahi-Belkaoui, 1995; O'Hanlon and Whiddett, 1991; Patz, 1989; Rike, Meeyanssen, and Chadwick, 1993; Cho, 1994; Das and Saudaragan, 1997). Determining the variables causing these differences is important to those users who rely on the earnings forecasts for their resource allocation decisions, and to policymakers in each country affected who need to improve the accuracy of earnings forecasts. Accordingly, this study considered whether disclosure policy, level of economic risk, and the level of alignment of financial and tax accounting explain differences in financial analysts' forecast (FAF) error internationally. The results on fourteen countries for the 1992–1994 period suggest that levels of FAF error are negatively related to the level of disclosure requirements of global stock exchanges, and positively related to the levels of economic risk and alignment of financial and tax accounting.

Adapted from Ahmed Riahi-Belkaoui, "Determinants of Prediction Performance of Earnings Forecasts Internationally: The Effects of Disclosure, Economic Risk, Alignment of Financial and Tax Accounting" *Advances in International Accounting* Vol. 11, copyright 1998, pp. 69–79, with permission from Elsevier Science.

BACKGROUND AND HYPOTHESES

The study proposes three determinants of prediction performance of earnings forecasts internationally: disclosure policy, economic risk, and level of alignment of financial and tax accounting.

Disclosure Policy

The empirical evidence is consistent with the notion that the generally accepted accounting principles (GAAP) rules in each country reflect the specific and unique set of institutional features relevant to each country (Gernon and Wallace, 1995; Wallace and Gernon, 1991). Among the institutional differences advanced by Riahi-Belkaoui (1994), Edwards (1993), Jacobson and Aaker (1993), and Falk (1994) are those relating to political structures, linguistic and cultural affiliation, tax structures, intercorporate ownership, industrial relations, type of economic system, and economic, social, and religious policies. The end result is that the level of disclosure in general and the mandated disclosures by stock exchanges in particular will differ (Adhikari and Tondkar, 1992). The differences in the disclosure levels mandated by stock exchanges lead to a difference in the level of informativeness about future earnings, a situation likely to affect the accuracy of analysts' earnings forecasts. This leads to the following hypothesis:

> H_1: The financial analysts' forecast error is negatively associated with the level of disclosure requirements of stock exchanges.

Economic Risk

Economic risk arises from instability in economic factors. It is manifest in higher inflation and debt servicing costs (Janah, 1991). The likely relation between economic risk and forecast accuracy is straightforward. To the extent that instability in economic factors is not very informative about future earnings, analysts' forecast accuracy will decrease with the low informativeness created by economic risk. Given that the instability in economic factors is definitively not useful to analysts, it is not difficult to imagine scenarios in which an increase in economic risk in a given country systematically reduces the accuracy of analysts' earnings forecasts. The strength of the relation between economic risk and financial analysts' forecast error is, however, an empirical one. This leads to the following hypothesis:

> H_2: The financial analysts' forecast error is positively associated with the level of the country's economic risk.

Alignment of Financial and Tax Accounting

A major variable differentiating the level of disclosure between countries is the important role played by tax rules in the production of financial statements. Generally labeled as tax relativism, it implies that the level of alignment between financial and tax accounting determines the level of disclosure in each country. The difference between the level of conformity between financial and tax accounting raises questions about the value relevance of financial data in high-alignment countries (Joos and Lang, 1994; Alford et al., 1993). High-alignment countries are more likely to be associated with concentrated ownership (Muller, Gernon, and Meek, 1994), with owners likely to have access to the information before its publication (Ashiq and Hwang, 1996), and are more likely to have creditor orientation and put more emphasis on valuing balance sheets (Gray et al., 1984). In addition, firms in high-alignment countries have more incentives to manipulate income downward to minimize taxes (Joos and Lang, 1994; Alford et al., 1993). All of the above arguments contribute further toward decreasing the value relevance of financial data used by financial analysts in the determination of financial forecasts. The strength of the relation between the level of alignment of financial and tax accounting and financial analysts' forecast error needs, however, to be tested. This leads to the following hypothesis:

H_3: The financial analysts' forecast error is positively associated with the level of alignment of financial and tax accounting.

EMPIRICAL ANALYSIS

Sample

Countries were selected on the basis of available data from the 1994 domestic and international Institutional Brokers Estimate System (IBES) tapes. Countries and firms (in parentheses) included in the analysis were : Australia (50), Canada (97), Denmark (60), France (60), Germany (60), Italy (60), Japan (183), the Netherlands (60), Spain (60), Switzerland (60), the United Kingdom (125), and the United States (450). The number and choice of firms were motivated by the following criteria: (a) The number of firms for each country reflects the capital market size with a higher number allocated to countries with large capital market size, and (b) the firms included had available and valid data for the analysis, and more than two analysts making earnings forecasts.

Financial Analysts' Forecast Error

The financial analysts' predictions of annual earnings for the firms of each country in the sample and the actual earnings reported by the firms were used to determine the dependent variable: the average mean squared forecast error

(MS). It is used as a measure of the forecast error. Reference for this measure is based on its mathematical and statistical tractability and the more than proportional weight given to large error, a desirable assumption in economic forecasting (Theil, 1966). It is defined as follows:

$$MS = 1 \bigg/ N\sum_{j=1}^{N}(P_j - R_j)^2 \qquad\qquad (12.1)$$

where

j = firm

t = year (1992, 1993, 1994)

$P_j = F_{jt} - A_{jt}$

$R_j = F_{jt} - A_{jt-1}$

F_{jt} is the current forecast for firm j at time t

A_{jt} is the current period's earnings

A_{jt-1} is the prior period's earnings

N is the number of observations

Economic Risk

The study relies on the risk-rating scores provided by international country risk guide (ICRG) of International Business Communication Ltd. (Janah, 1991). ICRG receives the most attention from foreign investors (Kim and Kim, 1993). ICRG provides a composite risk rating, as well as individual ratings for political, financial, and economic risk. The interest in this study is with the economic component that is economic risk. This economic component includes such factors as inflation and debt service costs (Janah, 1991). The maximum or least risky score is 50 for economic risk. It is shown in Exhibit 12.1 for each of the countries used in the sample.

Alignment of Financial and Tax Accounting

The fourteen countries used in the analysis were classified as having either low or high alignment between financial and tax accounting (see Exhibit 12.1). "Book and tax differences" from the series of Price Waterhouse publications in business environment in different countries was used as the primary source of the classification. High-level countries were coded 1, and low-level countries were coded 0.

Exhibit 12.1
Sample Description

Country	Alignment of Financial and Tax Accounting	Economic Risk	Disclosure Score
Australia	low level	37.0	74.60
Canada	low level	37.0	79.00
Denmark	low level	37.0	67.20
France	high level	34.5	76.20
Germany	high level	38.5	67.20
Italy	high level	25.0	68.46
Japan	high level	39.0	77.68
Korea	high level	36.5	71.43
Netherlands	low level	40.5	73.19
South Africa	low level	37.5	74.50
Spain	high level	35.0	68.84
Switzerland	high level	39.5	52.24
United Kingdom	low level	36.0	86.21
United States	low level	39.5	90.31

Adhikari and Tondkar's Disclosure Index

Adhikari and Tondkar's composite disclosure index (1992), intended to measure the quantity and intensity of disclosure required as part of the listing and filing requirements of stock exchanges, includes a list of forty-four items. An actual score for each stock exchange was obtained by Adhikari and Tondkar by summing all the scores received by the stock exchanges for the forty-four information items that are required by a stock exchange as part of its listing and filing requirements. The disclosure score was obtained by dividing the actual score attained by a stock exchange by the maximum attainable score. To account for differences among different user groups, each disclosure score was weighted by its relevance to a host of experts from each of the countries examined. As a result, a weighted (WTDSCORE) score was computed. They are shown in Exhibit 12.1. The index, as based on 1989 data, reflects a disclosure culture assumed to be rigid and slow to change, justifying its use to analyze 1994 analysts' errors.

Procedures

Cross-sectional regressions are run between the average mean squared forecast error of each country on one hand and the corresponding level of disclosure requirements of stock exchanges, economic risk, and level of alignment of financial and tax accounting on the other hand. The model is as follows:

$$MS_t = A_{r0} + A_{r1} \, WTDSCORE_t + A_{r2}ER + A_{r3}LOA_t \qquad (12.2)$$

Exhibit 12.2
Multiple Regression of MS$_t$ on Disclosure Score, Economic Risk, and Level of Alignment

$MS_t^2 = A_{t0} + A_{t1}$ WTDSCORE$_t$ + A_{t2}ER + A_{t3}LOA + R						
Years	A_{t0}	A_{t1}	A_{t2}	A_{t3}	F-Value	R^2 Adjusted
1992-94	-0.0229	-0.0810	0.1596	0.0608	8.569*	63.59%
	(0.213)	(4.291)*	4.168*	2.254**		

Notes: *Significant at 0.01
**Significant at 0.05

where

MS$_t$ = average mean square forecast error
WTDSCORE$_t$ = weighted disclosure score
ER   = economic risk
LOA   = level of alignment of financial and tax accounting

RESULTS

The three hypotheses state that the financial analysts' forecast error internationally is related negatively to the level of disclosure requirements of stock exchanges and positively to the level of economic risk and the level of alignment of financial and tax accounting.

Exhibit 12.2 presents the results of the regression analysis. As the F-statistic indicates, the general regression is significant with the three independent variables explaining 63.59 percent of the financial analysts' forecast error. The level of disclosure requirements of stock exchanges was significant in the exact direction to the stated Hypothesis 1. In other words, the results show that the higher the level of disclosure requirements for stock exchanges, the lower the financial analysts' forecast error. It shows that the level of disclosure requirements of a stock exchange, as an expression of the informativeness of each country's disclosure policy, increases the accuracy of analysts' earnings forecasts. This result is in conformity with U.S.-based findings on how disclosure affects favorably analysts' forecasts (Baginski and Hassell, 1990; Jennings, 1987; Waymire, 1986; Brown and Han, 1992; Swaminathan, 1991; Baldwin, 1984; Brown and Rozeff, 1979; Lang and Lundholm, 1996).

Economic risk was significant in the exact direction to the stated Hypothesis 2. In other words, the results show that the higher the level of economic risk, the higher the financial analysts' forecast error internationally. It indicates that, in economically risky situations, financial analysts deal with more uncertainties and have a more complex environment for the forecasting of earnings, which reduces their forecasting abilities and yields a higher forecast error.

The level of alignment of financial and tax accounting was significant in the exact direction of the stated hypotheses. In other words, the results show that the higher the level of alignment of financial and tax accounting, the higher the level of financial analysts' forecast error. This is in conformity with the thesis that firms in high-alignment countries have the incentive to manipulate income downward to minimize taxes, contributing further toward decreasing the value relevance of financial data used by financial analysts in the determination of earning forecasts (Joos and Lang, 1994; Alford et al., 1993).

CONCLUSIONS

The results of this study indicate that the level of financial analysts' forecast error internationally is negatively related to the level of disclosure requirements of global stock exchanges, and positively related to the levels of economic risk and alignment of financial and tax accounting. The results are consistent with earlier studies in the U.S. context with the view that more forthcoming disclosure policies lead to more accurate forecasts. They are also consistent with the established theses connecting economic risk and alignment of financial and tax accounting with reduced relevance of financial accounting data, leading also to less accurate forecasts. To the extent that the behavior of analysts internationally captures the disclosure policy and the levels of economic risk and alignment of financial and tax accounting, these results have implications for users of international forecasts and standard setters in each country as they set disclosure policy. Users of financial analysts' forecasts should put more weight on the forecasts originating from countries with a high level of disclosure, a low level of economic risk, and a low level of alignment of financial and tax accounting. Standard setters in each country need to set a higher level of disclosure policy and reduce the alignment of financial and tax accounting to increase the relevance of accounting data and reduce the level of forecast error.

REFERENCES

Adhikari, A. and R. H. Tondkar. 1992. "Environmental Factors Influencing Accounting Disclosure Requirements of Global Stock Exchanges." *Journal of International Financial Management and Accounting* 4: 76–105.

Alford, A., J. Jones, R. Leftwich, and M. Zmigewski. 1993. "Relative Informativeness of Accounting Disclosures in Different Countries." *Journal of Accounting Research* 31:183–223.

Arnold, J. and P. Moizer. 1984. "A Survey of the Methods Used by U.K. Investment Analysts to Appraise Investments in Ordinary Shares." *Accounting and Business Research* 14: 195–207.

Ashiq, A. and L.-S. Hwang. 1996. "The Effect of Alignment of Financial and Tax Accounting on the Value Relevance of Financial Accounting Data: Evidence from Cross-Country Comparison." Working Paper, University of Arizona, July.

Baginski, S. and J. Hassell. 1990. "The Market Interpretation of Management Earnings Forecasts as a Predictor of Subsequent Financial Analyst Forecast Revision." *The Accounting Review* 65: 175–190.

Baldwin, B. 1984. "Segment Earnings Disclosure and the Ability of Security Analysts to Forecast Earnings per Share." *The Accounting Review* 59: 376–389.

Brown, L. and J. Han. 1992. "The Impact of Annual Earning Announcements on Convergence of Beliefs." *The Accounting Review* 67: 862–875.

Brown, L. and M. Rozeff. 1979. "The Predictive Value of Interim Reports for Improving Forecasts of Future Quarterly Earnings." *The Accounting Review* 56: 585–591.

Capstaff, J., K. Paudyal, and W. Rees. 1995. "The Accuracy and Rationality of Earnings Forecasts by U.K. Analysts." *Journal of Business Finance and Accounting* 22(1): 67–85.

Cho, J. Y. 1994. "Properties of Market Expectations of Accounting Earnings by Financial Analysts: U.K. versus U.S." *Accounting and Business Research* 24: 230–240.

Das, S. and S. M. Saudagaran. 1997. "Properties of Analysts' Earnings Forecasts for Cross-Listed Foreign Firms." *Contemporary Accounting Research* 15: 62–71.

Edwards, P. 1993. "Listing of Foreign Securities on U.S. Exchanges." *Journal of Applied Corporate Finance* 5: 28–36.

Falk, H. 1994. "International Accounting: A Quest for Research." *Contemporary Accounting Research* 11: 595–615.

Gernon, H. and R. S. Olusegun Wallace. 1995. "International Accounting Research: A Review of Its Ecology, Contending Theories and Methodologies." *Journal of Accounting Literature* 14: 54–106.

Gray, S. J., L. G. Campbell, and J. C. Shaw. 1984. *International Financial Reporting: A Comparative International Survey of Accounting Requirements and Practices in 30 Countries*. England: Macmillan.

Jacobson, R. and D. Aaker. 1993. "Myopic Management Behavior with Efficient but Imperfect, Financial Markets: A Comparison of Information Asymmetries in the U.S. and Japan." *Journal of Accounting and Economics* 16: 383–405.

Janah, M. 1991. "Rating Risk in Hot Countries." *Wall Street Journal* September 20.

Jennings, R. 1987. "Unsystematic Security Price Movements, Managerial Earnings Forecasts and Revisions in Consensus Analysts Earning Forecast." *Journal of Accounting Research* 25: 90–110.

Joos, P. and M. Lang. 1994. "The Effects of Accounting Diversity: Evidence from the European Union." *Journal of Accounting Research* 32(Supplement): 141–176.

Kim, S. H. and S. H. Kim. 1993. *Global Corporate Finance: Text and Cases*, 2nd ed. Miami: Kolb Publishing.

Lang, M. H. and R. J. Lundholm. 1996. "Corporate Disclosure Policy and Analyst Behavior." *The Accounting Review* 4: 467–492.

Mande, V. 1996. "A Comparison of U.S. and Japanese Analysts' Forecasts of Earnings and Sales." *International Journal of Accounting* 16: 143–160.

Muller, G.G., H. Gernon, and G. Meek. 1994. *Accounting and International Perspective*. New York: Business One Irwin.

O'Hanlon, J. and R. Whiddett. 1991. "Do U.K. Security Analysts Overact?" *Accounting and Business Research* 22: 63–74.

Patz, D.H.K. 1989. "Analysts' Earnings Forecasts." *Accounting and Business Research* 19: 267–275.

Riahi-Belkaoui, A. 1994. *International and Multinational Accounting*. London: Dryden.

————. 1995. "Prediction Performance of Earnings Forecast of U.S. Firms Active in Developed and Developing Countries." *Advances in Accounting in Emerging Economics* 3: 85–97.

Rike, R., J. Meeyanssen, and L. Chadwick. 1993. "The Appraisal of Ordinary Shares by Investment Analysts in the U.K. and Germany." *Accounting Business Research* 24: 489–499.

Rivera, J. M. 1991. "Prediction Performance of Earnings Forecasts: The Case of U.S. Multinationals." *Journal of International Business Studies* 22: 265–288.

Swaminathan, S. 1991. "The Impact of Sec Mandated Segment Data on Price Variability and Divergence of Beliefs." *The Accounting Review* 66: 23–41.

Theil, H. 1966. *Applied Economic Forecast.* Amsterdam: North-Holland.

Wallace, R.S.O. and H. Gernon. 1991. "Frameworks for International Comparative Financial Accounting." *Journal of Accounting Literature* 10: 209–264.

Waymire, G. 1986. "Additional Evidence on the Accuracy of Analyst Forecasts before and after Voluntary Management Earnings Forecasts." *The Accounting Review* 59:129–142.

13

Economic, Political, and Civil Indicators and Reporting and Disclosure Adequacy: An Empirical Investigation

INTRODUCTION

That accounting objectives, standards, policies, and techniques differ among various countries is an established and proven fact in international accounting. As a result, the comparative accounting literature includes various attempts to classify the accounting patterns in the world of accounting in different historical "zones of accounting influence" (American Accounting Association, 1977, 1978; Mueller, 1967, 1968; Seidler, 1967; Previts, 1975; Da Costa et al., 1978; Frank, 1979). A general explanation for the various zones of accounting influence obtained is that the accounting objectives, standards, policies, and techniques result from the environmental factors in each country, and if "these environmental factors differ significantly between countries, then it would be expected that the major accounting concepts and practices in use in various countries also differ" (Frank, 1979, p. 593).

That accounting objectives, standards, policies, and techniques reflect the particular environment of the standard-setting body is also an accepted thesis in international accounting. Various attempts were made to identify the environmental conditions likely to affect the determination of national accounting principles (Choi and Mueller, 1978; Seidler, 1967; Frank, 1979). Two major remarks may be made about these studies. First, it was implicitly assumed that cultural, social, as well as economic factors may explain the differences in accounting

Adapted from *Journal of Accounting and Public Policy* Vol. 2, No. 3, Ahmed Belkaoui, "Economic, Political and Civil Indicators and Reporting and Disclosure Adequacy: Empirical Investigation" pp. 207–221, copyright 1983, with permission from Elsevier Science.

principles and techniques between the various countries. Second, two important environmental factors that may affect business behavior in general and accounting development in particular have not been included in these studies, namely, the degree of political rights and civil liberties of individuals. Two questions are open to empirical examination. First is the relative importance of economic factors in general and the extent of economic liberalism in particular on accounting development as compared with other environmental factors. Basically, besides the conventional economic indicators such as, for example, per capita GNP and growth rate of income, the impact of the economic system on accounting development is in need of empirical investigation. Second is the relative importance of the political atmosphere in general and political rights and civil liberties in particular on accounting development. Basically, the impact of the political system and the extent of political and civil freedom on accounting development is also in need of empirical investigation. Consequently, the objective of this study is to examine the international differences in reporting and disclosure adequacy and to relate these differences to the economic and political environment of each country.

ELEMENTS INFLUENCING THE DEVELOPMENT OF ACCOUNTING

The development of accounting may be viewed in terms of the development of an accounting profession and systems of accounting education, or in terms of the development of an adequate reporting and disclosure tradition. Both features of accounting development are certainly positively related. One may expect and safely assume that a well-developed accounting profession and system for accounting education in a given country leads to a tradition and/or effort of providing adequate reporting and disclosure. However, when comparing the development of accounting among various countries, reliable information on the development of adequate reporting and disclosure is more easily found than information on the development of an accounting profession and systems of accounting education. Therefore, in attempting to identify the elements influencing the development of accounting, this study considers a reporting and disclosure index as one of the representatives of the state of accounting development in a given country. If we view this reporting and disclosure index as an expression of a social behavior, then based on a well-accepted thesis in sociology that social structure determines social behavior, we may hypothesize that the index is a direct product of its environment. This index, as shown in Exhibit 13.1, may then be represented as being influenced by the political, economic, and demographic environment in a given country.

Political Environment

The political freedom of a country is important to the development of accounting in general and reporting and disclosure in particular. When people

Exhibit 13.1
Model of Accounting Development

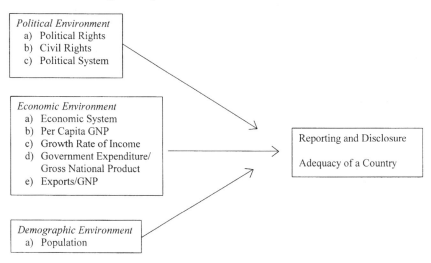

cannot choose the members of government or influence government policies, they are less likely to be able to create an accounting profession based on the principle of full and fair disclosure. Political repression involves a general loss of freedom, which may hinder to some extent the development of the profession of accounting. There is likely to be a positive relationship between accounting freedom to report and disclose and political freedom. As Exhibit 13.1 shows, the degree of political freedom in a given country is assumed to depend on the degree of political rights, the civil liberties, and the type of political system. Violations of political rights and civil liberties associated with various forms of political structure restrict political freedom in general and may act as a hindrance to the tradition of a full and fair disclosure. While these propositions may be viewed as intuitive and hardly self-evident, the objective of the study is to empirically test their validity.

Economic Environment

The economic environment is also important to the development of accounting in general and reporting and disclosure in particular. Economic development constitutes economic growth and various structural and social changes. One of the structural and social changes is the need for financial and reporting devices to measure the performance of each sector of the economy in terms of efficiency and productivity. Lowe notes that, from a historical point of view, accounting development is an evolutionary process dependent upon, and interwoven with, economic development (Lowe, 1967, p. 360). Similarly, Elliot et al. (1968, p. 764) state that the "social function of accounting, to measure and to communicate economic data, cannot be considered simply as the effect promoting the development process." However, economic development may be achieved by various forms of economic policies depending on the type of economic system chosen, the level and growth rate of income, the extent of government intervention and expenditures, and the level of exports. Each of these factors may imply a specific impact on accounting development. The following discusses possible impacts:

A. *Ceteris paribus*, a capitalist system, may be more favorable to accounting development than other economic systems. In a capitalist economic system, the survival of private enterprises depends not only on the production of goods and services but also on adequate information to various interest groups from investors and creditors to the capital market in general. In a similar vein, Quereshi draws attention to the relationship between financial accounting, capital formation, and economic development as follows:

The choice is based on the idea that financial reporting is closely dependent upon financial mechanisms and institutions. Studies by such eminent monetarists such as Kuznets, Goldsmith, and McKinnon provide a convincing evidence of the parallel between the development of capital markets and economic growth. The development and functioning of capital markets in turn is intimately related to the availability of financial information which is provided by the accounting proper function of reporting. (Quereshi, 1975, p. 71)

B. The higher the per capita GNP, and the higher the level and growth of income, the higher the political and economic freedom and, as suggested in the preceding arguments, the better the adequacy of reporting and disclosure. This may apply to any economic system since economic growth in some socialist countries was often followed by an effort to liberalize the regimes.

C. The higher the level of government expenditures, the higher the level of government intervention and the better the adequacy of reporting and disclosure. Government intervention is dictated by a need to provide economic security to all classes of society and takes the form of industry and opportunity creation. Because government is assumed to be accountable to the people, its intervention may be followed by an effort to report and disclose, and may be favorable to the development of an accounting profession and reporting and disclosure tradition. This is applicable today to the economic system in the United States, a capitalist economic system; governmental agencies all employ accounting as a tool to accomplish the regulatory mandate placed upon them by Congress (Bedingfield, 1982). The socialist countries developed unique accounting systems and procedures in the furtherance of their own centrally managed economies. Finally, the role of governments in developing accounting principles and providing legal authority is assumed to result in a higher reliability of financial disclosures in the developing countries. As stated by Jaggi, the "interference by governments may be essential to ensure higher reliability (which is vital for the expression of industries in these countries), for creating public confidence and trust in corporations, for creating an atmosphere where industrialization can progress, and for making economic and social decisions" (Jaggi, 1975, p. 84).

D. The higher the level of exports, the higher the need for better reporting and disclosure. Free-trade policies in general and export promotion in particular increase the cooperation with other countries, the flows of human and physical capital, and the need for comparable reporting and disclosure adequacy. For example, Kraayenhof argues that the international flow of capital for financing and participation creates more interest in the soundness of financial presentations and the intelligibility of the explanatory notes (Kraayenhof, 1960, p. 36).

Demographic Environment

The population in a given country could also be important to the development of accounting. The larger the population, the greater the number of people to be interested in the accounting profession, to feel the need for a well-developed accounting profession and the need for full and fair disclosure. For example, India, Egypt, and Pakistan, which are usually classified as developing countries, have developed accounting professions and also well-developed systems for accounting education (American Accounting Association, 1978, p. 13).

On the basis of these a priori analyses, the following hypothesis is proposed:

H_0: The reporting and disclosure adequacy will differ with differences in the political, economic, and demographic environments of different countries.

PROCEDURES

Methodology and Sample

The dependent variable in this study is a reporting and disclosure adequacy index. Independent variables are the following: (1) political rights, (2) civil liberties, (3) political system, (4) economic system, (5) per capita GNP, (6) growth rate of income, (7) government expenditures/GNP, (8) exports/GNP, and (9) population. First, each of these variables is explained and measured. Second, various regression models are run to identify the significant clements influencing the development of accounting internationally.

To be included in our sample a country must have available data to measure both the dependent and the independent variables. Fifty-five countries met this test. They are shown in Exhibit 13.2.

Reporting and Disclosure Adequacy Index

Adequacy refers to the coverage of events and transactions in the financial statements. A financial statement is considered adequate if all the relevant information has been reported and disclosed. The measurement of actual adequacy

Exhibit 13.2
Countries Included in the Study

1. Argentina	29. Malawi
2. Australia	30. Malaysia
3. Austria	31. Morocco
4. Bahamas	32. Mexico
5. Belgium	33. Netherlands
6. Bolivia	34. New Zealand
7. Botswana	35. Nicaragua
8. Brazil	36. Nigeria
9. Canada	37. Norway
10. Chile	38. Pakistan
11. Costa-Rica	39. Panama
12. Dominican Republic	40. Paraguay
13. Ecuador	41. Peru
14. El Salvador	42. Philippines
15. Fiji	43. Portugal
16. France	44. Singapore
17. Germany	45. South Africa
18. Greece	46. Spain
19. Guatemala	47. Sweden
20. Honduras	48. Switzerland
21. India	49. Taiwan
22. Iran	50. United Kingdom
23. Ireland	51. United States
24. Italy	52. Uruguay
25. Jamaica	53. Venezuela
26. Japan	54. Zaire
27. Kenya	55. Zambia
28. Korea	

is then determined quantitatively as the extent of coverage of relevant information. The same approach is used here to compute an actual disclosure index for a country. The first requirement was to select a set of reporting and disclosure practices on which countries were likely to differ.

Price Waterhouse's *International Survey of Accounting Principles and Reporting Practices* provides such a database (Price Waterhouse International, 1979). It indicates for each of 267 accounting principles and practices the extent of application in each country in terms of a sevenfold classification: (1) required, (2) insisted upon, (3) predominant practice, (4) minority practice, (5) rarely or not found, (6) not accepted, or (7) not permitted. In this study each of the seven classifications is coded as follows:

Classifications	Scale for the Extent of Application
1 = required	T
2 = insisted upon	G
3 = predominant practice	5
4 = minority practice	4

5 = rarely or not found	3
6 = not accepted	9
7 = not permitted	1

Then the scale for the extent of application of each of the 267 accounting principles and reporting practices constitutes a separate observation for each of the 55 countries. The sum of these observations per country is used as the actual reporting and disclosure adequacy index.

A high score on the "actual reporting and disclosure adequacy index" suggests a willingness by a given country to adhere to and enforce 267 accounting principles and practices deemed necessary for enhancing the quality of accounting practice and helping the move toward a greater degree of harmonization (Price Waterhouse, 1979, p. 3). Where differences in accounting principles and financial reporting practices exist, this either reflects the economic, political, and social environment of separate nations and regions or indicates that a different measure of reporting adequacy is considered appropriate. This study is based on the former interpretation, which is first that the conformity with each of the 267 practices and principles by the business community and accountancy profession is a desired goal of each of the countries in the study, and second that the degree of conformity depends on the economic, social, and political environment. That conformity is the desired goal is evident in the efforts of various organizations aimed at a greater harmonization of international reporting which include the United Nations Commission on Transnational Corporations, the Organization for Economic Cooperation and Development, the European Economic Community, and the International Accounting Standards Committee. That the degree of conformity is a reflection of the economic, political, and social environment is the subject of this study.

Political and Civil Indicators

In the model presented in Exhibit 13.1, the political environment is assumed to depend on political rights, civil liberties, and the political system. Although political rights and civil liberties are abstract concepts without natural units of measurement, various attempts are made in the sociology and political science literature to rank countries in terms of their degree of political rights and civil liberties, and to construct appropriate indices (Bollen, 1980). These indices should measure political democracy, rather than some particular aspects connected with the total level of freedom (Bilson, 1982).

With the same emphasis on freedom, to connote political democracy, Dr. Raymond Gastil, as director of the Freedom House, has constructed and published since 1973 indices of political rights and civil liberties (Gastil, 1978).

Gastil defines civil liberties as the rights of the individual against the state and the rights to freedom of expression and a fair trial (Gastil, 1978, p. 7). He then develops a civil liberties index composed of seven following levels:

1. Level (1) for states where the rule of law is not mistaken and which include various news media and possible and evident freedom of expression.
2. Level (2) for states where civil liberties are less effective than in states ranked (1) because of violence and ignorance or lack of sufficient or free media of expression, created by either several special laws that restrain rights or authoritarian civic tradition, or the influence of religion.
3. Level (3) for states where the trapping of civil liberties exist but are hampered by serious imperfections such as repeated reliance on martial law jailing for sedition, or suppression of publications.
4. Level (4) for states where there are broad areas of freedom and free publication, along with broad areas of repression.
5. Level (5) for states where civil liberties are often denied and complaints of violation are ignored because of weak government control, or frequently censored media.
6. Level (6) for states where the right of the state and government are given legal priority over the rights of groups and individuals although a few individuals are allowed considerable freedom.
7. Level (7) for states where citizens have no rights vis-à-vis the state and where internal criticism is only known to the outside world because of the government's condemnation of it. (Gastil, 1978, p. 19)

Gastil defines political rights as the rights to play a part in determining the laws and the government of the community (Gastil, 1978, p. 7). He then develops a political rights index composed of seven following levels:

1. Level (1) for states where most everybody has both rights and opportunities to participate in the political process, to compete for political office, and to join freely formed political parties.
2. Level (2) for states where the effectiveness of the open electoral process is reduced by factors such as extreme poverty, a feudal social structure, violence, or agreements to limit opposition.
3. Level (3) for states where the effectiveness of the open electoral processes is reduced by nondemocratic procedures such as coups.
4. Level (4) for states where there is either a constitutional block to the full democratic significance of elections, or the power distribution is not affected by the elections.
5. Level (5) for states where elections are either closely controlled or limited, or the results have very little significance.
6. Level (6) for states where there is either no operational electoral system or opposition candidates are not allowed to compete.
7. Level (7) for states which may be characterized as tyrannies with little legitimacy either in a national tradition or a modern ideology. (Gastil, 1978, p. 19)

The 1979 values of both the civil liberties index and the political rights index for the nations in our sample are presented in Gastil (1978).

The political structure index suggested by Gastil and used in this study ranks countries (1) for multiparty systems, (2) for dominant party systems, (3) for one-party systems (4) for military dictatorship, and (5) for traditional monarchy. The higher the level of political freedom, the lower the rank of a country.

Economic Indicators

In the model presented in Exhibit 13.1, the economic environment is assumed to depend on (a) the economic system, (b) the per capita GNP, (c) the growth rate of income, (d) the government expenditures over GNP, and (e) the exports over GNP.

First, the economic system index, suggested by Gastil and used in this study, ranks countries (1) for capitalist system, (2) for capitalist-statist system, (3) for capitalist-socialist system, and (4) for socialist system. Capitalist states are those states that "rely on the operation of the market and on private provision for individual welfare" (Gastil, 1978, p. 46). Capitalist-statist states are those states that have very large government productive enterprises, because of either an elitist development philosophy or a major dependence on a key resource such as oil (Gastil, 1978, p. 46). Capitalist-socialist states are those states that "provide social services on a large scale through governmental or other nonprofit institutions, with the result that private control over property is sacrificed to egalitarian purposes" (Gastil, 1978, p. 46). Finally, socialist states are those states that "strive programmatically to place an entire national economy under direct or indirect control" (Gastil, 1978, p. 47).

Second, the per capita GNP for 1978 and the growth rate of income from 1970 to 1976 were selected from the *World Bank Atlas* (1978).

Third, the ratio of total government expenditures to gross national product and the ratio of exports to GNP were collected from the IMF, International Financial Statistics (March 1980).

Demographic Environment

In the model presented in Exhibit 13.1, the demographic environment is solely represented by the population of each country. It was also collected from the *World Bank Atlas* (1978).

RESULTS: DETERMINANTS OF ACTUAL REPORTING AND DISCLOSURE ADEQUACY

A multiple-regression analysis was used to determine the association between the economic, civil, and political indicators with the actual reporting and disclosure adequacy index of each country in the sample. The correlation matrix

Exhibit 13.3
Correlation Matrix

Variables	PR	CL	ES	PS	POP	INC	GRR	GY	XY
PR	1.000								
CL	0.912^a	1.000							
ES	0.235^b	0.229^a	1.000						
PS	0.846^a	0.651^a	0.197	1.000					
POP	-0.115	-0.137	0.016	-0.131	1.000				
INC	-0.682^a	-0.673^a	-0.096	-0.492^a	-0.011	1.000			
GRR	0.062	0.065	-0.061	-0.012	-0.125	-0.088	1.000		
GY	-0.187	-0.170	0.112	-0.050	-0.182	0.097	0.010	1.000	
XY	-0.107	-0.114	0.002	-0.070	-0.392^a	0.045	0.182	0.468^a	1.000

Note: ^{a}Significant at 0.01 level; ^{b}significant at 0.05 level.

and the coefficients of the nine independent variables are listed in Exhibits 13.3 and 13.4, respectively, along with other related statistics. The only significant variable appears to be the government expenditures over the GNP variable. It is positively related to the actual disclosure and reporting index. As the F-statistic indicates, the general regression model was not, however, significant. The lack of significance of some of the independent variables may be related to the significant correlation shown in Exhibit 13.3. Also, the lack of significance of the regression results may be due to various other factors such as misspecification of the disclosure adequacy scores, and the economic, political, and civil indicators, and misrepresentation of the countries included in the sample. Future research may inquire into a different formulation of disclosure adequacy, rely on other economic, political, and civil indicators, and include a more representative sample of countries in terms of economic system, political system, etc. In any case, the results pinpoint the need to look for the relations between measures of accounting development and adequacy on one hand and measures of political, civil, and economic development and adequacy as a first step in the formulation of a contingency theory of international accounting.

Limitations

Various limitations of the study may be recognized before any generalizations of the results are possible. The first limitation relates to the choice of the actual reporting and disclosure index based on a country's degree of compliance with 267 accounting principles and practices as a measure of accounting adequacy. This interpretation may be biased toward a notion of adequacy more appropriate to developed rather than developing countries. Other measures of accounting adequacy may be more appropriate to developing countries, and may have to be tailored to the specific information needs of business and governments in each of those countries. The second limitation relates to the existence of alternative indicators of political, civil, and economic factors that may be used as possible determinants of the actual reporting and disclosure adequacy of a given country. Gastil's indices and other economic and demographic indices used in this study offer the quality of being available for a wide variety of countries

Exhibit 13.4
Regression Results

Independent Variables	Intercept	PR	CL	ES	PS	POP	INC	GRR	GY	XY
Coefficients	883.79	−21.11	35.16	19.68	−30.5	0.00002	0.0049	0.6512	535.35	38.14
T-statistic		−0.435	0.938	0.722	−0.725	0.082	0.434	0.434	1.96[a]	0.171
R^2	0.2090									
F	1.321[b]									
N	55									

Notes: PR, political rights index; CL, civil liberties index; ES, economic system; PS, political system; POP, population; INC, per capita GNP; GRR, growth rate of income; GY, government expenditures/GNP; XY, exports/GNP.
[a]Significant at $\alpha = 0.057$; [b]not significant.

and well accepted as political, civil, and economic indicators. Other indicators are hampered by concern as to their validity, their unknown reliability, and their limited sample and temporal coverage (Bollen, 1980, p. 370).

SUMMARY AND CONCLUSIONS

This study examines the international differences in reporting and disclosure adequacy and relates these differences to the economic and political environment of each country. The main hypothesis is that the reporting and disclosure adequacy in terms of conformity to a set of 267 principles and techniques is likely to differ with differences in the political, economic, and demographic environment from different countries. While the results of the overall regression model were not significant, the study indicates the need for research in an important, but relatively unexplored area.

REFERENCES

American Accounting Association, Committee on International Accounting Operations and Education, 1976–1978. 1978. *Accounting Education and the Third World*, p. 6. Sarasota, Fla.: American Accounting Association.
———. 1977. "Report of the American Accounting Association Committee on International Accounting Operations and Education, 1975–1976." *The Accounting Review* 4 (Supplement): 67–119.
Bedingfield, J. P. 1982, *Accounting and Federal Regulation*. Reston, Va.: Reston Publishing Company.
Bilson, J. F. O. 1982. "Civil Liberty—An Econometric Investigation." *KYKLOS* 3: 94–114.
Bollen, K. A. 1980. "Issues in the Comparative Measurement of Political Democracy." *American Sociological Review* June: 370–390.
Choi, F. D. S., and G. G. Mueller. 1978. *An Introduction to Multinational Accounting*. Englewood Cliffs, N.J.: Prentice-Hall.
DaCosta, R. C., J. C. Bourgeois, and W. M. Lawson. 1978. "A Classification of Inter-

national Financial Accounting Practices." *International Journal of Accounting* 10: 73–85.

Durkheim, E. 1933. *The Division of Labor in Society*, translated by George Simpson. New York: Macmillan.

———. 1964. *The Rules of Sociological Method*, translated by S. S. Solovay and J. H. Mueller and edited by G.E.G. Catlin. New York: Free Press.

Elliot, E. L., J. Larrea, and J. M. Rivera. 1968. "Accounting Aid to Developing Countries: Some Additional Considerations." *The Accounting Review* October: 763–768.

Frank, W. G. 1979. "An Empirical Analysis of International Accounting Principles." *Journal of Accounting Research* Fall: 593–605.

Gastil, R. D. 1973. *Freedom in the World—Political Rights and Civil Liberties 1978.* New York: Freedom House.

Jaggi, B. L. 1975. "The Impact of the Cultural Environment on Financial Disclosures." *International Journal of Accounting Education and Research* Spring: 75–84.

Kraayenhof, J. 1960. "International Challenges in Accounting." *Journal of Accountancy* 3: 34–38.

Lenski, G. 1976. "The Need for Reader-Access to the Measures of Variables Used in Quantitative Cross-National Studies." *American Sociological Review* 15: 741–751.

Lipset, S. 1963. *Political Man*. Garden City, N.Y.: Anchor.

Lowe, H. D. 1967. "Accounting Aid for Developing Countries." *The Accounting Review* April: 356–360.

Mueller, G. G. 1967. *International Accounting*. New York: Macmillan.

———. 1968. "Accounting Principles Generally Accepted in the United States versus Those Generally Accepted Elsewhere." *International Journal of Accounting Education and Research* Spring: 92–93.

———. 1977. "The State of the Art of Academic Research in Multinational Accounting." *Canadian Chartered Accountant Magazine* February: 15–22.

Parsons, T. 1971. *The System of Modern Societies*. Englewood Cliffs, N.J.: Prentice-Hall.

Previts, G. J. 1975. "On the Subject of Methodology and Models for International Accountancy." *International Journal of Accounting* Spring: 1–12.

Price Waterhouse International. 1979. *International Survey of Accounting Principles and Reporting Practices*. Scarborough: Butterworths.

Qureshi, M. A. 1975. "Economic Development, Social Justice and Financial Reporting: Pakistan's Experience with Private Enterprise." *Management International Review* 5: 71.

Ritzer, G. 1975. *Sociology: A Multiple Paradigm Science*. Boston: Allyn & Bacon.

Seidler, L. J. 1967. "International Accounting: The Ultimate Theory Course." *The Accounting Review* October: 775–781.

World Bank Atlas. 1978. Washington, D.C.: International Bank for Reconstruction and Development.

14
Disclosure Adequacy and Country Risk

INTRODUCTION

Disclosure adequacy of a given country refers to the coverage of events and transactions in financial statements. Financial statements are considered adequate if all the relevant information has been reported and disclosed. The measurement of actual adequacy is then determined quantitatively as the extent of coverage of relevant information. The disclosure adequacy for a country can be measured by the listing and filing requirements of stock exchanges (Adhikari and Tondkar, 1992). International accounting research mainly examined the environmental determinants of disclosure adequacy (Meek and Saudaragan, 1990; Wallace and Gernon, 1991). The focus of this chapter is different. It examines disclosure adequacy as the determinant of country risk. The hypothesis of this chapter is that disclosure adequacy as measured by the accounting requirements of global stock exchanges implies more information and therefore risk in volatility.

RATIONALE

International Asset Pricing

Research to date indicates an increasingly world capital market whose integration has been strengthened by increasing cross-border capital flows (Gultekin et al., 1983, 1985; Harvey, 1991; Solnik, 1977; Stulz, 1981, 1984; Wheatley, 1988). It points to the need for recognition of the effect of global factors in risk management. Harvey and Zhou (1993) explored the use of the simple version of the Sharpe (1964) capital asset pricing model in an international setting. The Morgan Stanley Capital International (MSCI) index is used as a value-weighted market portfolio. Basically, each country has a risk exposure to the world portfolio and differential expected returns across countries are determined by the relative risk exposures. The empirical results show the efficiency of the MSCI index cannot be rejected at standard significance levels when all seventeen country portfolios (sixteen OECD countries plus Hong Kong) are used in the tests. The quality of an investment in a given country can then be characterized by a country return and risk exposure as determined by an international capital asset pricing model (CAPM).

Disclosure and Country Risk

Disclosure adequacy as measured by the accounting requirements of global stock exchanges indicates the level of the flow of information available in a given country. The announcement of the level of the flow of information to the market is expected to be directly related to the volatility of prices (Ross, 1989). More precisely, the flow of information helps in the resolution of uncertainty that influences cash flows and generally alters values (Robichek and Myers, 1966; Epstein and Turnbull, 1980). One would then expect a positive relationship between a country disclosure adequacy and its risk exposure. The country risk is measured by its systematic risk. The following hypothesis is offered:

H_0: The country risk exposure is positively related to the level of disclosure requirements of a global stock exchange.

PROCEDURES

Methodology and Sample

The dependent variable in this study is the country risk exposure, as measured by the systematic risk. The independent variable is the level of disclosure requirements of a stock exchange. To be included in our sample a country must have available data to measure both the dependent and independent variables. Sixteen countries met this test. The data set used is shown in Exhibit 14.1. The independent variables are derived from Harvey and Zhou's (1993) study and the disclosure scores from Adhikari and Tondkar's (1992) study. The Harvey and Zhou study uses seventeen country portfolios. Belgium was dropped from the study because of the unavailability of disclosure scores.

Adhikari and Tondkar's Disclosure Index

Adhikari and Tondkar's composite disclosure index, intended to measure the quantity and intensity of disclosure required as part of the listing and filing

Exhibit 14.1
Data Used

Stock Exchange (Country)	Disclosure Score (a)		Country Return (b)	Systematic Risk	Market Model	
	Weighted	Unweighted				Unsystematic Risk
1. Australia (Sydney)	74.60	74.64	0.423	1.1254 (0.160)		-0.0015 (0.004)
2. Austria (Vienna)	54.17	53.52	0.50	0.3741 (0.075)		0.0036 (0.003)
3. Canada (Toronto)	79.00	78.64	0.447	1.0428 (0.071)		-0.0008 (0.002)
4. Denmark (Copenhagen	67.20	66.86	0.715	0.6150 (0.081)		0.0040 (0.003)
5. France (Paris)	76.20	76.16	0.658	1.0067 (0.093)		0.0012 (0.003)
6. Germany (Frankfurt)	67.20	66.86	0.477	0.7799 (0.086)		0.0008 (0.003)
7. Hong Kong (Hong Kong)	77.04	75.77	1.699	1.2247 (0.193)		0.0108 (0.007)
8. Italy (Milan)	68.46	68.39	0.235	0.7639 (0.102)		-0.0015 (0.004)
9. Japan (Tokyo)	77.68	77.68	1.326	0.9184 (0.093)		0.0086 (0.003)
10. The Netherlands (Amsterdam)	73.19	72.84	0.739	0.9837 (0.068)		0.0024 (0.002)
11. Norway (Oslo)	60.63	60.59	0.940	0.9882 (0.130)		0.0044 (0.004)
12. Spain (Madrid)	68.84	68.36	0.368	0.6344 (0.106)		0.0005 (0.003)
13. Sweden (Stockholm)	60.54	60.05	0.915	0.7407 (0.087)		0.0054 (0.003)
14. Switzerland (Zurich)	52.24	52.39	0.447	0.9162 (0.075)		-0.0002 (0.002)
15. United Kingdom (London)	86.21	84.86	0.728	1.2627 (0.147)		0.0009 (0.003)
16. United States (New York)	90.31	90.75	0.339	0.9733 (0.042)		-0.0015 (0.001)

Note: [a]Data are provided in Adhikari and Tondkar (1992). [b]Data are provided in Harvey and Zhou
    (1993). Standard errors are in parentheses.

requirements of stock exchanges, includes a list of forty-four items. An actual
score for each stock exchange was obtained by summing all the scores received
by the stock exchange for the forty-four information items that are required by
the stock exchange as part of its listing and filing requirements. The disclosure
score was obtained by dividing the actual score attained by a stock exchange
by the maximum attainable score. To account for differences among user groups,
each disclosure score was weighted by its relevance to a list of experts from
each of the countries examined (Adhikari and Tondkar, 1992). As a result, a
weighted (WTDSCORE) and an unweighted (UNWTSCORE) were computed.
They are shown in Exhibit 14.1.

Country Return and Risk

To compute the country return and risk, Harvey, and Zhou (1993) relied on
the data from Morgan Stanley Capital International on equity indices for a sample of seventeen country portfolios available from December 1969 to May 1989.
These indices are value weighted and calculated with dividend reinvestment. A
value-weighted world equity index that serves as the market portfolio is also
available from Morgan Stanley. The MSCI international indices include stocks
that broadly represent stock composition in different countries.[1]

The country returns are computed in excess of the U.S. Treasury bill that is
closest to thirty days to maturity on the last trading day of the month. The return
data are shown in Exhibit 14.1.

The country risks are computed on the basis of ordinary least squares regres-

Exhibit 14.2
Results of Cross-Sectional Regressions

Dependent Variable	Intercept	WTDSCORE	UNWTSCORE	Adjusted R^2	F
1. Model 1	-0.09862	0.01410	----------	.3947	9.244*
(WTDSCORE[2])	(-0.297)	(3.040)*			
2. Model 2	-0.08925	---------	0.01404	.3917	9.014*
(UNWTSCORE[3])	(-0.269)		(3.002)*		

Note: t-statistics are in parentheses. [2]With weighted score as independent variable. [3]With unweighted score as independent variable. *Significant at alpha = 0.01.

sions (OLS) of the country index excess returns (calculated in U.S. dollars) on
the excess return on the world market portfolio. The regressions are based on
monthly data from January 1970 to May 1989. The country risks obtained from
the regressions are shown in Exhibit 14.1.

RESULTS AND DISCUSSIONS

Two multiple regression models, one with the weighted disclosure score
(WTDSCORE) and the other with the unweighted disclosure score (UNWT-
SCORE) as the independent variable, were tested to investigate the relationships
of country risk with disclosure levels in different stock exchanges. Exhibit 14.2
reports cross-sectional regression results using both WTDSCORE and UNWT-
SCORE as the independent variables. The results of both models are significant
(F values of 9.244 and 9.014 significant at a 0.01 level). Exhibit 14.2 provides
evidence that the levels of disclosure requirements of stock exchanges in different countries explain a significant amount of the variance in country risk. The
first model has an R^2 of 0.3947 and the second model has an R^2 of 0.3917. The
regression coefficient of disclosure level is significant and has the predicted sign
in both models. The positive sign of the disclosure levels of stock exchanges is
consistent with more extensive disclosure from countries with higher risk.

SUMMARY AND CONCLUSIONS

This study examines the international differences in the level of disclosure
requirements of stock exchanges in relation to country risks. The results show
that the level of disclosure requirements of stock exchanges was positively related to country risk. Differences in the demand of information by global stock
exchanges create different conditions for country risk. Basically a stock
exchange's level of mandatory disclosure requirements is aimed at controlling
the conflicts created by favorable or unfavorable signals about the country risk
in a given country. Higher levels of disclosure by stock exchanges implied more
information and more risk in volatility.

NOTE

1. There is a 99.1 percent correlation between the MSCI U.S. excess return and the New York Stock Exchange value-weighted return calculated by the Center for Research in Security Prices (CRSP) at the University of Chicago (Harvey, 1991). There is also a 95 percent correlation between the MSCI Japanese excess return and the Nikkei 225 return (Harvey and Zhou, 1993). Use of the MSCI data is reported by McDonald (1989), French and Poterba (1991), and Fedenia, Hodder, and Triantis (1991).

REFERENCES

Adhikari, Ajay and Rasoul H. Tondkar. 1992. "Environmental Factors Influencing Accounting Disclosure Requirements of Global Stock Exchanges." *Journal of International Financial Management and Accounting* Summer: 75–105.

Epstein, L. G. and S. M. Turnbull. 1980. "Capital Asset Prices and the Temporal Resolution of Uncertainty." *Journal of Finance* June: 627–643.

Fedenia, Mark, James E. Hodder, and Alexander J. Triantis. 1991. "Cross-Holding and Market Return Measures," Graduate School of Business, Stanford University.

French, Kenneth R. and James M. Poterba. 1991. "Were Japanese Stock Prices Too High?" *Journal of Financial Economics* 29: 337–363.

Gultekin, Mustafa N. and N. Bulent Gultekin. 1983. "Stock Market Seasonality: International Evidence." *Journal of Financial Economics* 12: 469–481.

Gultekin, N. Bulent, Mustafa N. Gultekin, and Alessandro Penati. 1985. "Capital Controls and International Capital Market Segmentation: The Evidence from the Japanese and American Stock Markets." *Journal of Finance* 44: 849–869.

Harvey, C. R. 1991. "The World Price of Covariance Risk." *Journal of Finance* 46: 111–157.

Harvey, C. R. and G. Zhou. 1993. "International Asset Pricing with Alternative Distributional Specifications." *Journal of Empirical Finance* June: 107–131.

McDonald, Tack. 1989. "The Mochiai Effect: Japanese Corporate Cross Holdings." *Journal of Portfolio Management* 15: 90–94.

Meek, G. K. and S. M. Saudaragaran. 1990. "A Survey of Research on Financial Reporting in a Trans-national Context." *Journal of Accounting Literature* 9: 145–182.

Riahi-Belkaoui, Ahmed. 1994. *International and Multinational Accounting*. London: Dryden Press.

Robichek, A. A. and S. C. Myers. 1966. "Valuation of the Firm: Effects of Uncertainty in a Market Context." *Journal of Finance* May: 215–227.

Ross, S. A. 1989. "Information and Volatility: The No-Arbitrage Martingale Approach to Timing and Resolution Irrelevancy." *Journal of Finance* March: 1–16.

Sharpe, William. 1964. "Capital Asset Prices: A Theory of Market Equilibrium under Conditions of Risk." *Journal of Finance* 19: 425–442.

Solnik, Bruno. 1977. "Testing International Asset Pricing: Some Pessimistic Views." *Journal of Finance* 32: 503–511.

Stulz, Rene. 1981. "A Model of International Asset Pricing." *Journal of Financial Economics* 9: 383–406.

———. 1984. "Pricing Capital Assets in an International Setting: An Introduction." *Journal of International Business Studies* Winter: 55–73.

Wallace, R.S.O. and H. Gernon. 1991. "Frameworks for International Comparative Financial Accounting." *Journal of Accounting Literature* 19: 209–264.

Wheatley, Simon. 1988. "Some Tests of International Equity Integration." *Journal of Financial Economics* 21: 177–212.

15

The Effects of Country Return and Risk Differences on Prediction Performance of Earnings Forecasts

INTRODUCTION

Earnings forecasts are next to stock recommendation the most prominent output of the financial analysts' industry. The accuracy of the forecasts is important not only to the industry's credibility but also to the investors' reliance on the forecasts. The studies of the determinants of forecast error have been limited to the American context. In addition, the impact of the investment climate in a given country on financial analysts' prediction has not been investigated. Accordingly, this study considers whether country return and risk explain differences in financial analysts' forecast (FAF) error. A study of the FAF error for eleven countries showed that the FAF errors were negatively related to country return and positively to country risk. In the case of high country return and low country risk, financial analysts in the particular country form more accurate earnings expectations.

The chapter is organized as follows: sections are included on the rationale, the empirical research design, the empirical results, and, finally, conclusions.

RATIONALE

Background

Prior research suggests that analysts' forecasts of earnings are associated with significant security price revisions (e.g., Beaver et al., 1979; Elton et al., 1981; Givoly and Lakonishok, 1979; Patell, 1976; Penman, 1980; Imhoff and Lobo,

1980; Waymire, 1984; Fried and Givoly, 1982). The more accurate the earnings prediction, the more information content the management forecast carries (Patell, 1976, p. 248). Various factors are expected to influence the accuracy of analysts earnings forecast, including industry, size of firm, variability of earnings, and forecasting horizon (e.g., Albrecht et al., 1977; Baginski, 1987; Baldwin, 1984; Barefield and Comiskey, 1975; Brown et al., 1985, 1987; and Imhoff and Pare, 1982).

Rivera (1991) found that the accuracy of earnings predictions as well as the level of agreement in earnings predictions is lower for purely domestic U.S. firms than for U.S. multinationals. Riahi-Belkaoui (1995), following up on Rivera (1991), compared U.S. multinationals operating in developing countries. Using domestic firms as benchmark, Riahi-Belkaoui found significant differences in accuracy among U.S. multinationals.

All the cited studies investigated financial analysts' forecasting behaviors in the United States. The exception is a study by Cho et al. (1993) that found that the magnitude of financial analysts' forecast errors do vary across countries. This study extends Cho et al.'s study by examining country return and risk as possible determinants of differences in forecast errors across countries.

Country's Quality of Investment

Research in international finance investigated whether markets are segmented internationally or not (Stulz, 1984; Gultekin et al., 1983, 1989; Solnik, 1977; Wheatley, 1988; Harvey, 1991). While the results are not conclusive, there is growing evidence, on the other hand, of different average stock returns among countries. From the asset pricing theory perspective, and viewing countries as stock portfolios in a global market, the cross-sectional variations in expected returns should be explained by country risk exposures (Harvey, 1991). Country risk is defined as the conditional sensitivity (or covariance) of the country return to the world stock return. The reward per unit of risk is the world price of covariance risk. Harvey (1991) tested whether conditional versions of the Sharpe (1964) and Lintner (1965) asset pricing model are consistent with the behavior of returns in seventeen countries, and provide evidence that countries' risk exposure helps explain differences in performance. The quality of investment in a given country can then be characterized by a country return and risk exposure as determined by an international capital asset pricing model (CAPM).

Earnings Prediction Performance

The quality of investment in a given country is signaled by the country return and risk exposure. Financial analysts form an opinion of the investment climate through the information conveyed by signals. The implication for financial analysts in each country is to control the conflicts created by either favorable or unfavorable information about the general investment climate. The control is contingent on whether the information is conveyed by the return or the risk signals. More specifically, if a country return is high (low), financial analysts in the particular country are prone to less (more) forecast error; in other words, a negative relationship exists between the forecast error and the country return. Similarly, if a country risk exposure is high (low), financial analysts in the particular country are prone to more (less) forecast error; in other words, a positive relationship exists between the forecast error and low country risk. In the case of high (low) country return and low (high) country risk, financial analysts in the particular country form more (less) confident earnings expectations. The following hypothesis is offered:

H$_0$: The accuracy of analysts' earnings forecast in a given country is negatively related to the country return and positively related to the country risk.

METHODS

Earnings Predictions Performances

The financial analysts' predictions of annual earnings for the firms of each country in the sample and the actual earnings reported by the firms were used to determine the dependent variable: the average mean squared forecast error (MSFE).

The MSFE is used as a measure of forecast error. Reference for this measure is based on its mathematical and statistical tractability and the more than proportional weight given to large error, a desirable assumption in economic forecasting (Mincer and Zamovitz, 1969; Theil, 1966). It is defined as follows:

$$\text{MSFE} = 1/N \sum_{j=1}^{N} (Pj - Rj) \tag{15.1}$$

where

j = firm, t = year (1992, 1993, 1994)
$Pj = Fjt - Ajt$
$Rj = Ajt - Ajt - 1$
Fjt is the current forecast for firm j at time t.
Ajt is the current period's earnings.
$Ajt - 1$ is the prior period's earnings.

Measurement of Country Return and Risk

Country returns are drawn from Morgan Stanley Capital International (MSCI), and monthly data on the equity issues for the countries are included in this study from the 1992–1994 revised data. These indices are composed of stocks that broadly represent stock composition in each of the countries. The international model gives estimates of a conditional CAPM with time varying expected returns and a constant price of covariance risk. Three sets of instrumental variables Z are used in the estimation: a common instrument and two local instruments (Harvey, 1991). The common set of predetermined instrumental variables includes a constant, the excess return on the world index, a dummy variable for the month of January, the 1-month return for holding a 90-day U.S. Treasury bill less the return on the 30-day bill, less the yield on Moody's Baa rated bonds, and the dividend yield on the Standard and Poor's 500 stock index less the return on a 30-day bill. Local instrument one includes the common instrument set augmented with the country-specific dividend yield and the country-specific excess return in place of the world excess return (Harvey, 1991, p. 144).

Sample

Countries were selected on the basis of available data from the 1994 domestic and international *Institutional Brokers Estimate System* (UB/E/S) tapes and Morgan Stanley Capital International equity indices. Countries and firms (in parentheses) were included in the analysis: Australia (50), Canada (97), Denmark (60), France (60), Germany (60), Italy (60), Japan (183), the Netherlands (60), Spain (60), Switzerland (60), United Kingdom (125), and United States (450). The number and choice of firms were motivated by the following criteria: (a) the number of firms for each country reflects the capital market size with a higher number allocated to countries with large capital market size and (b) the firms included had available and valid data for the analysis and more than two analysts making earnings forecasts.

Procedure

Cross-sectional regressions are run between the average mean squared forecast error of each country on one hand and the corresponding country return and risk on the other hand. The model is as follows:

$$\text{MSFE}_t = at_0 + a_{t1}\text{CRET}_t + a_{t2}\text{CRISK}_t + E_t \tag{15.2}$$

where

MSFE = average mean squared forecast error
CRET   = country return
CRISK = country risk

Exhibit 15.1
Multiple Regression of MSFE on Country Return and Risk
$(MSFE_1 = at_0 + a_{t1} CRET_1 + a_{t2} CRISK_t + E_t)$

Years	at_0	at_1	at_2	F	Readjusted
1992–	8.748	−830.849	1.7762	(3.206)***	26.92%
1994	(6.929)*	(−2.386)	(2.388)**		

T-statistics are in parentheses.
*Significant at alpha = 0.01; **significant at alpha = 0.05; ***significant at alpha = 0.10.

RESULTS AND DISCUSSION

Exhibit 15.1 reports the results of the multiple regressions of the mean square forecast errors (MSFE) per country risk and return. The results are statistically significant. The independent variables of country return and risk have statistically significant coefficients. The negative sign of the country return coefficient and positive sign of the country risk coefficient are consistent with (a) less forecasting errors by financial analysts from countries with higher return, and (b) more forecasting errors by financial analysts from countries with higher risk. The stated hypothesis H_0 is verified.

This study shows that the extent of forecast errors of the financial analysts internationally is negatively related to country return and positively related to country risk. The investment climate, as conveyed by the signals of country return and country risk, appears to affect the accuracy of financial analysts' forecasts of earnings internationally. Financial analysts in an environment of high return and low risk seem to develop a better expectation of the future performance of firms. In an environment of low return and high risk, financial analysts need to adjust their expectations and confidence in their forecast to reflect the higher degree of uncertainty in their particular country.

CONCLUSIONS

This study found that the levels of FAF errors are negatively related to country return and positively related to country risk. In the case of high country return and low country risk, financial analysts in the particular country form more accurate earnings expectations. The findings point to more research on the determinants of FAF errors internationally in order to get a better appreciation of the differential information content of financial analysts' forecasts of earnings internationally.

REFERENCES

Albrecht, W. S., O. Johnson, L. L. Lookabill, and D.J.H. Watson. 1977. "A Comparison of the Accuracy of Corporate and Security Analysts' Forecasts of Earnings: A Comment." *The Accounting Review* July: 736–740.

Baginski, S. P. 1987. "Intra-industry Information Transfers Associated with Management Forecasts of Earnings." *Journal of Accounting Research* Autumn: 196–216.

Baldwin, B. A. 1984. "Segment Earnings Disclosure and the Ability of Security Analysts to Forecast Earnings per Share." *The Accounting Review* July: 376–389.

Barefield, R. M. and E. E. Comiskey. 1975. "The Accuracy of Analysts' Forecasts of Earnings per Share." *Journal of Business Research* July: 241–252.

Beaver, W. H., R. Clarke, and W. F. Wright. 1979. "The Association between Unsystematic Security Returns and the Magnitude of Earnings Forecast Errors." *Journal of Accounting Research* 1: 316–340.

Brown, L. D., R. L. Hagerman, P. A. Griftin, and M. E. Zmijewski. 1987. "Security Analyst Superiority Relative to Univariate Time-Series Models in Forecasting Quarterly Earnings." *Journal of Accounting and Economics* January: 61–81.

Brown, P., G. Foster, and B. Noreen. 1985. *Security Analysts Multiyear Earnings Forecasts and the Capital Markets*. Studies in Accounting Research No. 21. Sarasota, Fla.: American Accounting Association.

Cho, J., K. Jung, and A. Allen. 1993. "Pattern of Forecast Errors and Superiority of Analysts' Forecast: The International Domain." Working Paper, University of Nebraska–Lincoln.

Elton, E. J., M. J. Gruber, and M. Gultekin. 1981. "Expectations and Share Prices." *Management Science* September: 975–987.

Fried, Dov and Dan Givoly. 1982. "Financial Analysts' Forecasts of Earnings: A Better Surrogate for Market Expectations." *Journal of Accounting and Economics* 4: 95–108.

Givoly, Dan and Joseph Lakonishok. 1979. "The Information Content of Financial Analysts' Forecasts of Earnings." *Journal of Accounting and Economics* December: 165–185.

Gultekin, Mustafa N. and N. Bulent Gultekin. 1983. "Stock Market Seasonality: International Evidence." *Journal of Financial Economics* 12: 469–481.

Gultekin, M. N., N. Bulent Gultekin, and Allessandro Penati. 1989. "Capital Controls and International Capital Market Segmentation: The Evidence from the Japanese and American Stock Markets." *Journal of Finance* 44: 849–870.

Harvey, Campbell R. 1991. "The World Price of Covariance Risk." *Journal of Finance* 15: 111–158.

Imhoff, E. A., Jr. and G. J. Lobo. 1980. "Information Content of Analysts' Composite Forecast Revisions." *Journal of Accounting Research* Autumn: 541–545.

Imhoff, E. A., Jr. and P. V. Pare. 1982. "Analysis and Comparison of Earnings Forecast Agents." *Journal of Accounting Research* Autumn: 429–439.

Lintner, John. 1965. "The Valuation of Risk Assets and the Selection of Risky Investments in Stock Portfolios and Capital Budgets." *Review of Economics and Statistics* 47: 13–37.

Mincer, J. and V. Zarnowitz. 1969. "The Valuation of Economic Forecasts. In J. Mincer (ed.), *Economic Forecasts and Expectations*. New York: National Bureau of Economic Research.

Patell, James M. 1976. "Corporate Forecasts of Earnings per Share and Stock Price Behavior: Empirical Tests." *Journal of Accounting Research* Autumn: 246–276.

Penman, S. H. 1980. "An Empirical Investigation of the Voluntary Disclosure of Corporate Earnings Forecasts." *Journal of Accounting Research* Spring: 132–160.

Riahi-Belkaoui, A. 1995. "Prediction Performance of Earnings Forecasts of U.S. Firms

Active in Developed and Developing Countries." *Research in Accounting in Emerging Economies* 3: 85–97.

Rivera, Juan M. 1991. "Prediction Performance of Earnings Forecasts: The Case of U.S. Multinationals." *Journal of International Business Studies* 22: 265–288.

Sharpe, William. 1964. "Capital Asset Prices: A Theory of Market Equilibrium under Conditions of Risk." *Journal of Finance* 19: 425–442.

Solnik, Bruno. 1977. "Testing International Asset Pricing: Some Pessimistic Views." *Journal of Finance* 32: 503–511.

Stulz, Rene. 1984. "Pricing Capital Assets in an International Setting: An Introduction." *Journal of International Business Studies* 1: 55–73.

Theil, H. 1966. *Applied Economic Forecasting.* Amsterdam: North-Holland.

Waymire, G. 1984. "Additional Evidence on the Information Content of Management Earnings Forecasts." *Journal of Accounting Research* Autumn: 703–718.

Wheatley, Simon. 1988. "Some Tests of International Equity Integration." *Journal of Financial Economics* 21: 177–212.

16

Cultural Studies and Accounting Research

INTRODUCTION

This chapter elaborates on the basic knowledge and ideas from the fields of cross-cultural studies and global awareness deemed of importance to international accounting research. First, concepts of culture are introduced before a coverage of the main issues encountered in cross-cultural research. Various recommendations are made, which are intended to guide the accounting researchers through some of the main problems and issues in cross-cultural research.

CONCEPTS OF CULTURE AND ACCOUNTING RESEARCH

When studying culture, anthropologists are constantly concerned with comparison between and among different societies. In effect, the central theoretical concept of anthropology is "culture." Anthropologists study humans as cultural beings. They examine the whole array of human societies from a social, biological, and humanistic perspective. As stated eloquently by Swartz and Jordan:

Anthropology is a social science in that it studies the social arrangements found in human groups, how individuals live in these different sorts of groups, and the means by which the different ways of life found in these groups come to be, persist, and change. It is a biological science in that it is concerned with human evolution and with human physical

Adapted from Ahmed Riahi-Belkaoui, C. Perochon, M. A. Mathews, B. Bemardi, and Y. A. El-Adly, "Report of the Cultural Studies and Accounting Research Committee of the International Accounting Section," *Advances in International Accounting* Vol. 4, copyright 1991, pp. 175–198, with permission from Elsevier Science.

variation as this occurs in different parts of the world at different times. It is also a humanistic discipline that examines the values, art, and philosophy of people—wherever and whenever they live or lived—for the beauty, richness and meaning they have.

Culture is, therefore, the basis of anthropological research. Anthropologists differ as to what the concept of culture means, although they generally agree that it is learned rather than biologically transmitted, that it is shared by the members of a group, and that it is the foundation of the human way of life. (Swartz and Jordan, 1980, p. 8)

Various concepts of culture exist in anthropology suggesting different themes for accounting research (Smircich, 1983). First, following Malinowski's (1944) *functionalism*, culture may be viewed as an instrument serving biological and psychological needs. Adapting this definition for accounting research suggests: (a) the perception of accounting in each culture as a specific social instrument for task accomplishment and (b) the analysis of *cross-cultural* or *comparative accounting*. This field of accounting research will be concerned with differences in accounting practices and attitudes across countries, locate clusters of similarities, and draw implications for accounting effectiveness in each culture.

Second, following Radcliffe-Brown's (1968) *structural functionalism*, culture may be viewed as an adaptive regulatory mechanism that unites individuals in social structures. Adapting this definition for accounting research suggests (a) the perception of accounting in each culture as adaptive instruments existing by process of exchange with the environment, and (b) the analysis of an *accounting culture*. Basically accounting is viewed as culture producing phenomena, producing distinctive cultural artifacts such as rituals, legends, and ceremonies (Gambling, 1983):

Third, following Goodenough's (1971) *ethnoscience*, culture may be viewed as a system of shared cognitions whereby the human mind generates culture by means of a finite number of rules. Adapting this definition for accounting research suggests (a) viewing each culture's accounting as a system of knowledge that members of that culture share to varying degrees, and (b) the analysis of *accounting and cognition* among different cultures. The task of the accounting researcher following this interpretation is to determine what the rules are, to find out how the members of each culture see and describe accounting phenomena.

Fourth, following Geertz's (1973) *symbolic anthropology*, culture may be viewed as a system of shared symbols and meanings. Adopting this definition for accounting research suggests (a) viewing accounting as a pattern of symbolic discourse or language, and (b) the analysis of *accounting as language*.

Fifth, following Levi-Strauss' (1983) *structuralism*, culture may be viewed as a projection of mind's universal unconscious infrastructure. Adopting this definition for accounting research suggests (a) accounting viewed in each culture as the manifestation of unconscious processes, and (b) the analysis of *unconscious processes in accounting*. For this perspective, accounting phenomena may be viewed as projections of unconscious processes to be analyzed with reference to the dynamic interplay between out-of-awareness processes and their conscious manifestation. The purpose of the study of accounting in each culture using structural analysis is to unravel the hidden universal dimensions of the mind. As stated by Turner, the task of structural analysis is to "discover an order of relations that turns a set of bits, which have limited significance of their own, into an intelligible whole. This order may be termed 'the structure' " (Turner, 1977).

OBJECTIVE VERSUS SUBJECTIVE CULTURE

Culture is sometimes confused with nation, and cross-cultural differences considered merely cross-national differences. To clarify the true action of culture, Triandis (1980, p. 3) used the concept of *subjective culture* defined as follows:

Subjective culture refers to variables that are attributes of the cognitive structures of groups of people. The analysis of subjective culture refers to variables extracted from consistencies in their responses and results in a kind of "map" drawn by a scientist which outlines the subjective culture of a particular group. In short, when we observe consistent responses to claims of stimuli that have some quality in common, we assume that some "mediators" (attitudes, norms, values, etc.) are responsible for their consistencies. It is the cognitive structures which "mediate" between stimuli and responses in different cultural settings that we wish to study.

This implies that national groups may belong to different subjective cultures given the several groups' different characteristic ways of perceiving the same social environment, resulting in differences in their belief systems, attitude structures, stereotype formations, norms, roles, ideologies, values, and task definitions. Therefore, a nation may have one distinct objective culture and many subjective cultures. The objective culture is symbolized by the same language, climate, and/or ecology, while the subjective culture refers to each group's characteristic way of perceiving its social environment (Bhagat and McQuaid, 1982, p. 155). It is then the study of differences in subjective cultures that is the interest of cross-cultural research. As stated by Bhagat and McQuaid (1982, p. 655):

Examination of differences in subjective cultures explores differences in belief systems, attitude structures, stereotypes, norms, roles, ideologies, values and task definition. When differences on many of these constructs fall into a pattern, we can identify genuine cross-cultural differences, as opposed to cross-national differences.

In accounting research it is, therefore, the role of subjective culture in accounting that is the most important for the identification of cross-cultural differences as opposed to cross-national differences.

The same point is made for cross-cultural organization research as follows:

Cross-cultural researchers often compare mean group differences without attempting to understand or to explain why the cultures should differ on the variables being studied. We argue that the goal of comparative organizational research should be to replace the general and rather vague term *culture*, which often translates into simply the names of the countries being studied, with more refined, theoretically meaningful explanatory constructs. (Bhagat and McQuaid, 1982, p. 675)

REASONS FOR CROSS-CULTURAL RESEARCH IN ACCOUNTING

Reasons for cross-cultural research in accounting include the following. The first reason is to establish the boundary conditions for accounting models and theories (Wilier, 1967). This research would proceed with the testing of the validity of a model or a theory in another culture to determine the cultural groups where the model or theory is valid and to specify the variables for which the model is not valid in some cultural groups. Basically, the discovery of the limits of accounting theories is an important part of accounting research.

The second reason is to evaluate the impact of cultural and ecological factors on behavior in accounting contexts (Strodtbeck, 1964). Between-cultural-group mean comparisons are used to demonstrate cultural differences in the dependent variable. If these comparisons cannot be made because of the absence of score equivalence, then the strategy should be to test the *universality* of an accounting model or theory. Triandis, Malpass, and Davidson (1972) made a crucial distinction between cross-cultural research aimed at proving the cross-cultural generality of a relationship or phenomena and studies that attempt to show differences in the relationship of phenomena that depend on cultural factors as follows:

The former study can be done with relatively loose methodology, since if the same finding is obtained in spite of differences in the stimuli, responses and people, it must be a strong finding. The latter requires extremely stringent controls and a multi-method approach, since there are many competing hypotheses that can account for the observed differences. The best kind of study of the second type is more likely the one where the differences have been predicted on theoretical grounds.

The third reason is, while variables are often generally confounded, the confounding is not complete, as a few cultunits may present deviant cases. Cultunits as the object of study of some cross-cultural psychologists have been defined by Naroll (1970/1973, p. 248) as "people who are domestic speakers of a common district dialect language and who belong either to the same state or the same contact group." As stated by Triandis (1980, p. 2): "So, even if variables A and B are highly positively correlated, there are nevertheless a few cultunits that are high on A and low on B, and a few that are low on A and high on B. If we study the deviant cultunits we can establish whether relationships between dependent variables Y and the independent variables A and B are caused by A, caused by B, or caused by both A and B. This is information that is most valuable."

The fourth reason is that cultunits act as "natural grain-experiments" by being high or low on variables of particular interest (Triandis, 1980, p. 4). For example, some cultures may focus on some aspects of accounting more than others. As a result, perceptual and decision styles may differ and can be traced to ecological differences.

The fifth reason is that cultures determine aspects of psychological functioning (Triandis, 1980, p. 4). For example, some cultures may deem certain accounting functions to be useless or unnecessary for their particular context. As a result, those functions are not practiced as they are not rewarded. Triandis, Vassilion, Vassilion, Tanaka, and Shanmugam (1972) give the example of the low probability of the planning function in cultures where belief in the unpredictability of events is extremely high. The study of behavior in cross-cultural accounting contexts needs to match the particular nature of the ecology with the particular nature of the participants.

The sixth reason is that the frequency of different accounting methods and behavior in different cultures need to be identified.

CROSS-CULTURAL RESEARCH ISSUES

Approaches for Studying Accounting across Cultures

There are at least five possible approaches to cross-cultural research in accounting [Adler, 1984]:

1. *Parochial studies* is the approach comprising studies of the United States conducted by Americans.

2. *Ethnocentric studies* comprise studies that attempt to replicate American accounting research in foreign countries.

3. *Polycentric studies* comprise studies that describe accounting phenomena in foreign countries.

4. *Comparative accounting studies* focus on identifying the similarities and dissimilarities in accounting phenomena in cultures around the world.

5. *Culturally synergistic studies* focus on creating universality in accounting while maintaining an appropriate level of cultural specificity.

Each of these types of research addresses a different set of accounting questions and is based on different sets of assumptions.

Methodological Problems in Cross-Cultural Research

The methodological problems in cross-cultural research have been examined in most social science disciplines, including political science (Ross and Homer,

1976), criminology (Vigderhous, 1978), economics (Wagner, 1969), sociology (Bendix, 1969), psychology (Whiting, 1968), anthropology (Naroll, 1968), social psychology (Berry, 1979), public administration (Riggs, 1969), and management (Nath, 1968; Roberts, 1970; Sekaran, 1983). A note of pessimism seems to pervade these articles as a result of the gravity of some of the problems.

The first problem is how to sample (a) cultures (Strauss, 1968) and (b) respondents within each culture. One strategy proposed by Naroll (1968) is to sample *cultunits*, defined as "people who are domestic speakers of a common district dialect language and who belong to either the same state or the same contact group." The other problem of how to sample stimuli and responses is solved, according to Triandis and Malpass (1970), by a focus on representative sampling of the stimuli in particular domains, and also of the responses allowing each cultural group the opportunity to provide natural kinds of responses. One also needs to be aware of the differences that cultural groups show in the probability of their choice of "agree" or "yes" response or in the extremity of the judgments they make.

The second problem is that there is a need in cross-cultural research to de-center the instrument used in the sense that the items generated in one culture are adapted to suit the other culture. Brislin (1970) presents a methodology of decentering that may lead to adequate translation.

The third problem is that the establishment of the equivalence of measure is a serious methodological problem in cross-cultural research, as equivalent bases are needed to make comparisons across cultural boundaries. Four types of equivalence have been examined: functional, conceptual, linguistic (or translation), and metric equivalence.

Functional equivalence indicates that the test provides a measurement of the same attribute in different groups of people. Functional equivalence should preexist as a naturally occurring phenomenon. As Prezeworski and Teune (1970) have so graphically put it: "For specific observation a belch is a belch and nepotism is nepotism. But within an inferential framework a belch is an 'insult' or a 'compliment' and nepotism is 'conception' or 'responsibility.' " The reasons are stated as follows:

> The lack of equivalence can be caused by unequal familiarity with test materials differences in the meaning of the test situation, unequal understanding of the test format and directions, differential susceptibility to response sets, differences in the connotative meaning of linguistically connected translated items, and [a] variety [of] other variables. The number of variables that might plausibly cause score nonequivalence is so great that it is probably not feasible to measure and control for all of them in any one study. (Davidson, 1977, p. 50)

Conceptual equivalence refers to the presence or absence of meanings that individuals attach to specific stimuli such as test items, certain words, the nature of contrived sound, psychological experiment, and so forth (Lonner, 1979, p. 77).

Linguistic or translation equivalence focuses on reaching equivalent statements following translation. Procedures such as back translation should be used to assure that equivalence has been reached (Brislin, 1976; Sechrest, Fay, and Zaidi, 1972).

Score or metric equivalence indicates that in addition to measuring the same attribute in different groups the quantitative scale is the same for each group. Unfortunately, score equivalence is rarely if ever achieved in cross-cultural research (Cole and Bruner, 1971; Jahoda, 1965).

Sekaran (1983) also identified several types of equivalences, such as "vocabulary equivalence or a translation that is equivalent to the original language in which the instrument was developed; idiomatic equivalence which could become a serious problem when some idioms unique to one language just cannot be translated properly in other languages; grammatical and syntactical equivalence, which is especially important when translating long passages; experiential equivalence or the equivalence of the inferences drawn by the respondents in various cultures from a given statement" (p. 62).

In correcting for the equivalence problem, there is, however, the risk that important cultural differences would be obliterated, or at least obscured, by the efforts made to achieve a rather misleading notion of equivalence. This is known as the paradox of equivalence (Sechrest et al., 1972). Basically there is a need to be sensitive to the paradox of equivalence, which amounts to a trap of attaining excessive equivalence.

The fourth problem is getting comparable samples from different cultures. One approach has been to tap groups of comparable educational or social levels. A second approach has been to select organizations having equivalent objectives in two or more cultures. The assumption in the second approach is that given comparable objectives, the organizational structure and methods of operation will reflect the cultural values (Berrian, 1967, p. 35).

The fifth problem is the ethnic influences in research questions (Berrian, 1967, pp. 37–38). What may appear to be significant research problems within one culture may not be researchable within another. Basically, researchers tend to choose subjects of research that are an outgrowth of their own cultural milieu.

The sixth problem is comparability of research instruments particularly when a questionnaire or a test standardized in one culture is modified (not just translated) to "fit" another culture (Berrian, 1967, p. 38). When the modification is made, the particular behaviors observed in one culture are no longer any more equivalent to those in another. This is particularly crucial with the transferability of U.S. concepts and measures to other cultures. The comparability of the research instrument may, however, be maintained if the following strategy is followed:

The way out of this dilemma is to ensure by both rational and empirical means that the construct is meaningful in the cultures under examination. This can be done whether the measures of the constructs vary in relation to some other independent variable(s) as hypothesized from some theory. Ideally, such a theory should specify fundamental behavioral dimensions whose definitions are culture free. (Berrian, 1967, p. 41)

The seventh problem is the interpretation of data where there may be biases in culturally bound judgments. Given the difficulty of finding variables that are universally applicable, the cross-cultural researchers are generally asked to minimize their ethnocentrism in the interpretation of results. The focus should be on "culturally free interpretation" to the extent possible.

The eighth problem is the nuances of scaling as important aspects of measurements. For example, a seven-point scale was found to be more sensitive than a four point scale (Barry, 1965). Some instruments may have more validity in one culture than another (Sekaran and Trafton, 1978; Sekaran and Martin, 1982).

The ninth problem is that cultures studied, as stated by Roberts (1970) and Sechrest (1977), are "targets of opportunity" in the sense that they are selected because it is practical to study them. As sadly commented by Sechrest (1977, p. 76): "Good research, or at least genuine contributions to theory, in other fields of psychology do not usually come about because of the chance availability of some apparatus or odd group of animals. If one accepts this analysis . . . then it follows that cultures should be selected rationally to represent certain variables when influence is to be tested."

The tenth problem is that most cross-cultural comparisons have been based on "static-group designs" (Campbell and Stanley, 1966; Malpass, 1977) in the sense that subjects are not randomly assigned to different levels of a treatment variable. As a result, any variable correlated with culture may explain differences between two or more populations. Another threat to internal validity arises from the absence of a control group (Brown and Sechrest, 1980).

Another methodological problem that arises in cross-cultural research relates to the lack of knowledge of others' viewpoints, in the sense that if the subjects from other cultures view objects and events differently from the researcher, the manipulation of the stimulus is not meaningful to them and the differences in their behavior are not necessarily due to cultural differences. For example, culturally sensitive topics will not elicit correct responses irrespective of the scaling techniques used. Similarly there are some cultural biases in certain types of responses. Mitchell gives the extreme example of the "sucker bias," where foreign researchers may be perceived as fair game for deception in some cultures (Mitchell, 1969).

Five main nonmethodological issues were also identified by Sekaran (1983). They refer to: (a) the absence of good definitions of the concept of culture; (b) the absence of good theories about cross-cultural management; (c) arbitrariness and opportunism in the choice of problems, countries, and samples; (d) the failure to take both macro variables and micro variables into consideration in cross-cultural research; and (e) the absence of innovation in cross-cultural research.

The Politics and Ethics of Cross-Cultural Research

Cross-cultural research, and especially field research, is assumed to raise both ethical and political issues because it involves a form of social intervention in another culture. Cross-cultural research has been considered political because

1. it reflects or affects the ability of actors to impose their will, pursue their interests, or enjoy legitimacy in the exercise of authority;
2. political influences may affect what is studied, how it is studied and what is done with the results; and
3. cross-cultural research is used sometimes as input into political processes. (Warwick, 1980, p. 320)

As a result of these three arguments, Warwick (1980, p. 321) concluded that "it is difficult to imagine any piece of cross-cultural psychological research that in its origins, implementation, and uses is completely immune to politics. . . . Whatever the likes and intentions of the researcher, cross-cultural psychological research is never a value-free, apolitical exercise. Even an attempt to make it so by choosing topics, methodologies, and sponsorship that will arouse the least controversy itself reflects the anticipatory influence of politics."

Cross-cultural research also raises some ethical questions. First, an ethical problem arises when the behavior of the investigator is considered insensitive to political repercussions. Warwick (1980, p. 321) warns that "a United States social psychologist who undertakes a cross-national study on a delicate subject without considerable advance knowledge of the countries is in serious need of ethical, if not psychiatric, counseling."

Second, an ethical problem arises when the funding for the cross-cultural study comes from a source devoted to political rather than scientific objectives. One is reminded here of the famous "Camelot" project where, supported by defense funding, the Research Office of the U.S. Army created a panel of social scientists aimed at creating a series of models into which could be fed data from accumulated historical and exploratory studies to identify types of social change, social conflict, and causal sequences in six countries, and to build models to predict social outcomes in those countries (Beals, 1969, pp. 6–7; Horowitz, 1981). The project was fortunately aborted in the planning stage, but, as put by Warwick: "It is clear, in retrospect that the design of the project involved a continuing tension between two sometimes incompatible sets of interests: those of the researchers, most of whom sought to explore generic questions of social change and political conflict; and those of the Army, which revolved around the practical questions of combating 'insurgency' in the developing countries" (Warwick, 1980, p. 325).

Third, an ethical problem arises when the behavior of the investigator infringes on the moral or ethical code of a given culture. "Recognizing cultural differences in what is experienced as stressful, embarrassing, or humiliating, the investigator should consult members of the host community about the potential for such reactions and the special areas of vulnerability for the host community and its members" (Tapp et al., 1974, p. 244).

Fourth, the research should be of benefit to humanity and the host community and local participation should be encouraged to ensure that the research does not damage colleagues and other members of the host community, and if local collaborators and the local research community wish to utilize the research findings, they are free to do so (Tapp et al., 1974, pp. 245–246). Failure to ensure the provision of these benefits presents an ethical problem in cross-cultural research. There is, however, the possibility that local researchers will not appreciate the potential benefits, especially given the general charge that "foreigners" can never understand the deeper meaning, the "true meaning," of a given national culture. Such charges have been made by Canadian critics of foreigners working in their universities; witness the following naive comments:

Immigrants who come to a country at mature age, especially with a completed formal education, *cannot* experience or know certain things about the country they come to. There is no point in singling out Joseph Conrad or Kenneth Galbraith as people who have crossed cultures and been successful. The generalization remains true. Generally speaking, immigrants coming mature, with their formal education completed, from foreign countries—especially chauvinistic foreign nations like the U.S.—cannot experience or know certain kinds of things about the country they come to. (Mathews, 1974, p. 61)

Canadian nationality is an essential condition of insight into Canadian society. . . . Canadian nationality, native or acquired, opens the door for an awareness of Canada's underclass, hinterland status in the American Empire. (Davis, 1974, p. 21)

Fifth, failure to secure adequate competence before engaging in cross-cultural research is also an ethical problem. "The investigator should maintain high standards of professional competence by not undertaking research without the necessary skills and knowledge, including sophistication in cross-cultural methodology and familiarity with the cultural context of the research setting. The investigator should exercise care in the selection of the measuring instruments, particularly when these are to be used for cross-cultural comparisons and in the interpretation of cultural differences (Davis, 1974, p. 21).

Sixth, one political and ethical problem of ethnocentrism arises when one "culturally dependent" scientific community uses its own paradigms to investigate problems in other cultures. Witness the reaction of the American-educated and -trained Chilean social psychologist Zuniga when trying to apply his professional skills to emerging reform programs in Chile:

A problem that was specific to the psychologists and that made their integration among the social sciences very difficult was the cultural homogeneity of their training or, to put it more bluntly, the unanalyzed "Americanness" of their science. Much of the theoretical background and the totality of the professional arsenal of Chilean psychologists was not only culturally derivative but also culturally dependent. . . . The ethnocentrism in the training of American *psychologists* which is ever-present but irrelevant for all practical purposes suffers a radical qualitative transformation when it is mechanically transported to a different cultural context. What was only a localized deficiency becomes a universalistic ideology and an unconscious (or guilt-ridden) advocacy of a cultural intrusion that is often extremely naive. It often isolates the psychologists from other social scientists with disciplines in which competing centers of production make comparative and critical modes of thought necessary. The production of psychologists is significantly more alienated from their national reality, and their dependency on culturally extrinsic thought patterns is often a source of friction with other disciplines. (Zuniga, 1975, p. 327)

The solutions to most of these political and ethical problems are summarized eloquently in Berrien's (1970, pp. 33–34) "superego" paper:

The best cross-cultural research is that which (1) engages the collaborative efforts of two or more investigators of different countries, each of whom is (2) strongly supported by institutions in their respective countries, to (3) address researchable problems of a common concern not only to the science of psychology but (4) relevant to the social problems of our time. Such collaborative enterprises would begin with (5) the joint definition of the problems, (6) employ comparable methods, (7) pool data that would be "owned" by the collaborators jointly who are free to (8) report their own interpretation to their own constituents but (9) are obliged to strive for interpretations acceptable to a world community of scholars.

"Etic" versus "Emic" Approaches in Cross-Cultural Research

A research strategy is best characterized by the way it treats the relationship between what people say and think as subjects and what they say and think and do as objects of scientific inquiry. The researcher may view the thoughts and behavior of participants from either (a) the perspective of the participants themselves, or (b) the perspective of the observers. The words "emic" and "etic," as introduced by Pike in *Language in Relation to a Unified Theory of the Structure of Human Behavior* (1967), allows such a distinction. He suggested that the linguistic distinction between phonemics and phonetics could be used to separate two different approaches to the study of cultural phenomena. Phonemics studies the sound in one particular language while phonetics focus on generalizing from phonemic studies in separate languages to a universal scheme relevant to all languages. Accordingly, the "emic" (from phonemics) differs from the "etic" (from phonetics) approach in cross-cultural research.

Berry (1969) characterizes the emic-etic distinction as follows:

Emic Approach	*Etic Approach*
studies behavior from within the system	studies behavior from a position outside the system

| examines only one culture structure discovered by the analyst | examines many cultures, comparing structure created by the analyst |
| criteria are relative to internal characteristics | criteria are considered absolute or universal |

The etic approach takes the perspective of the observer as the important ingredient for the generation of scientifically productive theories about the causes of sociocultural differences and similarities. Basically it studies behavior from outside the system, and examines facts from many cultures in order to extract common elements. It has been eloquently characterized as follows:

Rather than employ concepts that are necessarily real, meaningful, and appropriate from the native point of view, the observer is free to use alien categories and rules derived from the data language of science. Frequently, etic operations involve the measurement and juxtaposition of activities and events that native informants may find inappropriate or meaningless. (Harris, 1979, p. 321)

What it amounts to is that the person adopting the etic approach, as an outside researcher, has his/her own categories by which the subject world is organized. Extreme advocates of the etic approach elevate the researcher as the best judge of the adequacy of the description or the analysis and dismiss the subject's opinion as possibly interesting but not relevant (Harris, 1979). Cross-cultural research has warned against the use of a "pseudoetic" or, as Berry (1980) calls it, an "imposed etic" approach, which assumes that an emic dimension is etic when in fact there is no evidence to support the assertion. Triandis and Marin (1983, p. 490) give the example of taking an intelligence test to another culture without the construct-validation procedures outlined by Irvine and Carroll (1980) as an example of pseudoetic, given that cultures have different concepts of intelligence. Basically a pseudoetic approach would translate and use instruments composed of items reflecting Western conditions in other cultures with little regard for the reliability, validity, or relevance of the instrument in the new culture.

The emic approach takes the perception of the participants as the important ingredient for the generation of scientifically productive theories about a sociocultural system. Basically it studies behavior from within the cultural system centering on the native, that is, the insider's or the "informant's," view of reality, and is therefore based on data from any one culture. Extreme advocates of the emic approach elevate the subject as the best judge of the adequacy of the research and analysis and consider the subject's acceptance of the results of the research as a necessary and sufficient validation (Frake, 1980; Sturtevant, 1964). For example, *philotimo* is an emic concept that applies only in Greece. It refers to the extent to which the individual conforms to the expectation of his ingroup (Triandis and Triandis, 1968; Triandis, Davis, and Takezawa, 1965).

Emic research techniques, generally encompassed under the cover term of ethnoscience, include ethnosemantics, or ethnographic semantics, or ethnographic ethnoscience, formal analysis, and componential analysis (Morey and Luthams, 1984). Spradley has operationalized many of these techniques of ethnoscience in a series of books (Spradley, 1979, 1980; Spradley and McCurdy, 1972).

In the controversy centering on the choices of etic versus emic approaches, a consensus is emerging toward the use of combined etic and emic methods in cross-cultural research. For example, Pelto (1970) indicates that there is an "embedded Emicism" in most anthropological field work with a focus on the native viewpoints, meanings, and interpretations. It follows, however, that as the researcher starts moving inductively up the levels of analysis searching for universal categories, an etic approach emerges. The emic categories are added to the etic categories to allow for a testing of propositions about human behavior (Morey and Luthams, 1984, p. 30). Another example of the combination of the etic and emic measures is suggested by Triandis (1972) as a two-step approach: the first step for an elicitation of the concepts under study in both cultures, and the second step for an inclusion of the attributes that are common (etic) as well as frequently used in one culture but not in any other (emic).

Cross-cultural research in accounting will also be best served if it includes more emic (subjectivist/idiographic/qualitative/insider) perspectives to be later generally translated into etic (objectivist/quantitative/nomothetic/outsider) terms.

The Independent Variable in Cross-Cultural Research

The search for the independent variable in cross-cultural research is complicated by the vagueness and ambiguity of the "culture," a concept that is nothing more than a superordinate name for its component parts (Segall, 1982). Faucheux (1976, p. 278) asserted "that a theory of culture is not only possible but is essential for the social psychologist." While awaiting a theory of culture, Levine (1970, pp. 565–566) prescribes that cross-cultural research should start with the dependent variable:

Research into causal relations can begin with dependent or independent variables.... Starting with independent variables entails the risk that their effects will turn out to be trivial, irrelevant, or otherwise uninteresting according to the external criteria by which the scientist evaluates his research.... Beginning with dependent variables guarantees the scientist that his efforts will be directed toward explaining a phenomenon he considers important or interesting.

The truly interesting dependent variable that depicts differences in the ways people scattered all over the world react and/or act is what finally motivates the search for the independent variables. Culture, however, is composed of numerous, separable contextual dimensions. Each of the cultural dimensions can be thought of as the independent variable. Any of the variables that can provide a systematic fit is a candidate for a culture surrogate. One would then expect cross-cultural research to try each candidate for the independent variables of culture and eliminate all the competing hypotheses that do not provide a systemic fit. As concluded by Segall (1982, p. 124):

We can't expect culture, which is an inherently ambiguous concept, to serve as an independent variable. The independent variable is to be found among the numerous environmental factors, both physical and cultural, that provide the contexts in which all behaving humans live. In conducting our search among those factors, we should be guided by a search for adaptiveness, or for systemic fit.

Cross-Cultural versus Subcultural Research

Some of the research termed cross-cultural is better termed subcultural or cross-ethnic, where the emphasis is on various ethnic groups in the same country. An examination of accounting phenomena in the United States, using such major subcultural groups as blacks, Chicanos, and American Indians would qualify as subcultural research. Berry (1980) suggested the use of the "ethunit" for research done with ethnic groups within pluralistic societies. There is, however, the risk in subcultural research of simultaneously diminishing the levels of conceptual, functional, and metric equivalence that are the main requirements for making acceptable comparisons. As stated by Lonner (1979, p. 38):

A serious shortcoming of subcultural, cross-ethnic or cross-national research (to the extent that we are aiming for cross-cultural purity) is that the psychological variables or constructs chosen are for the most part so deeply confounded that any number of alternative hypotheses could account for the result.

Cultural Relativism versus the Convergence Hypothesis

Cross-cultural research in accounting is still in an early stage of scientific development. This assessment applies as well to comparative management research. Cross-cultural research aims at determining to what extent culture impacts on individual actions. There are, however, competing hypotheses in cross-cultural research. Cultural relativism or determinism holds that culture determines and/or influences management practices. As stated by Oberg: "Cultural differences from one country to another are more significant than many writers now appear to recognize. A [universalistic claim] is hardly warranted by either evidence or institution at this stage in the development of management theory" (as quoted in Berry, 1980, p. 1).

A competing hypothesis, known as the convergence hypothesis, maintains that people, irrespective of culture, are compelled to adopt industrial attitudes and behaviors such as rationalism, secularism, and mechanical time concerns in order to comply with the imperatives of industrialization (Kelly et al., 1987, p. 18). For example, Harbison and Myers maintained that managerial beliefs are correlated into the stages of industrial development (Harbison and Myers, 1959). The evidence on the convergence hypothesis is rather mixed. For example, Child provided evidence of convergence at the organizational level (e.g., structure, technology) but divergence at the personal level (e.g., culturally derived attitudes and values) (Child, 1981). Of sixteen studies examined, England and Lee (1974) found that eleven indicated that country and/or culture made a difference while three indicated that country and/or culture made little difference in the variables studied. Similarly, Laurent (1983), Hofstede (1983), and Redding and Martyn-Johns (1979) provided evidence of the important role of culture on attitudes, behaviors, and functions.

The controversy between cultural relativism and the convergence hypothesis concerning the importance of culture found itself illustrated in the theoretical models of Negandhi-Prasad and Farmer-Richman. While Farmer and Richman describe culture as a major variable in determining both managerial and organizational effectiveness, Negandhi and Prasad identified management philosophy as a major independent factor. Empirical investigation of both models identified a persistent effect of culture on managerial attitudes after successful isolation of the culture factor (Kelly, Whatley, and Worthley, 1987; Kelly and Worthley, 1981).

CULTURE AND ORGANIZATIONAL STUDIES

Organizations and Culture

Three main theories of organization are of interest in this study: (1) universal theories of organization, (2) political economy theory of organizations, and (3) cultural theory of organization (Tayeb, 1988). First, the universal theories of organization started with a bureaucracy as the rational and efficient model of organizations and "one best way" of organizing firms, to be challenged later on human relations grounds and a call for a focus on human needs and abilities. Both theories were challenged by the contingency perspective that focuses on the need for a "matching" between structural characteristics and contextual and other environmental variables (Lawrence and Lorsh, 1967). Factors considered to be important to the organizational structure included technology, size, environmental uncertainty, strategy, and dependence. Of particular interest to the report is the emergence within the contingency perspective of a universal "culture-free thesis" with the argument that the relationships between organizational characteristics and their contextual variables is stable across cultures. As noted by Hickson et al. (1974, pp. 63–64):

[Our] hypothesis rests on the theory that there are imperatives, or "causal" relationships, from the resources of "customers," of employees, of materials and finance, etc. . . . , and of operating technology, to its structure, which take effect whatever the surrounding social differences. . . . Whether the culture is Asian or European or North American, a large organization with many employees improves efficiency by specializing their activities but also by increasing controlling and coordinating specialties.

The "culture-free thesis" assumes a certain universalism by testing the stability of the relationship between organizational structure and its environmental variables. The focus is on similarities rather than differences in organizations operating in different cultures. Their methodology rely on concepts and indicators that are by definition universal and preclude the detection of cultural differences (Maurice, 1976).

Second, the political economy theory of organization proposes broad environmental factors as potential determinants of organizational structure and management practices. These include, for example, (a) the degree and process of industrialization (Harbison and Myers, 1959; Dore, 1973), (b) the macroeconomic structure (Child and Tayeb, 1983), and (c) the type of labor market (Friedman, 1977a, 1977b; Watson, 1980).

Third, the cultural theory of organization proposes the existence of cultural differences in organizational structure and management practices. Two strands of research emanated from this school: one, known as "the ideationalist," focuses on the attitudes and values expressed by organizational members; the other, known as "the institutionalist," focuses on structural aspects within organizations, such as the division of labor, career, status, and reward structures. An evaluation of cultural theory follows:

The major strength of the cultural perspective as a whole is its recognition of (a) the important role that culture plays in shaping work-related values, attitudes and behaviors of individual members of various societies; (b) the fact that cultural values and attitudes are different in degree from one society to another; and (c) the fact that different cultural groups behave differently under similar circumstances because of differences in their underlying values and attitudes. (Tayeb, 1988, p. 401)

Cross-Cultural Research Related to Organization

A review of the cross-cultural research related to organizations identified twenty-six substantive areas studied: attitudes and values; attitude change; bibliographies; conflict resolution and ethnocentrism; decision making and bargaining; economics; education, creativity, and intelligence; efficiency and productivity; general; international business; interpersonal behavior; labor; language and communication; leadership (small group); management; management development; motivation and achievement; national character and stereotypes; occupational prestige; organizational structure; perception; personality; personnel selection and testing; satisfaction; social and technical change; training for cross-cultural contacts (Roberts, 1970). This research was conducted either at the micro level, where the focus was on the effect of culture on individual attitudes or variables, or at the macro level, where the focus was on the effect of culture on organizational, structural, environmental, and transaction variables. Basically the dependent variable was either individual or organizational variables and the independent variable was culture. Two assumptions were implicit:

One underlying assumption is that we have a fairly adequate understanding of the variability in the dependent variable within a single culture, and that we have some reason to be interested in its range across cultures. Another assumption is that we know what the independent variable means. At least we should be able to define "culture," for without this definition, a theory of culture is impossible to derive. Without some theoretical notions explaining culture and predicting its effects on other variables, we cannot make sense of cross-cultural comparisons. The problem is to explain the effects of culture on behavior, not to make inferences about behavior in spite of culture. (Roberts, 1970, p. 330)

Cross-cultural research on microorganizational behavior has examined various issues including (a) cognitive style, (b) work motivation, and (c) job satisfaction (Bhagat and McQuaid, 1982). First, research on cognitive style focused on the cultural differences in the structural aspects of an individual's cognitive system. It relied on the concept of psychological differentiation introduced by Witkin, Dyk, Fakerson, Goodenough, and Karp (1974) and used by Witkin and Berry (1975) for an understanding of the effects of subjective culture on individual behavior in general. Known as the *theory of psychological differentiation*, it relies on a central construct of field dependence and field independence, to categorize people along the level of field articulation. Cultural differences were found in the level of field articulation among cultural groups in several countries (Greenfield, 1973).

Besides the concept of field dependence, another cognitive style approach known as "individual modernity" was used in cross-cultural research, with the purpose of explaining how cultures change from traditional to modern (Inkeles and Smith, 1974). Evidence was found of some impact of modernity for some behavioral responses in the organization.

Second, research on attitudes and values focuses on cultural differences rather than similarities in personal, work-related, and ancestral values and attitudes. Various studies focused on a clustering of countries in terms of managerial and worker attitudes and values. Ronen and Shenkar (1985) presented a recent review of the published literature on country clustering and proposed a map that integrates and synthesizes the available data. The variables examined in these clustering studies include: (a) work goals importance, (b) need deficiency, fulfillment, and job satisfaction, (c) managerial and organizational variables, and (d) work role and interpersonal orientation. The resulting clusters were found to discriminate on the basis of language, religion, and geography. Well-defined clusters were the Anglo, Germanic, Nordic, Latin-European, and Latin-American ones. Ill-defined clusters were those describing the Far East and Arab countries as well as countries described as independent (e.g., Israel and Japan). Areas in Africa have not been studied at all and those in the Middle East and the Far East have not been studied sufficiently. The review was, however, criticized by Blunt (1986) for alleged (a) ethnocentrism and (b) technocentrism defined as a lack of interdisciplinary approach in organizational studies.

Third, research on work motivation examined cross-cultural differences in motivation using one of the following theoretical bases: (a) Atkinson's version of expectancy theory, (b) McClelland's (1961) achievement motivation theory, (c) vocational and achievement-related motivation (Smith, Kendall, and Hubir, 1969), and (d) Adam's equity theory.

Fourth, research on job satisfaction focused on the cross-cultural differences in the relationship between satisfaction and other variables of interest, such as absenteeism or productivity. The studies relied on one of the following theoretical bases: Maslow's need theory, importance of various job dimensions (Sahili, 1979), frame-of-reference theory, environmental theory (Soliman, 1970), Herzberg's two-factor theory (Herzberg, Mausner, and Snyderman et al., 1959), and an "alienation hypothesis" (Hubir and Blood, 1968).

CONCLUSION

Cross-cultural research in accounting is urgently needed to establish the bounding conditions for accounting models and theories. Researchers in this new domain of accounting should, however, be aware of the cross-cultural research issues to ensure the validity of their endeavors.

REFERENCES

Adler, Nancy J. 1984. "Understanding the Ways of Understanding: Cross-Cultural Management Methodology Reviewed." In R. Farmer (ed.), *Advances in International Comparative Management*, Vol. 1, pp. 31–67. Stamford, Conn.: JAI Press.

Barry, H. 1965. "Cross-Cultural Research with Matched Pairs of Societies." *Journal of Social Psychology* October: 25–33.

Beals, R. L. 1969. *Politics of Social Research*. Chicago: Aldine.

Bendix, R. 1969. "Contributions of the Comparative Approach." In J. Boddewyn (ed.), *Comparative Management and Marketing*, pp. 10–13. Glenview, Ill.: Scott, Foresman.

Berrian, P. Kenneth. 1967. "Methodological and Related Problems in Cross-Cultural Research." *International Journal of Psychology* 2(1): 13–22.

Berrien, F. K. 1970. "A Super-Ego for Cross-Cultural Research." *International Journal of Psychology* 5: 33–34.

Berry, J. W. 1969. "On Cross-Cultural Research." *International Journal of Psychology* 4: 119–128.

———. 1979. "Research in Multicultural Societies: Implications of Cross-Cultural Methods." *Journal of Cross-Cultural Psychology* December: 415–434.

———. 1980. "Introduction to Methodology." In H. C. Triandis and J. W. Berry (eds.), *Handbook of Cross-Cultural Psychology*, Vol. 2. Boston: Allyn & Bacon.

Bhagat, Rabi S. and Sara J. McQuaid. 1982. "Role of Subjective Culture in Organizations: A Review and Directions for Future Research." *Journal of Applied Psychology Monograph* October: 155, 653–685.

Blunt, Peter. 1986. "Techo- and Ethnocentrism in Organizational Studies: Comment and Speculation Prompted by Ronen and Shenkar." *Academy of Management Review* 11(4): 857–859.

Brislin, R. W. 1970. "Back-Translation for Cross-Cultural Research." *Journal of Cross-Cultural Research* 1: 297–318.

———. 1976. *Translation: Application and Research*. New York: Gardner.

Brown, E. and L. Sechrest. 1980. "Experiments in Cross Cultural Research." In H. C. Triandis and J. W. Berry (eds.), *Handbook of Cross-Cultural Psychology-Methodology*, Vol. 2, pp. 297–318. Boston: Allyn & Bacon.

Campbell, D. T. and J. Stanley. 1966. *Experimental and Quasi-Experimental Design for Research*. New York: Rand-McNally.

Child, J. D. 1981. "Culture, Contingency and Capitalism in the Cross-National Study of Organizations." In L. L. Cummings and B. M. Staw (eds.), *Research in Organizational Behavior*, pp. 303–356. Stamford, Conn.: JAI Press.

Child, J. and M. H. Tayeb. 1983. "Theoretical Perspectives in Cross-National Organizational Research." *International Studies of Management and Organization* 12: 23–70.

Cole, M. and J. S. Bruner. 1971. "Cultural Differences and Inference about Psychological Processes." *American Psychologist* 26: 867–876.

Davidson, Andrew R. 1977. "The Etic-Emic Dilemma: Can Methodology Provide a Solution in the Absence of Theory?" In Y. H. Poortinga (ed.), *Basic Problems in Cross Cultural Psychology*. New York: Swets & Zeitlinger.

Davis, A. G. 1974. "Letter to the Editor." *Bulletin of the Canadian Association of University Teachers* 22: 21.

Deloria, V., Jr. (1969). *Custer Died for Your Sins: An Indian Manifesto*. New York: Collier-Macmillan.

Dore, R. 1973. *British Factory—Japanese Factory*. Boston: Allen & Unwin.

England, G. W. and R. Lee. 1974. "The Relationship between Managerial Values and Managerial Success in the United States, Japan, India, and Australia." *Journal of Applied Psychology* 59(4): 411–419.

Faucheux, C. (1976). "Cross-Cultural Research in Experimental Social Psychology." *European Journal of Social Psychology* 6: 278.

Frake, C. O. 1980. "Cultural Ecology and Ethnography." In S. A. Sil (ed.), *Language and Cultural Description: Essays by Charles O. Frake*, pp. 18–25. Stanford, Calif.: Stanford University Press.

Friedman, A. F. 1977a. *Industry and Labor*. New York: Macmillan.

———. 1977b. "Responsible Autonomy versus Direct Control over Labor Process." *Capital and Class* 1: 43–45.

Gambling, Trevor. 1983. "Magic, Accounting and Morale." *Accounting, Organizations and Society* July: 244–247.

Geertz, Clifford. 1973. *The Interpretation of Cultures*. New York: Basic Books.

Goodenough, Ward H. 1971. *Culture, Language and Society*. Reading, Mass.: Addison-Wesley.

Greenfeld, L. W. 1973. "Field Dependence and Field Independence as a Framework for the Study of Task and Social Orientations in Organizational Leadership." In D. Graves (ed.), *Management Research: A Cross-Cultural Perspective*. Amsterdam: Ekenei-North Holland Biomedical Press.

Harbison, F. and C. A. Myers. 1959. *Management in the Industrial World*. New York: McGraw-Hill.

Harris, Marvin. 1979. *Cultural Materialism: The Struggle for a Science of Culture*. New York: Random House.

Herzberg, F., B. Mausner, and B. Snyderman. 1959. *The Motivation to Work*. New York: Wiley.

Hickson, D. J., C. R. Hinnings, C. J. McMillan, and J. P. Schwitter. 1974. "The Culture Free Context of Organizational Structure: A Tri-National Comparison." *Sociology* 8: 63–64.

Hofstede, G. 1983. "The Cultural Relativity of Organizational Practices and Theories." *Journal of International Business Studies* Fall: 25–89.

Horowitz, Irving Louis. 1981. "The Life and Death of Project Camelot." In Jean Guillemin (ed.), *Anthropological Realities: Readings in the Science of Culture*, pp. 476–492. New York: Transaction Books.

Hubir, C. L. and M. R. Blood. 1968. "Job Enlargement, Individual Differences and Worker Responses." *Psychological Bulletin* 69: 41–55.

Inkeles, A. and D. H. Smith. 1974. *Becoming Modern: Individual Change in Six Developing Countries*. Cambridge, Mass.: Harvard University Press.

Irvine, S. H. and W. K. Carroll. 1980. "Testing and Assessment across Cultures: Issues in Methodology and Theory." In H. C. Triandis and J. W. Berry (eds.), *Handbook of Cross-Cultural Psychology*, Vol. 2. Boston: Allyn & Bacon.

Jahoda, G. 1965. "Psychology and Social Change in Developing Countries." In *Proceedings of the XVI International Congress of Applied Psychology*. New York: Swets & Zeitlinger.

Kelly, L., A. Whatley, and R. Worthley. 1987. "Assessing the Effects of Culture on Managerial Attitudes: A Three-Culture Test." *Journal of International Business Studies* Summer: 15–32.

Kelly, L. and R. Worthley. 1981. "The Role of Culture in Comparative Management: A Cross-Cultural Perspective." *Academy of Management Journal* March: 164–173.

Laurent, A. 1983. "The Cultural Diversity of Management Conceptions." *International Studies of Management and Organization* Spring: 22–31.

Lawrence, P. R. and J. W. Lorsh. 1967. *Organization and Environment: Managing Differentiation and Integration*. Cambridge, Mass.: Harvard University Press.

Levi-Strauss, Claude. 1983. *Structural Anthropology*. Chicago: University of Chicago Press.

Levine, R. A. 1970. "Cross-Cultural Study in Child Psychology." In Ph. H. Mussen (ed.), *Carmichael's Manual of Child Psychology*, Vol. 2. New York: Wiley.

Lonner, Walter J. 1979. "Issues in Cross-Cultural Psychology." In A. J. Marsella, R. G. Tharp, and T. J. Aborowski (eds.), *Perspective on Cross-Cultural Psychology*, pp. 38, 77. New York: Academic Press.

Malinowski, B. 1944. *A Scientific Theory of Culture*. Chapel Hill: University of North Carolina Press.

Malpass, R. S. 1977. "Theory and Method in Cross-Cultural Psychology." *American Psychologist* 32: 1069–1079.

Mathews, R. 1974. "Canadianization." *Bulletin of the Canadian Association of University Teachers* 23: 6.

Maurice, M. 1976. "Introduction: Theoretical and Ideological Aspects of the Universalistic Approach to the Study of Organizations." *International Studies of Management and Organization* 6: 3–10.

McClelland, D. C. 1961. *The Achieving Society*. New York: Van Nostrand.

Mitchell, R. E. 1969. "Survey Materials Collected in Developing Countries: Sampling, Measurement and Interviewing Obstacles to Intra- and International Comparisons." In J. Boddewyn Scott (ed.), *Comparative Management and Marketing*, pp. 232–252. Glenview, Ill.: Scott, Foresman.

Morey, Nancy C. and Fred Luthams. 1984. "An Ernie Perspective and Ethnoscience Methods for Organizational Research." *Academy of Management Review* 9(1): 27–36.

Naroll, R. 1968. "Some Thoughts on Comparative Methods in Cultural Anthropology." In H. M. Blalock and A. B. Blalock (eds.), *Methodology in Social Research*, pp. 236–277. New York: McGraw-Hill.

———. 1970/1973. "The Culture-Bearing Unit in Cross-Cultural Surveys." In R. Naroll and R. Cohen (eds.) *Handbook of Method in Cultural Anthropology*. New York: Columbia University Press.

Nath, R. 1968. "A Methodological Review of Cross-Cultural Management Research." *International Social Sciences Journal* 20(1): 37–61.

Pelto, P. J. 1970. *Anthropological Research: The Structure of Inquiry*. New York: Harper & Row.

Pike, K. L. 1967. *Language in Relation to a Unified Theory of the Structure of Human Behavior*, 2nd ed. New York: Morton.

Prezeworski, A. and H. Teune. 1970. *The Logic of Comparative Social Inquiry*. New York: Wiley.

Radcliffe-Brown, A. R. 1968. *Structure and Function in Primitive Society*. New York: Free Press.

Redding, G. S. and T. A. Martyn-Johns. 1979. "Paradigm Differences and Their Relation to Management, with Reference to South-East Asia." In *Organizational Functioning in a Cross-Cultural Perspective*. Miami, Ohio: CARI, Kent State University.

Riggs, R. W. 1969. "Trends in the Comparative Study of Public Administration." In J. Boddewyn (ed.), *Comparative Management and Marketing*, pp. 273–283. Glenview, Ill.: Scott, Foresman.

Roberts, K. H. 1970. "On Looking at an Elephant: An Evaluation of Cross-Cultural Research Related to Organization." *Psychological Bulletin* 74: 327–350.

Ronen, Swicha and Oded Shenkar. 1985. "Clustering Countries as Attitudinal Dimensions: A Review and Synthesis." *Academy of Management Review* 10(3): 435–454.

Ross, M. H. and E. Homer. 1976. "Gallon's Problem in Cross-National Research." *World Politics* October: 1–28.

Sahili, F. 1979. "Determinants of Achievement Motivation for Women in Developing Countries." *Journal of Vocational Behavior* 14: 297–305.

Sechrest, L. 1977. "On the Death of Theory in Cross-Cultural Psychology: There Is Madness in Our Method." In Y. H. Poortinga (ed.), *Basic Problems in Cross-Cultural Psychology*. New York: Swets & Zeitlinger.

Sechrest, L., T. Fay, and H. Zaidi. 1972. "Problems of Translation in Cross-Cultural Research." *Journal of Cross-Cultural Psychology* 3: 41–56.

Segall, M. S. 1982. "On the Search for Independent Variables in Cross-Cultural Psychology." In S. H. Irvine and J. W. Berry (eds.), *Human Assessment and Cultural Factors*. London: Academic Press.

Sekaran, Uma. 1983. "Methodological and Theoretical Issues and Advancements in Cross-Cultural Research." *Journal of International Business Studies* Fall: 62, 66–67.

Sekaran, U. and H. J. Martin. 1982. "An Examination of the Psychometric Properties of Some Commonly Researched Individual Differences, Job and Organizational Variables in the Cultures." *Journal of International Business Studies* Spring: 51–66.

Sekaran, U. and R. S. Trafton. 1978. "The Dimensionality of Jobs: Back to Square One." *Twenty-First Midwest Academy of Management* 15: 249–262.

Smircich, Linda. 1983. "Concepts of Culture and Organizational Analysis." *Administrative Science Quarterly* 28: 339–358.

Smith, P. C., L. M. Kendall, and C. L. Hubir. 1969. *The Measurement of Satisfaction in Work and Retirement: A Strategy for the Study of Attitudes*. Chicago: Rand McNally.

Soliman, H. 1970. "Motivation-Hygiene Theory of Job Satisfaction: An Empirical Investigation and an Attempt to Reconcile Both the One- and Two-Factor Theories of Job Attitudes." *Journal of Applied Psychology* 54: 452–461.

Spradley, J. P. 1979. *The Ethnographic Interview*. New York: Holt, Rinehart & Winston.

———. 1980. *Participant Observation*. New York: Holt, Rinehart & Winston.

Spradley, J. P. and D. W. McCurdy. 1972. *The Cultural Experience: Ethnography in Complex Society*. Chicago: Science Research Associates.

Strauss, M. A. 1968. "Society as a Variable in Comparative Study of the Family by Replication and Secondary Analysis." *Journal of Marriage and Family* 30: 565–570.

Strodtbeck, F. L. 1964. "Considerations of Metamethod in Cross-Cultural Studies." *American Anthropologist* 66 (part 2): 223–229.

Sturtevant, W. C. 1964. "Studies in Ethnoscience." In A. K. Ronney and R. G. D'Andrade (eds.), *Transcultural Studies in Cognition*, pp. 99–131. New York: American Anthropologist Special Publication.

Swartz, Marc J. and David K. Jordan. 1980. *Culture: The Anthropological Perspective*. New York: Wiley.

Tapp, June Louis, H. C. Kelman, H. C. Triandis, L. S. Wrightsman, and G. V. Coellue. 1974. "Continuing Concerns in Cross-Cultural Ethics: A Report." *International Journal of Psychology* 9(3): 15–32.

Tayeb, Monir H. 1988. *Organizations and National Culture: A Comparative Analysis*. Beverly Hills, Calif.: Sage.

Triandis, H. C. 1972. *The Analysis of Subjective Culture*. New York: Wiley.

———. 1980. "Introduction to Cross-Cultural Psychology." In H. C. Triandis and W. W. Lambert (eds.), *Handbook of Cross-Cultural Psychology*. Boston: Allyn & Bacon.

Triandis, H. C., E. E. Davis, and S. I. Takezawa. 1965. "Some Determinants of Social Distance among American, German and Japanese Students." *Journal of Personality and Social Psychology* 2: 540–551.

Triandis, H. C. and R. S. Malpass. 1970. *Field Guide for the Study of Subjective Culture*. Urbana: University of Illinois Press.

Triandis, Harry C., Roy S. Malpass, and Andrew R. Davidson. 1972. "Cross-Cultural Psychology." In B. J. Siegel (ed.), *Biennial Review of Anthropology 1971*. Stanford, Calif.: Stanford University Press.

Triandis, Harry C. and Gerardo Marin. 1983. "Etic plus Emic versus Psendoetic: A Test of a Basic Assumption of Contemporary Cross-Cultural Psychology." *Journal of Cross-Cultural Psychology* 14 (4): 489–500.

Triandis, H. C. and L. M. Triandis. 1968. "A Cross-Cultural Study of Social Distance." *Psychological Monographs* 76: 62–71.

Triandis, H. C., V. Vassilion, G. Vassilion, Y. Tanaka, and A. V. Shanmugam. 1972. *The Analysis of Subjective Culture*. New York: Wiley.

Turner, Stephen P. 1977. "Complex Organizations as Savage Tribes." *Journal of the Theory of Social Behavior* 7: 99–125.

Vigderhous, G. 1978. "Methodological Problems Confronting Cross-Cultural Criminological Research Using Official Data." *Human Relations* March: 229–247.

Wagner, P. L. 1969. "On Classifying Economics." In J. Boddewyn (ed.), *Comparative Management and Marketing*, pp. 122–134. Glenview, Ill.: Scott, Foresman.

Warwick, Donald P. 1980. "The Politics and Ethics of Cross-Cultural Research." In H. C. Triandis and W. W. Lambert (eds.), *Handbook of Cross-Cultural Psychology*. Boston: Allyn & Bacon.

Watson, T. O. 1980. *Sociology, Work and Industry*. London: Routledge & Kegan Paul.

Whiting, J.W.M. 1968. "Methods and Problems in Cross-Cultural Research." In G. Lindzey and E. Aronson (eds.), *The Handbook of Social Psychology*. Reading, Mass.: Addison-Wesley.

Wilier, D. 1967. *Scientific Sociology: Theory and Method*. Englewood Cliffs, N.J.: Prentice-Hall.

Witkin, H. A. and J. W. Berry. 1975. "Psychological Differentiation in a Cross-Cultural Perspective." *Journal of Cross-Cultural Psychology* 6: 4–87.

Witkin, H. A., R. B. Dyk, H. F. Fakerson, E. R. Goodenough, and S. A. Karp. 1974. *Psychological Differentiation*. New York: Erlbaum.

Zuniga, R. B. 1975. "The Experimenting Society and Radical Social Reform: The Role of the Social Scientist in Child's Unidad Popular Experience." *American Psychologist* 30: 71–83.

17
Cultural Determinism and Systematic Risk of Global Stock Exchanges

INTRODUCTION

Viewing countries as stock portfolios in a global market, asset pricing theory suggests that cross-sectional differences in countries' risk exposures explain the cross-sectional variation in expected returns (Harvey and Zhou, 1993). This evidence begs a more crucial question. In a world with increasing integrated financial services, why do industrialized countries have different systematic risks? While economic and political risks may easily appear as candidates for providing an answer, they are themselves a by-product of the cultural dimensions present in each country. Culture is viewed as the key determinant of the economic and political atmosphere and the important determinant of the systematic risk of the global stock exchanges of industrialized countries. This study seeks to examine this cultural determinism thesis for the explanation of differences in systematic risks. The hypothesis is that the observed difference in countries' risk exposures is attributable to culture.

CULTURAL AND COUNTRY RISK

Culture is the basis of anthropological research. Anthropologists differ in the exact meaning of culture, although they generally agree that it is learned rather than biologically transmitted, that it is shared by the members of a group, and

This chapter is adapted from "Cultural Determinism and Systematic Risk of Global Stock Exchanges" by Ahmed Riahi-Belkaoui. *International Journal of Commerce and Management* 8 (1998): 102–108. Used by permission of *International Journal of Commerce and Management*.

it is the foundation of the human way of life (Swartz and Jordan, 1980, p. 8). There are various concepts of culture. In functionalism, culture is viewed as an instrument serving biological and psychological needs (Malinowski, 1944). In structural functionalism, culture is viewed as an adaptive regulatory mechanism that unites individuals in social structures (Radcliffe-Brown, 1968). In ethnoscience, culture may be viewed as a system of shared cognition whereby the human mind generates culture by means of a finite number of rules (Goodenough, 1971). In symbolic anthropology, culture is viewed as a system of shared symbols and meanings (Geertz, 1973). In structuralism, culture is viewed as a projection of mind's universal unconscious infrastructure (Levi-Strauss, 1983). Using any of these definitions, culture appears as a formidable instrument for shaping social environments in different countries. One crucial element of the social environment is the risk exposure of the global stock exchanges. This study uses this cultural determinism to investigate the observed differences in countries' risk exposures or systematic risk. More specifically, four cultural dimensions proposed by Hofstede (1991), namely, power distance, individualism, masculinity, and uncertainty avoidance, are investigated in terms of their impact on the level of systematic risk of global stock exchanges. They can be explained as follows.

Large versus small power distance is a dimension that represents the extent to which less powerful members of institutions and organizations within a country expect and accept that power is distributed unequally (Hofstede, 1991, p. 28). In large power distance societies, there is a tendency for people to accept a hierarchical order in which everybody has a place that needs no justification whereas in small power distance, there is a tendency for people to ask for equality and demand justification for any existing power inequalities.

Individualism versus collectivism is a dimension that represents the degree of integration a society maintains among its members. While individualists are expected to take care of themselves and their immediate families only, collectivists are expected to remain emotionally linked in cohesive groups that protect them in exchange for unquestioning loyalty. In individualist societies, individual interests prevail over collective interests and the economy is based on these individual interests (Hofstede, 1991, p. 78).

Masculinity versus femininity is a dimension that represents the nature of social divisions of sex roles. Masculine roles imply a preference for achievement, assertiveness, making money, sympathy for the strong, and so forth. Feminine roles imply a preference for warm relationships, modesty, care for the weak, preservation of the environment, quality of life, and so forth. In masculine societies the dominant values in society are material success and progress; they also stress equity, competition among colleagues, and performance (Hofstede, 1991, p. 96).

Strong versus weak uncertainty avoidance is a dimension that represents the degree to which members of a society feel uncomfortable with uncertain and ambiguous situations. In strong uncertainty avoidance societies, people are intolerant of ambiguity and try to control it at all cost, whereas in weak uncertainty avoidance, people are more tolerant of ambiguity and accept living with it. In strong uncertainty avoidance societies there is a focus on many precise laws and rules that cannot be changed.

The systematic risk of a country captures that aspect of investment that cannot be eliminated by diversification. The cultural dimensions of large power distance, individualism, masculinity, and lower uncertainty avoidance are likely to create an economic, social, and political climate conducive to frequent instability in the capital market and therefore to higher systematic risk. Accordingly, the following four hypotheses are offered for testing:

H_1: The greater the power distance within a society, the higher the level of systematic risk of its stock exchange.

H_2: The greater the individualism within a society, the higher the level of systematic risk of its stock exchange.

H_3: The greater the masculinity within a society, the higher the level of systematic risk of its stock exchange.

H_4: The greater the uncertainty avoidance within a society, the lower the level of systematic risk of its stock exchange.

PROCEDURES

Methodology and Sample

The independent variable in this study is the level of systematic risk of stock exchanges. Independent variables are the four dimensions identified by Hofstede (1991) as reflecting the cultural orientations of a country. These are individualism versus collectivism, large versus small power distance, strong versus weak uncertainty avoidance, and masculinity versus femininity.

To be included in our sample a country must have available data to the dependent and independent variables. Sixteen countries met this test. They are shown in Exhibit 17.1. The cultural scores are derived from Hofstede (1991).

Country Risk

To compute the country return and risk, Harvey and Zhou (1993) relied on the data from Morgan Stanley Capital International (MSCI) on equity indices for sixteen OECD countries and Hong Kong available from December 1969 to May 1989. These indices are value weighted and calculated with dividend reinvestment. A value-weighted world equity index that serves as the market portfolio is also available from Morgan Stanley. The MSCI international indices include stocks that broadly represent stock composition in different countries.

The country returns are computed in excess of the U.S. Treasury bill that is

Exhibit 17.1
Data Used

Stock Exchange (Country)	Country Return	Market Model Systematic Risk(1)	Unsystematic Risk	Cultural Scores			
				PDI(2)	IDV(3)	MAS(4)	UNA(5)
1. Sydney (Australia)	0.423	1.1254 (0.160)	-0.0015 (0.004)	36	90	61	51
2. Vienna (Austria)	0.550	0.3741 (0.075)	0.0036 (0.003)	11	55	79	70
3. Toronto (Canada)	0.447	1.0428 (0.071)	-0.0008 (0.002)	39	80	52	48
4. Copenhagen (Denmark)	0.715	0.6150 (0.081)	0.0040 (0.003)	18	74	16	23
5. Paris (France)	0.658	1.0667 (0.093)	0.0012 (0.003)	68	71	43	86
6. Frankfurt (Germany)	0.477	0.7799 (0.086)	0.0008 (0.003)	35	67	66	65
7. Hong Kong (Hong Kong)	1.699	1.2247 (0.193)	0.0108 (0.007)	68	25	57	29
8. Milan (Italy)	0.235	0.7639 (0.0102)	-0.0015 (0.004)	50	76	70	75
9. Tokyo (Japan)	1.326	0.9184 (0.093)	0.0086 (0.003)	54	46	95	92
10. Amsterdam (The Netherlands)	0.739	0.9837 (0.068)	0.0024 (0.002)	38	80	14	53
11. Oslo (Norway)	0.940	0.9882 (0.130)	0.0044 (0.004)	31	69	58	50
12. Madrid (Spain)	0.368	0.6344 (0.106)	0.0005 (0.003)	57	51	49	86
13. Stockholm (Sweden)	0.915	0.7407 (0.087)	0.0054 (0.003)	31	71	5	29
14. Zurich (Switzerland)	0.447	0.9162 (0.075)	-0.0002 (0.002)	34	68	70	58
15. London (United Kingdom)	0.728	1.2627 (0.147)	0.0009 (0.003)	35	89	66	35
16. New York (United States)	0.339	0.9733 (0.042)	-0.0015 (0.001)	40	51	62	46

Notes: [1]Standard errors are in parentheses; [2]power distance index; [3]individualism index; [4]masculinity index; [5]uncertainty avoidance index.

closest to thirty days to maturity on the last trading day of the month. The return data are shown in Exhibit 17.1.

The country risks are computed on the basis of ordinary least-square regressions of the country index excess returns (calculated in U.S. dollars) on the excess return on the world market portfolio. The regressions are based on monthly data from January 1970 to May 1989. The country risks obtained from the regressions are shown in Exhibit 17.1.

RESULTS AND DISCUSSION

A multiple-regression analysis was used to determine the association between the country systematic risk with the cultural dimensions of power distance, uncertainty avoidance, individualism, and masculinity. Exhibit 17.2 presents the results of the regressions.

The effect of the independent variable of masculinity was not significant but

Exhibit 17.2
Results of Cross-Sectional Regression

Dependent Variable F Value	Intercept	Power Distance	Individualism Index	Masculinity Index	Uncertainty Avoidance	R^2
Systematic Risk 5.752	0.2400	0.0129	0.0058	0.0023	-0.0068	0.6765
B		(0.3874)	(4.339)[*] (2.303)[**]	(1.366)	(-2.986)	

Notes: *Significant at 0.01 **Significant at 0.05

had the correct sign. The three independent variables of power distance, individualism, and uncertainty avoidance were significant and had the correct sign. As hypothesized, power distance and individualism were positively related to a country's systematic risk while uncertainty avoidance was negatively related. The overall regression was significant (*F* significant at $\alpha = 0.05$) and the four independent variables explained 67.65 percent of the variations in the systematic risk of stock exchanges.

The results of the study suggest that the systematic risk of stock exchanges is positively influenced by power distance and individualism dimensions and negatively influenced by uncertainty avoidance. Basically, societies in which people accept a hierarchical order in which everyone has a place that needs no justification, is expected to take care of himself and his immediate family, and is tolerant of ambiguity have strong conditions for high systematic risk. These results support the cultural determinism thesis and contribute to an explanation of the international differences in the systematic risk of stock exchanges. Basically, cultural differences in the level of systematic risk of stock exchanges from one country to another are significant. An unrealistic claim is not warranted on the basis of this evidence and at this stage in the integration of stock exchanges internationally. This cultural determinism is not to be taken as a fixed phenomenon. A competing hypothesis, known as the convergence hypothesis, maintains that cultural and managerial beliefs are correlated with stages of industrial development (Harbison and Myers, 1959; Kelly Whatley, and Worthley, 1987). One could expect that as countries reach similar stages of development and as capital markets get more integrated, the level of systematic risk among countries would tend to converge. Further research is needed to test the cultural determinism versus the convergence hypothesis by examining the changes in the level of systematic risk of stock exchanges and changes in the stages of industrial development internationally.

REFERENCES

Fedenia, M., J. E. Hodder, and A. J. Triantis. 1991. *Cross-Holding and Market Return Measures*. Stanford, Calif.: Graduate School of Business, Stanford University.
French, K. R. and J. M. Poterba. 1991. "Were Japanese Stock Prices Too High?" *Journal of Financial Economics* 29: 337–363.

Geertz, C. 1973. *The Interpretation of Cultures.* San Francisco: Basic Books.

Goodenough, W. H. 1971. *Culture, Language and Society.* Reading, Mass.: Addison-Wesley.

Harbison, F. and C. A. Myers. 1959. *Management in the Industrialized World.* New York: McGraw-Hill.

Harvey, C. R. 1991. "The World Price of Covariance Risk." *Journal of Finance* 46: 111–157.

Harvey, C. R. and G. Zhou. 1993. "International Asset Pricing with Alternative Distributional Specifications." *Journal of Empirical Finance* June: 107–131.

Hofstede, G. 1991. *Cultures and Organizations: Software of the Mind.* London: McGraw-Hill.

Kelly, L., A. Whatley, and R. Worthley. 1987. "Assessing the Effects of Culture on Managerial Attitudes: A Three Culture Test." *Journal of International Business Studies* Summer: 17–31.

Levi-Strauss, C. 1983. *Structural Anthropology.* Chicago: University of Chicago Press.

Malinowski, B. 1994. *A Scientific Theory of Culture.* Chapel Hill: University of North Carolina Press.

McDonald, Jack. 1989. "The Mochiai Effect: Japanese Corporate Cross Holding." *Journal of Portfolio Management* 15: 90–94.

Radcliffe-Brown, A. R. 1968. *Structure and Function in Primitive Society.* New York: Free Press.

Swartz, M. J. and D. K. Jordan. 1980. *Culture: The Anthropological Perspective.* New York: Wiley.

18

Cultural Determinism and Compensation Practices

INTRODUCTION

Labor cost is a major determinant of the competitiveness of firms in the global economy. Research to date reveals a wide range of compensation practices in different countries within the same industries (Tung, 1981; White, 1981; Hashimoto and Raisian, 1985; Nelson and Reeder, 1985; Bowey and Thorpe, 1986). These variations in compensation practices can be an important factor in firms' decisions on new investments on their production and/or distribution facilities, favoring countries with lower compensation practices. An understanding of the international differences in compensation practices can be useful for multinational corporations in meeting employees' expectations about pay equity. Townsend et al. (1990) show the differences in pay policies to be dependent on culture based on the cultural cluster model described by Ronen and Shenkar (1985). While the cultural cluster model has some merits in segmenting countries into culturally related groups for purposes of understanding work values and the relationship of culture to those values, it fails to account for the intracultural differences that make every nation a specific subcultural entity. Following this concern with the level of "national culture," Hofstede (1980, 1983, 1991) empirically identified four dimensions of national value patterns. Accordingly, these four cultural dimensions as proposed by Hofstede are investigated in terms of their impact on compensation practices internationally.

This chapter is adapted from "Cultural Determinism and Compensation Practices" by Ahmed Riahi-Belkaoui. *International Journal of Commerce and Management* 4, no. 3 (1994): 76–83. Used by permission of *International Journal of Commerce and Management*.

THEORETICAL JUSTIFICATION AND HYPOTHESES

Culture is "the learned, socially acquired traditions, and life styles of the members of a society, including their patterned, repetitious way of thinking, feeling, and acting (i.e., behaving)" (Harris, 1979, p. 6). It has been considered as an important environmental factor affecting business practices. It has also been argued that business practices are in fact determined by the culture of the country (Riahi-Belkaoui et al., 1991). The argument reflects a cultural determinism in international management and accounting. This study uses the first part of the cultural determinism thesis to investigate the observed international differences in the level of compensation. More specifically, the four cultural dimensions proposed by Hofstede, namely: (a) power distance, (b) individualism, (c) masculinity, and (d) uncertainty avoidance, are investigated in terms of their impact on the level of compensation internationally. Four hypotheses are proposed:

H_1: The greater the power distance within a society, the lower the level of compensation.

Large versus small power distance centers on the issue of inequality within a society. It is a dimension that represents the extent to which power in institutions and organizations is distributed unequally. Large power distance societies freely accept a hierarchical order in which everybody has a place that needs no justification, whereas small power distance societies demand equality and justification for any existing power inequalities. Therefore, the greater the power distance within a society, the greater is the compliance with the hierarchical order and the acceptance of the unequal distribution of power, and consequently, the lower is the level of compensation. Individuals in large power distance societies will refrain from asking for equality and from demanding justification for any existing power inequalities, which make them more amenable to accept lower levels of compensation than individuals in small power distance societies.

H_2: The greater the uncertainty avoidance within a society, the higher the level of compensation.

Strong versus weak uncertainty avoidance centers on the issue of anxiety within a society due to uncertainty about the future. It is a dimension that represents the degree to which members of a society feel uncomfortable with uncertain and ambiguous situations. In strong uncertainty avoidance societies, people are intolerant of ambiguity and try to control it at all cost whereas in weak uncertainty avoidance societies, people are more tolerant of ambiguity and accept living with it. Therefore, the greater the uncertainty avoidance within a society, the greater its intolerance of ambiguity created by lower levels of compensation and the greater the need to control it. Lower levels of compensation would thrive best in weak uncertainty avoidance societies which are flexible enough to accept living with the ambiguities created by the low compensation practices.

H₃: The greater the individualism within a society, the lower the level of compensation.

Individualism versus collectivism centers on the relationships between the individual and the collectivity prevailing in a given society. It is a dimension that represents the degree of integration a society maintains among its members. In collectivist societies, individuals remain emotionally integrated in cohesive groups, like unions or professions, which protect them in exchange for unquestioning loyalty. In individualist societies, people are more concerned with themselves and their families and claim to be able to take care of themselves. The reality is that the concessions on compensation are best obtained when groups rather than separate individuals bargain for a level of compensation. One would expect a higher level of compensation in collectivist societies.

H₄: The greater the "masculinity" within a society, the higher the level of compensation.

"Masculinity" versus "femininity" is a dimension that represents the nature of social divisions of sex roles. Masculine roles as often defined in the West imply a preference for achievement, assertiveness, making money, sympathy for the strong, and so forth. Feminine roles imply a preference for warm relationships, modesty, care for the weak, preservation of the environment, quality of life, and so forth. Masculine societies are tough competitive societies where individuals place a high value on achievement and the acquisition of money as a measure of strength. One would expect the masculine societies to value a higher level of compensation than feminine societies.

PROCEDURES

The analyses relied on regressions between measures of compensation on one hand and values for the four cultural dimensions of power distance, individualism, uncertainty avoidance, and masculinity on the other hand.

The compensation measures were derived from a compensation cost report prepared by the U.S. Department of Labor, Bureau of Labor Statistics, Office of Productivity and Technology (1990). The data included international comparisons of hourly compensation costs, hourly direct pay, and pay for time worked for production workers in manufacturing in thirty-four countries or areas. Accordingly, hourly compensation costs, pay for time worked, and hourly direct pay were used as dependent variables. They are defined as follows:

Exhibit 18.1
List of Countries Used

1. Australia	12. Hong Kong	23. Pakistan
2. Austria	13. India	24. Portugal
3. Belgium	14. Ireland	25. Singapore
4. Brazil	15. Israel	26. Spain
5. Canada	16. Italy	27. Sweden
6. Denmark	17. Japan	28. Switzerland
7. Finland	18. Korea	29. Taiwan
8. France	19. Mexico	30. Turkey
9. Germany	20. Netherlands	31. United States
10. Great Britain	21. Norway	32. Venezuela
11. Greece	22. New Zealand	

Hourly compensation is defined as: (1) all payments made directly to the worker, before payroll deductions of any kind; and (2) employer social insurance expenditures, that is, expenditures for legally required insurance programs and contractual and private benefit plans. This variable is measured on an hours-worked basis for every country.

Hourly direct pay includes pay for time worked (basic time and piece rates plus overtime premiums, shift differentials, other premiums and bonuses paid regularly each pay period, and cost-of-living adjustments), and other direct pay—pay for time not worked (vacations, holidays, and other leave, except sick leave), seasonal or irregular bonuses and other special payments, selected social allowances, and the cost of payments in kind, before deductions of any kind. This variable is also measured on an hours-worked basis for every country.

Pay for time worked includes only basic time and piece rates, overtime premiums, shift differentials, other premiums and bonuses paid regularly each pay period, and cost-of-living adjustments.

These three measures of compensation are measured on an hour-worked basis for every country. The independent variables were the four dimensions identified by Hofstede (1983) as reflecting the cultural orientations of a country. To be included in our sample a country must have available data to measure both the dependent and independent variables used in this study. Thirty-two countries met this test. They are shown in Exhibit 18.1.

RESULTS AND DISCUSSION

Multiple regression analyses were used to determine the association between three measures of compensation and the cultural dimensions of power distance, uncertainty avoidance, individualism, and masculinity. Exhibits 18.2–4 present the results of the regressions. The effects of the independent variable of power distance was neither significant nor had the right sign. The three independent variables of uncertainty avoidance, individualism, and masculinity were significant and had the correct sign in the three cases and for the five years examined.

Exhibit 18.2
Pay for the Time Worked in U.S. Dollars

	1985	1986	1987	1988	1989
Intercept	1.6240	1.7050	2.8590	3.0087	2.1860
	(1.1290)	(1.3620)	(1.7470)***	(1.8170)***	(1.4520)
Power Distance	-0.0130	-0.0070	-0.0044	-0.0065	-0.0048
	(-0.9940)	(-0.6170)	(-0.2860)	(-0.4180)	(-0.3390)
Uncertainty Avoidance	0.0440	0.0410	0.0399	0.0402	0.0590
	(2.6390)	(2.8400)*	(2.0920)**	(2.0850)**	(3.3630)
Individualism	-0.0111	-0.0180	-0.0370	-0.0320	-0.0370
	(-0.7860)	(-1.4920)	(-2.2970)	(-2.0030)***	(-2.5320)**
Masculinity	0.0001	0.0002	0.0002	0.0003	0.0003
	(2.1440)**	(4.0410)*	(3.7500)*	(4.2590)*	(4.3940)*
R^2	61.88%	76.80%	73.64%	75.83%	81.79%
F	5.682*	11.580	9.779*	10.979*	15.650*

*   **Significant at $\alpha = 0.01$**
**   **Significant at $\alpha = 0.05$**
*** **Significant at $\alpha = 0.10$**

Exhibit 18.3
Pay for the Time Worked in U.S. Dollars

	1985	1986	1987	1988	1989
Intercept	0.4581	-0.1420	0.0046	0.3970	9.8900
	(0.4450)	(-0.1330)	(0.0030)	(0.2640)	(1.6890)***
Power Distance	-0.0050	0.0051	0.0104	0.0099	0.1680
	(-0.4970)	(0.4890)	(0.7420)	(0.6700)	(2.9100)*
Uncertainty Avoidance	0.0472	0.0440	0.0450	0.0449	0.1250
	(3.6164)*	(3.1340)*	(2.3980)**	(2.2580)**	(1.6210)
Individualism	-0.0090	-0.0169	-0.0300	-0.0310	-0.0990
	(0.8500)	(-1.4330)	(-1.9130)***	(-1.8660)***	(-1.5290)
Masculinity	0.0002	0.0004	0.0005	0.0005	0.0000
	(4.7380)*	(7.2970)*	(7.0920)*	(7.1970)*	(-0.7160)
R^2	85.53%	89.00%	87.24%	87.27%	36.80%
F	26.620*	42.480*	35.907*	35.920*	3.057**

*   **Significant at $\alpha = 0.01$**
**   **Significant at $\alpha = 0.05$**
*** **Significant at $\alpha = 0.10$**

As hypothesized, the level of compensation, as measured by hourly compensation, pay for time worked, and hourly direct pay, was negatively related to individualism and positively related to both uncertainty avoidance and masculinity. The overall regression was also highly significant for all cases and for the five years examined (F significant at $\alpha = 0.01$), and the four independent

Exhibit 18.4
Pay for the Time Worked in U.S. Dollars

	1985	1986	1987	1988	1989
Intercept	0.2490	-0.7570	-0.7910	-0.3380	0.3930
	(0.2090)	(-0.5590)	(0.4370)	(-0.1860)	(0.2310)
Power	0.0018	0.0187	0.0285	0.0289	0.0262
Distance	(0.1590)	(1.4070)	(1.5990)	(1.6160)	(1.5660)
Uncertainty	0.0639	0.6350	0.0671	0.0688	0.0747
Avoidance	(4.0560)*	(3.5390)*	(2.7990)*	(2.8570)*	(3.3250)*
Individualism	-0.0191	-0.0304	-0.0487	-0.0519	0.0551
	(-8.4530)**	(-2.0350)**	(-2.4340)**	(-2.5820)*	(-2.9350)*
Masculinity	0.0003	0.0005	0.0006	0.0006	0.0006
	(4.9700)*	(7.0.250)*	(6.8300)*	(7.2920)*	(7.2240)*
R^2	85.51%	88.86%	87.12%	88.32%	89.08%
F	30.980*	41.861*	35.500*	39.710*	42.820*

* Significant at $\alpha = 0.01$
** Significant at $\alpha = 0.05$

variables explain a significant proportion of the variations in the level of compensation (a minimum R^2 of 36.08 percent and a maximum R^2 of 89 percent). The results of the study suggest that the level of compensation internationally is negatively influenced by individualism and positively by both uncertainty avoidance and masculinity. Basically, societies where people are collectivist in their relations with others, intolerant of ambiguity, and show a preference for competitiveness, achievement motivation, assertiveness, and the enjoyment of material success have strong conditions for a high level of compensation.

These results support the cultural determinism thesis in setting compensation practices, and contribute to an explanation of the differences in international compensation practices. Basically, cultural differences in the level of compensation from one country to another are significant. These results support previous findings and are centered on Ronen's and Shenkar's (1985) model and on the Townsend group's work (1990). The results show, however, that there are differences in the cost of labor between countries within a culture depending on the level of three of the cultural dimensions provided by Hofstede (1980, 1983). Labor costs are not only determined by market forces but are also influenced by the cultural dimensions of individualism, uncertainty avoidance, and masculinity. The results refute the assertion that employment practices are only marginally affected by cultural affiliation (Neghandi, 1973). This cultural determinism thesis is not to be taken, however, as a fixed phenomenon. In the long run, people, irrespective of their culture, may be compelled to provided similar levels of compensation to comply with similar imperatives of industrialization (Kelly et al., 1987).

This competing hypothesis, generally labeled the convergence hypothesis, argues for the convergence of managerial practices and stages of industrial development (Harbison and Myers, 1959). It calls for an investigation of the relationships between changes in the level of compensation and changes in the stages of industrial development internationally. Another worthwhile avenue of research is to investigate the combined effect of cultural and economic variables on compensation practices internationally.

REFERENCES

Bowey, A. and R. Thorpe. 1986. *Payment Systems and Productivity*. New York: St. Martin's.

Harbison, F. and C. A. Myers. 1959. *Management in the Industrial World*. New York: McGraw-Hill.

Harris, M. 1979. *Cultural Materialism*. New York: Random House.

Hashimoto, M. and J. Raisian. 1985. "Employment Tenure and Earnings Profiles in Japan and the United States." *American Economic Review* September: 721–735.

Hofstede, G. 1980. *Culture's Consequences: International Differences in Work Related Values*. Beverly Hills, Calif.: Sage Publications.

———. 1983. "Dimensions of National Cultures in Fifty Countries and Three Regions." In J. B. Deregowski, S. Dziurawiee, and R. C. Annis (eds.), *Explications in Cross-Cultural Psychology*, pp. 335–355. Lisse, The Netherlands: Soviets & Zeilinger.

———. 1991. *Cultures and Organizations: Software of the Mind*. London: McGraw-Hill.

Kelly, L., A. Whatley, and R. Worthley. 1987. "Assessing the Effects of Culture on Managerial Attitudes: A Three Culture Test." *Journal of International Business Studies* Summer: 17–31.

Neghandi, A. 1973. "Cross Cultural Studies: Too Many Conclusions." In A. Neghandi (ed.), *Modern Organizational Theory*. Kent, Ohio: Kent State University Press.

Nelson, J. and J. Reeder. 1985. "Labor Relations in China." *California Management Review* 27(4): 13–32.

Riahi-Belkaoui, A., C. Perochon, M. A. Mathews, B. Bemardi, and Y. A. El-Adly. 1991. "Report of the Cultural Studies and Accounting Research Committee of the International Accounting Section." *Advances in International Accounting* 4: 175–198.

Ronen, S. and O. Shenkar. 1985. "Clustering Countries on Attitudinal Dimensions: A Review and Synthesis." *Academy of Management Review* 10: 435–454.

Townsend, A. M., K. D. Scott, and S. E. Marrkham. 1990. "An Examination of Country and Culture-Based Differences in Compensation Practices." *Journal of International Business Studies* 21(4): 667–678

Tung, R. 1981. "Patterns of Motivation in Chinese Industrial Enterprises." *Academy of Management Review* 6(3): 15–34.

White, M. 1981. *Payment Systems in Britain*. Aldershot, U.K.: Gower.

19

Cultural Determinism and Professional Self-Regulation in Accounting: A Comparative Ranking

INTRODUCTION

Regulation of accounting standard setting and of the accounting profession is recognized internationally as a way of securing the reliability of accounting statements (Buckley and Weston, 1980). The type of regulation differs from one country to another varying in general in the degree of professional self-regulation (Al-Hashim, 1980; Gray et al., 1984). The hypothesis of this paper is that these differences are attributable to culture. Culture is "the learned, socially acquired traditions and life styles of the members of a society, including their patterned, repetitive way of thinking, feeling and acting (i.e., behaving)" (Harris, 1971, p. 15).

Culture has been considered an important environmental factor impacting the accounting environment of the country (Mueller, 1967; Nobes 1983, 1984; Hofstede, 1987; Schreuder, 1987; Belkaoui, 1984, 1985, 1988, 1989, Perera and Mathews, 1987). It has also been argued that (a) accounting is in fact determined by the culture of the country (Violet, 1983), and (b) the lack of consensus across different countries on what represents proper accounting methods is because the purpose of accounting is cultural not technical (Hofstede, 1985). These arguments reflect a cultural determinism in accounting, in the sense that the culture of a given country determines the type of standard setting and working of accounting institutions. This study uses the latter part of the cultural determinism

Adapted from Ahmed Riahi-Belkaoui, "Cultural Determinism and Professional Self-Regulation of Accounting Concepts" *Research in Accounting Regulation* Vol. 3, copyright 1989, pp. 93–101, with permission from Elsevier Science.

thesis in accounting to investigate the observed differences in professional self-regulation internationally. More specifically, four cultural dimensions proposed by Hofstede (1983), namely (a) individualism, (b) power distance, (c) uncertainty avoidance, and (d) masculinity, are investigated in terms of their impact on the degree of professional self-regulation of the accounting profession internationally.

THEORETICAL JUSTIFICATION AND HYPOTHESES

Culture has been defined as the collective mental programming, a part of the conditioning that people of a nation share among themselves but not with members of other regions, nations, or groups (Hofstede, 1983, p. 337). Hofstede identified four dimensions that reflect the cultural orientations of a country and explain 50 percent of the differences in value systems among countries (Hofstede, 1980, 1983). These are: (a) individualism versus collectivism, (b) large versus small power distance, (c) strong versus weak uncertainty avoidance, and (d) masculinity versus femininity.

Individualism versus collectivism is a dimension that represents the degree of integration a society maintains among its members. While individualists are expected to take care of themselves and their immediate families only, collectivists are expected to remain emotionally linked in cohesive groups that protect them in exchange for unquestioning loyalty.

Large versus small power distance is a dimension that represents the extent to which members of a society accept the fact that power in institutions and organizations is distributed unequally. In large power distance societies, there is a tendency for people to accept a hierarchical order in which everybody has a place that needs no justification, whereas in small power distance, there is a tendency for people to ask for equality and demand justification for any existing power inequalities.

Strong versus weak uncertainty avoidance is a dimension that represents the degree to which the members of a society feel uncomfortable with uncertain and ambiguous situations. In strong uncertainty avoidance societies, people are intolerant of ambiguity and try to control it at all cost, whereas in weak uncertainty avoidance, people are more tolerant of ambiguity and accept living with it.

Masculinity versus femininity is a dimension that represents the nature of social divisions of sex roles. Masculine roles imply a preference for achievement, assertiveness, making money, sympathy for the strong and so forth. Feminine roles imply a preference for warm relationships, modesty, care for the weak, preservation of the environment, quality of life, and so forth.

The cultural determinism thesis espoused in this study postulates that these four cultural dimensions determine the degree of professional self-regulation in accounting internationally as depicted in Exhibit 19.1. Four hypotheses are proposed:

Exhibit 19.1
Model of Accounting Professional Self-Regulation

Cultural Dimensions

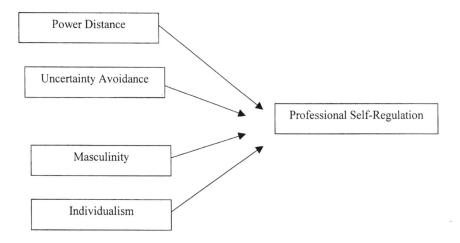

H₁: The greater the power distance within a society, the lower is the degree of professional self-regulation in accounting.

In effect, the greater the power distance within a society, the greater is the compliance with legal requirements, statutory control, and governmental regulation, and consequently the lower the degree of professional self-regulation in general and in accounting in particular. Gray (1985) argued that the degree of professionalism preferred in an accounting context would influence the nature of authority for the accounting system. Professionalism works best when there is a preference for the exercise of individual professional judgment and the maintenance of self-regulation. Accordingly, Gray (1985) argued for a negative relationship between professionalism and uncertainty avoidance.

H₂: The greater the uncertainty avoidance within a society, the lower the degree of professional self-regulation in accounting.

In effect, the greater the uncertainty avoidance within a society, the greater its intolerance of the ambiguity created by professional autonomy and independence and the greater the need to control through governmental regulation. Professional self-regulation in general and in accounting in particular would thrive best in weak uncertainty avoidance societies that are flexible enough to accept the ambiguities created by the professional autonomy of the profession and to accept living with them. Hofstede (1987, p. 8) argued that in large power distance countries, the accounting system will be used more frequently to justify the decisions of top power holders, and as a tool to present the desired image and to twist the figures to this end. The described scenario calls for weak professional self-regulation and a loss of independence by the accounting profession.

H₃: The greater the individualism within a society, the lower the degree of professional self-regulation in accounting.

Professional membership arises partly from the need of professionals to remain emotionally integrated into cohesive groups, like a profession, which protect them in exchange for unquestioning loyalty. In individualist societies, the need for professionalism and professional self-regulation is less pronounced as the individuals claim to be able to take care of themselves.

H₄: The greater the masculinity within a society, the higher the degree of professional self-regulation in accounting.

In a masculine society characterized by competitiveness, achievement motivation, assertiveness, and the enjoyment of material success, the professions need to be able to protect their members' trade monopoly, achievement, and the nature and quality of their service, hence a strong need for self-regulation. Only then can the profession create the appropriate institutional arrangement to harness both the egoistic motives for career success and altruistic motives for helping others, and to channel them into professionally competent behavior (Merton, 1982).

PROCEDURES

Methodology and Sample

The dependent variable in this study is a professional self-regulation score. Independent variables were the four dimensions identified by Hofstede (1983) as reflecting the cultural orientations of a country. These are: (a) individualism versus collectivism, (b) large versus small power distance, (c) strong versus weak uncertainty avoidance, and (d) masculinity versus femininity.

To be included in our sample a country must have available data to measure both the dependent and independent variables. Twenty-eight countries met this test. They are shown in Exhibit 19.2.

Variable Measurement

A recent study presented a survey of international accounting principles and techniques and environmental conditions (Gray, Campbell, and Shaw, 1984;

Exhibit 19.2
Countries and Professional Self-Regulation Score

Countries	Professional Self-Regulation Score	Countries	Professional Self-Regulation Score
Argentina	2	Malaysia	2
Australia	3	Mexico	3
Belgium	2	New Zealand	3
Brazil	1	Philippines	3
Chile	2	Portugal	1
Colombia	2	South Africa	2
Denmark	2	Spain	1
Finland	1	Switzerland	3
France	1	Thailand	3
Germany	2	United Kingdom	3
Indonesia	2	United States	3
Ireland	3	Uruguay	1
Italy	1	Zambia	3
Japan	2	Zimbabwe	3

hereafter GCS). The first chapter of the GCS database included questions on influences on accounting development. The extent of professional self-regulation was determined by the following question: "To what extent can it be said that the government keeps its intervention to a minimum relying instead on self-regulation within the financial community (based on professional standards, training, and a high standard of ethical behavior)?" There were three kinds of professional self-regulation for this study: (1) high, (2) medium, and (3) low. For the purposes of this study these levels were coded as follows:

Classification	Professional Self-Regulation Score
1. High	3
2. Medium	2
3. Low	1

The professional self-regulation scores are shown in Exhibit 19.1. The independent variables of individualism, power distance, uncertainty avoidance, and masculinity were provided in Hofstede's study of the dimensions of national cultures in fifty countries and three regions (Hofstede, 1983).

RESULTS AND DISCUSSION

A multiple-regression analysis was used to determine the association between the professional self-regulation score with the cultural dimensions of power distance, uncertainty avoidance, individualism, and masculinity. The use of a discontinuous dependent variable creates, however, three problems: nonnormal error terms, nonconstant error variance, and constraint on the response function. When the error term is not normal, the least-squares method still provides un-

Exhibit 19.3
Regression Results

Independent	Intercept	Power Distance	Uncertainty Avoidance	Individualism	Masculinity
Coefficients	3.3909	-0.0068	-0.0206	-0.0215	0.0188
T statistic	5.10*	-0.99	-3.94*	-2.38**	2.74*
R^2	51.06%				
F	6.26*				
N	28				

Note: *Significant at $\alpha = 0.01$; **significant at $\alpha = 0.05$.

biased estimates, which under general conditions are asymptotically normal (Neter and Wasserman, 1974, pp. 323). The solution adopted for the other two problems was to use a weighted least-squares method. Exhibit 19.3 presents the results of the regression.

The effect of the independent variable of power distance was not significant but had the correct sign. The three independent variables of uncertainty avoidance, individualism, and masculinity were significant and had the correct sign. As hypothesized, uncertainty avoidance and individualism were negatively related to the extent of professional self-regulation while masculinity was positively related. The overall regression was also significant (*F* significant at $\alpha = 0.01$) and the four independent variables explain 51.06 percent of the variations in the dependent variable of professional self-regulation.

The results of the study suggest that the degree of professional self-regulation in accounting internationally is negatively influenced by the uncertainty avoidance and individualism dimensions and positively by the masculinity dimension. Basically, societies where people are essentially tolerant of ambiguity, are collectivist in their relations with others and show a preference for competitiveness, achievement motivation, assertiveness, and the enjoyment of material success have strong conditions for professional self-regulation. This result supports the cultural determinism in accounting, and contributes to an explanation of the difference in the degree of professional self-regulation internationally. Basically, cultural differences in the degree of professional self-regulation from one country to another are significant. A universalistic claim is not warranted on the basis of this evidence and at this stage in the development of professional self-regulation internationally. One consequence of this situation is the difficulty countries may encounter in their efforts to harmonize accounting and auditing principles and facilitate the exchange of accounting services internationally. This cultural determinism is not to be taken, however, as a fixed phenomenon. In the long run, people, irrespective of culture, may be compelled to adopt industrial attitudes and behaviors such as rationalism, secularism, and mechanical time concerns in order to comply with the imperatives of industrialization (Kelly, Whatley and Worthley, 1987). This competing hypothesis, known as the convergence hypothesis, maintains that basically managerial beliefs are correlated with stages of industrial development (Harbison and Myers, 1959).

As a result of these changes, one may expect in the future a convergence toward a greater degree of professional self-regulation in accounting as countries reach similar stages of industrial development. Further research is needed to test the cultural determinism versus the convergence hypothesis by examining the relationships between the changes in the degree of professional self-regulation in accounting and changes in the stages of industrial development internationally.

REFERENCES

Al-Hashim, Ahia. 1980. "Regulation of Financial Accounting: An International Perspective." *International Journal of Accounting* Fall: 47–68.

Belkaoui, Ahmed. 1984. *Public Policy and the Problems and Practices of Accounting.* Westport, Conn.: Greenwood Press.

———. 1985. *International Accounting.* Westport, Conn.: Greenwood Press.

———. 1988. *The New Environment in International Accounting.* Westport, Conn.: Quorum Books.

———. 1989. *International Accounting.* Westport, Conn.: Greenwood Press.

Buckley, J. W. and J. P. Weston. 1980. *Regulation and the Accounting Profession.* Belmont, Calif.: Lifetime Learning Publications.

Gray, S. J. 1985. "Cultural Influences and the International Classification of Accounting Systems." Paper presented at EIASM Workshop on "Accounting and Culture," Amsterdam, June.

Gray, S. J., L. G. Campbell, and J. C. Shaw. 1984. *Information Disclosure and the Multinational Corporation.* Chichester: Wiley.

Harbison, F. and C. A. Myers. 1959. *Management in the Industrial World.* New York: McGraw-Hill.

Harris, M. 1971. *Culture, Man and Nature.* New York: Thomas Y. Crowell.

Hofstede, Geert. 1980. *Culture's Consequences: International Differences in Work-Related Values.* Beverly Hills, Calif.: Sage Publications.

———. 1983. "Dimensions of National Cultures in Fifty Countries and Three Regions." In J. B. Deregowski, S. Dziurawiec, and R. C. Annis (eds.), *Explications in Cross-Cultural Psychology*, pp. 335–355. Lisse, The Netherlands: Soviets & Zeilinger.

———. 1985. "The Ritual Nature of Accounting Systems." Paper presented at EIASM Workshop on "Accounting and Culture," Amsterdam, June 5–7.

———. 1987. "The Cultural Context of Accounting." In Barry E. Cusing (ed.), *Accounting and Culture*, pp. 1–11. Sarasota, Fla.: American Accounting Association.

Kelly, L., A. Whatley, and R. Worthley. 1987. "Assessing the Effects of Culture on Managerial Attitudes: A Three Culture Test." *Journal of International Business Studies* Summer: 17–31.

Merton, R. K. 1982. *Social Research and the Practicing Professions.* Cambridge, Mass.: Abt Books.

Mueller, Gerhard G. 1967. *International Accounting.* New York: Macmillan.

Neter, John and William Wasserman. 1974. *Applied Linear Statistical Models.* Homewood, Ill.: Irwin.

Nobes, C. W. 1983. "A Judgmental International Classification of Financial Reporting Practices." *Journal of Business Finance and Accounting* Spring: 15–33.

————. 1984. *International Classification of Financial Reporting*. London: Croom Helm.

Perera, M.H.B. and M. R. Mathews. 1987. "The Interrelationship of Culture and Accounting with Particular Reference to Social Accounting." Discussion Paper No. 59, Palmerston, N.Z.: Massey University, Department of Accounting and Finance.

Schreuder, Hein. 1987. "Accounting Research, Practice and Culture: A European Perspective." In Barry E. Cushing (ed.), *Accounting and Culture*, pp. 12–22. Sarasota, Fla.: American Accounting Association.

Violet, William J. 1983. "The Development of International Accounting Standards: An Anthropological Perspective." *International Journal of Accounting, Education and Research* Spring: 1–13.

20
Cultural Determinism and the Perception of Accounting Concepts

INTRODUCTION

Culture has been considered an important environmental factor influencing the accounting system of the country (Mueller, 1967; Nobes, 1983, 1984; Hofstede, 1987; Schreuder, 1987). It was also argued that (a) accounting is in fact determined by culture (Violet, 1983), and (b) the lack of consensus across different countries as to what represents proper accounting methods is because their purpose is cultural not technical (Hofstede, 1985). These arguments represent an acceptance of a cultural determinism in accounting whereby the culture of a given country determines the choice of its accounting techniques and the perception of its various accounting phenomena. This study investigates the hypothesis that accountants from different cultural groups will have different perceptions of accounting phenomena. Specifically using a concept perception experiment, we found differences in perceptions of accounting concepts among managers and partners from the same Big Six CPA firm.

While several previous empirical and conceptual studies have examined the impact of national culture on accounting (Soeters and Schreuder, 1988; Chevalier, 1977; Acheson, 1972; Alhashim, 1973; Beazley, 1968; McComb, 1979; Bromwich and Hopwood, 1983; Choi and Mueller, 1984; Belkaoui, 1983, 1985a), we introduce a cognitive perspective to explain the different perceptions of accounting concepts by participants from different cultural groups.

This chapter is adapted from "Cultural Determinism and the Perception of Accounting Concepts" by Ahmed Riahi-Belkaoui and Ronald D. Picur. *International Journal of Accounting* 26 (1991): 118–130. Used by permission of CIERA.

THEORETICAL JUSTIFICATION AND HYPOTHESES

The concept of culture is not monolithic (Perera and Mathews, 1987). Each of the concepts of "culture" from anthropology created different metaphors and ends in organizational research (Smircich, 1983, p. 342). Malinowski's functionalism, with its view of culture as an instrument serving human biological and psychological needs, motivated cross-cultural or comparative management research (Malinowski, 1944). Radcliffe-Brown's structuralism, with its view of culture as an adaptive regulatory mechanism that unites individuals in social structures, motivated research on corporate culture (Radcliffe-Brown, 1968). Goodenough's ethnoscience, with its view of culture as a system of shared cognitions where the human mind generates culture by means of finite number of rules, motivated research on organizational cognition (Goodenough, 1971; Frake, 1968; Bock, 1980). Geertz's symbolic anthropology, with its view of culture as a system of shared symbols and meanings where symbolic action needs to be interpreted, read, or deciphered in order to be understood, motivated research on organizational symbolism (Geertz, 1973). Finally, Levi-Strauss's structuralism, with its view of culture as a projection of mind's universal unconscious infrastructure, motivated research on unconscious processes and organization (Levi-Strauss, 1983).

The interest in this chapter is concept perception; therefore, a cognitive functioning view of culture is adopted to explicate cultural determinism in accounting. Culture is viewed as a system of shared cognitions or a system of knowledge and beliefs: "a unique system for perceiving and organizing materials, phenomena, things, events, behaviors and emotions" (Goodenough, quoted in Rossi and O'Higgins, 1980, p. 63). It is generated in the human mind "by means of a finite number of rules or means of unconscious logic" (Rossi and O'Higgins, 1980, pp. 63–64).

Using the cognitive emphasis, national cultures act as networks of subjective meanings or frames of reference that members of each culture share to varying degrees and that, to an external observer, appear to function in a rule-like or grammar-like manner. Relating this to accounting and the cultural determinism thesis in accounting, we assume that different cultural groups in accounting create different cognitions or systems of knowledge for intracultural communications and/or intercultural communications. These, in turn, lead to a different understanding of accounting relationships. This led to the following research question: "Are the perceptions of accounting concepts, as measured by the individual weights assigned by the participants to the dimensions of a common perceptual space, a function of the cultural group membership?"

Multidimensional scaling techniques are used to evaluate the differences in accounting concept perceptions by participants from different cultural groups within the accounting profession. The presumed differences may be a function of certain psychological, perceptual, and background variables. The variables examined are: (1) the subject's age, (2) his/her academic degree, (3) his/her familiarity with financial statements, (4) the number of years of experience with the CPA firm, and (5) the number of years in the present position.

METHOD

Sample

The choice of subjects in our field experiment was motivated by the need to isolate the impact of national culture on the perception of accounting concepts from the potential impact of organizational culture and linguistic relativism. To control for the impact of organizational culture, respondents were recruited from three offices of the same international Big Six accounting firm, with a strong U.S. orientation in organizational philosophies and policies (Soeters and Schreuder, 1988). To control for the impact of linguistic relativism, the three offices were chosen in three Anglophone cities, namely Chicago, London, and Toronto. Therefore, English-speaking partners or managers from the local offices of a Big Six international firm located in three different national cultures, U.S., British, and Canadian, were asked to participate in our study and to indicate their perceptions of accounting concepts. The main difference in the subjects that may influence their perception of accounting concepts was the difference in their national culture.

A questionnaire was given to an official at the headquarters of the Big Six firm, who agreed to coordinate the distribution of the questionnaires in the three cities and to return them to the researchers. The official was instructed to include as respondents only the employees of the firm in the three cities who:

a. were active in the accounting and auditing practice (thus excluding tax and consulting practice as well as administrative and other supporting staff);
b. had reached the manager or partner level;
c. were born in the national culture of the country where the local office is located.

These criteria produced a population of 87 respondents composed of 47 U.S., 21 British, and 19 Canadian partners or managers.

Research Instrument

Subjects in the three cultural groups were given the same questionnaire written in English (Exhibit 20.1). The questionnaire required subjects to assign similarity judgments to paired sets of twelve concepts. In multidimensional scaling techniques, such similarity judgments are interpreted as "psychological distances" representing a "mental map" through which respondents view pairs of concepts that are "near" each other as similar and pairs of concepts that are "far apart" as dissimilar. If numerical measures are provided for the similarity judg-

Exhibit 20.1
Questionnaire

1. Name: _____
2. Age: _____
3. Area of Undergraduate Studies: _____
4. Number of Accounting Courses Taken: _____
5.

Based on your background and experience, indicate the degree of importance you would assign to each piece of the following information when comparing the financial performance of two firms.

Circle the number corresponding to your evaluation.

	NOT IMPORTANT						EXTREMELY IMPORTANT
Balance Sheet	1	2	3	4	5	6	7
Profit and Loss Statement	1	2	3	4	5	6	7
Funds Flow Statement	1	2	3	4	5	6	7

6. Consider the Following Accounting Hypotheses
   Hypothesis   No. 1 Entity Assumption
                     No. 2 Going Concern Assumption
                     No. 3 Stable Monetary Unit Assumption
                     No. 4 Period Assumption
                     No. 5 Cost Principle
                     No. 6 Revenue Principle
                     No. 7 Matching Principle
                     No. 8 Objectivity Principle
                     No. 9 Consistency Principle
                     No. 10 Full Disclosure Principle
                     No. 11 Materiality Principle
                     No. 12 Conservatism Principle

Assuming you are familiar with these accounting hypotheses, indicate the degree of similarity of each pair of concepts. The criteria to be used are left to your discretion - be consistent in your evaluation.
Example: If you think that hypotheses 1 and 2 are very dissimilar accounting concepts, circle 1.

Hypothesis 1 & Hypothesis 2

Very
Dissimilar   1   2   3   4   5   6   7   Very
                                                Similar

Hypothesis 1 & Hypothesis 3

Very
Dissimilar   1   2   3   4   5   6   7   Very
                                                Similar

Exhibit 20.1 (continued)

Hypothesis 1 & Hypothesis 4

| Very Dissimilar | <u>1</u> | 2 | <u>3</u> | <u>4</u> | <u>5</u> | <u>6</u> | <u>7</u> | Very Similar |

Hypothesis 10 & Hypothesis 11

| Very Dissimilar | <u>1</u> | 2 | 3 | 4 | 5 | 6 | 7 | Very Similar |

Hypothesis 10 & Hypothesis 12

| Very Dissimilar | <u>1</u> | 2 | 3 | 4 | 5 | 6 | <u>7</u> | Very Similar |

Hypothesis 11 & Hypothesis 1

| Very Dissimilar | <u>1</u> | 2 | <u>3</u> | <u>4</u> | <u>5</u> | 6 | <u>7</u> | Very Similar |

Hypothesis 11 & Hypothesis 12

| Very Dissimilar | <u>1</u> | 2 | <u>3</u> | <u>4</u> | <u>5</u> | 6 | 7 | Very Similar |

7. List the criteria used for assigning similarities in question no. 3.
   - _____
   - _____
   - _____
   - _____

8. Please provide the following background information.
   1. What year were you born? 19___.
   2. To the nearest year, how many years have you been employed in this firm? ___ years.
   3. To the nearest year, how many years have you been employed in the present position? ___ years.
   4. Describe the exact nature of the activities of your department or group. Be specific.

   _____
   _____
   _____
   _____

   5. The results of this research will be mailed to you if you indicate your name and address:

   _____
   _____
   _____

9. Thank you very much for your cooperation and support.

ments, multidimensional scaling techniques may be used to construct a "physical" multidimensional map whose interpoint distances closely relate to the input data.

One of the multidimensional scaling techniques used in the study is the TORSCA nonmetric scaling routine (Young, 1968). Given $\frac{n(n-1)}{2}$ similarity/dissimilarity measures, the TORSCA program first yields a set of orthogonal coordinates for the final configuration and then estimates the dimensionality of the data. The other algorithm used in this study is the INDSCAL model (Caroll and Chang, 1970). In contrast to the TORSCA solution, the stimulus configuration obtained from the INDSCAL algorithm is uniquely oriented. The INDSCAL model assumes that all individuals share a common perceptual space but assigns differential weights or saliences to the different dimensions of the group's stimulus space. The individual saliences provide an operational measure for an evaluation of the possible inter- and intracultural group perceptual differences.

Both these multidimensional scaling techniques, the TORSCA and INDSCAL models, were applied to individual similarity judgments to estimate the dimensions of the common perceptual space and each respondent's salience was then used to measure the relation between salience and selected background variables, which included the subject's age, the number of years employed in the firm, and the number of years employed in the present position.

Professional Concepts and Experimental Decisions

The twelve concepts used in the study were chosen to reflect two categories of accounting concepts of relevance to accounting theory construction. The terms "going concern," "entity," "stable monetary unit," and "periodicity" represent underlying assumptions of accounting theory, while the terms "cost principle," "revenue principle," "matching principle," "objectivity principle," "consistency principle," "full-disclosure principle," "materiality principle," and "conservatism principle" represent generally accepted accounting principles within the profession (Belkaoui, 1985a).

Each of the participants was asked to do the following: (1) provide information on certain background variables, (2) for each of the financial statements, assign familiarity rating ranging from "not familiar" to "extremely familiar," (3) for each of the pairs of twelve concepts used as stimuli, assign an integer rating on a seven-point scale ranging from "very dissimilar" to "very similar," and (4) list the criteria used for assigning the similarities.

Procedure

The input to the TORSCA is a single rank-ordered similarity matrix computed by averaging the cell ranks obtained across all participants. The measure of departure from perfect fit, the "stress of the configuration," is used. As suggested by Kruskal (1964a, 1964b), the departure from perfect fit (stress = 0) can be expressed as follows: 0.025 excellent; 0.05 good; 0.10 fair. The input to the INDSCAL is the $87 \times 12 \times 12$ matrix of similarity judgments for all participants. The measure of fit used is the squared correlation in distances (RSQ). The RSQ values are the proportion of variance of the scaled data (disparities) in the partition (row, matrix, or entire data) that is accounted for by their corresponding distances.

Both TORSCA and INDSCAL will yield a set of dimensions of a common configuration that need to be identified. One way to identify the dimensions is the "maximum congruence" method of Miller, Shepard and Chang (1969). The method correlates the coordinates of the solution with ratings obtained from the respondents on a set of candidate attributes. This method was not used in this study as the provision of a set of candidate attributes may potentially influence the responses of the subjects in their similarity rating task toward one single way of thinking. The method used in this study was to ask the participants to state in order of importance the criteria used in mating their similarity judgments. The rationale is that in assigning similarity ratings among concepts, a process of concept perception is generally used, consisting of either the recognition of shared or linked characteristics in the accounting concepts (stimulus generalization) or the recognition of shared differences (stimulus discrimination). In either case, the process of concept formation results in the grouping of experiences into conceptual classes on the basis of similarities in their characteristics (McDavid and Harari, 1974, pp. 78–79). Hunt and Hovland (1960) classified the concepts as being conjunctive, relational, or disjunctive. Conjunctive concepts are perceived as those sharing common perceptual characteristics. Relational concepts are those linked by some fixed relationships. Finally, disjunctive concepts are those concepts that differ on the basis of one or more characteristics.

RESULTS

Preliminary Findings

The use of TORSCA resulted in the average stress indices of 0.356, 0.092, and 0.868 for two, three, and four dimensions, respectively. Based on these results, a "goodness of fit" is provided by three dimensions (stress 1.10). Kruskal considered a stress index under 0.10 to be fair. In addition, Klahr (1969), measuring stress indices from random data, concluded that for twelve stimuli there was only a 5 percent chance that a solution is random, if the stress index is not greater than 0.118. The use of INDSCAL produced an RSQ of 0.965 for three dimensions. On the basis of these findings on stress and RSQ measures, the three-dimensional solution will be used in this study. Exhibit 20.2 shows the graphical portrayal of the three-dimensional solution.

Exhibit 20.2
Stimulus Configuration

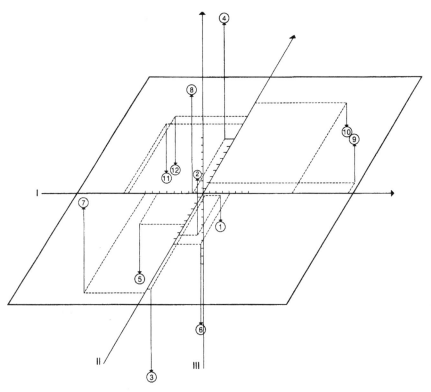

Note: I. Relational dimension; II. conjunctive dimension; III. disjunctive dimension; 1. entity as-
    sumption; 2. going concern assumption; 3. stable monetary unit assumption; 4. period as-
    sumption; 5. cost principle; 6. revenue principle; 7. matching principle; 8. objectivity principle;
    9. consistency principle; 10. full-disclosure principle; 11. materiality principle; 12. conservatism
    principle.

Identification of Perceptual Dimensions

The participants had indicated the criteria they used in making their similarity
judgments. An examination of the participants' answers revealed a consensus
toward assigning similarity judgments on the basis of the existence or absence
of common perceptual qualities between each pair of accounting concepts. An
examination of the answers showed evidence of a process of concept formation
used by the participants. It follows that the three-way concept perception classification is used to identify the three dimensions obtained in the INDSCAL
model solution listed in Exhibit 20.3 and portrayed in Exhibit 20.2.

An examination of the stimulus configuration in Exhibit 20.2 shows, for example, stable monetary unit and objectivity principle and consistency and ma-

Exhibit 20.3
Accounting Concepts' Salience in Three-Dimensional Space

Accounting Concepts	Salience		
	Dimension 1	Dimension 2	Dimension 3
1. The entity assumption	0.2413	-0.0190	0.3497
2. The going concern assumption	0.2353	-0.5982	0.8683
3. The stable monetary unit assumption	0.0022	-1.4585	-1.3549
4. The period assumption	-0.1446	0.9082	1.8595
5. The cost principle	-0.7469	-0.5209	-0.7631
6. The revenue principle	0.3756	-0.7796	-1.2843
7. The matching principle	-0.9497	-1.6190	1.3517
8. The objectivity principle	-0.2063	-0.0455	0.1575
9. The consistency principle	2.2555	0.2260	0.6949
10. The full disclosure principle	1.4267	1.4771	-0.3862
11. The materiality principle	-1.2672	1.1718	-0.7412
12. The conservation principle	-1.2220	1.2576	0.7518

teriality on opposite sides of dimension III. Similarly, revenue and cost principles and entity and objectivity are on opposite and equal sides of dimension I. Finally, materiality and conservatism and entity and going concern are the same equal side of dimension II. On the basis of these extrastatistical findings, dimension I may be labeled as the relational dimension, dimension II as the conjunctive dimension, and dimension II as the disjunctive dimension.

Intergroup Perceptual Differences

The INDSCAL model provides weights or saliences that each participant assigned to each of the three dimensions. A one-way analysis of variance for the three cultural groups of participants is used to determine whether they have different saliences on each of the three dimensions. The results of the analysis of variance are portrayed in Exhibit 20.4. The hypothesis of no differences in the intercultural group perceptual differences is rejected for both the conjunctive and relational dimensions, but not for the disjunctive dimension (at a level of confidence $\alpha = 0.10$). Basically, the different cultural groups in accounting created different cognitions or systems of knowledge for the perception of accounting concepts that share common perceptual characteristics (conjunctive concepts), or that are linked by some fixed relationship (relational concepts). The cognitive structure was not different among the three cultural groups for the accounting concepts that differ on the basis of one or more characteristics (disjunctive concepts). Therefore, a partial verification of the cultural determinism hypothesis is provided by the results in the sense that cultural affiliations lead to different cognitions or systems of knowledge, which, in turn, may lead to different approaches to the understanding of accounting relationships.

Exhibit 20.4
Results of the Analysis of Variances on Three Dimensions' Salience

Source of variation	Dimensions											
	Cognitive				Relational				Disjunctive			
	df	Sum of squares	Mean squares	F	df	Sum of squares	Mean squares	F	df	Sum of squares	Mean squares	F
Model	2	0.0047	0.0023	2.77**	2	0.0054	0.00270	2.61**	2	0.00011	0.00005	0.15
Error	84	0.0724	0.0008		84	0.0870	0.00103		84	0.03301	0.00039	
Total	86	0.0772			86	0.0924			86	0.03313		

Note: **Significant at a α = 0.10.

Exhibit 20.5
Regression Results on the Dimensions' Salience

Source of variation	Dimensions											
	Cognitive				Relational				Disjunctive			
	Df	Sum of squares	Mean squares	F	df	Sum of squares	Mean squares	F	df	Sum of squares	Mean squares	F
Model	4	0.0029	0.0073	2.77	2	0.00566	0.0014	1.28	4	0.0024	0.00061	0.59
Error	84	0.0739	0.0094		78	0.08645	0.0011		78	0.0302	0.00038	
Total	82	0.0769			82	0.09212			82			

Intragroup Perceptual Differences

To determine whether the observed difference in cognitions or systems of knowledge held, after allowing for the subject's background, the subject's salience for each of the three dimensions was regressed against the following variables: (1) the subject's age, (2) the number of years in the accounting firm, (3) the number of years in his/her present position, and (4) his/her familiarity with financial statements. Exhibit 20.5 reports the results of the regressions analysis. The four independent variables have no effect on the subjects' cognitions as represented by three-dimensional space. Therefore, the accounting concept perception and the resulting salience could be considered as independent of these variables.

DISCUSSION

The results suggest that intercultural differences exist in the perception of accounting concepts on two of the three dimensions of a common perceptual space. The results imply that the meanings of accounting concepts do vary in the manner with which they can be recognized, grasped, or understood by users from different cultural groups. These intercultural differences agree with the cultural determinism thesis that various cultural affiliations in accounting create different cognitions or systems of knowledge, which, in turn, lead to a different understanding of accounting constructs.

This study has isolated the effects of culture on the perception of accounting concepts by controlling for (a) organizational culture (the subjects were all from the same Big Six accounting firm), (b) occupational culture (the subjects were all professional accountants), (c) the managerial culture (the subjects were all partners or managers), and (d) linguistic relativism (the subjects were all anglophones). The results were indicative of communications problems that may arise in the perception of accounting concepts as a result of differences in the cognition or systems of knowledge of each particular culture.

The findings have general implications for the study and practice of accounting internationally. The general practice in international accounting has been for the observer to start with a set of assumed universal theoretical premises before attempting an inquiry across cultures. In doing so, an "etic" approach is adopted, taking the perspective of the observer as an important ingredient for the generation of scientifically predictive theories about the causes of sociocultural differences and similarities. Given the cultural relativism results found in this study, an "emic" approach is preferable as: (a) it studies behavior from within the system, (b) it examines one culture at a time, (c) it uses a structure discovered by the analyst (rather than created by the analyst), and (d) it uses criteria that are relative to the internal characteristics (rather than criteria that are assumed absolute or universal). The emic approach to cultural determinism to accounting, as advocated by this study's results, holds that culture determines and/or influences accounting techniques. An adoption of the emic approach to cultural relativism and cross-cultural research in accounting will allow the discipline to (a) establish the boundary conditions for accounting models and theories, (b) evaluate the impact of cultural and ecological factors in accounting contexts, and (c) identify the few cultunits that represent deviant cases.

CONCLUSION

A selected set of accounting concepts was subjected to analysis using multidimensional scaling techniques to evaluate the intercultural difference between three groups of partners and managers from the same Big Six accounting firm. Cultural relativism was used to justify the possible lack of consensus on the meaning of accounting concepts as a result of different cognitions or systems of knowledge in the three cultures. The INDSCAL model applied to the matrix of similarity judgments enabled the identification of three dimensions and subjects' salience. The dimensions were labeled as conjunctive, relational, or disjunctive, by analogy to the process of concept formation. An analysis of variance applied to the individual salience verified the cultural determinism thesis for two of three dimensions of a common cognitive space. These results indicate basic communication problems in the perceptions of accounting concepts as a result of differences in the cognition or system of knowledge of each particular culture. It appears, then, that the subjects from different cultures differ in their perception of accounting concepts independently of the differences in age, number of years in the accounting firm, number of years in the present position, and the degree of familiarity with financial statements. These differences are basic differences arising from cultural differences in the perception of accounting concepts. These differences may be explained by differences in value systems placing different emphasis on the meaning of each of the accounting concepts examined in this study. For example, differences in the perception of conservatism are consistent with the cultural differences on uncertainty avoidance. As stated by Gray: "A preference for more conservative measures of profits is consistent with strong uncertainty avoidance following from a concern with security and a perceived need to adopt a cautious approach to cope with uncertainty of future events" (Gray, 1988, p. 10). Therefore, the results observed in this study show that the differences in the perception of accounting concepts are reconcilable with differences in societal values that have a definite impact on accounting values. Given these communication problems, one may envision inconsistencies in audit behavior, financial analysis, accounting method choice, and so forth. Further research is needed on these subjects, especially in terms of allowing for the investigation of the combined effects of culture as cognition on the one hand, and organizational culture, occupational culture, managerial culture, and linguistic relativism on the other. In short, these preliminary results point to the need for more conceptual and empirical research on the nature and consequences of cultural determinism in accounting.

REFERENCES

Acheson, J. (1972). "Accounting Concepts and Economic Opportunities in a Tarascan Village: Emic and Etic Views." *Human Organization* Spring: 83–91.
Alhashim, D. 1973. "Accounting Control through Purposive Uniformity." *International Journal of Accounting Education and Research* Spring: 21–32.
Argyris, Chris and Donald Schon. 1978. *Organizational Learning*. Reading, Mass.: Addison-Wesley.
Beazley, Garnett F. 1968. "An International Implication for Accounting." *International Journal of Accounting Education and Research* Spring: 62–71.
Belkaoui, A. 1978. "Linguistic Relativity in Accounting." *Accounting, Organization and Society* 2: 97–104.
———. 1980. "The Interprofessional Linguistic Communication of Accounting Concepts: An Experiment in Sociolinguistics." *Journal of Accounting Research* Autumn: 362–374.
———. 1983. "Economic, Political and Civil Indicators and Reporting and Disclosure Adequacy: Empirical Investigation." *Journal of Accounting and Public Policy* Fall: 207–221.
———. 1985a. *Accounting Theory*. San Diego, Calif.: Harcourt Brace & Jovanovich.
———. 1985b. *International Accounting*. Westport, Conn.: Greenwood Press.
Bock, Phillip K. 1980. *Continuities in Psychological Anthropology*. San Francisco: W. H. Freeman.
Bougon, Michel. 1983. "Uncovering Cognitive Maps: The Self-Q Technique." In Careth Morgan (ed.), *Beyond Method: Social Research Strategies*. Beverly Hills, Calif.: Sage.
Bougon, Michel, Karl Weich, and Buikhost, Din. 1977. "Cognition in Organizations: An Analysis of the Utrecht Jazz Orchestra." *Administrative Science Quarterly* 22: 606–639.
Bromwich, M. and A. G. Hopwood (eds.). 1983. *Accounting Standard Setting: An International Perspective*. London: Pitman.
Caroll, J. D. and J. J. Chang. 1970. "Analysis of Individual Differences in Multidimensional Scaling via N-Way Generalization of 'Eckart-Young' Decomposition." *Psychometrika* 35: 238–319.
Chevalier, Gilles. 1977. "Should Accounting Practices Be Universal?" *Canadian Chartered Accountant Magazine* July: 47–50.
Choi, F.D.S. and G. G. Mueller. 1984. *International Accounting*. Englewood Cliffs, N.J.: Prentice-Hall.
Flamholtz, E. and E. Cook. 1978. "Cognitive Meaning and Its Role in Accounting Change: A Field Study." *Accounting, Organizations and Society* October: 115–140.
Frake, Charles. 1968. "The Ethnographic Study of Cognitive Systems." In Joshua A. Fishman (ed.), *Reading in the Sociology of Language*, pp. 434–446. The Hague, Netherlands: Mouton.

Geertz, Clifford. 1973. *The Interpretation of Cultures*. New York: Basic Books.

Goodenough, Ward H. 1971. *Culture, Language and Society*. Reading, Mass.: Addison-Wesley.

Grant, D. A. 1951. "Perceptual versus Analytical Responses to the Number Concept of a Weigel-type Card Sorting Test." *Journal of Experimental Psychology* 13: 23–29.

Gray, S. J. 1988. "Towards a Theory of Cultural Influence on the Development of Accounting Systems Internationally." *Abacus* March: 1–15.

Harris, Linda and Vemon Cronen. 1979. "A Rules Based Model for the Analysis and Evaluation of Organizational Communications." *Communications Quarterly* Winter: 12–28.

Heidbreder, E., M. Bensley, and M. Ivy. 1960. "The Attainment of Concepts. IV. Regularities and Levels." *Journal of Psychology* 12: 220–225.

Hofstede, G. 1985. "The Ritual Nature of Accounting Systems." Paper presented at EIASM Workshop, "Accounting and Culture," June 5–7.

———. 1987. "The Cultural Context of Accounting." In Barry E. Cushing (ed.), *Accounting and Culture*, pp. 1–11. Sarasota, Fla.: American Accounting Association.

Hunt, D. E. and C. I. Hovland. 1960. "Order of Consideration of Different Types of Concepts." *Journal of Experimental Psychology* 21: 220–225.

Klahr, David. 1969. "A Monte Carlo Investigation of the Statistical Significance of Kruskal's Nonmetric Scaling Procedure." *Psychometrica* September: 319–330.

Kruskal, J. B. 1964a. "Multidimensional Scaling by Optimizing Goodness of Fit to a Nonmetric Hypothesis." *Psychometrica* 29: 1–27.

———. 1964b. "Nonmetric Multidimensional: A Numerical Method." *Psychometrica* 29: 28–42.

Levi-Strauss, Claude. 1983. *Structural Anthropology*. Chicago: University of Chicago Press.

Litterer, Joseph A. and Stanley Young. 1981. "The Development of Managerial Reflective Skills." *Proceedings, Northeast AIDS* April: 16–23.

Malinowski, B. 1944. *A Scientific Theory of Culture*. Chapel Hill: University of North Carolina Press.

McComb, D. 1979. "International Harmonization of Accounting: A Cultural Dimension." *International Journal of Accounting Education and Research* Spring: 1–16.

McDavid, J. W. and H. Harari. 1974. *Psychology and Social Behavior*. New York: Harper & Row.

Miller, Joan E., Roger N. Shepard, and Jih-Jih Chang. 1969. "An Analytical Approach to the Interpretation of Multidimensional Scaling Solutions." *American Psychologist* September: 579–580.

Monti-Belkaoui, J. and Ahmed Belkaoui. 1983. "Bilingualism and the Perception of Professional Concepts." *Journal of Psycholinguistic Research* 2: 111–127.

Mueller, Gerhard G. 1967. *International Accounting*. New York: Macmillan.

Nair, R. D. and W. G. Frank. 1980. "The Impact of Disclosure and Measurement Practices on International Accounting Classification." *The Accounting Review* July: 426–450.

Nobes, C. W. 1983. "A Judgmental International Classification of Financial Reporting Practices." *Journal of Business Finance and Accounting* Spring: 15–26.

———. 1984. *International Classification of Financial Reporting*. London: Croom Helm.

Perera, M.H.B. and M. R. Mathews. 1987. "The Interrelationship of Culture and Accounting with Particular Reference to Social Accounting." Palmerston, N.Z.: Massey University, Department of Accounting and Finance, Discussion Paper No. 59.

Radcliffe-Brown, A. R. 1968. *Structure and Function in Primitive Society.* New York: Free Press.

Rossi, Ino and Edurin O'Higgins. 1980. "The Development of Theories of Culture." In Ino Rossi (ed.), *People in Culture*, pp. 31–78. New York: Praeger.

Schreuder, Hein. 1987. "Accounting Research, Practice and Culture: A European Perspective." In Barry E. Cushing (ed.), *Accounting and Culture*, pp. 12–22. Sarasota, Fla.: American Accounting Association.

Singhvi, S. Surendra. 1978. "Characteristics and Implications of Inadequate Disclosure: A Case Study of India." *International Journal of Accounting Education and Research* Spring: 29–43.

Smircich, Linda. 1983. "Concepts of Culture and Organizational Analysis." *Administrative Science Quarterly* September: 339–358.

Soeters, J. and U. Schreuder. 1988. "The Interaction between National and Organizational Cultures in Accounting Firms." *Accounting Organizations and Society* 13(1): 75–86.

Violet, William J. 1983. "The Development of International Accounting Standards: An Anthropological Perspective." *International Journal of Accounting Education and Research* Spring: 1–12.

Wacker, Gerald. 1981. "Toward a Cognitive Methodology of Organizational Assessment." *Journal of Applied Behavioral Science* 17: 114–129.

Weick, Karl E. 1979a. "Cognitive Processes in Organizations." In Larry L. Cummings and Barry M. Staw (eds.), *Research in Organizational Behavior*, pp. 41–74. Greenwich, Conn.: JAI Press.

———. 1979b. *The Social Psychology of Organizations.* Reading, Mass.: Addison-Wesley.

Young, F. W. 1968. "TORSCA-9: An IBM 360/7S FORTRAN IV Program for Nonmetric Multidimensional Scaling." *Journal of Marketing Research* 15: 319–320.

21

Economic Freedom and Macroeconomic Determinants of Economic Growth: Cross-Country Evidence

INTRODUCTION

What determines the rate of economic growth has been and is still a subject of research interest (Lucas, 1988; Romer, 1986; Stern, 1991; Barro, 1991: Ayal and Karras, 1998). The search is for empirical linkages between long-run average growth rates, and fiscal, trade, and monetary indicators as suggested by theory (Levine and Renelt, 1992). With very few exceptions, the research to date has not considered the potential impact of economic freedom on economic growth. Economic freedom is defined in terms of whether a country is relatively more or less reliant on private ownership and relatively more or less reliant on the market to allocate resources (Easton and Walker, 1997).

Economic research assumes either that economic freedom is given or that the impact of economic freedom is inconsequential, or both (Barro, 1996). As economic freedom is assumed to be central to economic growth (Ayal and Karras, 1998), its inclusion in macroeconomic models of growth is warranted. Accordingly, based on a set of hypotheses, this chapter examines the cross-sectional relationship between economic growth on one hand and macroeconomic and economic freedom variables on the other hand. Specifically, the chapter relies on 1980–1988 data from thirty countries to construct a pooled cross-sectional data set and examines the association of five variables with economic growth. These variables are: (1) gross domestic investment as a percentage of GDP, (2) annual rate of inflation, (3) terms of trade, (4) total expenditures on health and education as a percentage of GDP, and (5) an economic freedom index. The results support the significant impact of economic freedom, in addition to the other four macroeconomic variables, on economic growth.

HYPOTHESES AND EMPIRICAL DESIGN

General Growth Model

The empirical growth literature has relied on the following cross-sectional specification:

$$Y = B_i I + B_m M + B_z Z + u \qquad (21.1)$$

where Y is the per capita growth in GNP, I is a set of variables always included in the regression, M is a variable of interest, and Z is a subset of variables generally believed to be important explanatory variables of growth (Levine and Renelt, 1992). The I variables are inspired by new growth models that rely on constant returns to reproducible inputs or endogenous technological change (e.g., Romer, 1990b). Gross domestic investment as a percentage of GDP is used as the I variable in this study. The Z variables represent fiscal, trade, and monetary indicators as suggested by theory and earlier research. This study uses annual rate of inflation, terms of trade, and total expenditures on health and education as a percentage of GDP as Z variables included in the model. M, the variable of interest, is economic freedom. It is included in the model to test the currently spreading belief that economic freedom helps economic growth. This amounts to hypothesizing that economic freedom enhances the efficiency by which productive inputs are converted into output (Ayal and Karras, 1998). Under the hypothesis that multifactor productivity is enhanced by economic freedom, the latter is assumed to have a positive impact on economic growth after controlling for the Z variables representing fiscal, trade, and monetary policies. The next section considers a set of hypotheses that support the variables included in the model.

HYPOTHESES AND VARIABLES

The hypotheses are drawn upon the basis of the following characteristics: (1) they include the impact of economic freedom, (2) they rely on macroeconomic variables, (3) they yield testable implications for economic growth, and (4) they can be supported by available data.

Gross Domestic Investment as a Percentage of GDP

Out of forty-one growth studies, thirty-three included gross domestic investment as a percentage of GDP as an I variable. In addition, economic theory holds that higher rates of saving and investment are essential to the long-run rate of growth of a nation (Plossner, 1992). The intuition behind Solow's (1956) framework is that higher investment or saving rates lead to more accumulated capital per worker, resulting in an increase in the per capita output of the economy, but at a decreasing rate. In endogenous growth models with an emphasis on broader concepts of capital, such as Rebelo (1991) and Barro (1991), per capita growth and the investment ratio tend to move together. Delong and Summers (1992), looking at a cross-section of countries in the postwar period, find a positive association between investment in machinery and equipment and faster rates of growth. Based on the above empirical and theoretical evidence, this study relies on gross domestic investment as a percentage of GDP as a potential positive determinant of economic growth.

Annual Rate of Inflation

The Tobin-Mundell hypotheses imply that anticipated inflation causes more rapid shifts from real money balances toward real capital, raising investment, and economic growth. Conversely, Stockman (1981) implied that in economies with "cash-in-advance" constraints, anticipated inflation reduces economic activity and economic growth. Based on the above theoretical rationales, this study relies on the annual rate of inflation as a potential determinant of economic growth. A positive relationship will support the Tobin-Mundell hypotheses, while a negative relationship will support Stockman's hypothesis.

Terms of Trade

Export promotion policies have a beneficial impact on economic growth (Feder, 1982). Similarly, trade restrictions are expected to have an adverse effect on the efficiency of the economy by causing the failure to exploit comparative advantage and the reduction of aggregate output (Kormendi and Meguire, 1985). One factor associated with higher exports and lower trade restrictions is the commodity or net barter terms of trade. Terms of trade is the ratio of two indices: (1) the average price of a country's exports, which are approximated by dividing an index of export volume into an index of export revenue, and (2) the average price of its imports determined by the same method. Terms of trade is used as a determinant of economic growth. Thus countries in which terms of trade are greater may be expected to experience greater economic growth.

Total Expenditures on Health and Education as a Percentage of GDP

The impact of government expenditures on economic growth has led to a policy debate among developmental economists. Supply-side theorists argue that the taxes required for financing government expenditures distort incentives and reduce efficient resource allocation and the level of output (Grier and Tullock,

1989; Kormendi and Meguire, 1985; Denison, 1985). Basically, countries with greater mean growth in governmental expenditures experience lower economic growth. The empirical growth literature uses (1) measures of overall size of the government in the economy, (2) disaggregated measures of government expenditures, and (3) measures of growth rates of government expenditures. Disaggregated measures of government expenditures have been adopted in this study because of data availability. Thus, countries with greater total expenditures on health and education as a percentage of GDP should experience lower economic growth in the short run.

Economic Freedom

Sources of increases in productivity and income include: (a) improvements in the skills of workers, (b) investment and capital foundation, (c) advancements in technology, and (d) better economic organization (Gwartney, Lawson, and Block, 1996). A major influence on these four factors is the impact of economic freedom. Economic theory indicates that economic freedom will increase economic growth as it results in increases in the incentive to earn, higher productivity, and gains from trade and entrepreneurships. Several studies reported a very strong relationship between economic freedom and economic growth (Barro, 1996; Easton and Walker, 1997; Ayal and Karras, 1998).

EMPIRICAL DESIGN

The hypotheses were tested using the following regression model:

$$\text{GNPG}_j = a_0 + a_1\text{GDIG}_j + a_2\text{ARI}_j + a_2\text{TOT}_j + a_2\text{TEHEG}_j \qquad (21.2)$$
$$+ a_2\text{EF}_j + u_j$$

where

GNPG $\;=$ GNP per capital annual growth

GDIG $\;=$ gross domestic investment as a percentage of gross domestic product (GDP)

ARI_j $\;=$ annual rate of inflation

TOT $\;=$ terms of trade

TEHEG $=$ total expenditures in health and education as a percentage of GDP

EF $\;=$ economic freedom index

j $\;=$ country j

All the variables are measured as average data for the 1980–1988 period. This period includes a wide diversity in economic freedom among the nations in the sample. The data for the macroeconomic variables came from the *Human Development Report* of the United Nations (1990) and the *International Financial*

Exhibit 21.1
List of Countries

Australia	Hong Kong	Portugal
Austria	India	Singapore
Brazil	Italy	South Africa
Canada	Japan	Spain
Colombia	Korea	Sweden
Denmark	Malaysia	Taiwan
Finland	Mexico	Turkey
France	Netherlands	United Kingdom
Germany	Norway	United States
Greece	Pakistan	Venezuela

Statistics of the International Monetary Fund. The economic freedom index is made possible by the meticulous work of the Fraser Institute, the results of which were published in *Economic Freedom of the World: 1975–1995*, by James D. Gwartney, Robert Lawson, and Walter Block. To avoid some arbitrary benchmark of "socialism" or "capitalism," the index of economic freedom has seventeen components that are allocated to four major areas: (1) money and inflation, (2) government operations and regulations, (3) takings and discrimination taxation, and (4) international exchange. In aggregating these components of economic freedom into a summary index, various alternatives are used to attach different weights to the components. What results are five possible summary indices: (a) an equal impact index: Ie; (b) a survey of knowledgeable people index: Is1; (c) a survey of a large number of people index: Is2; (d) an average of the above three indexes: AVG; (e) a letter grade index: GRADE. Each of these five summary indexes—Ie, Is1, Is2, AVG, and GRADE—will be used in this study to evaluate the impact of economic freedom (EF) on economic growth (GNPC).

The thirty countries used were chosen because they had available data for all the variables used. The list of countries is shown in Exhibit 21.1.

THE EMPIRICAL RESULTS

The summary statistics and the correlation coefficients are reported in Exhibits 21.2 and 21.3, respectively. The RESET (regression specification error test), as suggested by Ramsey (1969) and Thursby (1981, 1985), and the Hausman test (1978), as suggested by Wu (1973) and Hausman (1978), were used to specification tests. The results of the RESET test, used to check omitted variables, incorrect functional form, and nonindependence of regressors, show that the model used in this study is not misspecified.

Exhibit 21.4 provides the results of estimating Equation (21.2), using five different measures of economic freedom. The model explains from 64.51 percent

Exhibit 21.2
Summary Statistics

Variables	Mean	Standard Deviation	Maximum	Median	Minimum
GDIG	23.72	4.81	37	23	15
ARI	16.23	33.84	188.7	7.1	1.2
TOT	96.99	23.32	152.0	103	41.0
TEHEG	9.86	4.53	18.0	10.5	2.4
GNPG	3.04	1.58	7.0	2.7	7.7
Ie	6.31	1.39	9.0	6.45	2.8
Is1	6.07	1.26	9.1	5.9	3.3
Is2	6.63	1.68	9.1	6.9	2.4
AVG	6.34	1.42	9.0	6.55	2.8
GRADE	3.73	1.63	6.0	4	1

Note: GDIG = Gross Domestic Investment as a Percentage of GDP; ARI = Annual Rate of Inflation; TOT = Terms of Trade; TEHEG = Total Expenditures in Health and Education as a Percentage of GDP; GNPG = Per Capita Annual Growth in GNP; Ie = Equal Impact Index of Freedom; Is1 = Survey of Knowledgeable People Adjusted Index of Freedom; Is2 = Survey of Large Number of People Adjusted Index of Freedom; AVG = Average Index of Freedom; GRADE = Letter Grade Index of Freedom (A = 6; B = 5; C = 4; D = 3; E = 2; F = 1)

Exhibit 21.3
Correlation Coefficients of Independent Variables

	GDIG	ARI	TOT	TEHEG	Ie	Is1	Is2	AVG	GRADE
GDIG	1.000	-0.1201	0.0567	-0.1616	0.2250	0.3129	0.1176	0.2165	0.2066
		(0.5123)	(0.2577)	(0.3758)	(0.2150)	(0.0812)	(0.5215)	(0.2340)	(0.2565)
ARI		1.000	0.0394	-0.3142	-0.5380	-0.4848	-0.5572	-0.5502	-0.4318
			(0.8277)	(0.0799)	(0.0007)	(0.0042)	(0.0008)	(0.0009)	(0.0121)
TOT			1.000	0.2598	0.2622	0.2265	0.2924	0.2688	0.3039
				(0.1509)	(0.1403)	(0.2041)	(0.0928)	(0.1303)	(0.0855)
TEHEG				1.000	0.5649	0.4199	0.6871	0.3800	0.6109
					(0.0008)	(0.016)	(0.0001)	(0.0005)	(0.0002)
Ie					1.000	0.9931	0.9725	0.9981	0.9527
						(0.0001)	(0.0001)	(0.0001)	(0.0001)
Is1						1.000	0.8981	0.9686	0.9123
							(0.0001)	(0.0001)	(0.0001)
Is2							1.000	0.9784	0.9480
								(0.001)	(0.0001)
AVG								1.000	0.9544
									(0.0001)
GRADE									1.000

Note: Variables are defined in Exhibit 21.2.

to 71.5 percent of the variation in measured economic growth. The F-statistics for the regression, F varying from 10.814 to 11.386, rejects the null hypothesis of no explanatory power for the regression as a whole at better than the 1 percent level.

Exhibit 21.4
Results of the Regression Model (t-coefficients are in parentheses)

	Regression 1	Regression 2	Regression 3	Regression 4	Regression 5
Intercept[1]	-4.592	-4.574	-4.382	-4.561	-3.059
	(-30114)	(-3.018)	(-3.182)*	(-3.133)*	(-2.483)**
GDIG	0.142	0.1397	0.1478	0.1425	0.1377
	(3.693)*	(3.520)*	(3.933)*	(3.697)*	(3.536)*
ARI	-0.008	-0.010	-0.008	-0.008	-0.011
	(-2.355)**	(-0.656)**	(-2.325)**	(-2.385)**	(-2.069)**
TOT	0.031	0.032	0.030	0.031	0.031
	(3.928)*	(4.025)*	(3.845)*	(3.938)*	(3.951)*
TEHEG	-0.1121	-0.093	-0.136	-0.115	-0.123
	(-2.371)**	(-2.122)**	(-2.585)**	(-2.408)**	(-2.498)
Ie	0.3798				
	(1.818)***				
Is 1		0.3635			
		(1.677)***			
Is 2			0.3583		
			(1.977)***		
AVG				0.3792	
				(1.850)**	
GRADE					0.3017
					(1.922)**
Adjusted R^2	64.51 %	63.81 %	65.33 %	71.21 %	71.52 %
F	10.814*	10.519*	11.178*	10.886*	11.049*

Notes: Variables are defined in Exhibit 21.2.
*Significant at 0.01
**Significant at 0.05
***Significant at 0.10

The individual coefficients in the macroeconomic variables were all significant with the expected sign: (1) positive for gross domestic investment as a percentage of GDP as expected from the new growth models, (2) positive for terms of trade as expected by the export promotion policy implications, (3) negative for inflation as advocated by Stockman's (1981) hypothesis, and (4) negative for total expenditures on health and education as a percentage of GDP, as expected from the "supply-side" hypothesis. Of more relevance to this study is the significant and positive influence of economic freedom as measured by each of the five measures of the economic freedom index on economic growth.

CONCLUSION

This study presents two empirical results on the impact of macroeconomic factors and economic freedom on economic growth. First, in accordance with macroeconomic hypotheses, economic growth was found to be positively related to gross domestic investment as a percentage of GDP and terms of trade, and negatively related to inflation rate and total expenditure on health and education as a percentage of GDP. Second, economic freedom, as measured by five different indexes, was found to be positively related to economic growth and provides the right climate for the efficient functioning of the investment, trade, fiscal, and monetary forces in the economy. The results are consistent with the spreading belief that economic freedom helps economic growth. It confirms the hypothesis that multifactor productivity is enhanced by economic freedom, with the latter having significant positive effects on economic growth. The essence of the results is that economic freedom is associated with faster rates of income growth. A freer economic structure contributes to prosperity and development, a result comparable to those associated with physical investment, schooling, and workforce growth. Future research needs to examine alternative measures for all the independent variables and different periods of analysis.

REFERENCES

Ayal, E. B. and G. Karras. 1998. "Components of Economic Freedom and Growth: An Empirical Study." *Journal of Developing Areas* 32:327–338.
Barro, R. 1996. "Democracy and Growth." *Journal of Economic Growth* 1: 1–27.
———. 1991. "Economic Growth in a Cross Section of Countries." *Quarterly Journal of Economics* May: 407–444.
Delong, J. B. and L. H. Summers. 1992. "Macroeconomic Policy and Long-Term Growth." *Policies for Long-Run Economic Growth*, pp. 93–128. Kansas City: Federal Reserve Bank of Kansas.
Denison, E. F. 1985. *Trends in American Economic Growth: 1929–82.* Washington, D.C.: The Brookings Institution.
Easton, S. T. and M. A. Walker, V. 1997. "Income, Growth, and Economic Freedom." *American Economic Review* 87: 328–332.
Feder, G. 1982. "On Exports and Economic Growth." *Journal of Development Economics* 12: 59–73.
Grier, K. B. and G. Tullock. 1989. "An Empirical Analysis of Cross-National Economic Growth, 1951–80." *Journal of Monetary Economics* 29: 259–276.
Gwartney, James, Robert Lawson, and Walter Block. 1996. *Economic Freedom of the World: 1975–1995.* Vancouver, B.C.: Fraser Institute.
Hausman, J. A. 1978. "Specification Tests in Econometrics." *Econometrics* 16: 1251–1270.
Kormendi, R. C. and P. G. Meguire. 1985. "Macroeconomic Determinants of Growth: Cross-Country Evidence." *Journal of Monetary Economics* 16: 141–163.
Levine, R. and D. Renelt. 1992. "A Sensitivity Analysis of Cross-Country Growth Regression." *American Economic Review* September: 942–963.
Lucas, R. 1998. "On the Mechanics of Economic Development." *Journal of Monetary Economics* July: 3–42.
Mankiw, N. G., D. Romer, and D. N. Weil. 1992. "A Contribution to the Empirics of Economic Growth." *Quarterly Journal of Economics* 107: 407–437.

Plossner, C. I. 1992. "The Search for Growth." In *Policies for Long-Run Economic Growth*, pp. 57–86. Kansas City: Federal Reserve Bank of Kansas.

Ramsey, F. I. 1969. "Test for Specification Errors in Classical Linear Least Squares Regression Analysis." *Journal of the Royal Statistical Society* 31 (Series B): 31.

Rebelo, S. 1991. "Long-Run Policy Analysis and Long-Run Growth." *Journal of Political Economy* 99: 500–521.

Romer, P. M. 1986. "Increasing Returns and Long-Run Growth." *Journal of Political Economy* October: 1002–1037.

———. 1990a. "Capital, Labor, and Productivity." *Brookings Papers on Economic Activity* 13: 337–420.

———. 1990b. "Endogenous Technological Change." *Journal of Political Economy* October: 71–102.

Solow, R. 1956. "A Contribution to the Theory of Economic Growth." *Quarterly Journal of Economics* 70: 65–94.

Stern, N. 1991. "The Determinants of Growth." *The Economic Journal* January: 122–123.

Stockman, A. 1981. "Anticipated Inflation and the Capital Stock in a Cash-in-Advance Economy." *Journal of Monetary Economics* 8:387–393.

Thursby, M. 1981. "A Test for Strategy for Discriminating between Auto-correlation and Misspecification in Regression Analysis." *Review of Economics and Statistics* 63: 117–123.

———. 1985. "The Relationship among the Specification Test of Hausman, Ramsey and Chow." *Journal of the American Statistical Association* 80: 926–928.

United Nations. 1990. *Human Development Report.* New York: United Nations.

Wu, P. 1973. "Alternative Tests of Independence between Stochastic Regressors and Disturbances." *Econometrics* 12: 733–750.

Index

Accounting concept perception study, 279–91; cognitive functioning view of culture in, 280; communication problems in, 290; and cultural determinism thesis, 289; findings and implications, 289–90; perceptual differences in, 287–89; perceptual dimensions in, 286–87; professional concepts in, 284

Accounting development: and accounting for inflation, 34–36; capital markets' role in, 26–28; cultural values and, 61–63; determinants of, 163–65; economic development and, 26–37; economic growth and, 155–57; economic systems and, 65–66, 208; environmental influences on, 163–64; and Gray's accounting values, 62, 64; and Hofstede's cultural values, 62, 64; human development and, 157; judgment/decision process in, 68–71; legal and tax relativism in, 60–61, 66–68; of micro- and macroaccounting systems, 30–32; political and civil relativism in, 63–65, 208; and professional self-regulation, 63; and welfare of the common man, 174, 175

Accounting diversity, 53–100, 154, 207; and accounting practice differences, 54; and accounting development patterns, 56; culture and, 61–63; definition and nature of, 53–54; and degree of flexibility, 54; economic and social welfare variables in, 65–66, 173; empirical research on, 61; elements of differentiation in, 54; environmental factors in, 153; in financial disclosure adequacy, 163–70; harmonization and, 74–92; historical zones of accounting influences in, 173; judgment diversity in, 68–74; levels of, 53; political and civil welfare and, 63–65, 173; presentation differences in, 54; research avenues and, 61; in standard setting, 74–92; welfare of the common man and, 173–74

Accounting education, financial disclosure adequacy and, 164, 169, 208

Accounting information adequacy thesis: and accounting information adequacy, 106, 110–12; and annual inflation rate, 105, 107, 110–12; as determinant of economic growth, 105–20; disclosure requirements as measure in, 108–9; and

About the Author

AHMED RIAHI-BELKAOUI is CBA Distinguished Professor of Accounting in the College of Business Administration, University of Illinois at Chicago. Author of numerous Quorum books, published or forthcoming, and coauthor of several more, he is an equally prolific contributor to the journals of his field, and has served on various editorial boards that oversee them.

About the Author